THE
SIERRA CLUB
GUIDE TO
THE
NATURAL AREAS
OF
NEW ENGLAND

OTHER NATURAL AREAS GUIDES

Guide to the Natural Areas of California

Guide to the Natural Areas of Oregon and Washington

Guide to the Natural Areas of New Mexico, Arizona, and Nevada

Guide to the Natural Areas of Colorado and Utah

Guide to the Natural Areas of Idaho, Montana, and Wyoming

Guide to the Natural Areas of New England

THE
SIERRA CLUB
GUIDE TO
THE
NATURAL AREAS
OF NEW ENGLAND

JOHN PERRY

AND

JANE GREVERUS PERRY

SIERRA CLUB BOOKS   SAN FRANCISCO

The Sierra Club, founded in 1892 by John Muir, has devoted itself to the study and protection of the earth's scenic and ecological resources—mountains, wetlands, woodlands, wild shores and rivers, deserts, and plains. The publishing program of the Sierra Club offers books to the public as a nonprofit educational service in the hope that they may enlarge the public's understanding of the Club's basic concerns. The point of view expressed in each book, however, does not necessarily represent that of the Club. The Sierra Club has some sixty chapters coast to coast, in Canada, Hawaii, and Alaska. For information about how you may participate in its programs to preserve wilderness and the quality of life, please address inquiries to Sierra Club, 730 Polk Street, San Francisco, CA 94109.

Library of Congress Cataloging-in-Publication Data

Perry, John, 1914-
The Sierra Club guide to the natural areas of
New England/John Perry and Jane Greverus Perry.

p. cm.
Bibliography: p.
Includes index.
ISBN 0-87156-744-X
1. Natural areas—New England—Guide-books.
2. Outdoor recreation—New England—Guide-books.
I. Perry, Jane Greverus. II. Sierra Club.
III. Title.
QH104.5.N4P47 1990   796.5'0974—dc20   89-35736 CIP

Production by Susan Ristow

Cover art by Bonnie Smetts

Book design concept by Lily Langotsky

Illustrations by Nancy Warner

Printed in the United States of America

10 9 8 7 6 5 4 3 2 1

CONTENTS

INTRODUCTION

This book is a guide to quiet places, away from crowds and city noises, places to enjoy trees and wildflowers, clear brooks, singing birds, and the flash of a deer's white tail. It is a guide for campers and hikers, birders and canoeists, fishermen and hunters.

We had known New England well, but for ten years our work had been in the West. So much had changed! From New York to Bar Harbor, spreading urban development surrounds choked highways. Lakes we remembered as pristine have become busy resorts.

Such contrasts between West and East! Montana's population density is less than 6 people per square mile. In Massachusetts it's 745; in the Connecticut county nearest New York City, it's 1,277. Distances seemed so short; one can cross Massachusetts in an hour. Spaces seemed so small; Montana is more than twice as large as all New England. Montana has 27 million acres of federal land open to recreation; all of New England, 1 million. We had written about western sites covering several million acres. New England's natural areas come in smaller packages.

Soon, in a few days of hiking and canoeing, we had put aside West-East comparisons. New England has its own unique natural qualities, its special ambience. Founded on the hemisphere's oldest rock, the landscape has been carved by a recent ice sheet. One mourns the destruction of the primeval forest but rejoices in its successor, risen from stony fields, approaching maturity.

New England has bush pilots that fly sportsmen and their canoes to otherwise inaccessible lakes. One can canoe-camp for days, running flatwater and whitewater, seldom meeting another party. New England has many miles of scenic mountain trails. With the returning forest has come a rejuvenated wildlife population, with increasing numbers of moose, bear, coyote, fisher, marten. Few regions have such a diversity of bird species, some at the northern or southern limits of their ranges, some seen only offshore, many breeding in the extensive wetlands. Few have such a diversity and abundance of seasonal wildflowers.

Don't come to New England with western expectations. This is a different kind of country, with different opportunities for enjoyment of nature.

QUALITY OF LIFE AND LANDSCAPE

Maps of New England states show many little patches of green: the parks and forests. As one drives the highways, however, most of the region looks green. The original forest was cut long ago, but the forest has returned. Four-fifths of the land again supports trees. However, less than one-tenth of the new forest is on publicly owned land. Most of it is at risk.

In our home state, Florida, one can't see the landscape for the billboards. They are wonderfully absent through most of New England. So is roadside litter, except where natives are outnumbered.

Hundreds of small towns have kept their colonial character: white-painted homes, many more than a century old; neat lawns and hedges; broad, tree-lined Main Streets with no flashing neon signs or golden arches. The character of these towns has been maintained not by ordinances but by the popular will.

New Englanders care about their land. Many landowners, unwilling to see their holdings subdivided and developed, bequeath them to Audubon Societies, The Nature Conservancy, Society for the Protection of New Hampshire Forests, or other groups for permanent protection.

Traditionally, much recreation has been on private land. In the north, this tradition continues. Many timber companies invite, welcome, or at least permit recreational use of their extensive holdings.

In the south, voluntary associations such as the Connecticut Forest and Park Association have developed networks of hiking trails, linking State lands, crossing private lands with owners' permission. Connecticut's Blue-Blazed Trails, the Appalachian Trail, Vermont's Long Trail, and many others have been planned, built, and maintained by citizen organizations, a remarkable achievement and testament to the neighborliness of New England landowners.

Of late, in some parts of New England, rapid growth has swept neighborliness aside. Developer money has overwhelmed tradition. The newcomers are less hospitable. Some resort areas have become gaudy, but not all. There are still natural areas to enjoy.

STATE LANDS

Out West, about half of the land is federally owned. The only large federal lands in New England are its two National Forests; all federal lands combined are less than 3 percent of the region.

Therefore, providing open green space in a period of rapid growth is a responsibility that has fallen on the States. They are responding by buying more land. Massachusetts, for example, now has over 200 State sites available for recreation, 45 of them larger than 2,000 acres. Most New England residents have a park, forest, or other green space less than 10 miles from home.

For residents, this is splendid, but what do these sites offer visitors? Should we include a small natural area within a metropolis? Why would visitors struggle through heavy traffic when they can find attractive sites more easily elsewhere? Should we omit everything within the congested coastal corridor?

The New England coast couldn't be overlooked. A beach that's crowded on the Fourth of July may be deserted after Labor Day. The salt marshes are special. So are the tidepools, dunes, islands, estuaries, rocky promontories. We've included the best of the natural areas on and near the coast, noting that one should choose the right time for a visit.

SOLITUDE IS THERE—IF YOU CAN FIND IT

State Parks are easy to find. They're shown on highway maps and usually have entrance signs. Finding a State Forest or Wildlife Management Area may be more difficult. Often there are no signs at access or entrance roads. Boundaries may be unmarked or marked in ways few visitors will recognize. Frequently we couldn't tell State from private land.

Chiefly, State recreation areas serve state residents. In State Parks we saw few out-of-state license plates. Not that New England lacks tourists, but most go to popular resorts, Acadia National Park, Cape Cod National Seashore, and such scenic areas as Mt. Washington and Franconia Notch.

Some State headquarters can provide site maps; others have none. At head-quarters, we asked how people find these sites. Acknowledging lack of maps and signs, our advisors said this is no great problem because most visitors come from nearby. Local hunters, fishermen, picnickers, and hikers know the areas.

You are not unwelcome, and the lack of publicity means you'll have less company. Except in hunting season, most State Forests and Wildlife Management Areas are quiet, many of them scenic and delightful. We hiked their trails and seldom met other hikers. Our entries will help you find these quiet places. When in doubt, ask locally. Folks who live nearby know where to go.

MAPS

Most U.S. roads aren't shown on standard State highway maps. Travelers venturing off main highways need more than these. Map resources differ greatly among the New England states. State prefaces say what's available.

We were delighted by the DeLorme atlases for Maine, New Hampshire, and Vermont. Rhode Island is so small its official highway map shows and names most streets. On a scale of about 3.5 miles per inch, Connecticut's official map is easy to read. At 5.8 miles per inch, the Massachusetts map is more difficult, and we could find nothing better.

National Forest maps show Forest roads; the highway maps don't. Entries note if site maps are available.

CAMPING

Out West, we seldom looked for a campsite until our day's work was done. Often, instead of campgrounds we found pleasant places on public land, perhaps beside a lake or stream. Such informal camping is forbidden in New England except in the two National Forests; one must use designated campgrounds.

A minority of State Parks and State Forests have campgrounds. Most of these were closed to us because we travel with a dog. Commercial campgrounds are usually available, but on summer weekends it's wise to have reservations. Because of our unpredictable schedule, we didn't make reservations, but we always found something.

Especially in southern New England, almost any campground can serve as a base. From a campground in west central Massachusetts, for example, any natural area in the western half of the state is within an hour's drive. Distances are greater in the north, but campsites are less crowded, and one can always camp in the National Forests.

Many State Forests and WMAs (Wildlife Management Areas) have small parking areas along interior dirt roads. They are used mostly by hunters. We often saw indications that people had camped, and we saw no signs prohibiting camping. At headquarters we were told camping is prohibited, and we asked if the rule is enforced. No one suggested ignoring the rule, but some answers were qualified:

- State agencies can't maintain regular patrols, especially on weekends. But some local managers make a point of patrolling.
- Parking a self-contained recreation vehicle overnight is less objectionable than other forms of camping.
- If asked, some local managers may suggest a place to park.
- Fires are strictly prohibited.

HIKING AND BACKPACKING

New England has several thousand miles of fine trails, short and long. Opportunities for day hikes are unlimited. Backpacking is a problem, even on the Appalachian Trail.

Informal trailside camping is prohibited on almost all State lands except in Vermont. Camping along the Appalachian and other long trails is limited to designated sites—State Park and Forest campgrounds and a few shelters—except in National Forests. Using designated sites, one can plan a weekend backpack, but more extensive hikes, even on the Appalachian Trail, require spending some nights off trail. Inn-to-inn hiking is popular in some areas.

The hiking guides noted in each state preface are indispensable. They describe the long trails and dozens of short trails to waterfalls, lookouts, ponds, and other places of special beauty or interest you're not likely to find without them. Without their descriptions of blazes, landmarks, side trails, and other highlights, you can lose your way.

CANOE COUNTRY

Carry a canoe if you can, possibly with camping gear. The canoeing guides noted in the state prefaces describe many spectacular trips through backcountry you can't get to by land. Many wetlands are best seen by canoe.

The rules prohibiting informal camping are less strictly applied to canoe camping. On a few popular waterways, canoeists are asked to use designated sites. More often you can find a suitable site on shore or on an island. If it seems to be private property and you can find the owner, it's good form to ask permission.

HOW TO USE THIS BOOK

Read the prefaces for each state! New England is not homogeneous—Maine doesn't resemble Rhode Island. The six states have great differences in their natural qualities and in opportunities for outdoor recreation.

The entries listed in each state preface, except Rhode Island's, are marked "North," "South," etc. The most populous areas, with the heaviest traffic, are eastern Rhode Island, Connecticut, and Massachusetts, southern New Hampshire, and southeastern Maine. The least populated areas with the most open space are northern Maine, New Hampshire, and Vermont.

WHAT'S IN THE ENTRIES

Entries tell how to get to principal site entrances.

A row of symbols shows at a glance the activities offered by each site. In addition to a general description of terrain and noteworthy features, information about flora and fauna is noted if it's available. Often it's not, but information from a similar site is usually applicable.

Some sites are included because of their interpretive programs. This is especially true of Audubon preserves and wildflower gardens where one can learn much about the ecology of a region and see labeled specimens of living plants.

Headings under ACTIVITIES match the symbols above. The symbol for ski touring (cross-country skiing) simply means it's permitted. The text doesn't add "If there's enough snow," and there's no promise of groomed trails.

PUBLICATIONS are those available in 1988 at the site or other headquarters. Most government publications are free and may be sent on request from State headquarters, especially if you send a self-addressed envelope. Site headquarters seldom have resources to respond to mail requests.

Some publications aren't free, especially those of private groups. We noted prices if asked to do so, but caution that prices often change.

REFERENCES are publications that were in print in 1988. A few out-of-print books or booklets are included because we found nothing comparable in print. We managed to find copies, so you might also.

Some regional references are listed in several entries and state prefaces, to provide the best service to readers.

HEADQUARTERS is the place to make inquiries. We asked each State headquarters to tell us whether to use site addresses, regional offices, or State headquarters and acted on their advice. Some sites have local managers but no offices. Some have only part-time or visiting managers.

WHAT'S NOT IN THE ENTRIES

Entries don't provide information about the following:

- *Entrance and camping fees.* Many State Parks and some forest recreation areas charge entrance fees. Almost all campgrounds do. Fees vary from place to place and year to year.
- *Campground facilities.* Standard campground directories and State-published leaflets provide the data.
- *Picnicking,* Except in a few private preserves where it's prohibited, one can picnic almost anywhere.
- *Hunting and fishing rules and regulations.* Each State publishes its own, annually.
- *Swimming,* unless there's a managed beach. It's prohibited in some public water supply reservoirs. For the most part, it's up to you and at your risk. Many beaches are used more for sunbathing than swimming because of cold water.
- *Winter sports.* Entries note downhill skiing if there's a ski area on the site. New England has many more ski areas, described in special directories. Ice skating is rarely mentioned by site managers because it's unmanaged; people skate at their own risk. Ice fishing is popular on some lakes, subject to State regulation.
- *Rules about pets,* except where they are firmly prohibited. Leashes are required where pets are permitted. Pets are almost always barred from public buildings and beaches. The rules in New England State Parks are changing from year to year. The trend has been toward exclusion, but one or two States are reconsidering, and enforcement is uneven. Except in crowded resort areas, few commercial campgrounds exclude pets.

HAZARDS

Entries note a few special hazards such as sudden weather on Mt. Washington. A more general admonition is not to plan mountain hiking trips during the mud season, generally from snowmelt until about the end of May. You won't enjoy it, and boots damage wet trails.

Late spring and early summer is usually the black fly season in the northern woods. Outfitters, pharmacies, and markets sell extra-strength repellents to ward off the vicious beasts. Better have some.

REFERENCES

In addition to standard field guides, we found these books useful to understanding the natural history of New England:

DeGraaf, Richard M., and Deborah D. Rudis. *New England Wildlife: Habitat, Natural History, and Distribution*. General Technical Report NE-108. Broomwall, PA: U.S. Department of Agriculture, Forest Service, Northeastern Forest Experiment Station, 1986.

Harris, Stuart K., and others. *AMC Field Guide to Mountain Flowers of New England*. Boston: Appalachian Mountain Club, 1982.

Jorgensen, Neil. *A Sierra Club Naturalist's Guide to Southern New England*. San Francisco: Sierra Club Books, 1978.

Kulik, Stephen, Pete Salmansohn, Matthew Schmidt, and Heidi Welch. *The Audubon Society Field Guide to the Natural Places of the Northeast: Coastal*. New York, Pantheon Books, 1984.

Kulik, Stephen, Pete Salmansohn, Matthew Schmidt, and Heidi Welch. *The Audubon Society Field Guide to the Natural Places of the Northeast: Inland*. New York, Pantheon Books, 1984.

References specific to states appear in state prefaces, references with site information in entries.

THE
SIERRA CLUB
GUIDE TO
THE
NATURAL AREAS
OF
NEW ENGLAND

MAINE

L arge as the rest of New England combined, Maine has less than a tenth of the region's population. Most of its people live in the coastal region from Portsmouth to Bar Harbor. The extreme south has merged with the Boston metropolis.

This is the part of Maine most tourists see. The number of 100,000-vehicle days on the Maine Turnpike doubled in two years. From the southern border to Bar Harbor, the Maine coast is busy in summer. We saw crowds at every sandy beach. Seaside State Parks were jammed, cars parked along the roads outside their gates. Traffic on the main roads was heavy. The unbelievable number of antique shops made us wonder if producing antiques is a major industry. The many lobster restaurants made it understandable that the lobster population has declined alarmingly.

Some speculators have made fortunes buying land and selling to developers. Lakes are the developers' prime targets as far north as Moosehead Lake. Lakes and ponds that were isolated a few years ago are surrounded by condominiums and tourist businesses. Our Maine advisors spoke of this change with shock and horror, calling it sudden, dramatic, unbelievable, overwhelming, terrifying. For the most part, it has been uncontrolled, or—as one state official put it—"plain crazy." Developers easily found loopholes in the state's environmental laws. Local governments couldn't cope. We were told that 80 percent of the developments are not reviewed.

"Those aren't our people buying the land," a Maine native said bitterly. "Maine folks don't have that kind of money." Frugal Maine natives are amazed to see costly houses built for only two weeks' occupancy in the year.

It's a fascinating coast, only 228 miles long but with a 3,478-mile shoreline. One can find quiet places even in summer. Avoid the sandy beaches. Rocky shores attract fewer people, and they have a greater diversity of flora and fauna. Acadia National Park has some splendid rocky shore. Beyond Acadia there's no crowding.

MAINE IS DIFFERENT

Away from the coast is a vast area unlike anything else in the United States, 300 mi. N–S, 300 mi. wide. The terrain is generally hilly and not high. Most of the SE half is below 500 ft. elevation. Most of the NW is a plateau between 1,000 and 1,500 ft. Mountains, extensions of the Appalachian chain, rise to peaks from 3,000 to 5,000 ft. in the central and western sectors. At 5,268 ft., Mt. Katahdin is Maine's highest point.

The landscape was shaped by glaciers. The state has more than 2,500 lakes and ponds distributed throughout the area, their combined surfaces totaling over 1.5 million acres. With more than 37,000 mi. of rivers, Maine has more canoe routes than any eastern state. Little known are its 700,000 acres of bogs and wetlands.

Much of the landscape one sees along inland highways is monotonous: mile after mile of second-growth forest on gently rolling land. Highway planners avoid mountains and ravines. Trees hide most of the lakes and rivers.

Most of this vast area was sold to timber companies and individuals in the nineteenth century. Maine was left with little public land, far less in relation to its size than any other woodland state. But it didn't seem to matter: for generations, most outdoor recreation—especially hunting, fishing, and canoeing—was on private land. The traditional pattern was based on the "camp," typically a lakeshore lodge that was often the only habitation on a backcountry lake. The camp provided guides, canoes, and equipment. Many a sportsman returned year after year to go out with the same guide, who paddled, made camp, cleaned fish, and cooked.

CLIMATE

Summer temperatures throughout Maine are generally cool, hot days unusual. In January average temperatures range from 10°F in the far north to over 20° along the coast. Total annual precipitation averages from 40 to 44 inches, with no pronounced wet or dry seasons. Except along the coast, most winter precipitation is snow. January is the snowiest month. The period of snow cover ranges from about 50 days near the coast to four months in the NW.

MAPS

Maine is singularly blessed with an array of excellent maps, produced by the DeLorme Publishing Company of Freeport. DeLorme's *The Maine Map and Guide* is the official State highway map. It is keyed to:

The Maine Atlas and Gazetteer. Freeport: DeLorme Publishing, 1983.

Similar to DeLorme's New Hampshire and Vermont atlases, the *Maine Atlas* has 70 full-page maps with symbols that include beaches, nature preserves, Wildlife Management Areas, Parks, boat launching sites, canoe trips, trails, and much more. It includes information about a range of subjects from campgrounds to charter fly-in services.

Maps and guides for hiking, canoeing, and fishing are noted under those headings.

FLORA AND FAUNA

About 85 percent of Maine is forested. Only a few remnants remain of the primeval forest, predominantly spruce and white pine. The timber industry is now cutting second- and third-growth spruce and pine, as well as poplar, fir, hemlock, and some hardwoods, chiefly maple, beech, and birch.

Although this forest is by far the most extensive plant community, there are many others, from coastal tidepools to subarctic flora on high mountains. Much of the northern region is poorly drained, creating swamps and bogs with their special plant species.

We didn't find a popular guide to Maine plants. Entries note what is available for sites such as Baxter State Park, which suggests species one could expect to find in similar habitats. Fox Forest is one of several sites that provides good information. A good regional reference is

Harris, Stuart K., and others. *AMC Field Guide to Mountain Flowers of New England.* Boston: Appalachian Mountain Club, 1982.

Nor did we find popular guides to the state's birds and mammals. The Maine Audubon Society has a field checklist of birds.

The state's mammals include three big game species: deer, black bear, and moose. Small mammals include bobcat, weasel, squirrel, snowshoe hare, coyote, fox, skunk, fisher, marten, raccoon, beaver, mink, otter, and muskrat. Marine mammals are often seen along the coast and its many islands. Large remote areas with little hunting pressure are valuable reservoirs.

Some of the larger sites, notably Acadia National Park and Baxter State Park, have information about their fauna. The most comprehensive information is provided by:

DeGraaf, Richard M., and Deborah D. Rudis. *New England Wildlife: Habitat, Natural History, and Distribution,* General Technical Report NE-108. Broomwall, PA: U.S. Department of Agriculture, Forest Service, Northeastern Forest Experiment Station, 1986.

TRAILS

An estimate of total trail mileage wouldn't mean much in Maine. In the vast region of commercial forest land, hikers use logging roads, many of which are busy during timber cutting, then abandoned until the next cutting cycle years later.

The state's four great trail systems are
- The Appalachian Trail, which begins in Baxter State Park
- Other Baxter trails
- Acadia National Park trails
- White Mountain National Forest trails

Trail information is noted in entries. Also see:

- AMC Maine Mountain Guidebook Committee. *Maine Mountain Guide.* Boston: Appalachian Mountain Club, 1985.
- ATC Committee. *Appalachian Trail Guide to Maine.* Harpers Ferry, WV: Appalachian Trail Conference, 1983.

Although these attract most of the backpackers, there are also many fine trails for day hikes. Even in midsummer we often hiked for several hours without meeting others. Look at the *Maine Atlas* to see what trails are in the region that interests you. Then consult one of the following booklets, which have trail maps, in color, and directions:

Hiking. Vol. 1: *Coastal and Eastern Region;* Vol. 2: *Western Region;* Vol. 3: *Northern Region.* Freeport: DeLorme Mapping, 1983.

Trails in Baxter, the SW region, and the south coast are described, with maps, in:

Gibson, John. *Fifty Hikes in Maine.* Woodstock, VT: Backcountry Publications, 1983.

PRIVATE LANDS

The use of private land for public recreation continues today, with increasing controls. The North Maine Woods (see entry), 2.8 million acres, has entrances where visitors register and select campsites. Some timber companies also have entrance gates and fees. Several didn't respond to our inquiries. One manager telephoned to explain why he wouldn't answer in writing: "We still let people hunt and fish and camp on our land, but we must be free to close gates or areas whenever we need to. We don't want anyone to think he has a right to be on our land."

The general rule seems to be: If a gate or sign tells you to keep out, do so. Otherwise, it's probably OK to enter, but act like a guest. If you're on a canoe trip, riparian camping is permissible unless there's a posted prohibition.

THE PUBLIC RESERVED LANDS

Several years ago it was discovered that the State had not, in fact, sold all that land in the 1800s. In some cases it had sold only the rights to the timber then standing. Having reestablished its title to 450,000 acres, the State began trading and consolidating. Now available to visitors are 21 large parcels, from 2,200 acres to over 35,000 acres. Multiple-purpose management plans call for a minimum of development, preservation of natural qualities, and opportunities for primitive recreation. If you visit one of these units, you're on your own. (The reacquisition process continues. We have a last-minute entry: Donnell Pond/Tunk Lake.)

We visited most of these new sites and pronounce them splendid. The Maine Bureau of Public Lands has a leaflet, *Recreational Opportunities on Maine's Public Reserved Lands.*

STATE PARKS

The Maine Bureau of Parks and Recreation operates 29 State Parks, large and small, serving a variety of purposes. They total about 25,000 acres, almost two-thirds of this total in the five largest Parks. Size isn't always significant. Some of the smaller Parks adjoin or are within larger areas available for recreation.

Preservation of green space hasn't kept up with development in the south. Areas of private land once freely used for recreation are fast being developed. As the need increases, land prices soar. One town paid over half a million dollars for 1,400 feet of lakefront. The federal funds once available to States for land acquisition have stopped coming. Bond issues have been proposed as an alternative. Developers and their political allies are, of course, opposed to State acquisition of any tract that could be a building site.

Maine has no State Forests.

COASTAL ISLANDS

The Maine Bureau of Public Lands (BPL) manages several hundred small State-owned coastal islands. Hundreds more are State or federal wildlife refuges with restricted access. Most of the BPL islands are rocky and barren, some inundated by high tides. Some are off limits because of seabird colonies. A few, however, are large enough to support some visitation and have interesting features. The BPL leaflet, *Your Islands on the Coast,* includes warnings that should be heeded. Also available is

Monegain, Bernie. *Coastal Islands, a Guide to Exploring Maine's Offshore Isles.* Freeport: DeLorme Publishing, 1985.

The Illustrated Map of the Maine Coast. Freeport: DeLorme Mapping, 1987.

WILDLIFE MANAGEMENT AREAS

We were given information about 8 WMAs, totaling 12,081 acres. Maine, with its many wetlands, is an important waterfowl production area, and several of the WMAs are wetlands. See entries.

CAMPING

Of the State Parks, 13 have campgrounds. Most are open May 15–Oct. 15. A new reservation system was introduced in 1988. Reservations can be made by telephone (1-800-332-1501 within Maine, 1-207-289-3824 outside Maine), using VISA or MasterCard, but we suggest asking for the system information first, by telephone or writing to the Bureau of Parks and Recreation.

Pets are not allowed at Sebago Lake State Park or on beaches in other Parks.

Camping is permitted only in campgrounds in State Parks and Acadia National Park. Campsites are assigned at entrance gates of the North Maine Woods. Informal camping is permitted in the Public Reserved Lands and in the White Mountain National Forest.

Forest campsites are available at 88 locations on private lands in northern Maine. The Maine Forest Service no longer publishes a list of these sites, but information is available at Forest Service regional offices in Island Falls, Greenville, and Old Town.

Maine has many commercial campgrounds, but the vocabulary often confuses strangers. A "camp" may offer cabins, guides, fishing, boating, and more—but not campsites for tents or RVs. Consult a campground directory or consult the Maine Campground Owners Association, 655 Main St., Lewiston, ME 04240; (207) 782-5874. For a broader picture, the promotional brochure, *Maine Invites You,* has much useful information. It's available from:

Maine Publicity Bureau
97 Winthrop St.
Hallowell, ME 04347
(207) 289-2423

It includes a list of Chambers of Commerce, several of which we found remarkably well informed about local trails and other outdoor features.

CANOEING

Maine is canoe country, none finer. We saw ten canoes on passing cars for every motorcraft towed or carried. The most famous canoe trips are the Allagash Wilderness Waterway and the St. John River. We have entries for them and a number of others. Many trips are described and mapped in various publications, including those we list. The North Woods has countless backcountry water routes known only to professional guides, who know the best places to fish and camp.

AMC River Guide, Maine. Boston: Appalachian Mountain Club, 1986.
Kellogg, Zip. *Canoeing.* Vol. 1: *Coastal and Eastern Rivers.* Freeport: DeLorme Publishing, 1985.

Kellogg, Zip. *Canoeing.* Vol. 2: *Western Rivers.* Freeport: DeLorme Publishing, 1985.

Kellogg, Zip. *Canoeing.* Vol. 3: *Northern Rivers.* Freeport: DeLorme Publishing 1986.

FISHING, BOATING

Three volumes of fishing maps have descriptions of the waters and tell what species inhabit them. The maps show public launching sites. The Bureau of Parks and Recreation leaflet, *Outdoors in Maine,* has a long list of boat-launching sites.

Vanderweide, Harry. *Maine Fishing Maps.* Vol. 1: *Lakes and Ponds.* Freeport: DeLorme Publishing, 1986.

Vanderweide, Harry. *Maine Fishing Maps.* Vol. 2: *Rivers and Streams.* Freeport: DeLorme Publishing, 1984.

Vanderweide, Harry. *Maine Fishing Maps.* Vol. 3: *Salt Water Areas.* Freeport: DeLorme Publishing, 1984.

Vanderweide, Harry, ed. *The Maine Sportsman Fishing Trip Planner.* Yarmouth: All Outdoors, annual.

STATE AGENCIES

Bureau of Parks and Recreation
State House Station 22
Augusta, ME 04333
(207) 289-3821

Department of Inland Fisheries and Wildlife
State House Station 41
Augusta, ME 04333
(207) 289-3371

Bureau of Public Lands
Maine Department of Conservation
State House Station 22
Augusta, ME 04333
(207) 289-3061

PRIVATE ORGANIZATIONS

Maine Chapter, The Nature Conservancy
122 Main St.
P.O. Box 338

Topsham, ME 04086
(207) 729-5181

The Nature Conservancy's mission is to identify and preserve unusual natural areas. In Maine, TNC has acquired or received numerous parcels of land subsequently transferred to federal or State agencies. It owns and manages 70 preserves totaling about 12,000 acres. We have entries for several. The publication cited looks too expensive to be a handout:

Lannon, Mary Minor C. S. *Maine Forever.* Topsham: The Nature Conservancy, 1984.

Maine Audubon Society
Gilsland Farm
118 US Route 1
Falmouth, ME 04105
(207) 781-2330

The society operates a number of preserves and nature centers. We have entries for several.

MAP NOTES IN TEXT

All map references (e.g., "Map 34, B-3") are to the DeLorme Publishing Company's *Maine Atlas and Gazetteer* (Freeport: 1983). *Coastal:* Maps 1–9, 12–17, 22–27, and 36–37. *West:* Maps 10–11, 18–21, and 28–35. *North:* Maps 38–69.

NORTH

Presque
Isle ●

95

WEST

Skowhegan ●

Bangor ●

COASTAL

Augusta ●

Bar Harbor ●

Lewiston ●

Portland ●

0   40 MI.

0   40 KM

An Alphabetical Listing

Acadia National Park
Coastal
Allagash Wilderness Waterway
North
Appalachian Trail
West
Baxter State Park
North
Bigelow Preserve
West
Bradbury Mountain State Park
Coastal
Brownfield Bog Wildlife
Management Area
Coastal
Camden Hills State Park
Coastal
Chamberlain Lake Management
Unit *North*
Chesterville Wildlife Management
Unit *West*
Cobscook Bay State Park
Coastal
Deboullie Management Unit
North
Donnell Pond/Tunk Lake
Coastal
Duck Lake Management Unit
West
Eagle Lake Management Unit
North
East Point Sanctuary
Coastal
Fernald's Neck Preserve
Coastal
Four Ponds Management Unit
West
Frye Mountain Wildlife
Management Area
Coastal

Gardner-Deboullie Management
Unit *North*
Georgia-Pacific Corporation Lands
West/North
Gero Island Management Unit
North
Gilsland Farm
Coastal
Grafton Notch State Park
West
Great Wass Island Preserve
Coastal
Gulf Hagas Area
North
Holeb Management Unit
North
Howard L. Mendall Wildlife
Management Area
Coastal
Indian Point/Blagden Preserve
Coastal
Josephine Newman Sanctuary
Coastal
La Verna and Rachel Carson Salt
Pond Preserves
Coastal
Leavitt Wildlife Management Area
West
Lily Bay State Park
North
Little Squaw Management Unit
North
Lt. Gordon Manuel Wildlife
Management Area
North
Machias Seal Island
Coastal
Mahoosuc Mountains Management
Unit *West*
Mast Landing Sanctuary
Coastal

Mattawamkeag Wilderness Park
North
Moosehead Lake
North
Moosehorn National Wildlife
Refuge   *Coastal*
Morse Mountain Preserve
Coastal
Mount Blue State Park
West
Mullen Woods Preserve
Coastal
North Maine Woods
North
Peaks-Kenny State Park
West
Petit Manan National Wildlife
Refuge   *Coastal*
Pond Farm Wildlife Management
Area   *West*
Popham Beach State Park
Coastal
Quoddy Head State Park
Coastal
Rachel Carson National Wildlife
Refuge   *Coastal*
Rangeley Lake State Park
West
Reid State Park
Coastal
Richardson Lake Management Unit
West
Rocky Lake Management Unit
Coastal
Round Pond Management Unit
North
Ruffingham Wildlife Management
Area   *Coastal*

R. Waldo Tyler Wildlife
Management Area
Coastal
Sawtelle Deadwater Wildlife
Management Area
North
Scarborough Marsh
Coastal
Scraggly Lake Management Unit
North
Sebago Lake State Park
Coastal
Seboeis Lake Management Unit
North
Seboeis River
North
Squa Pan Lake
North
Steep Falls Wildlife Management
Area   *Coastal*
Steve Powell Wildlife Management
Area   *Coastal*
St. John River
North
Sugar Island Management Unit
North
Telos Lake Management
Unit/Chamberlain Lake
Management Unit
North
The Great Heath
Coastal
Vaughan Woods
Coastal
Vernon S. Walker Wildlife
Management Area
Coastal
White Mountain National Forest
West

NATURAL AREAS IN MAINE
by Zone

North Zone

Allagash Wilderness Waterway
Baxter State Park
Chamberlain Lake Management
 Unit
Deboullie Management Unit
Eagle Lake Management Unit
Gardner-Deboullie Management
 Unit
Georgia-Pacific Corporation Lands
Gero Island Management Unit
Gulf Hagas Area
Holeb Management Unit
Lily Bay State Park
Little Squaw Management Unit
Lt. Gordon Manuel Wildlife
 Management Area
Mattawamkeag Wilderness Park
Moosehead Lake
North Maine Woods
Round Pond Management Unit
Sawtelle Deadwater Wildlife
 Management Area
Scraggly Lake Management Unit
Seboeis Lake Management Unit
Seboeis River
Squa Pan Lake
St. John River
Sugar Island Management Unit
Telos Lake Management
 Unit/Chamberlain Lake
 Management Unit

Coastal Zone

Acadia National Park
Bradbury Mountain State Park
Brownfield Bog Wildlife
 Management Area
Camden Hills State Park
Cobscook Bay State Park
Donnell Pond/Tunk Lake
East Point Sanctuary
Fernald's Neck Preserve
Frye Mountain Wildlife
 Management Area
Gilsland Farm
Great Wass Island Preserve
Howard L. Mendall Wildlife
 Management Area
Indian Point/Blagden Preserve
Josephine Newman Sanctuary
La Verna and Rachel Carson Salt
 Pond Preserves
Machias Seal Island
Mast Landing Sanctuary
Moosehorn National Wildlife
 Refuge
Morse Mountain Preserve
Mullen Woods Preserve
Petit Manan National Wildlife
 Refuge
Popham Beach State Park
Quoddy Head State Park
Rachel Carson National Wildlife
 Refuge
Reid State Park
Rocky Lake Management Unit
Ruffingham Wildlife Management
 Area
R. Waldo Tyler Wildlife
 Management Area
Scarborough Marsh

Sebago Lake State Park
Steep Falls Wildlife Management
Area
Steve Powell Wildlife Management
Area
The Great Heath
Vaughan Woods
Vernon S. Walker Wildlife
Management Area

West Zone

Appalachian Trail
Bigelow Preserve
Chesterville Wildlife Management
Unit

Duck Lake Management Unit
Four Ponds Management Unit
Georgia-Pacific Corporation Lands
Grafton Notch State Park
Leavitt Wildlife Management Area
Mahoosuc Mountains Management
Unit
Mount Blue State Park
Peaks-Kenny State Park
Pond Farm Wildlife Management
Area
Rangeley Lake State Park
Richardson Lake Management Unit
White Mountain National Forest

ACADIA NATIONAL PARK
National Park Service   Coastal
35,000 acres.

On Mt. Desert Island. From US 1 at Ellsworth, S on SR 3 to visitor center.
(Map 16.)

Open all year. Some roads may be closed by snow in winter and early spring.

This is the only National Park in New England, on the largest rock island
off the U.S. Atlantic coast. It includes parts of several smaller islands and a
mainland peninsula. It is second only to Great Smoky Mountains National
Park in number of visitors, about 4 million per year.

Uplift, subsidence, glaciation, and erosion have produced a rugged, rocky
shoreline. Mountains up to 1,530 ft. rise abruptly from the sea. At low tide,
countless pools are exposed, lively with marine creatures. The island is cut
by many deep sounds, harbors, and coves. Somes Sound, a fjord, almost bisects the island. Several freshwater lakes are on the island. Uplands are heavily forested, but mountain summits are often open and rocky, providing for
great vistas.

Most National Parks were carved from the public domain. Acadia was created by conservation-minded citizens who contributed most of the land and
persuaded Congress to establish, in 1919, the first National Park east of the
Mississippi.

The Park doesn't occupy all of Mt. Desert Island. The town of Bar Harbor is at the gateway. A map makes the Park look like an unfinished jigsaw puzzle, several large masses and a number of smaller ones, with gaps between, the accumulation of land gifts. Indeed, the boundaries were not fixed by law until 1986. In coming years, the Park may acquire some of the inholdings within these boundaries.

Thanks to good signs and good Park planning, the jigsaw pattern isn't too confusing on the ground. The island has 200 mi. of paved state and town roads, the Park only 25 mi., including the Loop Road, the principal tour route. Many portions of the Park are roadless, linked by state and town roads.

For the summer visitor, the first question is where to stay. The Park has two campgrounds, one with a Ticketron reservation system. The other is first come, first served, but it is often full in summer. Nearby are 11 private campgrounds, plus motels and other accommodations, where reservations are necessary in the busy season.

At the Grand Canyon of the Colorado, visitors may be satisfied that they have "seen" the canyon if they have spent an hour at the South Rim. Acadia has no such central feature, but a great diversity of natural splendors. Many visitors don't know what to do or where to go.

Stop at the visitor center first. Here one quickly realizes that Acadia can't be fully seen in a day or a week. Last year's schedule of naturalist programs had 120 activities weekly, including mountain hikes, boat cruises, beaver watches, and amphitheater slide presentations. On your own you can travel the 25 mi. of paved roads, 120 mi. of hiking trails, and 44 mi. of carriage paths used by hikers, cyclists, horseriders, and—in winter—skiers.

If you have only one day, see the sights along the 27-mi. Park Loop Road: spectacular mountains, beaches, and cliffs. There's enough time to walk up Cadillac Mountain, visit the Shore Path, stop at the Jordan Pond Nature Trail, and end the day at one of the amphitheater programs. We spent much of our first day exploring tidepools.

Climate: Summer temperatures vary from 45° to 85°F, spring and fall from 30° to 70°. Annual precipitation is about 49 in. Rain and fog may occur at any time. Mosquitoes and black flies are most common in June.

FEATURES

The largest mass of the Park is on the E side of the island, beyond the visitor center. Near the middle of the E side are two of the largest water bodies: *Eagle Lake,* about 1 3/4 mi. long, and *Jordan Pond,* about 1 1/4 mi. long. The *Loop Road* circles the area E of these lakes, enclosing the Park's highest mountain. Along the route are *Sieur de Monts Spring,* with a Nature Center and wildflower garden; *Sand Beach,* one of ME's few sandy beaches, popular with sunbathers; *Thunder Hole, Otter Cliffs, Jordan Pond,* and *Bubble Pond.* On the W side of this portion of the Park is *Sargent Drive,* overlooking *Somes Sound.* A spur road goes to the top of 1,530-ft. *Cadillac Mountain.*

In the early days of the Park, *carriage paths,* a unique way of providing access to automobile-free areas, were financed and planned by John D. Rockefeller, Jr. The paths extend from near the visitor center to the S coast, chiefly to the W of the Loop Road.

The smaller mass, W of Somes Sound, has fewer roads and fewer visitors. At the far S is *Seawall Campground.* Bicycles can be rented at *Southwest Harbor.* A nature trail is at *Ship Harbor.* Swimming at *Echo Lake.*

FEATURES OUTSIDE MT. DESERT ISLAND

Isle au Haut is about 18 mi. to the SW by water, more than 70 by road and the mail boat from Stonington. (Map 15, E-4.) There is no car ferry. This remote, densely forested island, a bit over 6 mi. long, has long had a small fishing community and summer colony. In 1943 the S half of the island was given to the Park. It's an island for hikers, with numerous trails to explore the rocky shoreline, marshes, bogs, a narrow lake, and forested hills. A campground near the Duck Harbor landing has five lean-tos, each accommodating 6 people, available by reservation only. No other accommodations are available. (The Duck Harbor landing is used only July–August. The town landing is 5 mi. from the campground.)

The number of visitors on the island is limited, and on rare occasions daytrippers may be excluded.

Schoodic Peninsula lies E of Bar Harbor. The Park area is reached from US 1 at West Gouldsboro, S on SR 186. (Map 17, A-1.) Few Park visitors go there. It's a small piece of the peninsula, about 1 1/2 by 3 mi., with a one-way scenic drive. It preserves a fine section of the coast, and the peninsula as a whole has the flavor of rural, small-town Maine, unlike the bustle of Bar Harbor. There is no campground in the Park.

The *Islesford Historical Cruise* lands at Little Cranberry Island for a visit to the *Islesford Museum.*

Plants: 95% of the Park is forested, an intermingling of northern coniferous and temperate deciduous types. 35% of the area is predominantly coniferous, 40% mixed forest, 20% deciduous. The most common tree species are eastern white pine, pitch pine, red spruce, white spruce, eastern hemlock, quaking aspen, American beech, pin cherry, red maple, striped maple, northern red oak, balsam fir, northern white-cedar.

About 1,500 plant species occur in the Park. A three-page checklist of common flowering plants is available, grouped by habitat: coniferous woods, mountains and dry rocky sites, deciduous woods, marsh and pond, bog, roadside, and meadow.

Birds: Birding is exceptional. The Park's checklist shows seasonal abundance, habitats, and confirmed breeding. About 336 species have been reported, an extraordinarily high number that reflects both the diverse nature of the site and the quality of observation. The list includes 70 species reported less than five times, such as the magnificent frigatebird, greater white-fronted goose, sandhill crane, South-Polar skua, ivory gull, sooty tern, and yellow-headed blackbird, all well out of their normal ranges.

Mammals: The Park's checklist shows common species, those which are rare, and those which have been extirpated, such as the timber wolf, lynx, and cougar. Common species include red fox, raccoon, whitetail deer, shorttail and longtail weasels, mink, otter, striped skunk, porcupine, woodchuck, beaver, eastern chipmunk, red and gray squirrels, northern flying squirrel, deer mouse, boreal redback and meadow voles. Shrews: masked, northern water, pygmy, shorttail. Starnose and hairytail moles, snowshoe hare, red and hoary bats, harbor seal, harbor porpoise, minke whale.

INTERPRETATION
Visitor center at entrance has orientation film, publications, information about walks, hikes, boat cruises, evening programs, and much more. *Closed Nov.–Apr.; then see Park HQ on SR 233, 3 mi. W of Bar Harbor.*
Tape tour, on cassette, is available at the visitor center.
Nature center, wildflower garden, and *Abbe Museum* at Sieur de Monts Spring.
Nature trails at Jordan Pond and Ship Harbor.

ACTIVITIES
Camping: Two campgrounds, 541 sites. Blackwoods is open all year. Reservations through Ticketron are required at Blackwoods June 15–Sept. 15. No reservations at Seawall campground, which is open late May through late Sept.
Hiking: 120 mi. of trails, throughout the Park. No trailside camping.
Fishing: Fresh and salt water. Freshwater species include trout, salmon, bass.
Swimming: Lifeguards at Echo Lake and Sand Beach.
Boating: Courtesy moorings at Schoodic Peninsula (Winter Harbor), Baker Island, Isle au Haut (Duck Harbor) and near the entrance to Somes Sound. Launching on lakes and ponds. Marinas and other commercial facilities at Bar Harbor and other coast towns.
Horse riding: Stable on Loop Road near Seal Harbor.
Bicycling: Rentals at Bar Harbor and Southwest Harbor. All carriage paths suitable for balloon-tire bikes, 16 mi. for thin tires.
Pets must be kept on leash.

PUBLICATIONS
Park leaflet with map.
Acadia's Beaver Log has visit-planning information, activity schedules.
Information pages:
Welcome to Acadia National Park!

Freshwater fishing.
List of publications.
Winter activities guide.
Geology.
History.
Bicycle guide.
Isle au Haut.
Private campground list.
Boat cruise and ferry list.
Schoodic Peninsula (with map).
Camping: Ticketron reservation form.
Plant checklist.
Bird checklist.
Mammals, reptiles, and amphibians checklist.

REFERENCES
AMC Maine Mountain Guidebook Committee. *AMC Trail Guide to Mount Desert Island and Acadia National Park.* Boston: Appalachian Mountain Club.

Gibson, John. *Fifty Hikes in Maine.* Woodstock, VT: Backcountry Publications, 1983.

Monegain, Bernie. *Natural Sites, A Guide to Maine's Natural Phenomena.* Freeport: DeLorme Publishing, 1985.

Mt. Desert Island—Acadia National Park Map. Freeport: DeLorme Mapping, 1987.

NEARBY: Indian Point/Blagden Preserve (see entry).

HEADQUARTERS: Box 177, Bar Harbor, ME 04609; (207) 288-3338.

ALLAGASH WILDERNESS WATERWAY
Bureau of Parks and Recreation   North
92 mi. waterway; 200,000 acres, including 30,000 acres of water.

In the North Maine Woods (see entry). All access is by float plane or private road; landowners permit public use but control access. Upstream access at Telos Lake or Chamberlain Lake (see entries). Other access points from Ashland, Allagash Village. See Maps 50, 55, 56, 61, 62, 66.

This fabulous waterway through the forests of northern ME was established by state legislation in 1966 and included in the National Wild and Scenic Rivers System in 1970. It is a protected corridor, not a vast pristine region. Private roads cross or parallel it at several places. Development or other habitat disturbance is prohibited within 500 ft. of the waterway. Only state-approved timber harvesting is permitted in areas visible from the river within 1 mi. of the shore.

Most of the surrounding land is owned by timber companies. This was once the domain of giant white pines. Now spruce, fir, and other softwood species supply the pulp and paper industries.

However, since the Waterway was established ME's Bureau of Public Lands has acquired nearly 30,000 acres at Telos and Chamberlain lakes and Round Pond (see entries). Here the mandate is multiple-use management, giving full weight to wildlife and recreation values along with timber production.

For those who travel the waterway, it is a wilderness experience. Only canoes are permitted N of Chamberlain Lake, although canoes may have motors up to 10 hp. (Inflatable craft are not permitted.) Canoeing the entire route takes 7 to 10 days. The linear trip is only one of many possibilities. The complex includes a variety of lakes, ponds, and streams on either side of the main route. One can make a camping trip of a day, a week, or more, returning to the put-in point.

Allagash Lake, for example, is about 6 mi. W of the main route, linked to Chamberlain Lake by Allagash Stream. This is the only part of the Waterway where all motors are prohibited. Eight campsites are distributed around the lake. "Ice caves" are on the NE side.

Water conditions vary from year to year, but they are usually favorable from late May into Oct. Ice sometimes persists into late May. In side streams, flow may become inadequate late in the season. High flow rates require extra skill at Chase Rapids.

Drinking water can usually be obtained from a spring or lake. Normal purification methods are recommended. Food, fuel, and other supplies aren't available along the way. You should have both the Waterway schematic map and topos.

FEATURES

From the put-in on Telos Lake, it's 5 mi. to the foot of Chamberlain Lake, then 10 mi. to Lock Dam and a short portage. Then comes 12 mi. on Eagle Lake, and 7 more mi. to Churchill Dam. Below the dam is the 9-mi. run through Chase Rapids to Umsaskis Lake. Portage service is available in season for those who wish to avoid the rapids. Rapids are rated to Class II.

From this point on to Allagash Falls, there are no large lakes. The falls, a 40-ft. drop, are one of the scenic features of the route. The portage around the falls is 1/8 mi. Then it's 13 mi. to Allagash Village, where most cruises end. Return transportation can be arranged privately at Allagash Village or at towns on the St. John River.

Guide service is available. Outfitters offer trips, supplying all but personal gear.

ACTIVITIES

Camping: Only authorized campsites may be used. They are scattered along the waterway, signed, and marked on maps. Sites cannot be reserved, and sharing sites is a wilderness courtesy. Most sites have tables, fireplaces, and pit toilets.

Hiking: There are a few trails to fire towers, providing fine viewpoints.

Hunting: Firearms may not be carried or used within the waterway boundaries May 1–Oct. 1. Otherwise state game laws apply.

Fishing: Brook trout, togue, lake whitefish.

Canoeing: Each party must register at the first contact point.

In winter: Snowmobiles may use unplowed roads (most of which are outside Waterway boundaries) or frozen lakes. Stream channel ice is likely to be thin; some channels remain open.

Strict rules govern use of the Waterway. HQ will supply copies of the regulations.

The black fly season is June, extending into July in wet years. Bring an effective repellent.

PUBLICATIONS

Waterway folder with map
Regulations

REFERENCES

Allagash & St. John Map and Guide. Freeport: DeLorme Mapping Company, 1987.

AMC River Guide: Maine. Boston, MA: Appalachian Mountain Club, 1980.

Kellogg, Zip. *Canoeing.* Vol. 3: *Northern Rivers.* Freeport: DeLorme Publishing, 1986.

Vanderweide, Harry. *Maine Fishing Maps.* Vol. 1: *Lakes and Ponds;* Freeport: DeLorme Publishing, 1986.

Vanderweide, Harry. *Maine Fishing Maps.* Vol. 2: *Rivers and Streams.* Freeport: DeLorme Publishing, 1984.

HEADQUARTERS: Bureau of Parks and Recreation, State House Station 22, Augusta, ME 04333; (207) 289-3821.

APPALACHIAN TRAIL

Mixed ownerships   West
279 mi. in ME.
(Maps 18, 29-31, 41-42, 50.)

From Mt. Katahdin in Baxter State Park to the NH border.

We walked one section of the famous Trail along the main street of Monson. Two hikers with destinations more distant than ours were replenishing their food stocks. Most of the Trail is in backcountry, following the ridges, crossing the state's highest peaks, often far from any road or shop.

Some day the entire Trail, from Maine to Georgia, may be on public land or protected by easements. Today Maine has more unprotected trail miles than any other state. Until recently there has been no pressing need. Much of the Trail is on land owned by timber companies that permit recreation on their holdings.

Getting permission to maintain the Trail across private land isn't the only issue. The National Park Service hopes to make the trail a scenic corridor. In 1987 this aim conflicted with the plans of a commercial ski area. The proposed hillside clearings, lift towers, and other structures wouldn't block the Trail, but would spoil its backwoods character. NPS was trying to acquire enough land to protect the view.

Our entries note if the Trail crosses or passes nearby. Many other trails, most of them blue-blazed, intersect the Appalachian, linking it with various parks, preserves, and trailheads.

ACTIVITIES

Backpacking: More than three dozen campsites and shelters are maintained along the Trail. Other camping possibilities are on side trails.

Fishing: Many streams, ponds, and lakes are along the route.

REFERENCE: ATC Committee. *Appalachian Trail Guide to Maine.* Harpers Ferry, WV: Appalachian Trail Conference, 1983.

BAXTER STATE PARK

Bureau of Parks and Recreation   North
201,108 acres.

From Greenville (Map 41, D-2), N on Lily Bay Rd. to Togue Pond Gatehouse. (Map 50, A-D, 4-5; Map 51, A-D, 1.)

In season, gates are open 6 A.M. to 10 P.M.

We've never been there, although we've been close half a dozen times. Baxter's roads are so narrow that most trailers and motor homes are barred. So are motorcycles, off-road vehicles, and pets. We travel in a motor home with a black Labrador, both disqualifying us. This is not a complaint; we hope it's kept that way. Our entry is based on information from the Bureau of Parks and Recreation, maps, and talks with people who know the Park well.

Few state governors have left such a legacy. Former ME Governor Percival P. Baxter gave his state the first portion of the Park, including Mt. Katahdin, in 1931. His final gift of 7,764 acres in 1962 brought the Park to its present size, one of the largest State Parks in the United States.

It is surrounded by a vast area of timber company land extending to the Canadian border, crossed by private roads open to public use subject to owners' regulations. (See entry, North Maine Woods.) Like the surrounding lands, portions of the Park were cut over in the past, but the exceptional ruggedness of the terrain protected much of it from ax and saw.

Mt. Katahdin, 5,267 ft. high, in the SW quadrant, is the highest point in Maine. Almost the entire Park is mountainous, except for the valleys of Trout Brook, Nesowadnehunk Stream, Wassataquoik Stream, and Katahdin Stream. Of the 46 peaks and ridges, 18 are higher than 3,000 ft. The Park's lowest elevation is 550 ft.

From the Togue Pond gatehouse, the S entrance, a dead-end road goes to Roaring Brook, trailhead for the Mt. Katahdin and Chimney Pond trails. Mt. Katahdin is the northern terminus of the Appalachian Trail. It is fitting that such a magnificent achievement should end at the highest point, but one can continue to hike north, all the way to a trailhead at South Branch Pond.

Also from the Togue Pond gatehouse, a road follows the stream valleys northward near the W boundary, turning NE along Trout Brook. Just at the turn, a road to the W exit is a route to the Allagash Wilderness Waterway (see entry). The Trout Brook road ends at the Matagamon gatehouse on Matagamon Lake, the boundary, meeting the road to Shin Pond. Most of the Park is roadless wilderness, accessible only on foot.

Not by canoe. Although there are streams everywhere—the map suggests there are over 200 mi. of streams, perhaps much more—most aren't canoeable. There is a short canoe run from Nesowadnehunk Lake to the campground, but that seems to be the only one of note. Lakes and ponds are numerous, but the largest within the Park isn't much over a mile long.

Over 170 mi. of trails are within the Park, offering opportunities for short day hikes from the perimeter road or extended backpacking in the interior.

Plants: Over 90% of the Park is forested, chiefly with the northern spruce/fir type. Principal tree species include red, black, and white spruce; balsam fir; eastern white, red, and jack pines; hemlock, sugar and red maples, beech, birches, aspen. The forest is far from uniform. On the South Branch Nature Trail, one can see the traces of a fire that burned over 80,000 acres in 1903. Here and there are the stumps of great white pines cut long ago. Especially on the upper slopes are stands of old-growth timber.

A list of 112 wildflowers doesn't note abundance or blooming season. Among them are pink moccasin-flower, white rein orchid, several violets, Dutchman's-breeches, cardinal flower, nightshade, blue flag, painted trillium, fireweed, evening primrose, fringed gentian, purple clematis, Indian-pipe, round-leaved sundew, pitcher plant, trailing arbutus, wild columbine, yellow avens, spring beauty.

Birds: A checklist of 177 bird species does not give abundance or seasonality, and thus may include species seldom seen. A selection indicating the range of habitats includes common loon, pied-billed grebe, green heron, least and American bitterns, Canada and snow geese, green-winged and blue-winged teal, wood duck, common and hooded mergansers. Hawks: goshawk, sharp-shinned, Cooper's, red-tailed, red-shouldered, broad-winged, rough-legged. Bald eagle, osprey, peregrine falcon, merlin, American kestrel, spruce and ruffed grouse, Virginia and sora rails, American woodcock, yellow-billed and black-billed cuckoos. Owls: screech, great horned, snowy, hawk, barred, great gray, short-eared, boreal, saw-whet. Woodpeckers: northern flicker, pileated, yellow-bellied sapsucker, hairy, downy, black-backed, and northern three-toed. Swallows: tree, bank, rough-winged, barn, cliff. Bohemian and cedar waxwings, loggerhead and northern shrikes. Vireos: yellow-throated, solitary, red-eyed, Philadelphia, warbling. Warblers: black-and-white, Tennessee, Nashville, northern parula, yellow, magnolia, Cape May, black-throated blue, yellow-rumped, black-throated green, blackburnian, chestnut-sided, bay-breasted, blackpoll, pine, palm, ovenbird, northern waterthrush, mourning, common yellowthroat, Wilson's, Canada, American redstart. Sparrows: tree, chipping, white-crowned, white-throated, fox, Lincoln's, field, swamp, song.

Mammals: The available list isn't a complete inventory of mammals, but it names those the visitor is most likely to see, with information on when and where. Moose, black bear, and deer are the common big game mammals. Other common species include beaver, muskrat, otter, raccoon, bobcat, lynx, red fox, fisher, marten, snowshoe hare, porcupine, red squirrel, chipmunk, mink, coyote.

FEATURES

Mt. Katahdin, just under a mile high, is the prime attraction. Tell someone you've visited Baxter, and the first question is "Did you climb Katahdin?" Then the next question: "Did you cross the Knife Edge?" One need not, although alternative routes aren't easy. The Cathedral Trail gains 2,300 ft. in 1 3/4 mi. At Knife Edge, two cirques meet, forming a narrow ridge, in places less than a yard wide with precipices on each side, one of them almost 2,000 ft. down. It's jagged, bare rock, far from level, and often swept by strong winds. Our daughter crossed it sitting down and said she was terrified. No one should try it in bad weather.

Blueberry Knoll is only one of numerous day hikes that offers splendid scenery with moderate rather than strenuous effort. From Roaring Brook campground, it's 3.2 mi., with an elevation gain of 1,600 ft.

Great Basin is the largest of the 7 cirques forming Mt. Katahdin. Several trails cross this great U-shaped valley. Two tarns, steep-banked mountain ponds, are within the basin.

Katahdin Stream Falls is on the Hunt Trail about 1 1/2 mi. from the perimeter road. Four vertical drops totaling about 80 ft. are in a mossy gorge.

Green Falls is more remote, near the center of the Park on Wassataquoik Stream near Wassataquoik Lake. It's a two-stage drop in a handsome setting. Trail access.

Little Niagara and *Big Niagara Falls* are on Nesowadnehunk Stream in the SW corner of the Park. They were named in jest—"Big" Niagara drops less than 20 ft.—but it's a delightful area with many ponds and streams, surrounding the Daicey Pond campground.

INTERPRETATION

Visitor center is at Millinocket on SR 11/157. Displays, slide show, literature. It's a good idea to stop here for information before proceeding to the Park.

Daicey Pond Nature Trail circles Daicey Pond in the SW corner of the Park, just off the Appalachian Trail. Many wildflowers.

Roaring Brook Nature Trail is near the Roaring Brook Campground. Habitats include forest, bog, stream, pond.

South Branch Nature Trail begins at the South Branch Pond campground parking lot. This was the area of the 1903 burn. Many wildflowers, birds.

ACTIVITIES

Camping: 6 campgrounds accessible by road, plus cabins at Daicey Pond. Facilities vary, including lean-tos, tent space, bunkhouses, fireplaces, tables. Essentially primitive. Reservations recommended. Open May 15–Oct. 15.

Reservations can be requested as early as Jan. 1, by mail or in person, from Millinocket HQ. ME residents have limited priority.

Hiking, backpacking: 178 mi. of trails, including the first 10.4 mi. of the Appalachian Trail. All hikers must register at the nearest campground. Backpackers must use authorized sites. This includes 2 backcountry campgrounds in addition to the 6 accessible by road. Hikers should have topos. *No children under age 6 are permitted above timberline.*

Hunting: In designated sections only; inquire. Firearms are prohibited elsewhere.

Fishing: Excellent. Streams and ponds. Chiefly brook trout.

Boating: No trailer-access ramps. Motors are permitted on Matagamon and Webster lakes.

Canoeing, boating: Boats with motors can be used on Webster and Matagamon lakes, and on Nesowadnehunk Lake, outside the boundary. Canoes can be rented at South Branch, Russell, Trout Brook Farm, and Daicey ponds; all have campgrounds. Day use canoe rentals at Kidney and Togue ponds. *Ski touring:* Season is generally Dec. 1–Mar. 31. Snowmobiles are permitted on the perimeter road only.

All persons entering or leaving the Park must stop and register at the gatehouse or Park HQ.
Special rules govern activities in the Park. Obtain a copy from HQ before making the trip. Vehicles more than 7 ft. wide, 9 ft. high, or 22 ft. long are prohibited.
Gasoline is not available.
Pets are prohibited.
The Park is open for general use May 15–Oct. 15; day use only Oct 15–Dec. 1, and Apr. 1–May 15. Winter use is subject to special regulations; camping, climbing, or mountain hiking requires a permit requested 4 weeks in advance; permits are issued only to parties deemed qualified and properly equipped.

PUBLICATIONS
General information page with trail information and map.
Rules and regulations.
Wildflower list.
Bird and mammal lists.
Nature trail guides: Daicey Pond, Roaring Brook, South Branch.
Map, Baxter Park and Katahdin. $4.15, plus $1 postage.

REFERENCES
Baxter State Park and Katahdin Map and Guide. Freeport: DeLorme Publishing, 1987.
Feller-Roth, Barbara, ed. *Hiking.* Vol. 3: *Northern Region.* Freeport: DeLorme Publishing, 1983.
Kulik, Stephen, Pete Salmansohn, Matthew Schmidt, and Heidi Welch. *The Audubon Society Field Guide to the Natural Places of the Northeast: Inland.* New York: Pantheon Books, 1984.
Monegain, Bernie. *Natural Sites, a Guide to Maine's Natural Phenomena.* Freeport: DeLorme Publishing, 1985.

HEADQUARTERS: Baxter State Park Authority, 64 Balsam Dr., Millinocket, ME 04462; (207) 723-5140.

BIGELOW PRESERVE
Bureau of Public Lands   West
29,578 acres.

W central ME. SR 16/27 NW from New Portland. In about 25 mi. look for gravel road on right at Stratton Brook with Appalachian Trail sign. For lake access, Long Falls Dam Road runs N from North New Portland on SR 16 to the E end of the lake. (Maps 29, B-4; 30, B-1.)

The principal features of this unit are Flagstaff Lake and Bigelow Mountain. The unit occupies much of the land between SR 16/27 and the lake, with additional State acreage on islands and a peninsula on the N shore. The 10-mi. W–E range offers some of ME's finest alpine scenery. The Appalachian Trail crosses the high country.

Elevation at the lake is 1,146 ft. Avery and West peaks are both over 4,000 ft., two others above 3,500. Timberline here is about 3,800 ft. Avery and West peaks have extensive subalpine heaths. Several glacial tarns are near timberline.

The S slope drops from the ridge irregularly in a series of terraces and cliffs to the Stratton Brook and Huston Brook valleys. Hikers and campers generally enter the unit on the Stratton Brook Road to trailheads where the Appalachian Trail crosses or at the outlet of Stratton Brook Pond; both have limited parking.

The N slope is a more continuous grade down to the lake and adjoining swamp. Flagstaff Lake is sometimes labeled Dead River Flowage. North and South Branches of the Dead River join at Stratton. The dam is at the E end. The lake is about 20 mi. long, up to 3 mi. wide, with numerous bays, coves, and islands. Much of the shoreline, especially on the S, is marshy. The lake is shallow.

Plants: Northern hardwood forests predominate at lower elevations, beech/birch/maple intermixed with spruce/fir. From 2,000 to 2,700 ft. this gives way to a boreal forest of red spruce/balsam fir/white birch. Still higher the trees become smaller, until in the subalpine zone they are low, matted, and shrublike, the pattern called *krummholz.* The highest peaks are treeless; patches of low shrubs, herbs, grasses, and sedges broken by rock outcrops.

Other habitats in the Preserve include the following:
- *Cedar swamp:* northern white-cedar with red spruce, balsam fir, yellow birch, and eastern hemlock. The shrub understory includes blueberry. Growing on the sphagnum mat are three-seeded sedge, sensitive fern, cinnamon fern, ostrich fern, goldthread, and starflower.
- *Black spruce bog:* with black spruce, red maple, northern white-cedar, and larch.
- *Heath and open bog:* shrubs including leatherleaf, sheep laurel, labrador tea, bog laurel, blueberry, cranberry.
- *Wet meadow:* with sedges, grasses, cattail, blue flag.

Birds: A preliminary list records only those species seen or heard during the site inventory. They include common loon, black duck, red-tailed and Cooper's hawks, ruffed and spruce grouse, spotted sandpiper, American woodcock, common snipe, northern flicker; pileated, hairy, and downy woodpeckers; yellow-bellied sapsucker, alder and olive-sided flycatchers, tree and bank swallows, gray and blue jays, common raven, American crow, black-capped and boreal chickadees. White-breasted and red-breasted nuthatches, winter wren. Thrushes: wood, hermit, Swainson's, and gray-cheeked. Veery, golden-crowned and ruby-crowned kinglets, solitary and red-eyed vireos. Warblers: Tennessee, Nashville, yellow, magnolia, black-throated blue, black-throated green, yellow-rumped, bay-breasted, blackpoll, yellowthroat, ovenbird, Canada, American redstart. Red-winged blackbird, scarlet tanager, pine and evening grosbeaks, purple finch, pine siskin, slate-colored junco; chipping, white-throated, and eastern song sparrows.

Mammals: The site inventory listed mammals likely to occur here, then noted those whose presence was confirmed. The latter, certainly an incomplete account, includes shorttail shrew, little brown myotis, snowshoe hare, eastern chipmunk, woodchuck, gray and red squirrels, beaver, deer mouse, meadow and rock voles, muskrat, meadow and woodland jumping mice, porcupine, coyote, red fox, black bear, raccoon, marten, fisher, mink, striped skunk, bobcat, whitetail deer, moose.

ACTIVITIES

Camping: Campsites at Stratton Brook Pond, Huston Pond, and along the shore of Flagstaff Lake. Camp in any suitable place, but a permit is required for fires except at the designated campsites.

Hiking, backpacking: The Bigelow Mountain Trails, from Stratton E along the ridge, are joined by the Appalachian Trail, Firewarden's Trail, and others. Two lean-tos are on the ridge.

Fishing: Warmwater species, chiefly pickerel and yellow perch, in the lake. The North Branch of the Dead River is good for brook trout, the South Branch somewhat less so.

Boating: Ramps near Stratton and at Bog Brook, on the E end. Drawdowns, especially in the fall, may impede launching.

Canoeing: Whitewater runs on both the North and the South branches and on the Lower Dead River below the dam. Rapids to Class IV.

PUBLICATION: Information page.

REFERENCES
ATC Committee. *Appalachian Trail Guide to Maine.* Harpers Ferry, WV: Appalachian Trail Conference, 1983.

Feller-Roth, Barbara, ed. *Hiking.* Vol. 3: *Northern Region.* Freeport: DeLorme Publishing, 1983.

Gibson, John. *Fifty Hikes in Maine.* Woodstock, VT: Backcountry Publications, 1983.

Kellogg, Zip. *Canoeing.* Vol. 2: *Western Rivers.* Freeport: DeLorme Publishing, 1985.

HEADQUARTERS: Bureau of Public Lands, Maine Department of Conservation, State House, Station 22, Augusta, ME 04333; (207) 289-3061.

BRADBURY MOUNTAIN STATE PARK
Bureau of Parks and Recreation   Coastal
272 acres.

On SR 9 about 15 mi. N of Portland. (Map 5, C-5.)

Open about May 15 to Oct. 15.

This small park offers camping on 41 wooded sites and a pleasant day hike up through open forest to a bald top with a view over Casco Bay. The round trip is less than a mile, with a rise of about 200 ft. 4 mi. of other trails.

HEADQUARTERS: Pownal, ME 04069; (207) 688-4712.

BROWNFIELD BOG WILDLIFE MANAGEMENT AREA
Department of Inland Fisheries and Wildlife   Coastal
5,454 acres.

SE of Fryeburg. Just off SR 160 about 1 1/2 mi. NE of East Brownfield Village. (Map 4, B-2.)

The Saco River Valley is a picturesque and popular waterfowl hunting area. The Saco River flows into and through Brownfield Bog, to and beyond Lovewell Pond. The WMA, its terrain relatively flat, is at about 360 ft. above sea level. It includes 1,100 acres of floodplain, 970 acres of marshland, 3,384 acres of upland. An access road from SR 160 passes Bald Bog, skirts the river channel, and ends at Great Bog.

No lists of fauna are available, but the diversity of habitats indicates a good variety of species.

Birds: Nesting waterfowl include black duck, ring-necked duck, wood duck. Introduced Canada geese have nested.

ACTIVITIES

Camping: Nearby, the Appalachian Mountain Club has a site at Walker's Falls, chiefly for canoeists on the Saco River.

Hunting: Deer, waterfowl, grouse, woodcock.

Fishing: Brown trout and smallmouth bass in the river and pond, pickerel and bullhead in bogs.

Boating: Ramp near point where the river enters the pond. Pond is about 2 1/2 mi. long.

Canoeing: A popular 33-mi. canoe route on the Saco River passes the bog. Put-in off SR 160 or at Lovewell Pond.

CAMDEN HILLS STATE PARK

Bureau of Parks and Recreation   Coastal

5,500 acres.

On US 1 just N of Camden. (Map 14, C-4.)

Park open all year, campground May 15–Oct. 15.

Maine's largest coastal park has a quarter-million visitors a year. The campground is usually full from mid-July to Labor Day, often by noon. Most campers are transients, and 85% of all visitors are from other states.

Almost all of the visitors come through the main entrance. The great majority drive the scenic road to the top of Mt. Battie. About 30,000 per year hike to the top. It's not to be missed, even if you're there on a crowded day, but there's much more to the Park, large areas most visitors don't see.

The Park extends about 5 mi. on an axis parallel to US 1, although it has less than half a mile of highway frontage. Its boundaries are very irregular, touching or crossing other roads at several places. The trail system extends throughout the Park. A small block opposite the main entrance extends to the sea. The shore is a steep, rocky bluff offering no access to the water. The land rises to Megunticook Mountain, which overlooks Lake Megunticook.

About 85% of the Park is forested, a mixed forest with northern red oak, American beech, red maple, white ash, white birch, red spruce, white pine, balsam fir, eastern hemlock, northern white-cedar.

FEATURES

Mt. Battie attracted visitors long before there was a park. The view from the top, 1,380 ft. above the sea, is magnificent, encompassing sea islands, the lake, and distant mountains. The stone tower was built in 1921 at the site of a former hotel. The auto road to the summit is open May 1–Nov. 1, 9 A.M. to sunset.

Maiden Cliff is a sheer drop of 800 ft. down to SR 52 on the shore of Lake Megunticook. Ridge Trail leads to the cliff top.

ACTIVITIES

Camping: 112 sites. Reservations by Ticketron. There is no overflow campground, but campers will be referred to private campgrounds when sites are full.

Hiking: 25 mi. of trails.

Hunting: In undeveloped areas. Inquire.

Ski touring, snowmobiling: Popular in winter. A ski shelter is at the center of the Park, access from Youngtown Rd.

PUBLICATIONS

Park leaflet.
Trail map.
Information: Mt. Battie.
Snowmobile trails map.

REFERENCE: Gibson, John. *Fifty Hikes in Maine.* Woodstock, VT: Backcountry Publications, 1983.

NEARBY: *Warren Island State Park* is on a 70-acre spruce-covered island in Penobscot Bay. It has docking and mooring facilities, 10 campsites, 2 shelters, water. Use your own boat, or ask Camden Hills HQ about transportation.

HEADQUARTERS: S.C.R. 60, Box 3110—Belfast Rd., Camden, ME 04843; (207) 236-3109.

CHAMBERLAIN LAKE MANAGEMENT UNIT

See Telos Lake Management Unit.   North

CHESTERVILLE WILDLIFE MANAGEMENT AREA

Department of Inland Fisheries and Wildlife   West
468 acres.

From Farmington, SE on US 2 to Farmington Falls, then S on Pope Rd. and Valley Rd. to Chesterville. Dam is on Little Norridgewock Stream in Chesterville. (Map 20, E-1.)

The WMA is long and narrow, following the stream for 3 mi. A canoe is the preferred craft, especially at low water. Access is limited to the dam site, where a few cars can be parked and small boats launched. (With two cars, leave one at the dam; put in at Parker Pond in Jay, and canoe downstream.)

From a canoe, wildlife viewing is likely to be good. The waterway is quiet, no roads nearby.

Birds: Wood duck and black duck are common. One may also see hooded merganser, great blue heron, osprey, warblers, flycatchers, red-winged blackbird, ring-necked duck, and blue-winged teal, all of which nest here. In uplands, ruffed grouse, occasional woodcock.

Mammals: Canoeists often see deer, beaver, muskrat, moose. Present but less often seen: mink, otter, bobcat, raccoon, red fox, weasel, snowshoe hare.

ACTIVITIES
  Hunting: Most hunting is for deer.
  Fishing: Pickerel, largemouth and smallmouth bass.
  Canoeing: May require hauling across old or new beaver dams.

COBSCOOK BAY STATE PARK
Bureau of Parks and Recreation   Coastal
868 acres.

On US 1 20 mi. N of Machias. (Map 26, A-2.)

"This is the unappreciated part of Maine," said one advisor. "This part of the coast, from Bar Harbor to Canada, hasn't had the surge of development you see in the south." Traffic on US 1 is light to moderate, even on weekends, and the roadside isn't lined with antique shops and lobster restaurants. Cobscook is a coastal park, but on a fine July weekend there were a few vacant campsites.

The Park is on Whiting Bay, an arm of Cobscook Bay, where the tide fluctuation is 24 to 28 ft. The coast is steep and rocky, the upland hilly, with fine views from hilltops, although none rise much over 400 ft. From the campground, we found a trail down to a stony beach, where our presence seemed to interest a loon.

Adjoining the Park is the 6,600-acre Edmunds Unit of the Moosehorn National Wildlife Refuge (see entry). Park employees can provide maps and information. The Refuge offers extensive hiking opportunities.

Plants: About 75% of the Park is forested, spruce and balsam predominating. The Park has a list of 50 flowering plant species: wild cherry, pear, and apple blossom in late May–early June, daisy, buttercup, Indian paintbrush, and others June–Aug.

Wildlife: See the species lists for Moosehorn NWR. Coastal and many of the upland species are seen in the park.

ACTIVITIES
  Camping: 100 sites. May 15–Oct. 15. Sites are usually available.
  Hiking: Trails in the park, up to a locked fire tower, and in the NWR, including its wilderness area.
  Fishing: Stream and ocean.
  Boating: Launching ramp on Whiting Bay. Boaters should be aware of the rapid tide changes, swift currents, and eddies.
  Ski touring, snowmobiling: On groomed trails.

PUBLICATION: Leaflet with map.

HEADQUARTERS: R.F.D., Dennysville, ME 04628; (207) 726-4412.

DEBOULLIE MANAGEMENT UNIT
Bureau of Public Lands   North
21,871 acres.

N central ME. From Portage on SR 11, Haul Road, a private road, W and N. (Map 63, A-1.) Or see Map 66, 5-E, for an access road S from SR 161.

This area of steep mountains, forests, and crystal lakes is within the North Maine Woods (see entry). It was managed as commercial forest before the State acquired it, with extensive logging in the 1950s and 1960s, but new growth is vigorous and the landscape shows few scars.

Although fishing here is very good, camping and hiking delightful, visitation has been light because of the site's remoteness and poor access roads. State managers were concerned that road improvements and publicity would attract too many people, with consequent damage to the fragile environment, especially around the four principal ponds. A management plan published in 1987 divides the site into six zones, categories that provide special protection for rare and endangered species, a backcountry closed to motor vehicles, preferred wildlife habitats, recreation sites, scenic areas, and—finally—timber production zones. Only one interior road will be maintained, with temporary logging roads permitted as needed.

The principal mountains, ponds, and other scenic features of the site are in the SE third of the unit. So are the established campsites. The interior road cuts across the corner of this portion. Thus it is here that protection of natural qualities is most needed. A strip along the road is zoned for recreation sites, as is the N shore of Togue Pond. Most of the SE third will be kept roadless and closed to motor vehicles.

Red River Camps is a traditional sportsman's camp, predating State ownership, now commercially operated under lease. It provides rustic accommodations, meals, canoe rentals, and guide services. Lease terms require that it be kept simple and that some services, such as canoe rentals, be available to all visitors. The operator also maintains some short trails to ponds.

FEATURES

Deboullie Mountain, 1,981 ft., is the site's highest point, with a fire tower on top that offers fine views. Gardner Mountain isn't quite as high: 1,817 ft. The word *deboullie* is French for "rock slide"; the mountains have steep sides with cliffs and talus slopes.

Elevations of the ponds range from 1,107 to 1,189 ft. Gardner, Togue, and Deboullie ponds are the three largest, from 1 1/4 to 1 3/4 mi. long, each a bit under 300 acres. A dozen other ponds are large enough to appear on the site map.

Cliffs on the S shore of Togue Pond are included in the scenic zone. The N shore of Deboullie Pond has "ice caves," small openings in rock crevices that remain frosty into the summer.

Five tracts of old-growth spruce/fir have been designated as Critical Areas, worthy of preservation. All are in the SE portion of the site.

The acreage to the N and W is said to have no features of interest to visitors other than hunters. This portion of the site will be managed for timber production, with due regard for environmental quality.

Plants: Logging began here in the late 1800s and continued into the 1960s. Cutting, governed by market demand, was mostly for softwoods and high-quality hardwoods. This history has produced a forest that is 42% mixed woods, 33% softwoods, 25% hardwoods. Most softwood species here are in the 30- to 80-year age classes, while about a third of the hardwoods are over 100 years old. Softwoods are chiefly fir and spruce, with some cedar. Hardwoods include sugar maple, yellow birch, beech, red maple, white birch, and poplar.

Wildlife: Little information is available on the birds and mammals of the area, other than game species.

ACTIVITIES

Camping: 17 primitive campsites. The North Maine Woods manages recreation use throughout the private lands that surround Deboullie and collects fees at their gatehouses. Although fees are not charged at other Bureau of Public Lands sites, that would be poor policy here, and North Maine Woods collects the usual fee. There are no reservations. One can camp elsewhere, with no facilities and without open fires. Sites are too small for motor homes and large trailer combinations.

Hiking: The principal hiking trails were developed by and for fishermen, linking the several ponds. One trail ascends to the fire tower on Deboullie Mountain. The BPL has proposed a 10-year plan for extension of the trail network.

Hunting: Deer, moose, snowshoe hare, and grouse are present. The limited diversity of habitat conditions makes this a relatively poor area for game production. Most hunters go elsewhere.

Fishing has long been the principal attraction here, and it is one of the BPL's chief concerns. Overfishing has already drastically reduced fish populations in one pond. The Department of Inland Fisheries and Wildlife is monitoring the ponds, with differing management goals. "Catch and release" is a possible option in one or more ponds.

Boating, canoeing: Canoe is the preferred craft. Hand-carried boats can be launched on the larger lakes. The rules on motors aren't yet in place, but it's probable that small motors will be allowed on Deboullie and Gardner, no motors elsewhere.

Ski touring: Remoteness and snow conditions make winter use less than popular.

HEADQUARTERS: Bureau of Public Lands, Maine Department of Conservation, State House, Station 22, Augusta, ME 04333; (207) 289-3061.

DONNELL POND/TUNK LAKE
Bureau of Public Lands   Coastal
7,200 acres.

From US 1 at Cherryfield, W on SR 182. The site lies S of SR 182 between Donnell Pond and Tunk Lake. (Map 24, 5-D.)

We were about to send this manuscript to the publisher when the Bureau of Public Lands sent a packet of information about this newly acquired site, the yield of several complex transactions. It includes 8 mi. of undeveloped frontage on the S and E shore of Donnell Pond, including two sand beaches over 1,000 ft. long. It has about 3 mi. of frontage on the SW shore of Tunk Lake, and the land between, including Schoodic, Black, and Caribou mountains and several ponds. Both lakes are almost entirely undeveloped, although Tunk is known to fishermen. The three mountain tops provide fine views of Acadia National Park, the ocean, and nearby mountains.

Unimproved access to the S end of Tunk Lake is via SR 183 from East Sullivan on US 1, to the N end of Donnell Pond from SR 182. There are no present plans to improve access. The site will remain wild, open to the adventurous.

HEADQUARTERS: Bureau of Public Lands, Maine Department of Conservation, State House, Station 22, Augusta, ME 04333; (207) 289-3061.

DUCK LAKE MANAGEMENT UNIT
Bureau of Public Lands   West
25,220 acres.

From Burlington (B-2), SE, around the N end of Nicatous Lake, to site. (Maps 34, C-5, and 35, C-1.)

The region NE of Bangor, bounded by US 2, SR 6, US 1, and SR 9, has many lakes, extensive wetlands, and few roads. The thousand-square-mile region is heavily forested, flat to rolling. Its lakes are generally at between 300 and 500 ft. elevation. Most of the upland is between 400 and 600 ft., with a few widely scattered mountains.

The Unit is at the center of this region, as remote as any part of it. It is accessible by road, according to one description "easily, albeit patiently." Patience here is well rewarded; the road passes through country as interesting as the destination. Along the route are several campsites, the put-in for the 23-mi. Narraguagus River canoe trip, and side roads to large and small lakes, wetlands, campsites, and hiking trails.

The road traverses the site, passing the E tip of Duck Lake. The Unit is somewhat higher and hillier than most of the region, with several hills at about 1,000 ft. elevation. Duck Mountain rises to 1,169 ft. Duck Lake has several unusual qualities. At 519 ft., it is one of the highest lakes of the region. It is a deep, coldwater fishery (salmon and trout), whereas most nearby lakes are shallower, offering bass, pickerel, and white perch. It has extensive sand beaches. The lake is about 1 3/4 mi. long, 1 mi. wide.

Gassabias Lake, in the S portion of the site, is almost as large. Two small lakes, Upper Unknown and Lower Unknown, are near the NE corner.

ACTIVITIES
Camping: One vehicle-access primitive site is on Duck Lake. Three boat-access sites (no latrines, no fires permitted) are on the lake. Two sites are on Gassabias. One is between the Unknown lakes. Visitors may camp anywhere, with no open fires.

Hiking: The site map shows a few short trails. Some seem to be related to fishing. There is no trail maintenance.

Hunting: Deer, ruffed grouse; but wildlife populations are relatively low in this region.

Fishing: Duck Lake isn't as well publicized as some of the larger lakes in this semiwilderness region. Fishing pressure is light to moderate. Gassabias and Unknown lakes have excellent warmwater fishing.

PUBLICATION: Information page with contour map.

HEADQUARTERS: Bureau of Public Lands, Maine Department of Conservation, State House, Station 22, Augusta, ME 04333; (207) 289-3061.

EAGLE LAKE MANAGEMENT UNIT
Bureau of Public Lands   North
23,287 acres.

The town of Eagle Lake is on SR 11 about 18 mi. S of Canada. Access to the Unit, across the lake, is from Fort Kent, on the border, via SR 161 and Sly Brook Road. (Maps 67, E-5, and 68, E-1.)

Not to be confused with the Eagle Lake on the Allagash, this one is narrow, L-shaped, about 15 mi. long, linked to the St. John River by Fish River. A minor part of the site is on the S side of the lake, near the town, but the main part, including the campsites, is across. To avoid the drive up to Fort Kent and back, one can launch at the town and reach campsites by boat.

The site has a few hills; its highest point is about 400 ft. above the lake. Blake Lake is a pond in the site's NW corner, 200 ft. above the lake, with a hike-in campsite. Alec Brook drops from Blake Lake to Eagle Lake. There are wetlands in the NE corner and between Eagle Lake and Square Lake. The two lakes appear to be linked by a canoeable water passage, another channel linking Square Lake and Cross Lake; campsites are on both of these lakes.

Fishing: Harry Vanderweide's *Maine Sportsman Fishing Trip Planner* (Yarmouth: All Outdoors, annual) calls this Fish River region "one of Maine's best landlocked salmon fisheries," adding that Eagle Lake also has lake trout.

HEADQUARTERS: Bureau of Public Lands, Maine Department of Conservation, State House, Station 22, Augusta, ME 04333; (207) 289-3061.

EAST POINT SANCTUARY

Maine Audubon Society   Coastal
30 acres.

From Biddeford, SE on Pool Rd., SR 208. (Map 3, C-3.)

Open dawn to dusk.

This small site on a point projecting into the Gulf of Maine is one of the best birding sites for migrants in southern ME. The rocky coastal headland is rimmed with steeply sloping shingle beaches grading up to open meadow and shrub thicket. From the entrance there is a 2-mi. loop trail.

FERNALD'S NECK PRESERVE

Maine Chapter, The Nature Conservancy   Coastal
315 acres.

From Camden, N on SR 52. Just beyond Youngstown Corner, turn left at Highway Marker 5016. Continue on road, which becomes dirt. Bear left at fork, or park if road is muddy. Pass the gray farmhouse into a hay field, and park near the woods. See a small TNC sign marking the entrance. (Map 14, C-3.)

Open dawn to dusk.

The Preserve is on a peninsula that almost bisects Megunticook Lake. Roads surround the lake, and developers have been active. Local residents bought the site to preserve it. The tip of the peninsula is a town park accessible only by water.

The 18,000-ft. shoreline of the Preserve is irregular, bordered by many plants such as pipewort, arrowhead, bur-reed, pondweeds, and bulrushes. Many visitors arrive by boat, and there are several suitable places to beach a canoe or other small craft. Back of the shore is forest, mostly white and red pine and hemlock in the N and W, mixed hardwoods and conifers in the S. A large wetland in the center has pitcher-plant, rose pogonia, blue flag iris, and various grasses, sedges, and rushes.

There's a well-marked trail system and a brochure in the registration box. *Pets are prohibited.*

NEARBY: Camden Hills State Park (see entry).

HEADQUARTERS: Maine Chapter, The Nature Conservancy, 122 Main St.,
P.O. Box 338, Topsham, MA 04086; (207) 729-5181.

FOUR PONDS MANAGEMENT UNIT
Bureau of Public Lands   West
4,026 acres.

Foot access only; no vehicles. S of Rangeley Lake. Appalachian Trail crosses the site, between SRs 17 and 4. Foot access from SR 17 by Appalachian
Trail or local trail. (Map 18, A-B, 4-5.)

The BPL plans to keep this site quiet, closed to vehicles. From SR 17 it's about
a 1 1/2 mi. walk. The N boundary is less than a mile from SR 4, but across
a lake. Hikers and fishermen are the principal visitors.
"Four Ponds"? We counted 7, although the two largest aren't entirely within the boundaries. The 3 on the W side of the site are relatively high, over
2,300 ft. elevation. The Appalachian Trail ascends to 2,970 ft. near the site's
midpoint. To the E, the terrain slopes downward. Long Pond, on the NE
boundary, is at 1,729 ft., a drop of some 600 ft. in 3 1/2 mi. (According to our
maps, the water body on the W side is also named "Long Pond." The former
has an alias: "Beaver Mountain Lake." Beaver Mountain, 3,160 ft., is N of
the Unit.)
The management plan permits timber harvesting, but not around the ponds
or near the trails. The AT passes beside attractive ponds, ascends gradually
through heavily shaded corridors, and emerges at viewpoints.

ACTIVITIES
Camping: An AT lean-to is near the W boundary. Trailside camping is per-
mitted anywhere. No open fires.
Fishing: Native and stocked brook trout.

HEADQUARTERS: Bureau of Public Lands, Maine Department of Conservation, State House, Station 22, Augusta, ME 04333; (207) 289-3061.

FRYE MOUNTAIN WILDLIFE MANAGEMENT AREA
Department of Inland Fisheries and Wildlife   Coastal
5,176 acres.

From Belfast, W on SR 3 beyond North Searsmont to SR 220. N on SR
220 about 7 mi. Site is on the right. A gravel road crosses the site to SR
137. (Map 14, A-2.)

This forested site is managed to promote wildlife production. Patches of timber are cut to create openings and new growth. Strips have been cut in reverting fields, followed by plantings of grasses and legumes. Beneficiaries of this
treatment include deer, pheasant, grouse, snowshoe hare, woodcock, and
squirrel.

The entrance road climbs the shoulder of the mountain, through a young
hardwood forest. We saw one grove of white pine and scattered hemlock,
spruce, and fir. The understory was heavy, with many ferns. Along the roadside were summer flowers, notably black-eyed susan and asters.

The site is moderately popular in all seasons. 12 mi. of gravel roads provide
good access to most of the site and include a spur to the top of Frye Mountain,
1,140 ft., the site's highest point, which has a fire tower. Hikers favor the late
spring and summer. Fishing for brook trout isn't great but good enough to
attract some anglers. Hunters come for deer and small game. When snow
falls, the Bureau of Parks and Recreation grooms snowmobile trails, and
cross-country skiers use unplowed roads.

HEADQUARTERS: Department of Inland Fisheries and Wildlife, 284 State St.,
Station 41, Augusta, ME 04333; (207) 289-5253.

GARDNER-DEBOULLIE MANAGEMENT UNIT
See Deboullie Management Unit.   North

GEORGIA-PACIFIC CORPORATION LANDS
450,000 acres, plus 350,000 acres in New Brunswick.   West/North

Numerous large and small landholdings on both sides of the U.S.-Canada
border, from the vicinity of Calais to the vicinity of North Amity on US
1 S of Houlton. Access from US 1, SR 6, and other routes. (Maps 36, 45,
46, 53.)

The company's Woodland Division operates these lands on a multiple-use
plan, making them available to the public for outdoor recreation. This water-

shed of the St. Croix River is a region of thick forests, many lakes and streams, including Grand Lake, Big Lake, and others.

To use these lands, write to the company's headquarters for the "Sportsmen's Map," then relate this to the corresponding maps in the DeLorme *Atlas.* Most other lands in this vast area are owned by other timber companies who generally permit public use. Keep in mind that these are private lands whose owners can restrict or prohibit use at will, and who can eject persons who misbehave.

For more information about these lands, including campsites, stop at the nearest local office of the Maine Forest Service.

ACTIVITIES

Camping is permitted in designated sites only. Open fires require a permit from the Maine Forest Service.

Fishing: East Grand Lake, also called Grand Lake, is one of several fine fishing areas. It covers over 16,000 acres, with a maximum depth of 128 ft. Salmon, brook trout, lake trout, small mouth bass, white and yellow perch, pickerel, hornpout, smelt, whitefish.

Boating: Ramps on East Grand Lake and others.

Canoeing: Grand Lake Stream is part of a complex of waterways, including lakes and streams.

Visitors are excluded from areas being logged. Private roads must be driven with caution. Trucks have the right-of-way—and their drivers expect it.

PUBLICATION: *Sportsmen's Map of Washington County and Western New Brunswick.*

REFERENCES

Kellogg, Zip. *Canoeing.* Vol. 1: *Coastal and Eastern Rivers.* Freeport: De-Lorme Publishing, 1985.

Vanderweide, Harry. *Maine Fishing Maps.* Vol. 1: *Lakes and Ponds.* Freeport: DeLorme Publishing, 1986.

Vanderweide, Harry. Vol. 2: *Rivers and Streams.* Freeport: DeLorme Publishing, 1984.

HEADQUARTERS: Georgia-Pacific Corporation, Woodland, ME 04694; (207) 427-3311.

GERO ISLAND MANAGEMENT UNIT

Bureau of Public Lands   North
3,185 acres.

Water access only. At the head of Chesuncook Lake, NW of Millinocket. A popular camping stop for canoeists on the West Branch of the Penobscot River. Launching at the S end of the lake is accessible by private road from

Millinocket. Also launching at the N end, W side, at campsite near Umbazooksus Stream. (Map 49, A,B-5. Map 50, D-1.)

Chesuncook Lake, ME's third largest lake, is one element in a complex of interconnected lakes and rivers in a region where travel is chiefly by water. Elevation at the lake is 942 ft. The lake is long, narrow, with several arms and bays. At the N end, the roughly circular Gero Island rises to a high point of 1080 ft. A grove of old-growth white pine is on the N end of the island.

The Unit includes a strip of land that faces the island on the W shore of the lake, the site of what was Chesuncook village. The village now has four year-round residents. It is dominated by a century-old hotel, still operating, reached only by water.

ACTIVITIES

Camping: 4 primitive campsites are on this side of the island. 3 private campsites are on the mainland. Many informal sites are available to canoe campers.

Fishing: Fine fishing for salmon, brook and lake trout, white and yellow perch.

Boating: The lake is about 24 mi. long, with little shoreline development. It can be very rough, which calls for sound boats with reliable motors.

REFERENCE: Vanderweide, Harry. *Maine Fishing Maps.* Vol. 1: *Lakes and Ponds.* Freeport: DeLorme Publishing, 1986.

HEADQUARTERS: Bureau of Public Lands, Maine Department of Conservation, State House, Station 22, Augusta, ME 04333; (207) 289-3061.

GILSLAND FARM
Maine Audubon Society   Coastal
70 acres.

From Portland, N on US 1 across the Presumpscot River, to 118 US Route 1, on left. (Map 5, E-5.)

Headquarters of the Maine Audubon Society, the site has self-guiding trails through diverse habitats beside the river: salt marsh, secondary hardwoods, red oak woodland, oak/hemlock woodland, shrubland, and open meadows. HQ has a list of 123 bird species recorded.

HEADQUARTERS: 118 US Rt. 1, Falmouth, ME 04105; (207) 781-2330.

GRAFTON NOTCH STATE PARK
Bureau of Parks and Recreation   West
3,112 acres.

On SR 26, N of Newry, near the NH border. (Map 18, D-1.)

SR 26 is one of ME's most scenic routes, and Grafton Notch is its principal feature. The notch is in the Mahoosuc Mountains (see entry). SR 26 crosses the Park. Indeed, the Park has no entrance. Along the road are parking areas for such features as Screw Auger Falls, Mother Walker Falls, and Moose Cave Gorge. Each is a short walk from the parking, and each has an exhibit panel.

Farther on are trailheads. The Appalachian Trail crosses SR 26 here. Within the Park are trails to Old Speck Mountain and Table Rock. The highway crosses the Park at 1,100 ft. elevation. The high country is on either side in the Mahoosuc Mountain Management Unit.

There is no camping here, no campground nearer than a commercial one at Newry.

NEARBY: *Step Falls Preserve* of the Maine Chapter, The Nature Conservancy, is on the N side of SR 26 just S of the Park. A trail through a dense stand of balsam fir and hardwood forest climbs about 1/2 mi. for a fine view of the falls, which cascade down 200 ft. in less than 1/8 of a mi.

REFERENCE: Monegain, Bernie. *Natural Sites, a Guide to Maine's Natural Phenomena.* Freeport: DeLorme Publishing, 1985.

GREAT WASS ISLAND PRESERVE
Maine Chapter, The Nature Conservancy   South
1,543 acres.

From Jonesport on SR 187, S over bridge to Beals Island. Continue through Beals to Great Wass Island and by dirt road to Black Duck Cove and parking. (Map 26, E-1.)

Open dawn to dusk.

Here one can enjoy a wild oceanic island without benefit of boat. The open exposure to the ocean makes this habitat unusual, with a shoreline more typical of the subarctic than of the temperate zone. The interior has one of the state's largest stands of jack pine, near the southern limit of its range. The coastal raised peat bogs are typical of Canada's Maritime Provinces. The intertidal zone has unusual algal species and several invertebrates usually found below the tidal zone.

The *Cape Cove Trail* traverses moss-floored spruce/fir forest, open jack pine woods, a point from which to observe a large bog, a swamp with pitcher plants and sundews, and ends at the eastern shore. The *Mud Hole Trail* traverses white birch woods and ends on the NE shore. Those who don't mind slippery rocks and frequent fogs can hike the shore between the two trails and to points south.

Wildlife includes species typical of northern bogs and boreal forests, as well as coasts. Harbor seals are often numerous on the ledges off the E coast.

Trail information is available at the registration box.

HEADQUARTERS: Maine Chapter, The Nature Conservancy, 122 Main St., P.O. Box 338, Topsham, ME 04086; (207) 729-5181.

GULF HAGAS AREA
Mixed ownerships   North

From Brownville Junction, N 5.5 mi. on SR 11, then left 6.8 mi. to Katahdin Iron Works. Pay the gate fee and ask about road conditions. Get map and directions. It's another 14 mi., with several turns. (Map 42, D-1.)

Gulf Hagas has been called "the Grand Canyon of Maine" and even "the Grand Canyon of the East." It's well worth the trip, but there's much more than the canyon to see and do in this region. Some day, perhaps, the roads will be paved and the roadsides commercialized. Today the region still has the beauty and flavor of backwoods Maine.

The Katahdin Iron Works is now restored as a State Historic Site. The rail siding that once served it is gone. This is the put-in for a run on the West Branch, Pleasant River, continuous steep rapids that can be run only at medium high water. Nearby Silver Lake has landlocked salmon.

Gulf Hagas is a rocky gorge in which the river drops 400 ft. in 4 mi. in a series of five waterfalls. The walls are sheer cliffs up to 125 ft. high. Several trails lead to viewpoints. It's a National Natural Landmark.

Just before arriving at the Gulf, the road crosses the *Appalachian Trail.* Not far off the road the trail crosses *The Hermitage,* a grove of 150-year-old white pines, a preserve of the Maine Chapter, The Nature Conservancy. Nearby is Screw Auger Falls. These are not the falls of the same name at Grafton Notch. There is no designated campsite beyond Brownville Junction.

REFERENCES

Feller-Roth, Barbara, ed. *Hiking.* Vol. 3: *Northern Region.* Freeport: De-Lorme Publishing, 1983.

Monegain, Bernie. *Natural Sites, a Guide to Maine's Natural Phenomena.* Freeport: DeLorme Publishing, 1985.

HOLEB MANAGEMENT UNIT
Bureau of Public Lands   North
16,129 acres.

From Jackman on US 201 the State highway map shows no roads in to Holeb Pond. The DeLorme *Maine Atlas* shows an unimproved road from US 201 near Dennistown, N of Jackman, to the Turner Brook Inlet camp-site on the NE shore, with boat launching nearby. Many people launch at Attean Pond. (Map 39, C-2.)

Holeb is best known for fishing and canoeing, especially for the Moose River Bow, a canoe-camping circuit. It's well known, so don't expect to be alone on a prime weekend.

W of Jackman are several lakes. Jackman is on Wood Pond, which is linked by streams to Attean Pond on the S and Little Big Wood Pond to the NW. Holeb is about a mile W of Attean. The Canadian Pacific RR runs near the S shore of Holeb and the N shore of Attean on its way to Jackman.

Holeb and Attean ponds are N of Attean Mountain, a small W–E range rising to a 2,453-ft. peak from the lake elevation of 1,231 ft. Holeb is over 3 mi. long, its widest point about 1 mi.

The boot-shaped Management Unit is on both sides of Holeb Pond, its larg-er portion extending S and W and including the first 6 mi. of the Moose River canoe run. The headwaters of the Moose are to the W, near the Quebec bor-der. The river passes close to the lake's W shore, with Holeb Stream as a con-necting passage.

The canoe trip, a scenic journey through mountainous country, is a circuit, requiring no car shuttle. Most canoeists who make the circuit begin at the NE corner of Attean Pond. The hard work is a portage from Attean to Holeb, which is 74 ft. higher. At the W end of Holeb is a short stream connection to the Moose River, which meanders around the S side of Attean Mountain to the SE corner of Attean Lake. The circuit is 34 mi. It can be done in two days, but why hurry?

The site includes several small ponds and bogs. The largest wetlands are on the N side and—outside the boundaries—along the Moose River to the SE. The area was timber company land and will continue under multiple-use management, timber harvesting harmonized with wildlife and recreation. Upland vegetation is mixed forest near the lake shore, giving way to spruce/fir on the higher slopes.

Little information on flora and fauna is available as yet, but it is probably similar to that of the lower elevations of the Bigelow Management Unit (see entry).

ACTIVITIES

Camping: The Turner Brook campsite at the NW corner of the lake is the only one accessible by car. Although one may camp anywhere, only 2 mi. of access road are within the site boundaries, with few feasible sites. For boat campers, several undeveloped sites are on the N shore. Canoeists have several sites along the Moose River.

Hiking: The site map shows only two short trails, their locations suggesting they were made by fishermen. The Atlas map shows a third along the S shore of the lake. We were told that hikers, chiefly fishermen, use the railroad right-of-way. (From Jackman, the Sally Mountain Trail, about 4 mi. long, leads to a fire tower overlooking Attean Pond, an ascent of about 1,000 ft.)

Hunting: Deer, bear, small game.

Fishing: Harry Vanderweide (see References) says that Holeb and other lakes of the region "have strong fisheries for brook trout and landlocks." Holeb and Attean are said to offer "a true Maine fishing experience for brookies."

Boating: Launching at Turner Brook for "modest-sized craft."

Canoeing: The Moose River trip includes some rips and drops to Class II and requires portaging around several waterfalls.

PUBLICATION: Information page with map.

REFERENCES

Kellogg, Zip. *Canoeing.* Vol. 2: *Western Rivers.* Freeport: DeLorme Publishing, 1985.

Vanderweide, Harry, ed. *The Maine Sportsman Fishing Trip Planner.* Yarmouth: All Outdoors, annual.

HEADQUARTERS: Bureau of Public Lands, Maine Department of Conservation, State House, Station 22, Augusta, ME 04333; (207) 289-3061.

HOWARD L. MENDALL WILDLIFE MANAGEMENT AREA

Department of Inland Fisheries and Wildlife   Coastal
242 acres.

Parking and boat launching on US 1A between Frankfort and Prospect. (Map 23, D-1.)

The Mendall Marsh occupies most of a peninsula between the Penobscot River and the South Branch Marsh River. The parking and boat-launching ramp are on the W side of the South Branch. Driving N, the first sign we saw marked a good dirt road that served as entrance to a parking area. Beyond, the road continued through a small grove of birch, maple, and aspen and out to the end of a short causeway in the river.

A hand-carried boat could be launched here; a ramp is further N. From US 1A, access to the site is by boat. It was too late in the day for us to explore the E side, but the map suggests taking SR 174 E from Prospect and looking for an unimproved road on the left.

The department began acquiring the site in 1970 as part of its effort to save ME's remaining coastal marshes from destruction. It includes open water, tidal flats, and salt marsh, an estuarine community with a rich flora and fauna. Typical marsh plants are cordgrass, black rush, salt grass, bayonet-grass, and many others.

Birds: In spring, many ducks and geese pause here for resting and feeding before proceeding N up the Penobscot River valley. They can find aquatic plants, snails, crustaceans, and small fish here while inland marshes are still frozen. Many shorebirds frequent the mud flats.

NEARBY: *Sandy Point Wildlife Management Area* (540 acres. Off US 1 N of Sandy Point. After going under a railroad bridge, first left turn, Muskrat Rd., unsigned. In 0.1 mi., see WMA sign and dirt road.)

It looked like just another freshwater marsh. A local resident stopped and told us it was once a muskrat farm. The birding is excellent, he said. (Includes black duck, ring-necked duck, blue-winged and green-winged teal, wood duck, hooded merganser, American goldeneye, and mallard.) The dirt road penetrates the marsh. A car can drive in to the turnaround, but we suggest caution if it looks muddy. Part of the marsh can be overlooked from the highway.

The wetland complex includes both shallow and deep marsh, 34 acres of open water, over a hundred acres of bog. Three streams flow from the N and NW, crossing Meadow Rd. and joining within the site. Below the wetland, the combined stream cuts through the hill to enter the Penobscot River. Hiking and hunting.

HEADQUARTERS: Department of Inland Fisheries and Wildlife, 284 State St., Station 41, Augusta, ME 04333; (207) 289-5253.

INDIAN POINT/BLAGDEN PRESERVE
Maine Chapter, The Nature Conservancy   Coastal
110 acres.

> On Mt. Desert Island. After crossing the SR 3 bridge to the island, bear right on SR 102. In 1.8 mi., turn right on Pretty Marsh Rd. In 1.7 mi., bear right at fork. Entrance is in 200 yds. (Map 16, B-2.)
>
> *Closed after 6 P.M.*

Visitors to Acadia National Park may enjoy a brief visit here. In 1947 a great fire burned much of central and eastern Mt. Desert Island. This area escaped and thus provides an interesting comparison of vegetation types. Most of the preserve is forest: tall coastal red spruce, white-cedar, and balsam fir. The Preserve has over 1,000 ft. of frontage on Western Bay, rocky, gravel beaches with schist outcrops. Harbor seals can often be seen on nearby small islands. Osprey nest near the shore.

Visitors are asked to register at the caretaker's house and to stay on the marked trails.

HEADQUARTERS: Maine Chapter, The Nature Conservancy, 122 Main St., P.O. Box 338, Topsham, ME 04086; (207) 729-5181.

JOSEPHINE NEWMAN SANCTUARY
Maine Audubon Society   Coastal
119 acres.

> From Woolwich on US 1, S on SR 127 9.1 mi. to Georgetown. Look for Sanctuary sign on right. (Map 7, D-1.)
>
> *Open daily, dawn to dusk.*

This small coastal site has remarkable natural diversity. It also has one of the most outstanding guides we've ever seen, a 60-page booklet that interprets every aspect of the site, excellent in concept, text, illustrations, and design. It begins with a "Sanctuary Almanac," a week-by-week calendar of natural events. In the third week of May, for example, "Yellow-rumped warblers arrive. Apple trees in flower. Trees leaf out."

On the E and W are two arms of Robinhood Cove. The land rises to 120 ft. Early efforts to farm are marked by crisscrossing stone walls. Bedrock outcrops are schist and granite. A small stream traverses wetlands before cascading into a saltwater cove. Bordering the site are mud flats and a rocky shore. Three marked, self-guiding trails total 2 1/2 mi.

Plants: The center spread of the booklet is a map of the plant communities, including cattail marsh, meadow, alder swamp, maple swamp, pine/alder shrub thicket, mixed forest, field pine and juniper, deciduous forest, hemlock ravine, coniferous forest, spruce/fir thicket, and salt marsh. Each community is described in considerable detail, making this booklet a useful guide far beyond the Sanctuary borders.

Also included are lists of the common wildflowers, grasses, and sedges; shrubs; trees; ferns; and mosses, lichens, club mosses, and horsetails.

Birds: The booklet has lists of 38 species known to breed in the Sanctuary and 31 visitors or migrants, with notes on seasons and preferred habitats.

Other fauna: Included are lists of mammals, amphibians, and reptiles.

NEARBY: Reid State Park (see entry).

PUBLICATION: *Forests, Fields, and Estuaries.* $2.50.

HEADQUARTERS: Maine Audubon Society, Gilsland Farm, 118 US Route 1, Falmouth, ME 04105; (207) 781-2330.

LA VERNA AND RACHEL CARSON SALT POND PRESERVES

Maine Chapter, The Nature Conservancy   Coastal
119 acres and 70 acres.

From Newcastle on US 1, S on SR 130 to New Harbor. For La Verna, 3 mi. N on SR 32. At Tibbitts Rd., park along SR 32 and walk 1/2 mi. to the shore, keeping right at the turnaround. For Rachel Carson, 1 mi. N on SR 32; park on the seaward side and use the steps. (Map 7, C-4.)

Both preserves front on Muscongus Bay. La Verna has 3,600 ft. of rugged shore, with cliffs and steep ledges on the N end, gravel beach on the S. Behind the shore are coniferous forest, swamp, freshwater marsh, and reverting farmland. Birding is good, and the site is excellent habitat for deer and small mammals.

At the 1/4-acre "salt pond" that now bears her name, author and naturalist Rachel Carson gathered some of the material for *The Edge of the Sea* (1955). Low tide exposes a variety of seaweeds with barnacles, blue mussels, hermit and green crabs, periwinkles, starfish, and green sea urchins.

Pets are prohibited.

HEADQUARTERS: Maine Chapter, The Nature Conservancy, 122 Main St., P.O. Box 338, Topsham, ME 04086; (207) 729-5181.

LEAVITT WILDLIFE MANAGEMENT AREA
Department of Inland Fisheries and Wildlife   West
6,408 acres.

From Dover-Foxcroft, 8 mi. SE on SR 15. The county line is the site's center. (Map 32, C-3.)

Between Dover-Foxcroft and Bangor, this is a place to hike with little likelihood of meeting other visitors except in hunting season. Primarily upland, it has a mixture of old fields and orchards and mixed forest. The highest terrain is Bull Hill, extending E from SR 15; some hawk watchers come here during the migration. Hatch Hill and High Cut are W of SR 15.

A small bog is also on the E side. Several streams have beaver dams, attracting waterfowl and aquatic furbearers.

ACTIVITIES
Hiking: Opportunities include interior roads, including old logging roads. Good berrying in season.
Hunting: Chiefly for deer, bear, and small game.

LILY BAY STATE PARK
Bureau of Parks and Recreation   North
924 acres.

From Greenville, 8 mi. N on Lily Bay Rd. (Map 41, C-3.)

Open May 1–Nov. 30.

This has long been one of our favorite parks. We're not alone; it's often full, but one can usually get a campsite, and all the sites are attractive. Many are on the shore where one can keep a boat and swim.

The chief attraction is Moosehead Lake, ME's largest, 30 mi. long, 20 mi. wide. (See entry.) Although the lake has attracted vacationers and fishermen for more than a century, until recently most development has been at the S end. Now development is spreading northward, but most of the shoreline is still wild, with no road access.

The shore is very irregular, with many bays, coves, and peninsulas. The Park itself has 7 mi. of shoreline. Near shore the water is generally shallow with numerous rocks and snags, but it's clear and one can navigate or wade, cautiously.

Many large and small islands are in the lake, some with private summer homes. Some have primitive campsites; others are available for picnics. Sugar Island (see entry) is just offshore from the Park.

Beyond the Park, the road extends NE into the region of almost unbroken forest, with countless lakes and streams, access to the North Maine Woods and Baxter State Park (see entries) and Ripogenus Dam between Chesuncook Lake and the West Branch of the Penobscot River. Several dirt roads to the left approach the lake shore at places where one can often see moose in the early evening. We've seen moose more closely from a canoe.

W of Greenville is a popular trail to the Big Squaw Mountain Fire Tower and the less-known Little Squaw Management Unit (see entry).

ACTIVITIES

Camping: 92 sites around two loops: Dunn Point and Rowell Cove. Arrive early in the day and take a number. While waiting, scout the area, identify sites you like, and see who's leaving. At the appointed hour, you'll be called in turn.

Hiking: Short hikes are possible within the Park, but there are unlimited opportunities nearby. Gatehouse has information.

Hunting: Prohibited during the Park's open season or when crews are working. Otherwise state regulations apply.

Fishing: Moosehead Lake is famous for its salmon, brook trout, and lake trout.

Boating: Ramp. Between the Park and Greenville, one could usually hail a passing boat for help. Further N, it might be a long wait. The lake can be very rough. Rocks and shoals are common near shore.

Canoeing: Rentals available. A Greenville outfitter will deliver a canoe to your campsite.

Ski touring: Popular in and near the Park. The Park facilities are closed during the winter.

PUBLICATION: Information page with sketch map of campground.

HEADQUARTERS: Greenville, ME 04441; (207) 695-2700.

LITTLE SQUAW MANAGEMENT UNIT
Bureau of Public Lands   North
12,584 acres.

From Greenville, W on SRs 15 and 6. Just outside of town, the road cuts across the NE corner of the site. Dyer Road, gravel surface, passes through the Unit. Just beyond the site is the road left to the Squaw Mountain Ski Area and Big Squaw Mountain Trail. (Map 41, D-1.)

The site is near the S end of Moosehead Lake. Big Squaw Mountain has been a popular day hike for vacationers. Little Squaw Mountain is a minor ridge trending WSW from near the highway, not as high as Big Squaw but offering a good view of the lake. The site is best known to fishermen, those who don't mind a bit of hiking. Little Squaw Pond is about 2 mi. from the road, Big Squaw Pond another half mile. Big Indian Pond, largest on the Unit, is at its far SW corner, accessible by a rough gravel road from Dyer Road. All the ponds are surrounded by forested hills, spectacular when the fall colors are at their best.

ACTIVITIES
Camping: Primitive campsites are at each of the principal ponds. Trailside camping is permitted anywhere, with no open fires.

Hiking: Chiefly on old logging roads. A new trail from a trailhead on the travel road leads to Big Squaw Pond, then Little Squaw Pond, then along the ridgeline to a trailhead behind the Greenwood Motel, where parking is available.

HEADQUARTERS: Bureau of Public Lands, Maine Department of Conservation, State House, Station 22, Augusta, ME 04333; (207) 289-3061.

LT. GORDON MANUEL WILDLIFE MANAGEMENT AREA
Department of Inland Fisheries and Wildlife   North
6,452 acres.

From Houlton, S on US 1, W on local road to Hodgdon. Parking, launching, and picnic area at the dam. Access to land area by Horseback Rd. and Town Line Rd. (Map 53, B-3.)

A water power dam on the South Branch of the Meduxnekeag River was built here in the late 1800s, forming a marsh that attracted waterfowl. Abandoned in the 1950s, the dam washed out, the marsh dried, and waterfowl declined. The site was acquired by the department, a new dam was built, and waterfowl returned.

From the dam, the marsh extends S for 2 1/2 mi., with a maximum width of 2,000 ft. Adjacent upland is a mixture of hardwood stands and reverting fields.

The marsh is best seen by boat. Motors are prohibited.

More recently about 6,000 acres of upland were added to the WMA. This upland is a mixture of old fields, woodlands, swamps, small wetlands, and streams.

Birds: Upland species include grouse, woodcock. Nest boxes have been placed for goldeneye, wood duck, and hooded merganser. Other waterfowl seen here include blue-winged and green-winged teal, black duck, ring-necked duck, American merganser, grebe, and Canada goose. Many shorebirds and songbirds frequent the area.

Mammals: Reported species include beaver, muskrat, mink, otter, red fox, coyote, fisher, marten, weasel, skunk, raccoon, snowshoe hare, deer, moose, black bear.

MACHIAS SEAL ISLAND

25 acres.   Coastal

At the mouth of the Bay of Fundy, between Maine and Nova Scotia. By charter boat from Lubec, Cutler, Jonesport. (Not shown on *Atlas* maps.)

Birding season is May to mid-Aug.

This tiny island is reached by boat from ports in ME. Each year it attracts several hundred birders because of its seabirds. More than 2,000 pairs of Arctic terns nest here, some 800 pairs of common puffins, with smaller numbers of many other species such as the common tern, razorbill, Leach's storm-petrel (seldom seen), and various land birds.

From the landing, visitors may use the boardwalk, footpaths to blinds, and a mowed area.

INFORMATION: It is not an Audubon Preserve, but the Maine Audubon Society (118 US Route 1, Falmouth, ME 04105; (207) 781-2330) has offered occasional tours. We also obtained information from a charter boat operator: Barna B. Norton, RR #1, 340 Main St., Jonesport, ME 04649; (207) 497-5933.

MAHOOSUC MOUNTAINS MANAGEMENT UNIT
Bureau of Public Lands   West
27,253 acres.

From Bethel, N on SR 26 to Grafton Notch. The Unit has two portions, W and E of the highway, separated by and adjacent to Grafton Notch State Park. (Map 18, D-E, 1-2.)

A major trailhead is in New Hampshire on Success Pond Rd. (DeLorme Publishing's New Hampshire Atlas, Map 51).

SR 26 is one of ME's most scenic highways. Grafton Notch has long been a famous resort because of its spectacular setting. The Mahoosuc Range is wild and rugged, with forested slopes, steep gorges, cataracts and waterfalls, cirques, glacial tarns, subalpine heaths, even a few "ice caves," small caves where ice forms and may last all summer. Several peaks rise to over 3,500 ft. Old Speck, 4,180 ft., is ME's third highest. On the E, Baldpate Mountain has twin peaks, both over 3,500 ft.

Most of the Unit is accessible only on foot. Bull Branch Road penetrates the W portion from the SE. East B Hill Road crosses the N tip of the E portion. Otherwise there are only a few logging roads, not shown on the site map and in uncertain condition.

It's a glorious place for hiking. The Management Units are the only State lands where one can camp almost anywhere, pitching a tent trailside or near one's car. (Fires require Forest Service permits except at designated campsites.) Most hiking has been on the Appalachian Trail, and trail sections near the highway have had heavy use. Recreation plans include loop trails, better trail maintenance, and more trailside campsites.

Plants: At the base of the mountains is mixed forest. At about 2,500 ft. this gives way to spruce/fir forest; this dominates the slopes to about 3,300 ft., where it becomes spruce/fir krummholz, trees reduced to the stature of shrubs by severe climate and thin soil. At the highest elevations are subalpine heaths and exposed rock covered with lichens. Here, too, are alpine bogs with delicate plant species.

Multiple use is the governing policy here. About 17,000 acres, the lower-elevation forest, are managed for commercial timber production. Harvesting is planned to promote growth of yellow and white birch and sugar maple. The high slopes won't be cut, nor will areas designated for recreation or buffer zones around lakes and streams. Cutting is planned in consultation with wildlife biologists, to maintain or improve habitats.

Birds: No bird list has yet been prepared. Most of ME's upland bird species should occur here, as well as species characteristic of more northern habitats, including the spruce grouse, gray jay, and boreal chickadee.

Mammals: No list has been made. Most upland species are probably here but not abundant.

FEATURES

The Cataracts are on a trail off East B Hill Rd. Frye Brook cascades over several falls in the gorge between Baldpate and Surplus mountains.

Speck Pond, a mountain tarn on Old Speck Mountain, is the highest lake in ME. On the Appalachian Trail, it's not far from the State Park and SR 26, but the trail is steep and difficult. A shelter is nearby.

Observation tower atop Old Speck Mountain has splendid views.

Mahoosuc Notch, 1,500 ft. below Mahoosuc Arm, is noted for lush growth of ferns and mosses and a nearby 250-year-old stand of yellow birch.

Alpine bog and heath areas are on Mahoosuc, Goose Eye, and Carlo mountains. Hikers are asked to keep off, as the plants are highly vulnerable to trampling. Walkways have been placed on a few.

ACTIVITIES

Camping: Car camping is difficult. The State Park has no campground. The nearest commercial campgrounds are about 10 mi. N or S. Roadside camping in the Management Unit isn't prohibited, but there isn't much road. Little more than 1 mi. of Bull Branch Rd. is inside the boundaries.

Most trailside camping is along the Appalachian Trail. Five lean-tos or shelters are along the Trail, with tent platforms at Speck Pond, all maintained by the Appalachian Trail Club.

Hiking, backpacking: The trail system was here before the State acquired the land. The principal trails originate outside the boundaries. The main stem is the Appalachian Trail, entering near Baldpate in the N, crossing the State Park, then following the Mahoosucs past Mt. Carlo to the New Hampshire border. The section at Mahoosuc Notch is said to be the most difficult mile anywhere on the Trail. Along the way are side trails suitable for day hikes as well as overnights. Several of these—Speck Pond, Mahoosuc Notch, Goose Eye, and Carlo Col—originate in NH. All are well described in hiking guides.

Hunting: Game species are very limited.

Fishing: Opportunities are limited. The principal fishing streams are along SR 26 and Bull Branch Rd.

Ski touring, snowmobiling: The State Park is the principal base for parking.

This is remote country. Hikers should know the degree-of-difficulty rating of any trail before starting and be prepared for contingencies, including weather changes.

PUBLICATION: Folder with map.

REFERENCES

AMC Maine Mountain Guidebook Committee. *Maine Mountain Guide.* Boston: Appalachian Mountain Club, 1985.

ATC Committee. *Appalachian Trail Guide to Maine.* Harpers Ferry, WV: Appalachian Trail Conference, 1983.

Feller-Roth, Barbara, ed. *Hiking.* Vol. 2: *Western Region.* Freeport: DeLorme Publishing, 1987.

Gibson, John. *Fifty Hikes in Maine.* Woodstock, VT: Backcountry Publications, 1983.

Kulik, Stephen, Pete Salmansohn, Matthew Schmidt, and Heidi Welch. *The Audubon Society Field Guide to the Natural Places of the Northeast: Inland.* New York: Pantheon Books, 1984. Pp. 298–308.

HEADQUARTERS: Bureau of Public Lands, Maine Department of Conservation, State House, Station 22, Augusta, ME 04333; (207) 289-3061.

MAST LANDING SANCTUARY

Maine Audubon Society   Coastal
140 acres.

From US 1 in Freeport, across from the L. L. Bean Company building, take Bow St. 1 mi. to Upper Mast Rd., on left. Up hill, and Sanctuary is on the right. (Map 6, C-1.)

Open dawn to dusk.

The site is operated as a nature day camp, but hikers are welcome. Wooded ridges, fields, and orchard slope down from 100 ft. above sea level to salt marsh along Mill Creek. Runoff has cut deep ravines, several of which have hemlock stands. Habitats include a red maple/alder swamp. Most of the site is forested. A brochure describes the Sanctuary's natural communities and cultural history.

The site has a well-developed system of trails.

HEADQUARTERS: Maine Audubon Society, Gilsland Farm, 118 US Route 1, Falmouth, ME 04105; (207) 781-2330.

MATTAWAMKEAG WILDERNESS PARK

Penobscot County   North
1,018 acres.

From US 2 at Mattawamkeag, local road E along the Mattawamkeag River. (Map 44, C-3.)

Open May 15–Oct. 15.

The Park is centered on a low hardwood ridge surrounded by softwood forest and wetlands, with 2 mi. of frontage on the river. The surrounding region, while not true wilderness, is largely roadless, flat to hilly, forested with extensive wetlands. The central feature is the Mattawamkeag River, a scenic fishing stream with rapids.

ACTIVITIES
Camping: 50 sites; 12 shelters.
Hiking: 15 mi. of trails.
Fishing: Brook trout and salmon. The river has large granite pools.
Canoeing: From Kingman on SR 170, a 12-mi. run to the Penobscot River at Mattawamkeag, passing the camp. Rapids to Class III. The river can be canoed later in the season than most.

PUBLICATIONS: Information leaflets.

REFERENCE: Kellogg, Zip. *Canoeing.* Vol. 3: *Northern Rivers:* Freeport: DeLorme Publishing, 1986.

HEADQUARTERS: Box 5, Mattawamkeag, ME 04459; (207) 736-4881.

MOOSEHEAD LAKE

30 mi. N–S, 20 mi. W–E.   North

Greenville is at the S end. (Map 41.)

Maine's largest lake lies between the state's developed and undeveloped areas. To the N are few paved roads and few towns; most of this territory is owned by timber companies, accessible by their private roads.

The lake's elevation is 1,029 ft. Surrounding it are forested hills, generally rising no more than 400 ft. above the shore. Behind them are a few mountains more than 3,000 ft. high.

The lake's shape is very irregular. So is that of a moose's head, but it requires great imagination to see a resemblance. The lake has many arms, bays, coves, and peninsulas, and in the lake are numerous large and small islands. Maximum depth is 246 ft. Many of the bays and coves are shallow, and boaters should beware of rocks near shore and occasionally well out.

Moosehead has been a famous resort for more than a century. Outfitters, inns, lodges, marinas, and other commercial development centered at Greenville, and this is still the primary point of access. SR 6/15 now runs halfway up the W side to Rockwood, which has similar but fewer services. Lily Bay State Park (see entry) is on the E side. Most of the shore beyond these points is roadless.

Primitive campsites are scattered around the lake and on several of its islands. We saw many quiet coves, far from any road, where one could camp from a boat or canoe. Sugar Island, off Lily Bay, is State land (see entry). Canoeing near dusk, we often paddled close to a moose.

Moosehead is one of the state's best fisheries for salmon, brook trout, lake trout, hornpout, smelt, lake whitefish, round whitefish, others.

Boaters venturing far from base should watch the weather. Storms can develop suddenly, and the lake can be very rough. However, it's almost always possible to find shelter behind an island or in a cove.

Ice-out is usually by mid-May.

REFERENCES

Kulik, Stephen, Pete Salmansohn, Matthew Schmidt, and Heidi Welch. *The Audubon Society Field Guide to the Natural Places of the Northeast: Inland.* New York: Pantheon Books, 1984.

Monegain, Bernie. *Natural Sites, a Guide to Maine's Natural Phenomena.* Freeport: DeLorme Publishing, 1985.

Moosehead Lake Map and Guide. Freeport: DeLorme Publishing.

Vanderweide, Harry. *Maine Fishing Maps.* Vol. 1: *Lakes and Ponds.* Freeport: DeLorme Publishing, 1986.

INFORMATION: Moosehead Lake Region Chamber of Commerce, P.O. Box 581, Greenville, ME 04441; (207) 695-2702.

MOOSEHORN NATIONAL WILDLIFE REFUGE
U.S. Fish and Wildlife Service   Coastal
Baring Unit, 16,065 acres; Edmunds Unit, 6,600 acres.

Baring Unit: on US 1 SW of Calais. (Map 36, C-5.) Edmunds Unit: on US 1 about 2 mi. N of Whiting. (Map 27, B-2.)

This part of the ME coast is irregular, with countless bays, coves, and inlets, and many offshore islands. Tidal fluctuations are extreme, about 24 ft. in the Cobscook Bay area (Edmunds Unit).

Except for the coastline, it's not a dramatically scenic area, but it has natural diversity and rich wildlife. The land is highly glaciated, with low rolling hills, elevations from 50 to 480 ft. The two units, about 25 mi. apart, have about 100 water-marsh areas. Lakes and ponds range from 20 to 400 acres, with many smaller ponds and flowages. About a tenth of the Refuge area is wetlands.

Plants: The forest is easily accessible, so it's been cut more than once, and planned harvesting continues within the Refuge. Some scattered stands of old-growth white pine remain. Most of the cover is relatively young aspen, beech, birch, maple, spruce, fir, and pine. We saw one area that had been burned and was now green with weeds and dotted with wildflowers.

Birds: This is the only federal refuge where the American woodcock is intensively studied and managed. The average summer woodcock population is 1,800; more than 3,000 are here in spring and fall migrations. Their mating ritual can be seen in clearings in early spring.

The best birding season is May 10–30. A checklist of 209 bird species is available. Seasonally abundant or common species include common loon, pied-billed grebe, great and double-crested cormorants, American bittern, great blue heron, Canada goose, wood duck, green-winged and blue-winged teal, American black duck, ring-necked duck, common goldeneye, bufflehead, common and hooded mergansers.

Also osprey, bald eagle, northern harrier, broad-winged hawk, American kestrel, ruffed grouse, killdeer, greater and lesser yellowlegs; spotted, semipalmated, and least sandpipers; common snipe; Bonaparte's, herring, and great black-backed gulls.

Also great horned and barred owls, common nighthawk, whip-poor-will, chimney swift, ruby-throated hummingbird, belted kingfisher. Woodpeckers: yellow-bellied sapsucker, downy, hairy, black-backed, northern flicker. Flycatchers: olive-sided, eastern wood-pewee, alder, least, eastern phoebe, eastern kingbird. Tree, bank, cliff, and barn swallows; blue jay, American crow, common raven.

Also black-capped chickadee, red-breasted nuthatch, brown creeper, winter and sedge wrens, golden-crowned and ruby-crowned kinglets, veery; Swainson's, hermit, and wood thrushes; American robin, gray catbird, cedar waxwing, European starling, red-eyed vireo. Warblers: Tennessee, Nashville, northern parula, yellow, chestnut-sided, magnolia, black-throated blue, yellow-rumped, black-throated green, blackburnian, black-and-white, American redstart, ovenbird, northern waterthrush, common yellowthroat.

Sparrows: American tree, chipping, vesper, savannah, song, white-throated. Dark-eyed junco, snow bunting, bobolink, red-winged blackbird, common grackle, brown-headed cowbird, purple finch, common redpoll, pine siskin, American goldfinch, evening grosbeak, house sparrow.

Mammals: Annotated list available. Abundant or fairly abundant species include masked and shorttail shrews, hairytail and starnose moles, little brown myotis, snowshoe hare, woodchuck, eastern chipmunk, red squirrel, northern flying squirrel, beaver, deer and white-footed mice, boreal redback and meadow voles, muskrat, meadow and woodland jumping mice, porcupine, whitetail deer, black bear, red fox, raccoon, mink, river otter, harbor seal, coyote.

BARING UNIT

This is the larger of the two units. The entrance is off US 1, half a mile S of its junction with SR 191. Refuge headquarters is about 3 mi. from this turn. At HQ are a bulletin board and an exhibit with Refuge information and map. A nature trail is on the road leading in to HQ. One can hike on interior roads that are closed to vehicles. There is no tour route.

Of the Unit's 16,065 acres, 4,680 are Wilderness. HQ is near the edge of the Wilderness, and several trails lead from here to points of interest in the Wilderness, including Bearce Lake, largest in the Refuge. The Refuge has several miles of frontage on SR 191, with several trailheads.

EDMUNDS UNIT

We thought this unit was less interesting than Baring, except that it adjoins Cobscook Bay State Park (see entry) and provides good hiking opportunities for campers. The Park gatehouse can supply a map and information. N of the Park entrance, on the other side of US 1, is North Trail, the beginning of a 5 1/2 mi. auto loop, a pleasant but unexciting drive through the woods. On the E, the Unit borders on Cobscook Bay between the Dennys and Whiting rivers.

2,782 acres of the Unit are Wilderness. The loop route passes along the Wilderness boundary. Old roads provide hiking routes. The portion of the area we saw has an understory too dense for bushwhacking.

ACTIVITIES

Hiking: 60 mi. of trails in the two Wilderness Areas.
Hunting: For deer, with special regulations. Inquire at HQ.

Fishing: Smallmouth bass, yellow perch, pickerel, brook trout. Fishing areas are designated on the bulletin board at HQ.

Boating: On Bearce Lake and Vose Pond. No motors. Bearce Lake access from SR 191.

PUBLICATIONS
  Refuge leaflet with map.
  Unit maps.
  Bird checklist.
  Mammal checklist.

HEADQUARTERS: P.O. Box 1077, Calais, ME 04619; (207) 454-3521.

MORSE MOUNTAIN PRESERVE
Private   Coastal
600 acres.

From US 1 at Bath, S on SR 209. Where it turns left, continue straight on SR 216 for about 1 mi. Entrance is on left. (Map 6, E-5.)

We noticed this site on the DeLorme *Atlas* map. When Popham Beach and Reid State Parks (see entries) were overcrowded, we thought this might be a quiet seaside. The map shows 1 1/2 mi. of private dirt road crossing a salt marsh and wooded hill from the entrance to the mile of sandy beach.

We saw no sign, just a gap in a stone wall, but people knew about the place. The small parking area inside the wall was full, and many cars were parked along the road outside. This, too, seems to be a site worth exploring before or after the warm months.

MOUNT BLUE STATE PARK
Bureau of Parks and Recreation   West
4,398 acres.

From Dixfield on US 2, N on SR 142. For lakeside, turn left on West Rd. from Berry Mills. For mountain trails, continue to Weld, then on Maxwell Rd. (Map 19, C-3.)

Open May 15 to Oct. 15.

The Park is in two pieces, the smaller one on the shore of Webb Lake, the larger in mountainous terrain. The smaller attracts the campers, picnickers, fishermen, and swimmers; the larger attracts hikers and backpackers.

Webb Lake, elevation 678 ft., is about 4 mi. long. The Park has about 3/4 mi. of shoreline. Although there is some development around the lake, the surrounding country is largely roadless, most of it owned by timber companies.

The larger portion of the Park is mountainous, about 5 1/2 mi. W–E. From Maxwell Rd. one can drive to the base of Mt. Blue via Center Hill Rd. and Mt. Blue Rd. It is then a 3/4-mi. hike to the summit at 3,187 ft., a gain of 1,800 ft.

The Park, like the surrounding region, is almost entirely forested, spruce/fir with some hardwoods. Wildflowers, chiefly in openings and along roadsides, include trailing arbutus, lady's-slipper, violets, dogwood, wild rose, goldenrod, blue flag, jack-in-the-pulpit, daisies, buttercup. Several streams flow to the lake.

ACTIVITIES

Camping: 136 sites.

Hiking, backpacking: Trails and logging roads in the surrounding area offer opportunities for extensive hiking and backpacking, to such destinations as Tumbledown Mountain, Little Jackson Mountain, Rangeley Lake, and the Appalachian Trail.

Hunting: In designated sections. Deer, bear, raccoon, rabbit, coyote, partridge, woodcock, waterfowl.

Fishing: Lake and stream. Salmon, brown trout, bass, perch, pickerel. Ice fishing.

Swimming: Camp beach may be supervised.

Boating: Ramp. Rentals. Sailing.

Ski touring, snowmobiling: Snowmobile trail to Rangeley Lake, about 30 mi. Many opportunities on unplowed roads.

REFERENCE: Gibson, John. *Fifty Hikes in Maine.* Woodstock, VT: Backcountry Publications, 1983.

HEADQUARTERS: Center Hill, Weld, ME 04285; (207) 585-2261.

MULLEN WOODS PRESERVE
Maine Chapter, The Nature Conservancy   Coastal
117 acres.

From Newport, E on US 2. Where it bends right, just before East Newport, continue straight on Bangor Rd., then left on Stetson Rd. and left on Durham Bridge Rd. Just over the bridge, right on Rutland Rd. After a sharp left, go 1 mi. Park on Rutland Rd. and walk in. Entrance is a grassy track between fences on the right. (Map 22, A-2.)

Great white pines once were common in Maine forests. Although the original stand here was cleared in the eighteenth century, many of those now growing are over 150 years old, some taller than 100 ft. The forested area of the tract includes mixed conifers and hardwoods, a stand of younger white pine, and some mature hemlock. A small stream bounded by cedar thickets meanders through the N section. An old field is being used for silvicultural test plots.

Stay on the paths. Pets are prohibited.

HEADQUARTERS: Maine Chapter, The Nature Conservancy, 122 Main St., P.O. Box 338, Topsham, ME 04086; (207) 729-5181.

NORTH MAINE WOODS

North Maine Woods   North
2,800,000 acres.

Northern ME, roughly from Baxter State Park to Canada. The private road system is controlled at checkpoints. The one most used by recreationists is 6 Mile Checkpoint (Map 63, E-5), W of Ashland on American Realty Tote Rd.

Summer season: May opening to Sept. 30. Fall: Oct. 1–Nov. 30; summer season permits not valid.

This huge forested region is privately owned. The owners, individuals and corporations, chiefly timber companies, have formed the North Maine Woods organization to provide for multiple-use management, including recreation. It is open to public use, subject to rules and restrictions adopted by the owners.

Much of this land was sold at about the time Maine was separated from Massachusetts in 1820. It was usually sold in blocks of 36 sq. mi., called "townships," at the time often roadless and inaccessible. Even today many of these townships have only names like "T 12 R 15." Often several individuals joined in purchasing a township. Paper companies began large-scale acquisitions early in the twentieth century. Sales, transfers, and bequests have produced some complex partnerships, such as a paper company and a number of individuals.

Don't come here unless you understand the nature of the area and unless you've obtained the Guide Map, which includes the rules and regulations. Motorists sometimes plan to drive the American Realty Road (as labeled on state highway maps) from Ashland W to Quebec, only to discover that it can't be used as a through route; travelers must leave by the checkpoint through which they entered.

The region is commercial forest, not wilderness. Not shown on highway maps are more than 2,000 mi. of permanently maintained roads and additional miles of temporary roads built for forest operations. Large areas have been cut over twice, and a third growth is being harvested. Some sections are tree farms, plots clear-cut and supporting even-aged single-species stands. Earlier cutting in other large areas has been followed by natural succession, and a mixed forest is maturing.

Sculptured by the ice sheet, the terrain is hilly and irregular, most of it between 1,000 and 1,400 ft. elevation, cut by countless large and small stream valleys, with many rivers, lakes, and wetlands.

The north Maine woods have long been known to hunters and fishermen from throughout the United States and elsewhere. Before most of the present roads were built, parties were conducted by professional guides who paddled the canoes, made camp, cleaned fish, and cooked meals. In the 1920s John's great-uncle came here each summer, wearing his Norfolk jacket, knickers, and laced boots, carrying his cased salmon rods, meeting his favorite guide.

Huge areas are still roadless, and only those familiar with the area know the water trails and portages to the many quiet, isolated lakes and ponds. Registered guides still conduct parties.

With more roads came a rapid increase in the number of visitors. The ensuing problems compelled owners to control access. With the complex ownerships, the only feasible solution was a consortium to manage public use. Differences of viewpoint persist. Some owners would prefer to exclude visitors altogether, but all within the boundaries entrust the North Maine Woods consortium with publishing and administering public use regulations.

Despite the roads, the region is still huge, wild, and primitive. Fewer people live here than in the past. There are no motels, gas stations, shops, or tow trucks. The principal law officers are the State's fish and wildlife wardens and fire control rangers, each of whom has a large territory. Visitors who get in trouble are on their own.

Entrances are controlled. Visitors must register and pay fees. Those who wish to camp must obtain permits for use of authorized campsites.

The St. John River, Allagash Wilderness Waterway, and Deboullie Management Unit are within the North Maine Woods; see separate entries.

Flying service by floatplane—people, canoes, and gear—is available at Shin Pond, Portage Lake, Millinocket, and Greenville. Bush pilots know many out-of-the-way spots.

ACTIVITIES

Camping: Several hundred primitive campsites are available, most with fireplace, table, and privy. Camping is permitted only at authorized sites. Reservations can be made a minimum of one month before arrival, or one can chance what's available on entering. For sites inaccessible by motor vehicle, a fire permit must be obtained from the Maine Forest Service before entering.

Hiking, backpacking: Aside from abandoned roads and trails to a few fire towers, hiking routes are limited. Checkpoint attendants, wardens, and rangers can usually suggest something.

Hunting: Subject to state laws and local regulations of landowners. Inquire. Special entry permits may be required.

Fishing: As many perennial visitors know, it's great if you know where to go. The guides do.

Canoeing: Canoeing is the best way to travel off road, the only means of access to large areas. Good maps are essential, and many visitors depend on registered guides.

Ski touring, snowmobiling: Permitted on unplowed roads.

Trail bikes and all-terrain vehicles are prohibited. 4-wheel-drive vehicles must stay on rights-of-way. Mobile homes are prohibited. Travel trailers and vehicles up to 28 ft. are permitted through certain checkpoints only.

Quotas may limit visitor numbers. This usually happens only in hunting season.

May–June is black fly season.

PUBLICATIONS

Welcome to North Maine Woods. Basic information, map, regulations. $1.50 postpaid.

Lists of cooperating flying services, outfitters, guides.

List of campsites.

REFERENCE: Kulik, Stephen, Pete Salmansohn, Matthew Schmidt, and Heidi Welch. *The Audubon Society Field Guide to the Natural Places of the Northeast: Inland.* New York: Pantheon Books, 1984.

HEADQUARTERS: P.O. Box 421, Ashland, ME 04732; (207) 435-6213.

PEAKS-KENNY STATE PARK

Bureau of Parks and Recreation   West
839 acres.

From Dover-Foxcroft, N on SR 153. (Map 32, A-1.)

Open May 15–Oct. 1, 9 A.M. to sunset.

Most visitors come here for water-based recreation. The Park has a 2-mi. frontage on 6,000-acre Sebec Lake, which is over 10 mi. long. The park is attractive, with wooded campsites, a sand beach at the foot of an expanse of lawn. Most of the site is covered by young mixed forest: spruce/fir with northern hardwoods.

To the N of Sebec Lake is a vast region of forest and lakes, mostly land owned by timber companies, with extensive opportunities for primitive camping, backpacking, hunting, fishing, and canoeing.

ACTIVITIES

Camping: 56 sites. Likely to be full Sat. and holidays, sometimes on Fri.

Hiking: 3 trails are within the Park, 1/2 to 2 mi. Other opportunities are nearby.

Fishing: Lake and stream. Salmon, trout, togue, pickerel, smallmouth bass, perch.

Swimming: Lake. Beach may be supervised.

Boating: Power boats are allowed on the lake; a ramp is outside the Park at the end of SR 153. Sailing.

REFERENCE: Vanderweide, Harry. *Maine Fishing Maps.* Vol. 1: *Lakes and Ponds.* Freeport: DeLorme Publishing, 1986.

HEADQUARTERS: Dover-Foxcroft, ME 04426; (207) 564-2003.

PETIT MANAN NATIONAL WILDLIFE REFUGE

U.S. Fish and Wildlife Service   Coastal

3,335 acres.

From Ellsworth, about 30 mi. S on US 1. Just beyond Steuben, turn S on Pigeon Hill Rd. (Map 17, A-3.)

Open during daylight hours.

The Refuge occupies a peninsula between Dyer Bay and Pigeon Hill Bay and several nearby islands. Petit Manan Point is rugged, windswept, with a rocky shoreline, cobble beaches, fresh and saltwater marshes, beaver flowages, heath, and mixed forest. Small tidepools can be found on the E side of the

Point. The highest land is 144 ft. above sea level. Bois Bubert Island, on which the Refuge has 1,155 acres, is much like the Point; it can be reached only by boat. The other islands are much smaller and visiting is discouraged, especially in nesting season.

Birds: No checklist is available. About 250 species have been recorded, including black duck, eider; black-backed, herring, and laughing gulls; osprey, bald eagle, peregrine falcon, ruffed and spruce grouse, whimbrel; common, arctic, and roseate terns; black guillemot.

Mammals: Include deer, beaver, mink, muskrat, raccoon, weasel, red fox, striped skunk, snowshoe hare, porcupine, coyote.

An information exhibit is at the parking area. Two unimproved trails begin here: Shore Trail, 5 mi., to the shore of Pigeon Hill Bay; Birch Point Trail, 4 mi. loop to Dyer Bay.

The manager advises that the best time for a visit is late summer, when the weather is best and black fly and mosquito numbers have decreased.

Parts of the Point and Bois Bubert Island are private property. Please observe Refuge boundary signs.

PUBLICATIONS
Information page.
Map.

HEADQUARTERS: P.O. Box 279, Milbridge, ME 04658; (207) 546-2124.

POND FARM WILDLIFE MANAGEMENT AREA
Department of Inland Fisheries and Wildlife   West
450 acres.

From I-95 at Howland, Exit E on SR 6, the Trans-Maine Highway. In 1 mi. turn N on SR 116. In about 2 mi., fork left on North Howland Rd. In 1 1/2 mi., turn N on Seboeis Rd. In about 1 1/2 mi., see site on left at bridge. (Map 33, A-3.)

This site interested us because of its unusual history. Until the late 1800s, there was a large pond here, the water retained by an esker. Some men blasted through this glacial ridge, releasing a flood that caused downstream damage all the way to Bangor. Then followed ditching and unsuccessful farming, grazing, and mining enterprises, after which the land was allowed to revert, grasses and sedges growing in moist areas, woody plants where there was drier ground.

Title passed from owner to owner until someone in the Fish and Game Department observed that it had been State property all the time. All "great ponds," ponds larger than 10 acres, belong to the State. Draining a pond doesn't change its legal status.

So the department dammed the outlet, flooding the old bottom and creating a new pond and marsh. The WMA is near a waterfowl migration route, and its attraction was increased by developing goose pasture, building nesting islands, and blasting potholes. Nearly all species of ducks found in ME's freshwater wetlands now are seen here. Bald eagles are often sighted and ospreys nest. Standing near the bridge, we looked out over this restored habitat, which shows few signs of its past abuse.

Just beyond the bridge, a short dirt road leads to a parking area for about three cars and launching for hand-carried boats.

POPHAM BEACH STATE PARK

Bureau of Parks and Recreation   Coastal
529 acres.

From US 1 at Bath, S on SR 9 to beach. (Map 6, E-5.)

Open May 1–Sept. 30.

It is said to be a fine sand beach with tidepools and rock outcrops. We don't know. On a sunny day in August, the parking area was full and dozens of cars were parked along the road outside. Try it in the fall.

QUODDY HEAD STATE PARK

Bureau of Parks and Recreation   Coastal
481 acres.

From US 1 at Whiting, NE on SR 189 toward Lubec. Entering Lubec, S on South Lubec Rd., then E to Quoddy Head. (Map 27, B-4.)

Quoddy Head is the easternmost point of land in the United States. It's a scenic area, with cliffs 80 ft. high, Gulliver's Hole (a foaming sea pocket), a lighthouse, and a short trail that includes a boardwalk through a peat bog. It's an easy detour for visitors to Campobello Island. The nearest camping is at Cobscook Bay State Park (see entry).

RACHEL CARSON NATIONAL WILDLIFE REFUGE
U.S. Fish and Wildlife Service   Coastal
2,810 acres.

From Wells, N on US 1, then right a short distance on SR 9. (Map 3, D-1.)

The Refuge is a chain of small units, coastal marshes extending from near Kittery Point to the Spurwink River S of South Portland. Most of the units have little or no upland. The only visitor facilities are at the unit N of Wells.

Wells is a busy, congested resort town. Just outside, the Refuge is a quiet, delightful woodland overlooking salt marsh, tidal channels, and estuary. Exhibits at the parking area describe the site and its purpose. A loop trail passes through the white pine forest to overlooks and a boardwalk. The original trail was a dirt track, later covered with wood chips; when we visited, some sections were being paved.

An extensive bird list is available. At midday in August we saw more butterflies than birds. We enjoyed the visit.

Rachel Carson Salt Pond Preserve, 78 acres, is on Pemaquid Neck S of Bristol. (Map 7, C-4.) Overlook.

PUBLICATIONS
Information pages.
Annotated bird checklist.

HEADQUARTERS: Route 2, Box 751, Wells, ME 04090; (207) 646-9226.

RANGELEY LAKE STATE PARK
Bureau of Parks and Recreation   West
691 acres.

W central ME. From S of Rangeley on SR 4, W on South Shore Drive. (Map 28, E-4.)

An attractive camp on the shore of a lake that has been a well-known resort for more than a century. The lake is about 8 mi. long, covering 6,000 acres. Roads encircle it, and development is increasing. However, much of the surrounding territory is mountainous, forested, and undeveloped, with many isolated streams and ponds.

The Park has 1 1/2 mi. of lake shore, and most recreation is water-based. No trails are within the Park, but it's a good place to camp for day hiking at Sabbathday Pond, Elephant Mountain, Bald Mountain, and Saddleback Mountain, which is on the Appalachian Trail.

ACTIVITIES

Camping: 50 sites. May 15–Oct. 1.
Fishing: Chiefly salmon. Also brook trout.
Swimming: Supervised beach.
Boating: Ramp; dock; rentals.
Ski touring, snowmobiling: Marked snowmobile trail, 30 mi., to Mount Blue State Park.

REFERENCES

Gibson, John. *Fifty Hikes in Maine.* Woodstock, VT: Backcountry Publications, 1983.
Vanderweide, Harry. *Maine Fishing Maps.* Vol. 1: *Lakes and Ponds.* Freeport: DeLorme Publishing, 1986.

HEADQUARTERS: Rangeley, ME 04970; (207) 864-3858.

REID STATE PARK
Bureau of Parks and Recreation   Coastal
766 acres.

From Woolwich on US 1, S and E on SR 127, then S on Seguinland Rd. (Map 7, D-1.)

Open all year.

It is said to have 1 1/2 mi. of sand beaches, dunes, marshes, ledges, and other natural attractions, including spruce trees growing close to the high-tide mark. Birding is said to be good, in season, with gannet, eider, and scoter offshore, shorebirds in late summer, many upland species.

What we saw on a warm summer weekend was a roadside lined with cars that couldn't be parked inside and a beach thronged with people. One can usually find parking on weekdays, we were told. It could be quiet and pleasant in spring and fall.

RICHARDSON LAKE MANAGEMENT UNIT
Bureau of Public Lands   West
22,806 acres.

From Andover (at the intersection of SRs 120 and 5), N on South Arm Road to the private campground and boat ramp at the S end of Lower Richardson Lake. SR 16 W from Rangeley crosses the N end of the site; a boat launch site is at the N end of Upper Richardson Lake. (Map 18, A-2, 3.)

The 4,200-acre upper lake and 2,900-acre lower lake are joined at a shallow narrows. The upper lake is separated from Mooselookmeguntic Lake by a dam. All three are within the Rangeley Lakes complex, in a hilly, forested region with few roads. The lakes are noted for excellent salmon and trout fishing. The shore is undeveloped except for a few private cottages. Upper Richardson has numerous sand beaches.

The public land lies between the Richardson Lakes and Mooselookmeguntic. Land access is from the south. The gate shown on the *Atlas* map is not closed except possibly at spring breakup.

Elevation at the lakes is 1,448 ft. The public land is heavily forested, relatively flat, with isolated hills up to 2,130 ft. Three small ponds are in the N portion of the site near SR 16.

ACTIVITIES

Camping: Designated lakeshore sites are assigned at the South Arm campground.

Hiking: On woods roads.

Hunting: Deer, moose, bear, grouse, but in relatively low numbers.

Fishing: Lake, brown, and brook trout; salmon, hornpout, bullhead. Best fishing June–Sept. Excellent Sept. fly fishing in Rapid River, outlet of the lower lake. Marked fly fishing areas in upper lake.

Boating, canoeing: Launch at S and N ends. Ice out about May 5.

REFERENCE: Vanderweide, Harry. *Maine Fishing Maps.* Vol. 1: *Lakes and Ponds.* Freeport: DeLorme Publishing, 1986.

HEADQUARTERS: Bureau of Public Lands, Maine Department of Conservation, State House, Station 22, Augusta, ME 04333; (207) 289-3061.

ROCKY LAKE MANAGEMENT UNIT
Bureau of Public Lands   Coastal
9,904 acres.

From East Machias on US 1, N about 8 mi. on SR 191, which cuts across
the SE corner of the site. (Map 26, A-3.)

"I like this site," our advisor said. "It's underutilized. Excellent warmwater
fishing. Sand beaches. A good canoe trip."

The boundaries are well marked at the highway with blue-and-white signs.
About 3 by 6 mi., the site is in a region of lakes and wetlands. The land is
flat to gently rolling, the elevation about 200 ft. Rocky Lake, about 4 1/2 mi.
long, is in the E half of the unit. The W half is crossed by the East Machias
River and Huntley Brook, with associated wetlands. Second Lake, about 1 mi.
long, is on the N boundary. A launch site for hand-carried craft and a campsite are at the dam, on the E side of Rocky Lake, about 1/2 mi. off the access
road.

Rocky Lake is indeed rocky. Boats with motors must be operated cautiously. It has miles of undeveloped shoreline and many small islands.

ACTIVITIES

Camping: 4 vehicle-access campsites on Rocky Lake, one on Second Lake.
The Mud Landing site is marked at the highway. Walk down before trying
the road with a trailer. Camp in any suitable place; no open fires.

Hiking: A few short trails are within the boundaries, miles of back roads
and trails nearby.

Hunting: Game populations are generally low.

Fishing: Chiefly bass, white perch, pickerel. Called excellent. Atlantic salmon in the East Machias River.

Canoeing: A 50-mi. trip begins at the end of the lake, curves S into Second
Lake, then down the East Machias River through Hadley Lake to the ocean.
Some moderate whitewater and areas of open water.

HEADQUARTERS: Bureau of Public Lands, Maine Department of Conservation, State House, Station 22, Augusta, ME 04333; (207) 289-3061.

ROUND POND MANAGEMENT UNIT
Bureau of Public Lands   North
19,468 acres.

Most visitors are traveling the Allagash Wilderness Waterway (see entry).
Land access is from Ashland, W on American Realty Road through the

North Maine Woods (see entry), turning N at Musquacooks lakes. (Map 62, C-1.)

Maine is blessed with an abundance of "Round Ponds." We counted 3 on the Allagash Waterway, and there may be more. This one is at Mile 88 from Telos Landing. About 2 mi. long, the pond is a backwater surrounded by forested hills.

It's a pleasant, scenic rest stop for canoeists, with 4 campsites, a 2 1/2 mi. trail to an old fire tower, and abundant wildlife, including loons and other waterfowl.

The Waterway, managed by the Bureau of Parks and Recreation, has a protected corridor of 500 ft. on each side, which is managed by the Bureau of Public Lands.

HEADQUARTERS: Bureau of Public Lands, Maine Department of Conservation, State House, Station 22, Augusta, ME 04333; (207) 289-3061.

RUFFINGHAM WILDLIFE MANAGEMENT AREA
Department of Inland Fisheries and Wildlife   Coastal
610 acres.

From US 1 at Belfast, W on SR 3. At North Searsmont, site and dam are on the right. Access by canoe or along the shore. (Map 14, B-2.)

The region has many ponds and freshwater marshes but few are State-owned. This site, acquired as a waterfowl nesting area, has freshwater marsh, open water, and a strip of land as buffer. It offers an attractive opportunity for quiet walking, canoeing, and wildlife viewing.

Bartlett Stream and Thompson Brook flow from the N into the 386 acres of wetland, where principal plant species include grasses, cattail, bulrush, wild rice, pondweed, coontail, spatterdock, and water-lily.

Birds: Nesting species include black duck, ring-necked duck, blue-winged and green-winged teal, wood duck, hooded merganser, American goldeneye, Canada goose. Upland species include woodcock, American kestrel, owls, various songbirds.

Mammals: Include muskrat, otter, mink, flying squirrel, deer.

Canoeing: Put-in at the dam on SR 3.

R'. WALDO TYLER WILDLIFE MANAGEMENT AREA
Department of Inland Fisheries and Wildlife   Coastal
533 acres.

> From US 1 at Thomaston, E about 1 mi., then right (S) on Buttermilk Lane
> to Weskeag Marsh. Sign is on right on hill overlooking the marsh. (Map
> 8, A-3.)

The bridge at South Thomaston crosses the Weskeag River. A dam was built
near here around 1850 to hold tidewater for operation of a mill. Upstream is
an extensive salt marsh. From Buttermilk Lane, we looked out over rolling
fields and woodlands to the marsh below. The Weskeag complex covers about
900 acres. State acquisition began with 180 acres. It now includes 360 acres
of salt and fresh marsh, 120 acres of forest, about 50 of fields.

The WMA sign is the only marker. We saw no boundary postings. There's
no parking area, but one can pull off onto the shoulder or into a field.

Birds: No list is available. It's a migration and wintering area for teal, black
duck, and Canada goose. Also mentioned as common: yellowlegs, herons,
songbirds.

Salt marshes are a rich habitat for shellfish, eels, striped bass, and other
fauna.

HEADQUARTERS: Department of Inland Fisheries and Wildlife, 284 State St.,
   Augusta, ME 04333; (207) 289-5253.

SAWTELLE DEADWATER WILDLIFE MANAGEMENT AREA
Department of Inland Fisheries and Wildlife   North
300 acres.

> See entry, Scraggly Lake Management Unit. Huber Road passes the site.
> (Map 57, E-3.)

Our first draft didn't include this site. Then we had a note: "They should include Sawtelle—a great place to see moose, deer, and waterfowl from canoe!"

With the note came some history. The deadwater was formed by a dam that powered a sawmill. When the mill was moved in 1955, wildlife biologist Francis D. Dunn urged his department to buy or lease the site to manage it for waterfowl. Thirty years passed before the department agreed to buy and the owner agreed to sell. The Unit was dedicated to Dunn in 1985.

Since then the dam has been maintained, wild rice planted, Canada geese released, and nest boxes installed for wood ducks and hooded mergansers.

The best time to see moose is in July. Reports of 10 to 15 feeding at the same time are not uncommon.

Fishing is for brook trout and yellow perch.

Canoeing is the way to see the wildlife. There's little upland on the site.

SCARBOROUGH MARSH

(Scarborough Wildlife Management Area; Scarborough   Coastal
    Marsh Nature Center)
Department of Inland Fisheries and Wildlife; Maine Audubon Society
3,100 acres.

From US 1 between Saco and South Portland, E 3/4 mi. on SR 9. (Map 3, B-4.)

Nature Center is open 9:30 A.M.–5:30 P.M., in season.

The complex includes ME's largest salt marsh, tidal creek, fresh marsh, and uplands. From mid-June to Labor Day the Maine Audubon Society operates the Nature Center, which serves as the site's visitor center with many active programs. The center also has canoe rentals and a store. Parking at the center is limited to about 12 cars, but there's ample parking along the highway.

ME's coastal wetlands were being destroyed by dredging, drainage, filling, and polluting, depriving waterfowl of essential resting, nesting, and feeding habitat. Acting on a cooperative plan, the U.S. Fish and Wildlife Service assembled the Rachel Carson National Wildlife Refuge (see entry), while the (Maine) Department of Inland Fisheries and Wildlife acquired the Scarborough and improved nesting habitat with dams and dikes.

The marsh is at the confluence of the Dunstan and Nonesuch rivers, its soil held in place by cordgrass, cattails, rushes, and sedges. Its habitats, based on salt, brackish, and fresh waters, support a wide array of organisms.

Birds: A summer bird list is available. It includes (omitting uncommon and rare species), double-crested cormorant, Canada goose, mallard, American black duck, wood duck, green-winged and blue-winged teal, common eider, common merganser, Virginia and sora rails. Gulls: herring, great black-backed, ring-billed, Bonaparte's. Common tern; great blue, little blue, and green herons; black-crowned night-heron, snowy egret, American bittern, glossy ibis, northern harrier, sharp-shinned and red-tailed hawks, osprey, merlin, American kestrel, black-bellied and semipalmated plovers, killdeer, ruddy turnstone, common snipe, short-billed and long-billed dowitchers, Hudsonian godwit, whimbrel, willet, greater and lesser yellowlegs, sanderling; pectoral, least, spotted, and semipalmated sandpipers; dunlin, ruff, rock and mourning doves, belted kingfisher.

Also common nighthawk, common flicker, eastern kingbird, great crested flycatcher, eastern phoebe, eastern wood-pewee; tree, barn, and cliff swallows; blue jay, American crow, black-capped chickadee, marsh wren, northern mockingbird, gray catbird, brown thrasher, American robin, cedar waxwing, European starling. Warblers: Nashville, yellow, yellow-rumped, common yellowthroat, northern waterthrush, Wilson's, American redstart, chestnut-sided. House sparrow, bobolink, eastern meadowlark, red-winged blackbird, northern oriole, common grackle, brown-headed cowbird, northern cardinal, rose-breasted grosbeak, purple and house finches, American goldfinch, rufous-sided towhee. Sparrows: savannah, sharp-tailed, swamp, song.

Mammals: No checklist. Mentioned: vole, muskrat, woodchuck, raccoon, fox, deer, occasional river otter, seal, moose.

INTERPRETATION
Nature Center, has exhibits, slides, talks, literature.
Weekly programs include "Wildflowers and Wild Edibles," "Family Marsh Adventure," "Dusk and Dawn Birding," canoe tours, etc.
Nature trail into the marsh.

ACTIVITIES
Hiking: The site map shows one foot trail 2 mi. long crossing the marsh. We found other trails or little-used roads to explore the marsh, some of them outside the site boundaries.
Hunt: Waterfowl.
Canoeing: Rentals at the Nature Center, or bring your own canoe.

PUBLICATIONS
Nature Center folder.
Site map.
Nature trail guide.
Canoeing guide.
Summer bird list.

REFERENCE: Kulik, Stephen, Pete Salmansohn, Matthew Schmidt, and Heidi Welch. *The Audubon Society Field Guide to the Natural Places of the Northeast: Inland.* New York: Panthean Books, 1984.

HEADQUARTERS: Maine Audubon Society, 118 US 1, Falmouth, ME 04105; (207) 781-2330. Nature Center (seasonal): (207) 883-5100.

SCRAGGLY LAKE MANAGEMENT UNIT
Bureau of Public Lands   North
9,092 acres.

From I-95 N of Millinocket, W and N on SR 159 to Shin Pond, then NW on Huber Road about 15 mi. Lake-access road is on the right. (Map 57, E-2,3.) ("Huber Road" on the DeLorme map; other sources call it American Thread Road or Grand Lake Road.)

The SW corner of this unit touches the NE corner of Baxter State Park (see entry).

N central ME is a region of lakes and forests, with few roads or settlements. Scraggly Lake, only 3 mi. long, is not among the larger waters, nor is it famous for fishing, although the fishing is good. It is a quiet place, attractive to campers, hikers, and fishermen.

The lake is irregularly shaped, with many small islands and coves. At the E end are bluffs over 100 ft. high. Several small ponds are within the Unit. To the N and S are hills rising to about 400 ft. above the lake level. Land just to the W is flat to gently rolling. The surrounding land is heavily forested.

ACTIVITIES

Camping: 10 primitive sites with road access are in a campground on the E shore. Visitors may camp anywhere, with no open fires. 3 single water-access sites.

Hiking: The map shows several short trails with no apparent destinations, other than one to Ireland Pond near the N boundary of the unit. A trail loop is on Owl's Head, on the E end, water access. The region has many unmaintained logging roads, some of which can be hiked.

Fishing: Smallmouth bass, white perch, pickerel.

Boating: Ramp, trailer access, on the E shore.

NEARBY: Sawtelle Deadwater Wildlife Management Area (see entry). You pass it on the way. Don't miss it!

PUBLICATION: Information page with map.

REFERENCE: Vanderweide, Harry. *Maine Fishing Maps.* Vol. 1: *Lakes and Ponds.* Freeport: DeLorme Publishing, 1986.

HEADQUARTERS: Bureau of Public Lands, Maine Department of Conservation, State House, Station 22, Augusta, ME 04333; (207) 289-3061.

SEBAGO LAKE STATE PARK
Bureau of Parks and Recreation   Coastal
1,300 acres.

From Portland, NW on US 302. Park is on the N shore. (Map 5, C-1.)

The lake is New England's third largest. The state's record landlocked salmon was caught here in 1907, and the fishing is still good. Because of its proximity to Portland and other population centers, it's the most heavily used large lake, with increasing shoreline development. The Park is more heavily affected than any other inland ME park.

Camping: 250 sites, usually full in July–Aug. Season is May 1–Oct. 15.

Pets are prohibited.

REFERENCES
Sebago Lake Region Map and Guide. Freeport: DeLorme Publishing, 1987.
Vanderweide, Harry. *Maine Fishing Maps.* Vol. 1: *Lakes and Ponds.* Freeport: DeLorme Publishing, 1986.

SEBOEIS LAKE MANAGEMENT UNIT
Bureau of Public Lands   North
11,436 acres.

From Millicket, SW about 12 mi. Look for sign on left in Long A Township. S about 2 1/2 mi. on gravel road. (Map 43, D-1.)

The road leads to the N end of Seboeis Lake, a water body about 6 mi. long that is almost entirely within the boundaries. The lake is about 1 1/4 mi. across at its widest point. As the road approaches the lake, the right fork leads to a launching place for hand-carried boats and passes near two primitive campsites. The left fork continues S somewhat E of the lake, turning E to a primitive campsite on the S end of Endless Lake, outside the unit except for some frontage on the SW shore.

Camping and fishing are the principal activities here, with hunting in season. Maps show no hiking trails, but the east side road has little traffic unless loggers are active. Terrain is gently rolling rather than mountainous; elevation at the lake is 438 ft., at the hilltops only 745. Plant cover is chiefly forest in various stages of growth. The land near Endless Lake was heavily cut over shortly before the state acquired it. The woods around Seboeis are in better condition.

Seboeis is usually a quiet place. It is only one of many lakes near Millicket. Several others are larger, better known, with more dramatic scenery and with visitor facilities. Furthermore, Seboeis is subject to drawdowns in dry summers. In the lake are 250-acre Leyford Island and several others, including little Dollar Island, just big enough for one campsite.

ACTIVITIES

Camping: The two campsites near the head of the lake are small, primitive, only accessible by foot but not far from the road. The island site is accessible by boat. Camp anywhere, but with no open fire.

Hunting: Deer, bear, ruffed grouse, snowshoe hare.

Fishing: Both lakes offer good bass and salmon fishing.

Boating: Launching for hand-carried boats only. Some attractive campsites can be reached by boat.

Swimming: Sandy beaches at the N end of the lake.

PUBLICATION: Information page with map.

HEADQUARTERS: Bureau of Public Lands, Maine Department of Conservation, State House, Station 22, Augusta, ME 04333; (207) 289-3061.

SEBOEIS RIVER
Mixed ownerships   North
About 32 river miles.

From Shin Pond on SR 159, W on Baxter Park road (Grand Lake Road) about 6 mi. to the river. (Map 51, A-4.)

The crossing of road and river is the center of the Seboeis River Gorge Preserve of the Maine Chapter, The Nature Conservancy. Upstream is a deep V-shaped gorge, unusual in ME, with steep banks over 165 ft. high. In this section, Godfrey Pitch and Tiger Rips could be called either falls or rapids. Some whitewater experts might try the run, but it's not recommended. The TNC Preserve extends a few mi. downstream.

Next to the bridge is a Forest Service campground. This is the put-in for a 24-mi. canoe run in scenic mountain country ending just above Whetstone Falls, W of Stacyville, where there is another campground. This is a relatively easy 2-day run, with some Class II rapids and a short portage near the beginning.

This is wild, unspoiled country, black ash and white spruce trees beside the river, alders, sedges, and ferns where there is seasonal flooding, dense growths of mixed hardwoods and conifers on the hills and ridges. In some stretches, maples overarch the stream. Wildlife is abundant.

ACTIVITIES

Camping: Primitive campsites at each end of the run and along the river.

Hiking: Unimproved roads parallel part of the river, and there are a few informal fishermen's trails. Otherwise bushwhacking.

Fishing: Fishermen recommend 4 days for the run. Good fishing for brook trout.

REFERENCES

Kellogg, Zip. *Canoeing.* Vol. 3: *Northern Rivers.* Freeport: DeLorme Publishing, 1986.

Vanderweide, Harry. *Maine Fishing Maps.* Vol. 2: *Rivers and Streams.* Freeport: DeLorme Publishing, 1984.

SQUA PAN LAKE
Bureau of Public Lands   North
17,458 acres.

From Presque Isle, W on SR 163 to Mapleton. There, ask directions to Squa Pan Lake Association Road. (Maps 64, E-4, and 58, A-4.)

The lake is relatively shallow. The fishing might be acceptable elsewhere, but not in northern ME, which has such outstanding fishing waters. Nor is the area especially scenic. The terrain is flat to gently rolling except for Squa Pan Mountain, a N–S ridge rising to 1,460 ft.

However, the unit does offer quiet camping and hiking. The E shore is undeveloped. One can camp anywhere, without fire. The forest is sufficiently open to invite bushwhacking up to the ridge.

Boating: The Squa Pan Outing Club charges a fee for road access to the ramp on the NW shore.

HEADQUARTERS: Bureau of Public Lands, Maine Department of Conservation, State House, Station 22, Augusta, ME 04333; (207) 289-3061.

STEEP FALLS WILDLIFE MANAGEMENT AREA
Department of Inland Fisheries and Wildlife   Coastal
2,537 acres.

> About 20 mi. NW of Portland via SR 25 and SR 113 to Steep Falls. Just beyond the town, turn right on Turkey Farm Road, not named on the De-Lorme *Atlas* map but shown as an unimproved road to Adams Pond. (Map 4, D-5.)

Near Sebago Lake, the site is a mix of forest, wooded swamp, and wetland, with enough open water to attract waterfowl. In addition to Turkey Farm Road (reported to us as graveled) there are about 5 mi. of logging roads in various conditions. Tucker and Davis brooks cross the site.

Some hiking trails have been marked by the operator of a commercial campground on Adams Pond.

Birds: Game species include ruffed grouse, woodcock, wood duck, black duck, mallard, hooded merganser.

Mammals: Important deer habitat, especially for wintering. Species reported include snowshoe hare, fisher, red fox, coyote, raccoon, beaver, otter. Bobcat and bear sightings. Moose may visit.

NEARBY: Steep Falls, on the Saco River, is on the SW side of the town. The Saco is canoeable, the falls about a 6-ft. drop.

STEVE POWELL WILDLIFE MANAGEMENT AREA
Department of Inland Fisheries and Wildlife   Coastal
1,755 acres.

> From I-95, Exit 26, then E on SR 197 to Richmond. The landing is on the Kennebec River where SR 197 meets SR 24. (Map 6, A-5.)

Season: Weekends only, last Sat. in Apr. to first Sun. in June; daily, first Mon. in June through Labor Day. Day visits: 9 A.M. to sunset.

This unique WMA is on Swan Island, accessible by the Department of Inland Fisheries and Wildlife ferry. It is the only WMA that is a wildlife sanctuary and the only one where camping is allowed. It is the only WMA with a descriptive brochure, self-guiding tour, and guided tours of a restricted area.

Reservations are required. Reservations include a scheduled ferry trip. Only 60 visitors are permitted at one time. Camping is in 6-person Adirondack shelters.

The island was once the headquarters of Indian kings. Settlement by whites began in colonial times. Houses, ruins, wells, and other structures remain from the years of farming, fishing, lumbering, shipbuilding, and ice cutting. State purchase began in the 1940s. Until 1952 it was a game research experiment station. Since then management emphasis has been on providing forage crops for the thousands of Canada geese that arrive each spring.

The island (not to be confused with Swan's Island near Acadia National Park) is 4 mi. long, 1/4 to 3/4 mi. wide. The ferry landing is at the N end. The WMA includes Little Swan Island and over 500 acres of tidal flats.

Plants: The island has 840 acres of upland forest, 230 acres of improved pasture, with surrounding wetlands and fertile mud flats. Most of the forest is on the W side, the higher and steeper ground. Tree species include white oak, butternut, mulberry, black birch. On the uplands are deep freshwater marshes and areas of open water, with stands of wild rice, cattail, softstem bulrush, and other aquatic plants. Coastal marshes support pickerelweed, spatterdock, wild rice, duck potato, and bulrush. Goose pastures are on the E side.

The island flora has been greatly affected by logging, land clearing, and introduction of new species, and by the overpopulation of deer. Hunting was first prohibited in the 1890s, when deer populations were low, and the prohibition continued here after mainland hunting resumed. Trapping and relocating deer didn't reduce the overpopulation. A proposal to reduce the herd by hunting was bitterly opposed and abandoned. So damage to the habitat continues, and some deer die during severe winters. The island population ranges from 25 to 200.

Birds: As many as 5,000 Canada geese may be present in the spring migration, as well as a variety of ducks. A bald eagle nest on the island has been used for two decades. ME's eagle population declined sharply, largely because of pesticides in fish, but recovery efforts are showing some success. Wood ducks reproduce in the nest boxes at artificial ponds. Waterfowl include black duck, common goldeneye, bufflehead, mallard, blue-winged and green-winged teal, hooded merganser. Also common are many shorebirds, ruffed grouse, many songbirds.

Mammals: Include red and gray squirrels, woodchuck, beaver, red fox, raccoon, deer.

INTERPRETATION

The self-guiding tour follows the gravel road that runs the length of the island. No private vehicles use the road. The 18-page tour guide describes the island's history and natural features.

ACTIVITIES

Camping: From the ferry landing, campers and their gear are carried by Department vehicle to the campground. 10 open shelters accommodate 6 persons each. Tent camping is not permitted. Water and firewood are provided. Stays are limited to 2 nights. Reservations are made by written application with fee, submitted at least 7 days before the requested date.

Hiking: Visitors may hike anywhere on the N end of the island. The S end is restricted; visitors must be accompanied by the custodian or obtain permission.

Hunting: On tidal flats below the high-water mark, except in Maxwell Cove.

Boating: Visitors may bring boats, by prior arrangement. Because of tides up to 10 ft., small boats aren't recommended.

Swimming and fishing have been inadvisable because of river pollution. Efforts are being made to improve water quality. Inquire.

Pets are prohibited.

PUBLICATIONS

Information folder with application form.
Tour guide.

HEADQUARTERS: Steve Powell WMA, Swan Island, Richmond, ME 04357; (207) 737-4307.

ST. JOHN RIVER

North Maine Woods   North
134 river miles.

In the North Maine Woods, roughly paralleling the Quebec border. Access by private road or float plane.

The St. John is about 400 mi. long, the last half in Canada. In May–June it offers a unique opportunity for canoeing through an almost roadless forest on a swift-flowing stream with rapids to Class III. The longest run begins at Fifth St. John Pond. Here access is by vehicle or flying boat, bringing canoe and gear. Most trips begin at Baker Lake, 20 mi. downstream. Here there is road access, but the spring road conditions and the difficulties of arranging a car shuttle persuade many to fly in.

Most travelers take 7 to 10 days for the journey to the junction with the Allagash River. It's possible to continue farther, even on through New Brunswick.

The lakes and streams are State property, but the land is privately owned, managed by the North Maine Woods consortium (see entry). Once this was a forest of great trees. The river was the only way to transport huge logs to mills. Only traces remain of the small settlements of loggers and supporters. The present-day forest is mostly spruce/fir with aspen, birch, and alder. Through the North Maine Woods organization, the landowners permit public recreation, subject to their rules. The wilderness quality of the waterway is protected by the St. John River Resource Protection Plan, adopted by the Maine Land Use Regulation Commission.

It's a wilderness adventure, not to be taken casually, through seemingly endless forest with abundant wildlife. You're on your own. Although a few private roads cross the waterway, you might wait a long time to see a vehicle pass. The mile-long Big Black Rapids, Class III, is 30 mi. from a settlement.

Water conditions can change rapidly, so it's important to get last-minute advice from the North Maine Woods ([207] 435-6213) or Upper St. John District Headquarters, Maine Forest Service ([418] 244-6501). The season begins after ice-out, usually about May 1. By mid-June there may be too little water in the river for canoeing.

Everyone using the river must register at checkpoints or when meeting a ranger on the river.

Flying services at Greenville, Shin Pond, Portage Lake, Allagash Village, and other places can deliver you and your gear to any of several points on the river. Guides and outfitters also can arrange waterway trips.

ACTIVITIES

Camping: At designated sites only.

Hunting: The river isn't usually canoeable in hunting season.

Fishing: Chiefly brook trout. Possibly muskellunge, a new species migrating from Quebec.

The black fly season is May–June; ask locally about repellents.

PUBLICATIONS

St. John River. 12-page folder with map, information. On waterproof paper. $3 postpaid.

Welcome to North Maine Woods. Map, information, rules and regulations. $1.50 postpaid.

Lists of flying services, outfitters and guides.

REFERENCES

Allagash and St. John Guide. Freeport: DeLorme Publishing, 1987.

Kellogg, Zip. *Canoeing.* Vol. 3: *Northern Rivers.* Freeport: DeLorme Publishing, 1986.

HEADQUARTERS: North Maine Woods, P.O. Box 421, Ashland, ME 04732; (207) 435-6213.

SUGAR ISLAND MANAGEMENT UNIT
Bureau of Public Lands   North
4,208 acres.

In Moosehead Lake. Nearest boat ramp is at Lily Bay State Park (see entry). (Map 41, B-2.)

The island is 4 1/2 mi. long, up to 2 mi. wide. It is hilly, rising to about 400 ft. above the lake surface, and heavily forested. The shoreline is rocky, and many rocks lurk below the water; we lost a shear pin on one of them.

A number of private summer residences are along the shore, some of them quite impressive, with private docks. The rest of the land is State-owned. There is no public dock, but we had no difficulty getting ashore. Moosehead Lake can be stormy, and overnight campers should be careful about their moorings.

Campers at Lily Bay State Park often come here for picnics. There seem to be no trails, but much of the forest is parklike.

Camping: 3 primitive sites; 2 or 3 more may be added.

HEADQUARTERS: Bureau of Public Lands, Maine Department of Conservation, State House, Station 22, Augusta, ME 04333; (207) 289-3061.

TELOS LAKE MANAGEMENT UNIT/CHAMBERLAIN LAKE MANAGEMENT UNIT
Bureau of Public Lands   North
22,806 acres.

From Millinocket, NW on Golden Road to Ripogenus Dam, then N on Telos Road. (Map 50, A-2,3; Map 56, E-2.)

At the very edge of the North Maine Woods (see entry), Telos Lake is the gateway to the Allagash Wilderness Waterway (see entry). The Unit includes Chamberlain Bridge, a major put-in for the Waterway trip, and the Arm of Chamberlain.

Telos Lake itself is about 5 mi. long, linked to Chamberlain Lake by mile-long Round Pond. On Telos are put-ins for both the Allagash Waterway and for a lesser-known canoe trip eastward through Webster Lake and Webster Brook into Baxter State Park (see entry).

Normal pool elevation of Telos Lake is 945 ft. The surrounding land is forested, hilly to mountainous, from gradually sloping to steep at the shoreline. Highest nearby point is 1,329-ft. Telos Mountain.

The Chamberlain Lake unit is NW of Telos Lake. It includes tracts in Chamberlain, Eagle, and Allagash lakes. Access is by the Telos Road or by water.

ACTIVITIES

Camping: Primitive campsites at Telos Landing can be reached by gravel road. Numerous other sites are accessible by boat. Visitors may camp anywhere, without facilities and with no open fires.

Fishing: Chiefly lake and brook trout.

Boating: Launching at Chamberlain Bridge.

Canoeing: Many canoeists are heading for the Allagash. But those who want a circuit rather than a one-way trip can spend days exploring this area, of which the Management Units are only a part.

HEADQUARTERS: Bureau of Public Lands, Maine Department of Conservation, State House, Station 22, Augusta, ME 04333; (207) 289-3061.

THE GREAT HEATH
Bureau of Public Lands   Coastal
3,300 acres.

From US 1 at Harrington, about 5 mi. N. (Map 25, C-3.)

Maine has an estimated 5,000 bogs covering more than 700,000 acres. The Great Heath is the largest, one of the largest anywhere. Until recent years, bogs were considered to be wastelands, good for duck hunting or filling. The oil crisis changed that. One acre of bog may contain 1,600 tons of peat, the energy equivalent of 3,800 barrels of oil.

The prospect of extensive peat mining called attention to the natural values of bog ecosystems. The Land and Water Resources Council was directed to identify peatlands that should be preserved because of their rare flora and fauna. The Great Heath has been so identified, to be devoted exclusively to primitive recreation, scientific study, and education.

It is crossed by the Pleasant River, which provides canoe access. The river has a natural population of Atlantic salmon. Pineo Ridge, a noteworthy glacial feature, abuts the SW boundary.

No interpretive program has yet been developed. The best published information we've seen is in the cited reference.

REFERENCE: Kulik, Stephen, Pete Salmansohn, Matthew Schmidt, and Heidi Welch. *The Audubon Society Field Guide to the Natural Places of the Northeast: Inland.* New York: Pantheon Books, 1984.

HEADQUARTERS: Bureau of Public Lands, Maine Department of Conservation, State House, Station 22, Augusta, ME 04333; (207) 289-3061.

VAUGHAN WOODS
Maine Bureau of Parks and Recreation   Coastal
250 acres.

From junction of SR 4 and SR 236 in South Berwick, S 1 mi. on SR 236, then right 1 mi. on Brattle St. (Map 1, A-3.)

On Brattle St. one passes "the oldest water power site in America," where an old mill still stands. Vaughan Woods is on the shore of the Piscataqua River, here the boundary between ME and NH. The land was given to the State in 1949 with the proviso that it remain wild, "a sanctuary for the wild beasts and birds."

The handsome old-growth forest has moderately steep slopes. Several trails lead down to the river, including a 2-mi. loop trail. The riverside trail is said to be an authentic Indian route. When we visited, part of the trail was being improved, using a design to check erosion as well as provide better footing. A spacious parking lot and nearby tables suggest this is a popular picnic site for local residents.

VERNON S. WALKER WILDLIFE MANAGEMENT AREA
Department of Inland Fisheries and Wildlife   Coastal
4,937 acres.

Southern ME. From Sanford, N on SR 11 to North Shapleigh, then right on Mann Rd. Approximate boundaries are SR 11 on the W and N, Mann Rd. on the S. (Map 2, A-2.)

This is one of the largest WMAs and one we had inadequate time to explore. Access is somewhat limited. The management plan mentions 2 trails entering from Mann Rd. The map shows others entering from the N. In our brief visit, we identified only one of these. The management plan mentions "limited vehicle access"; we saw no entering road. According to the management plan, the site has 3 Management Area and 3 information signs; boundaries are marked in red.

It's worth exploring because of its size and diversity, a quiet area in the state's S portion, most of which is being developed rapidly. Both the Little Ossipee River and Branch Brook are canoeable. There's a put-in for the Little Ossipee on SR 11. The DeLorme *Atlas* mentions an 11 1/2-mi. canoe trip from here to Ossipee Mills (E of Newfield) with unrunnable rapids in Newfield.

The site is hilly. Much of the forest burned in 1947, so the woodland is chiefly young second growth. Within the site are 3 ponds and part of a fourth.

Data on flora and fauna are scanty but promising. There's enough wetland to attract some waterfowl. Mammals include snowshoe hare, beaver, otter, mink, racoon, deer, and occasional moose and bear. Fishing is chiefly for brook and brown trout.

WHITE MOUNTAIN NATIONAL FOREST
U.S. Forest Service   West
49,166 acres in ME.

On the NH border S and W of Bethel. (Map 10, B-C, 1-2.)

See entry in NH, where most of the Forest is located. The ME portion extends S along the border from the Androscoggin River. SR 113 crosses the W side through Evans Notch. The principal trailheads are on this route.

The area is mountainous and forested. High point is Speckled Mountain, 2,907 ft. Numerous streams and ponds. S of Bethel is a scenic drive along Patte Brook, with the Crocker Pond campground nearby.

Caribou/Speckled Mountain roadless area, 16,000 acres, is a candidate for Wilderness status. The area surrounds 2,828-ft. Caribou Mountain and Speckled Mountain. Terrain ranges from valley bottoms to mountain peaks, gentle slopes to rocky cliffs. Many streams flow from the area to the watersheds of the Androscoggin and Saco rivers. Vegetation is chiefly northern hardwoods with white pine at mid and lower elevations, spruce/fir on higher slopes, mountain blueberry, cranberry, other shrubs, and wildflowers on exposed mountain tops.

Visitor use is light, about 7,100 visitor-days per year, most of this June–Sept. Snowmobiling, ski touring, and snowshoeing vary with snowfall.

Speckled Mountain is at the center of an extensive network of trails. Trailheads are on SR 113 and US 2.

Camping: 2 campgrounds, 31 sites. Informal camping in almost any suitable place.

Hiking: Several attractive day hikes go E from SR 113. At least 5 trails ascend Speckled Mountain, including the Spruce Hill Trail from Evans Notch.

PUBLICATION: Forest map. $1.

REFERENCES

Trail Map and Guide to the White National Forest. Freeport: DeLorme Publishing, 1987.

Daniell, Eugene S., III, ed. *AMC White Mountain Guide.* Boston: Appalachian Mountain Club, 1987.

HEADQUARTERS: Evans Notch Ranger District, Bethel, ME 04217; (207) 824-2134.

VERMONT

On a map, Vermont and New Hampshire look much alike: about the same size, the Connecticut River a shared boundary, each with a National Forest (the only two in New England), each mountainous, each with many lakes and ponds. But Vermont has little more than half New Hampshire's population, and the difference is widening. In New Hampshire more than half of the population lives in urban areas; in Vermont, about one-third. Southern New Hampshire has been annexed by the Boston metropolis. Vermont is a safe distance away. And while both states are roughly triangular, New Hampshire's base is in the south; most of Vermont's area is in the less developed north. Unlike NH, VT has an income tax, small but helpful to State functions. Its tax revenues are 85 percent more per capita.

The Green Mountains divide the state, N–S. At 4,393 ft., Mt. Mansfield is the highest peak, but many others in the range exceed 3,000 ft. In the southwest, the Green Mountains merge with the N end of the Taconic Range, while in the NW the mountains drop down on the W to the Champlain Valley. The E and W boundaries are mostly water, Lake Champlain on the W, the Connecticut River on the E. Elevations below 500 ft. are found chiefly on the lowlands bordering Champlain and in the central and southern Connecticut River Valley.

Many rivers flow down the slopes of the Green Mountains. In addition to several hundred miles of rivers, VT has more than 400 lakes and ponds. Lake Champlain, 100 mi. long, is by far the largest. Largest of those wholly within the state is 2,360-acre Lake Bomoseen.

Like other New England forests, those of Vermont were heavily logged in the nineteenth century. A hundred years ago 80 percent of the forest had been cleared. As farming and grazing declined, forests regenerated, and today 80 percent of the land is again forested. Pristine conditions are not returning except in a few Wilderness Areas. Most forest areas are managed for timber production.

Like the climate of other New England areas, Vermont's is highly variable: daily, seasonally, annually, and from place to place. Summer temperatures are generally comfortable. January averages are below freezing statewide, with the lowest readings in the NE. Precipitation is well distributed seasonally and by region, annual averages ranging from 38 to 45 in. Snowfall varies from 55 in. in valleys to over 120 in. on high elevations.

By far the largest area available for recreation is the Green Mountain National Forest, 5 percent of the state's land, occupying much of the central and southern portions of the mountain range. Although less than half of the area within the authorized boundaries is government-owned, this is mostly the upper slopes, the rugged terrain of greatest interest to outdoorsmen. Vermont has no National Park, one National Wildlife Refuge.

STATE LANDS

When we asked for definitions of "State Park" and "State Forest," the reply was, "Don't worry about it." The leaflet *Vermont State Parks and Forest Recreation Areas* lists 42 State Parks, one of which is also a State Forest, 6 recreation areas within one State Forest, 5 Forest Recreation Areas, 3 of which— don't worry about it!

By our calculations, VT State Parks total about 26,000 acres, State Forests about 150,000 acres. We have entries for units that have significant natural areas. They're well distributed around the state.

By a 1986 count, the State has 60 Wildlife Management Areas with a total of 91,000 acres, 5 of the WMAs with more than 5,000 acres each.

MAPS AND PATHFINDING

The official highway map is available from

Vermont Travel Division
134 State St.
Montpelier, VT 05602

It includes information on recreation areas and outdoor activities.
This atlas is indispensable:

The Vermont Atlas and Gazetteer. Freeport, ME: DeLorme Publishing, 1986.

In addition to its 59 maps, it has information on campgrounds, canoe trips, fishing, hiking, parks and recreation areas, and much more.

Pathfinding in VT is uniquely difficult because of an admirable law that bans billboards, making the landscape wonderfully uncluttered. Current rules say an establishment may have two signs, each of a small, standard size, on the approaching State roads. In an even-handed way, the rule has been applied to the State's own properties, including Parks and Forests. Thus a large State Forest with miles of highway frontage and multiple entrances can post only the two small signs allowed a restaurant or antique shop!

The Department of Forests, Parks & Recreation uses the allowed signs to mark campgrounds and other recreation sites, where most visitors go. Elsewhere we couldn't distinguish State from private land. Without trail maps, it's difficult to find trailheads.

The DeLorme Publishing Company's *Atlas* is of considerable help in finding Parks and Forests, although it is somewhat out of date. For the Wildlife Management Areas, however, it shows only symbols, often well away from any mapped road.

The Department of Fish and Wildlife acknowledges that it's difficult, if not impossible, for a stranger to find most WMAs. The department has no maps to hand out. Its *Vermont Guide to Hunting* shows site outlines but on a small scale. Local hunters and fishermen know where to go. We usually found someone to ask.

We commented that even off State highways, where the signing rule doesn't apply, we rarely saw WMA signs. Many have been stolen, we were told. We often looked in vain for boundary markings or posted rules.

At headquarters, we were given information about some WMAs and told management plans are being developed for others. We were warned that even a large WMA may not be a good entry for us: The State may not own timber rights and thus may have no control over logging. We visited a number of WMAs enjoyed good hiking and birding, but we may have missed a few good ones.

FLORA AND FAUNA

Our bibliographic search turned up few references describing VT's flora and fauna, most of those technical or out of print. Several regional references are useful:

DeGraaf, Richard M., and Deborah D. Rudis. *New England Wildlife: Habitat, Natural History, and Distribution.* General Technical Report NE-108. Broomwall, PA: U.S. Department of Agriculture, Forest Service, Northeastern Forest Experiment Station, 1986.

Harris, Stuart K., and others. *AMC Field Guide to Mountain Flowers of New England.* Boston: Appalachian Mountain Club, 1982.

And this bird guide may be available:

Birds of Vermont. Green Mountain Audubon Society, P.O. Box 33, Burlington, VT 05401.

The Department of Fish and Wildlife has a number of useful information bulletins, including

Wild Mammals of Vermont.
Amphibians of Vermont.
Ask about others.

HIKING TRAILS

The 265-mi. Long Trail (see entry), extending from north to south along the Green Mountains, is the centerpiece of VT's trail system. Before it turns eastward, the Appalachian Trail coincides with the southern section of the Long Trail. The state has more than 700 miles of trails, about 512 miles on federal and State land, the rest on private land. The Green Mountain Club, established in 1910, was acclaimed by the State legislature as "founder, sponsor, defender and protector of the Long Trail system," which now includes a network of subsidiary trails. There are also interesting day hikes elsewhere in VT, especially in State Forests and State Parks. Hiking in Wildlife Management Areas is largely on used and overgrown back roads and informal trails.

Backpacking is possible both on the Long Trail and the Appalachian. The Green Mountain Club maintains many shelters, and trailside camping is permissible in the National Forest and in all or portions of most State Forests. The rules are in a leaflet, *Guide to Primitive Camping on State Lands,* available from the Department of Forests, Parks & Recreation. The department's *Hiking and Walking in Vermont* lists sources of trail guides and businesses offering conducted hiking tours and inn-to-inn hiking. Also available from the department is *Day Hiker's Vermont Sampler.*

Hikers are asked to stay off trails in the "mud season," usually from snow melt to Memorial Day.

These are basic references:

Fitzgerald, Brian T., ed. *Guidebook of the Long Trail.* Green Mountain Club, P.O. Box 889, Montpelier 05602. 1987.

Appalachian Trail Conference. *Appalachian Trail Guide to New Hampshire/Vermont.* Harpers Ferry, WV: Appalachian Trail Conference, 1985.

Day Hiker's Guide to Vermont. Green Mountain Club, P.O. Box 889, Montpelier 05602. 1987.

Sadlier, Heather and Hugh. *Fifty Hikes in Vermont.* Woodstock, VT: Backcountry Publications, 1985.

CAMPING

For information on camping in the Green Mountain National Forest, see entry.

The Department of Forests, Parks & Recreation operates 35 campgrounds with 2,186 sites in State Parks and State Forests. Most open on the Friday before Memorial Day. Some close on the Tuesday after Labor Day, others after the Columbus Day weekend. Most campgrounds have several lean-tos.

Campsites can be reserved by mail with fee. Ask for the leaflet, *Vermont State Parks and Forest Recreation Areas,* and reservation form.

Pets are allowed, on leash, in the campgrounds of most State Parks, not in day use areas. They are permitted on trails. A stricter rule is under consideration.

CANOEING, BOATING

Canoeists have a wide range of choices in VT, from challenging whitewater to canoe-camping trips of several days to quiet exploration of wildlife areas. Two basic references are

Schweiker, Roioli, ed. *AMC River Guide: New Hampshire, Vermont.* Boston: Appalachian Mountain Club, 1983.

Schweiker, Roioli. *Canoe Camping Vermont and New Hampshire Rivers.* Woodstock, VT: Backcountry Publications, 1985.

Entries describe other opportunities.

The primary boating water is Lake Champlain (see entry). The leaflet *Guide to Fishing* lists many lakes and rivers and boating access, as well as fishing information. Public boat launch sites are marked on the official highway map.

FISHING, HUNTING

A *Vermont Guide to Fishing* and a *Vermont Guide to Hunting* (leaflets) are both available from the Department of Fish and Wildlife. The latter has information on hunting areas, rules, and species.

STATE AGENCIES

Department of Forests, Parks & Recreation
Waterbury Complex, 10 South
Waterbury, VT 05676
(802) 828-3375

Department of Fish and Wildlife
Waterbury Complex, 10 South
Waterbury, VT 05676
(802) 244-7331

THE GREEN MOUNTAIN CLUB

The Green Mountain Club has, since 1910, been the principal force in preservation of Vermont forests and in the construction and maintenance of a statewide network of hiking trails. (See entry, Long Trail.) Its publications include

> *Day Hiker's Guide to Vermont.* Green Mountain Club, P.O. Box 889, Montpelier 05602. 1987.
> Fitzgerald, Brian T., ed. *Guidebook of the Long Trail.* Green Mountain Club, P.O. Box 889, Montpelier 05602. 1987.
> *Trail Maps: Mt. Mansfield, Camel's Hump.*
> *Tundra Trail.* (On Mt. Mansfield.)

Headquarters staff will gladly answer mail or telephone inquiries about trails, trail conditions, and shelters.

The Green Mountain Club
P.O. Box 889
Montpelier, VT 05602
(802) 223-3463

MAP NOTES IN TEXT

All map references (e.g., Map 26) are to the DeLorme Publishing Company's *The Vermont Atlas and Gazetteer* (Freeport, ME: 1986). *South:* Maps 1–29. *North:* Maps 30–59.

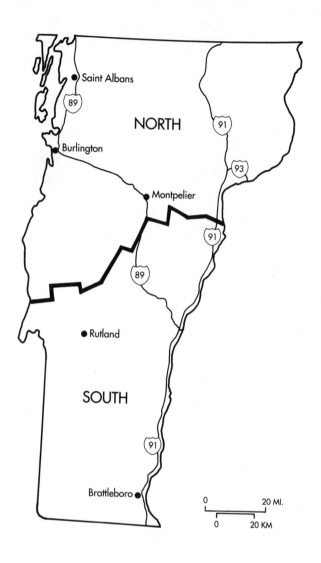

NORTH

SOUTH

Saint Albans

Burlington

Montpelier

Rutland

Brattleboro

89

91

93

91

89

91

0   20 MI.

0   20 KM

NATURAL AREAS IN VERMONT

An Alphabetical Listing

Ascutney State Park
South
Atherton Meadow Wildlife
Management Area
South
Bill Sladyk Wildlife Management
Area *North*
Bomoseen State Park
South
Branbury State Park
South
Burton Island State Park
North
Button Bay State Park
North
Calvin Coolidge State Forest
South
Camel's Hump Forest Reserve
North
Connecticut River
North/South
Cornwall Swamp Wildlife
Management Area
South
Dead Creek Waterfowl Area
South
Elmore State Park
North
Emerald Lake State Park
South
Gifford Woods State Park
South
Green Mountain National Forest
South
Groton State Forest
North
Jay Peak Area
North
Lake Champlain
North

Lewis Creek Wildlife Management
Area *North*
Little Otter Creek Wildlife
Management Area
North
Little River State Park
North
Long Trail *North/South*
Lower Otter Creek Wildlife
Management Area
North
Maidstone State Park
North
Missisquoi National Wildlife
Refuge *North*
Mount Mansfield State Forest
North
Mud Creek Wildlife Management
Area *North*
Pine Mountain Wildlife
Management Area
North
Plymsbury Wildlife Management
Area *South*
Putnam State Forest
North
Quechee Gorge State Park
South
South Bay Wildlife Management
Area *North*
Townshend State Park
South
Victory Basin Wildlife Management
Area *North*
Wenlock Wildlife Management
Area *North*
Willoughby State Forest
North
Woodford State Park
South

NATURAL AREAS IN VERMONT

by Zone

North Zone

Bill Sladyk Wildlife Management
Area
Burton Island State Park
Button Bay State Park
Camel's Hump Forest Reserve
Connecticut River
Elmore State Park
Groton State Forest
Jay Peak Area
Lake Champlain
Lewis Creek Wildlife Management
Area
Little Otter Creek Wildlife
Management Area
Little River State Park
Long Trail
Lower Otter Creek Wildlife
Management Area
Maidstone State Park
Missisquoi National Wildlife
Refuge
Mount Mansfield State Forest
Mud Creek Wildlife Management
Area
Pine Mountain Wildlife
Management Area
Putnam State Forest

South Bay Wildlife Management
Area
Victory Basin Wildlife Management
Area
Wenlock Wildlife Management
Area
Willoughby State Forest

South Zone

Ascutney State Park
Atherton Meadow Wildlife
Management Area
Bomoseen State Park
Branbury State Park
Calvin Coolidge State Forest
Connecticut River
Cornwall Swamp Wildlife
Management Area
Dead Creek Waterfowl Area
Emerald Lake State Park
Gifford Woods State Park
Green Mountain National Forest
Long Trail
Plymsbury Wildlife Management
Area
Quechee Gorge State Park
Townshend State Park
Woodford State Park

ASCUTNEY STATE PARK
Department of Forests, Parks & Recreation   South
1,984 acres.

From I-91, Exit 8, N 2 mi. on US 5, then 1 mi. NW on Brownsville Rd. (Map 16.)

This is said to be the first American mountain with a developed hiking trail, and thus the ancestor of the Long Trail and Appalachian Trail. The mountain is a monadnock, not part of a chain, and is visible for miles around. Its peak is 3,144 ft. elevation, almost half a mile above its base. Its slopes are generally moderate, steep in places. At one point water trickles over a steep ledge, forming an impressive ice sheet in winter.

The mountain forest is not pristine. It was severely burned in a summer-long forest fire in 1883, much of it flattened by a great hurricane in 1938. Its crest is decorated with television, radio, and microwave towers. A motor road goes almost to the top, a trail the rest of the way. It's a splendid view from there. The area has good hiking trails.

Features include *Gerry's Falls,* seen from a spur off the Windsor Trail, and *Crystal Cascade,* on the Weathersfield Trail, where Ascutney Brook plunges 84 ft. *West Peak,* near the end of the motor road, is a launch site for hang gliders.

ACTIVITIES
Camping: 49 sites, including 10 lean-tos. Approximate season: Memorial Day weekend through Columbus Day weekend. Reservations available.

Hiking, backpacking: Trailside camping is permitted. Trail guide available at entrance. Three trails go to the summit. Two can be combined in a 7-mi. circle hike. Snow may remain at high elevations until the end of May.

Hunting: Deer, wild turkey, grouse.

Ski touring: On scenic road when unplowed.

PUBLICATIONS
Site map.
Guide to the Trails of Ascutney Mountain. Ascutney Trails Association. Available at entrance. $1.50.

REFERENCES
Day Hiker's Guide to Vermont. Green Mountain Club, P.O. Box 889, Montpelier 05602. 1987.
Kulik, Stephen, Pete Salmansohn, Matthew Schmidt, and Heidi Welch. *The Audubon Society Field Guide to the Natural Places of the Northeast: Inland.* New York: Pantheon Books, 1984.

HEADQUARTERS: RD #2, Windsor, VT 05089; (802) 674-2060.

ATHERTON MEADOW WILDLIFE MANAGEMENT AREA
Department of Fish and Wildlife   South
1,042 acres.

Near the MA border, W of Whitingham on SR 100, S of the Harriman Reservoir. ("Whitingham Reservoir" on older maps.) Look for sign and parking area on the W about 6 1/2 mi. W of Jacksonville. (Map 2.)

The WMA has no frontage on the reservoir, but there is public access at the N end and the fishing is good. The reservoir covers 2,157 acres and is about 8 mi. long.

The WMA's terrain is moderately steep to steep, elevations from 1,500 to 2,078 ft. The site is largely forested with a mix of northern hardwoods and softwoods. Also fields and a large beaver meadow.

One source reports about 4 mi. of trails. Mostly these are routes used by hunters, and there are less or more depending on what you consider a trail. You can get around.

Birds: Include eastern bluebird, black-capped chickadee, brown creeper, goldfinch, purple finch, ruffed grouse, flycatchers, kinglets, vireos, cedar waxwing, American woodcock, woodpeckers, various wood warblers.

Mammals: Include deer, snowshoe hare, red and gray squirrels, chipmunk, red and gray foxes, coyote, black bear, bobcat, raccoon, otter, mink, weasel, fisher, beaver.

HEADQUARTERS: District Wildlife Biologist, RR #1, Box 33, North Springfield, VT 05150; (802) 886-2215.

BILL SLADYK WILDLIFE MANAGEMENT AREA
(formerly Hurricane Brook Wildlife Management Area)   North
Department of Fish and Wildlife
9,500 acres.

N VT. From Island Pond, N 8 1/2 mi. on SR 114. Just S of Norton Pond, turn W on access road and continue to entrance sign. (Map 58.)

The turn is onto an unmarked well-maintained gravel road. Just across rail-road tracks is a sign saying this is the road to the Hurricane Brook WMA (the former name). On the way in, we passed a marsh with some open water, one of a series of marshes along the Pherrins River, which parallels the road from Island Pond. In 2.4 mi. the entrance sign has the newer name. The road penetrates the WMA much farther than the map indicates. We parked and hiked on old logging roads. A broad swath was cleared on both sides of the road, creating a fine habitat for wildflowers, which were bright and abundant. Prominent were goldenrod, black-eyed susan, aster, pussytoes, lobelia, milkweed. The terrain is rolling, covered with young forest: northern hardwoods along the ridges, spruce/fir along stream bottoms and in swampy areas. Elevations range from about 1,450 ft. to just over 1,900 ft.

From the entrance, it's about 5 1/2 mi to the N boundary, which is the Canadian border. The northern 2/3 of the WMA is roadless. Holland Pond, Beaver Pond, Round Pond, and Halfway Pond, shown on *Atlas* Maps 57 and 58, are within the site and can be reached by trail.

On a fine day in August, we had the place to ourselves.

ACTIVITIES

Hiking: Miles of trails and woods roads.

Hunting: Deer, bear, grouse, woodcock, snowshoe hare.

Fishing: Ponds, some stream. Brook, brown, and rainbow trout; chain pickerel.

Ski touring, snowmobiling: Users are warned to stay on established trails and avoid areas used by wintering deer—places "well-laced with deer tracks."

REFERENCE: *Day Hiker's Guide to Vermont.* Green Mountain Club, P.O. Box 889, Montpelier 05602. 1987.

HEADQUARTERS: District Wildlife Biologist, 180 Portland St., St. Johnsbury, VT 05819; (802) 748-8787.

BOMOSEEN STATE PARK
Department of Forests, Parks & Recreation   South
2,739 acres.

From Hydeville on US 4, N 4 mi. on West Shore Rd. (Map 13.)

Lake Bomoseen, about 7 mi. long, covers 2,360 acres. Roads encircle much of the lake shore, with much lakeside development. The park is on an arm of the lake, between it and 191-acre Glen Lake. A separate block to the N, sometimes called Halfmoon Pond State Park, surrounds 23-acre Halfmoon Pond, with campground and trails.

The park is popular, most visitors coming for water-based recreation and camping, although there are hiking trails. It has an interesting nature trail. A park naturalist offers programs from mid-June to Labor Day.

Plants: The terrain is level to rolling, land that was once cleared for pasture and crops. Now it's a mixture of forest, reverting fields, and marsh. The forest is mostly hardwoods: beech, sugar maple, birches; red oak and hickory in the drier sites. Also hemlock, white pine. Many wildflowers appear in spring and summer, notably hepatica, bloodroot, wild rose, violets, jack-in-the-pulpit, goldenrod, asters. Woodland plants include goldthread, partridgeberry, wintergreen, royal fern, mosses. Yellow water-lilies in pond shallows. Bulrushes and cattails in marshes.

Birds: No checklist is available. Species noted include black duck, mallard, blue-winged teal, yellow-bellied sapsucker, wild turkey, eastern kingbird, red-winged blackbird, wood and hermit thrushes, veery, junco, towhee.

ACTIVITIES

Camping: 65 sites at Bomoseen, 69 at Halfmoon; each includes 10 lean-tos. Season is Memorial Day weekend through Columbus Day weekend. Reservations are available.

Hiking: About 10 mi. of trails, including nature trails.

Fishing: Brook and brown trout, yellow perch, northern pike, chain pickerel, largemouth and smallmouth bass, bullhead.

REFERENCES

Day Hiker's Guide to Vermont. Green Mountain Club, P.O. Box 889, Montpelier 05602. 1987.

Kulik, Stephen, Pete Salmansohn, Matthew Schmidt, and Heidi Welch. *The Audubon Society Field Guide to the Natural Places of the Northeast: Inland.* New York: Pantheon Books, 1984.

HEADQUARTERS: RFD 1, Box 2620, Fair Haven, VT 05743; (802) 265-4242.

BRANBURY STATE PARK

Department of Forests, Parks & Recreation   North
96 acres.

From Middlebury, S 7 mi. on US 7, then 2 mi. S on SR 53. (Map 25.)

This small park on 985-acre Lake Dunmore is a convenient base for hiking in the Green Mountain National Forest. It's not far from the Long Trail and several high peaks. It has a park naturalist in summer and a nature trail. There is also a scenic, rather steep hiking trail to a viewpoint in the National Forest.

Our copy of the Nature Trail Guide is 10 years old. If it's no longer available for distribution, ask if there's a copy you can see; it's excellent.

ACTIVITIES

Camping: 43 sites, including 3 lean-tos. Season is Memorial Day weekend through Columbus Day weekend.

Fishing: Rainbow trout, landlocked salmon, lake trout, smelt, yellow perch, northern pike, largemouth and smallmouth bass, bullhead.

PUBLICATION: *Day Hiker's Guide to Vermont.* Green Mountain Club, P.O. Box 889, Montpelier 05602. 1987.

HEADQUARTERS: RFD 2, Brandon, VT 05733; (802) 247-5925.

BURTON ISLAND STATE PARK

Department of Forests, Parks & Recreation North
253 acres.

From St. Albans Bay (Map 52), 3 1/2 mi. SW on local roads to Kamp Kill Kare State Park (Map 44). Passenger ferry to island runs 8:30 A.M.–6:30 P.M. at 1 1/2-hr. intervals.

This island in Lake Champlain has a 100-slip marina with power hookups and other facilities, making it a popular stop for cruisers. Landlubbers can take the park ferry. The island was once used for dairy and sheep farming. Now the fields are reverting and forest has reappeared on the higher ground.

The island has an abundant bird population as well as deer and small mammals. A nature trail explains the island's history and describes its present flora and fauna. A naturalist in residence mid-June through Labor Day offers walks and talks.

Camping: 42 sites, including 22 lean-tos. Season is Memorial Day weekend through Labor Day weekend. Reservations available.

HEADQUARTERS: Box 123, St. Albans Bay, VT 05481; (802) 524-6353.

BUTTON BAY STATE PARK
Department of Forests, Parks & Recreation   North
236 acres.

From Vergennes, 1/2 mi. S on SR 22A, then 6 1/2 mi. NW on local roads. (Map 30.)

Button Bay is on Lake Champlain. No doubt most visitors come for water-based recreation, but the site is noteworthy for its geological features, fossils of coral and sea plants from the period when this area was covered by a tropical sea. It is also a convenient base for visits to the Lower Otter Creek and Dead Creek Wildlife Management Areas (see entries).

The site is largely wooded with mixed hardwoods and conifers, including mature hemlock, maple, and beech.

INTERPRETATION

Nature trail and *nature museum* display fossils, remnants of coral reef, signs of later glaciation, present-day flora and fauna.

Naturalist, here in summer, offers guided walks, evening talks, other programs.

ACTIVITIES

Camping: 72 sites, including 9 lean-tos. Season is Memorial Day weekend to Columbus Day weekend. Reservations available.

Boating: Ramp. Rentals.

REFERENCE: Kulik, Stephen, Pete Salmansohn, Matthew Schmidt, and Heidi Welch. *The Audubon Society Field Guide to the Natural Places of the Northeast: Inland.* New York: Pantheon Books, 1984.

HEADQUARTERS: RFD 3, Box 570, Vergennes, VT 05491; (802) 475-2377.

CALVIN COOLIDGE STATE FOREST
Department of Forests, Parks & Recreation   South
17,949 acres.

From SR 100 at Plymouth, SW of Rutland, N 2 mi. on SR 100A. (Maps 15–16.)

The routing is to the Forest recreation area, not far from the birthplace of the former President. The Forest is made up of several blocks, irregular in shape, their largest boundary-to-boundary dimensions less than 2 mi. The DeLorme *Atlas* Maps 15 and 16 show all but one of these blocks.

Base elevation of the recreation area is about 1,500 ft., Nearby, 2,174-ft. Slack Hill is crossed by a loop trail from the camping area. The area has a small pond for swimming.

In general, all the blocks are forested with a mix of red spruce, hemlock, balsam fir, yellow and white birches, beech, and sugar maple, with some Norway spruce and pine plantations.

FEATURES

Shrewsbury Peak, 3,720 ft., NW of Plymouth, is one of the highest points in the Forest. A good trail leads to the summit. A connecting trail meets the Appalachian and Long trails, here running together.

Tinker Brook Natural Area, 45 acres, is about 2 mi. SW of Shrewsbury Peak, reached by SR 100 and local roads. Its pristine habitat features an old-growth stand of large red spruce and hemlock and the Tinker Brook ravine.

Killington Peak, 4,235 ft., is the highest in the Forest and second only to Mt. Mansfield in VT. Driving NW on US 4 from Rutland, pass through Mendon, turn right on Wheelerville Rd., and continue 4 mi. to the trailhead. The round trip is about 7 mi. The gondola and ski lift operate after the snow leaves, for those who don't wish to hike. The view from the top is superb, despite the towers, gondola terminal, and restaurant. The Appalachian and Long trails cross the mountain; they divide a short distance to the N.

ACTIVITIES

Camping: At the recreation area, 60 sites including 35 lean-tos. Season is Memorial Day weekend through Columbus Day weekend. Reservations available.

Hiking, backpacking: Trailside camping is permitted in some areas, chiefly along the major trails. Principal trails are the combined Appalachian and Long trails, the Shrewsbury and Killington peaks trails, and numerous side trails. Trail connections into other state lands, chiefly Wildlife Management Areas.

Hunting: Deer, bear, snowshoe hare, rabbit, turkey, grouse.

Fishing: We could not find any major fishery in the Forest, but sections of a number of streams are stocked with trout.

Ski touring, skiing, snowmobiling: Ski area on Killington. Ski touring and snowmobiling on trails and unplowed roads. Map available.

PUBLICATIONS

Recreation area leaflet with map.
Hiking trails leaflet with map.
Snowmobile trails leaflet with map.

REFERENCES

Fitzgerald, Brian T., ed. *Guidebook of the Long Trail.* Green Mountain Club, P.O. Box 889, Montpelier 05602. 1987.

Kulik, Stephen, Pete Salmansohn, Matthew Schmidt, and Heidi Welch. *The Audubon Society Field Guide to the Natural Places of the Northeast: Inland.* New York: Pantheon Books, 1984.

Sadlier, Heather and Hugh. *Fifty Hikes in Vermont.* Woodstock, VT: Backcountry Publications, 1985.

HEADQUARTERS: HCR Box 105, Plymouth, VT 05056; (802) 672-3612.

CAMEL'S HUMP FOREST RESERVE

Department of Forests, Parks & Recreation   North
14,789 acres.

From the McCullough Highway, SR 17, about 6 mi. W of Irasville, N to the Winooski River. S access on SR 17. Major N trailheads are E from Huntington Center and S from North Duxbury by local roads. (Map 31.) (The area S of SR 17 is Camel's Hump State Forest. The area N of SR 17 is Camel's Hump State Park, not shown on some lists because it has not been developed. "Monroe State Park," still shown on some maps, has been incorporated into Camel's Hump State Park.)

This is a preserve for hikers. The Long Trail crosses it N to S. SR 17 W from Irasville is access to several ski areas, nordic and cross-country. It climbs to Appalachian Gap, elevation 2,365 ft., just N of the Green Mountain National Forest (see entry). At the top is a parking area and an overlook; the view is attractive but not sweeping. The Long Trail crosses here; going N, the first bit is a rock scramble.

The Reserve was established by the legislature in 1969. The proponents' aims included preserving areas of near-wilderness but also recommended multiple-use management, providing for timber, water, wildlife, and recreation. The lack of roads N of SR 17 is in part because of legislation but also because of the mountainous terrain. Camel's Hump itself is 4,083 ft. high, third highest in VT, and the skyline is rugged from N to S.

The Hump receives an astonishing 100 in. of annual precipitation. Moisture falling on the peaks and ridges supplies high bogs and marshes, feeding numerous mountain streams that cascade down to rivers in the valleys below.

Plants: Steep terrain didn't dissuade the loggers who clear-cut many of the slopes in the 1800s, while more acres were denuded by fire. Now protected are three Natural Areas: a pristine stand of northern hardwoods on the W slope; a boreal forest of old-growth balsam fir; and the alpine tundra at the summit. Several thousand acres are now pine and spruce plantations, while others are in stages of natural succession with birch, beech, and maple, colorful in the fall.

Wildlife: The information for fauna in the Green Mountain National Forest is applicable here; the Preserve has comparable habitats. Birds include species favoring wetlands and forest to those that soar along the ridges. Mammals include black bear, porcupine, beaver, raccoon, red fox, bobcat, gray squirrel, chipmunk, mink, otter, occasional coyote. Deer are present but not in great numbers, because of the heavy tree cover.

ACTIVITIES

Hiking, backpacking: The trails up Camel's Hump are among the most popular in VT for day hikes. Each of the two principal trails offers about a 7-mi. round trip, with a vertical rise of over 2,600 ft. The Long Trail is favored by backpackers. Shelters are spaced along the route from SR 17 to the N boundary. Trailside camping is permitted except in the Research Area adjacent to Burrows Trail and in the Gleason Brook Drainage Area.

Hunting: Bear, deer, small game.

Fishing: Some brook trout fishing in mountain streams, but most of the action is in the Winooski and other valley rivers.

Canoeing: The Winooski River is canoeable for most of its length from Montpelier to Lake Champlain, with a few dams that require portages. Where the river cuts through the Green Mountains between rock cliffs, the current is strong, and there is one 3/4-mi. portage.

Ski touring: Ski trail in the NW sector.

PUBLICATIONS

A Promise Was Made.
Trail map, showing trailheads.

REFERENCES *Camel's Hump Trail Map.* Green Mountain Club, P.O. Box 889, Montpelier 05602. 1985.

Fitzgerald, Brian T., ed. *Guidebook of the Long Trail.* Green Mountain Club, P.O. Box 889, Montpelier 05602. 1987.

Sadlier, Heather and Hugh. *Fifty Hikes in Vermont.* Woodstock, VT: Backcountry Publications, 1985.

Schweiker, Roioli, ed. *AMC River Guide: New Hampshire, Vermont.* Boston: Appalachian Mountain Club, 1983.

Schweiker, Roioli. *Canoe Camping Vermont and New Hampshire Rivers.* Woodstock, VT: Backcountry Publications, 1985.

HEADQUARTERS: Department of Forests, Parks, & Recreation, 103 South Main St., 10 South, Waterbury, VT 05676; (802) 828-3375.

CONNECTICUT RIVER
235 river miles.   North/South

The VT-NH border.

The Connecticut River is no wilderness stream. In colonial times, rivers were the avenues of exploration, travel, commerce, and settlement. Dams provided power for mills. Towns and cities grew around the mills. Roads parallel the river for much of its course. Even so, the canoeist can enjoy quiet stretches, where the banks are greener than when nineteenth-century logging had stripped them of trees.

Along the VT-NH portion of the river are 13 dams, most operated by power companies. A few rapids are dangerous during the high water of spring run-off, but after mid-June most of it is easy going. The power dams usually retain water at night, releasing it by day. Canoeists should be aware of these fluctuations, lest a canoe beached at night float away when the water rises.

Efforts are being made to reduce pollution, but the river water isn't drinkable. Swimming is inadvisable without knowing local conditions; a stretch that may be safe enough one day can be polluted after a heavy rain.

ACTIVITIES

Camping: With some planning, it is possible to canoe-camp the entire 235 mi. Camping areas include commercial campgrounds, municipal campgrounds, several dam sites, and one State Park. Many owners of riparian land will permit camping, if asked. Superintendents at the dams are your best local information sources.

Towns are frequent enough for provisioning and refilling water jugs.

Fishing: Apparently the pollution isn't severe enough to makes fish inedible. The state fishing guide says the river has brook, rainbow, and brown trout; yellow perch, walleye, northern pike, chain pickerel, largemouth and small-mouth bass, bullhead, and panfish.

Boating: Chiefly in dam impoundments. Check locally.

Canoeing: Good information and preparation is essential. The references describe each river section.

REFERENCES

Canoeing on the Connecticut River. Department of Water Resources, Waterbury Complex, 1 South, 103 S. Main St., Waterbury, VT 05676. 1976.

The Connecticut River Guide. Connecticut River Watershed Council, 125 Combs Rd., Easthampton, MA 01027.

Happy Valley and *Home Again.* New England Power Company, P.O. Box 528, Lebanon, NH 03766.

Schweiker, Roioli, ed. *AMC River Guide: New Hampshire, Vermont.* Boston: Appalachian Mountain Club, 1983.

CORNWALL SWAMP WILDLIFE MANAGEMENT AREA
Department of Fish and Wildlife   South
1,384 acres.

> From US 7 about 7 mi. S of Middlebury, E through West Salisbury and Salisbury to covered bridge. (Map 24.)

The covered bridge, built in 1865, has a 136-ft. span. A sign posted inside invites you to join the society dedicated to preservation of such bridges. Otter Creek here is about 35 ft. wide and deep enough for canoeing, although a mat of litter had accumulated at the bridge. There's a parking area and the remains of a ramp, suitable now only for a hand-carried boat.

Most of the WMA is N of here, including wetlands on the W side of the creek. Supposedly there are 5 mi. of trails, and a posted sign asks that visitors stay on the trails. We saw only a track at the edge of an open field, parallel to the creek but separated from it by a fringe of trees.

Hunting: Deer, grouse, woodcock, waterfowl.

DEAD CREEK WATERFOWL AREA
Department of Fish and Wildlife   South
2,858 acres.

> N access: From Vergennes, about 2 mi. S on SR 22A, then W about 2 mi. to dead end. (Map 30.) S access: Continue S on 22A to Addison, then W on SR 17 to creek. (Map 23.)

Dead Creek (a branching, slow-moving stream) flows N for about 10 mi., joining Otter Creek W of Vergennes, about 3 mi. from Lake Champlain. (See entry, Lower Otter Creek.) The Waterfowl Area occupies the southern 6 1/2 mi., including marsh and a narrow strip of upland on each side.

The N access road ends at a parking area. On the E, the site borders a fenced field, with a jeep track, unused but mowed, going S. On the W side is a fringe of trees. A hand-carried boat could be launched here, although the water is shallow. Walking S, we saw two duck blinds.

The S access leads to a more interesting area. The creek is broader here, with more branches. One can launch a hand-carried boat. There are also greater opportunities to explore the area on foot. The S access road passes the manager's house.

Birds: This is a nesting area for Canada goose and other waterfowl. In season, shorebirds and marshland species are common.

Mammals: Although the upland is limited, reported species include deer, muskrat, cottontail, gray squirrel, woodchuck, otter, mink, weasel, red and gray foxes, coyote.

ACTIVITIES
   Camping: At Button Bay State Park (see entry).
   Hunting: Goose hunting requires permit and assigned blind. Black duck, mallard, wood duck, teal, pintail.
   Fishing: It's not great. Bullhead, pout, northern pike.
   Canoeing: The *Vermont Guide to Fishing* (available from the Department of Fish and Wildlife) marks the entire creek as canoeable, but there's a dam at the N end; when we visited, the water below the dam was too shallow for any craft. We were advised that some areas are posted.

REFERENCE: Schweiker, Roioli, ed. *AMC River Guide: New Hampshire, Vermont.* Boston: Appalachian Mountain Club, 1983.

HEADQUARTERS: RD #1, Box 130, Vergennes, VT 05491; (802) 759-2397.

ELMORE STATE PARK

Department of Forests, Parks & Recreation   North
709 acres.

From Montpelier, 20 mi. N on SR 12. (Map 39.)

The Park has frontage on the N end of 224-acre Lake Elmore. Most of the shoreline is privately owned, with increasing development. Most visitors come for camping and water-based recreation. Much of the surrounding area is hilly to mountainous forest, privately owned but available for hiking and ski touring. Base elevation at the Park is about 1,000 ft. A 1 1/2 mi. trail ascends 2,608-ft. Mount Elmore.

We found the drive N from Montpelier pleasant, traffic light, the road closely following the Winooski River—a good fishing stream—and its North Branch.

ACTIVITIES

Camping: 60 sites, including 13 lean-tos. Season is Memorial Day weekend through Columbus Day weekend. Reservations available.

Boating: Ramp. Rentals.

HEADQUARTERS: Box 93, Lake Elmore, VT 05657; (802) 888-2982.

EMERALD LAKE STATE PARK
Department of Forests, Parks & Recreation   South
430 acres.

From Manchester, Rutland, 22 mi. N on US 7. (Map 10.)

The Park is bisected by US 7. The lake covers only 28 acres. It's a pleasant area, however, with many local attractions. US 7 runs in the long, picturesque Valley of Vermont with Batten Kill, a well-known trout stream, and Otter Creek. The Emerald Lake Natural Bridge spans a deep ravine. US 7 is on or near the W boundary of the Green Mountain National Forest. To the N and S of the Park are trails connecting with the Long Trail. The 80-ft.-deep lake has a sand beach.

Elevation at the valley is about 1,000 ft. The nearby Dorset Area Trails lead to 3,770-ft. Dorset Peak and 3,230-ft. Mt. Aeolus. There is also a nature trail that explains, among other things, why the older rock of the Taconic Mountains is on top of younger rock.

Camping: 105 sites, including 36 lean-tos. Season is Memorial Day weekend through Columbus Day weekend. Reservations available.

REFERENCE: *Day Hiker's Guide to Vermont.* Green Mountain Club, P.O. Box 889, Montpelier 05602. 1987.

HEADQUARTERS: P.O. Box 485, East Dorset, VT 05253; (802) 362-1655.

GIFFORD WOODS STATE PARK
Department of Forests, Parks & Recreation   South
114 acres.

From the junction of US 4 and SR 100, N 1/2 mi. on SR 100. (Map 20.)

The Park itself isn't much more than an attractive wooded campsite, but it's a good base. Close by is Sherburne Pass, where the Long Trail and Appalachian Trail part company. Also nearby are the Pico and Killington ski areas, and trout and bass fishing in Kent Pond.

Camping: 47 sites, including 21 lean-tos. Season is Memorial Day weekend through Columbus Day weekend. Reservations available.

PUBLICATION: Local trail map.

REFERENCES

Appalachian Trail Conference. *Appalachian Trail Guide to New Hampshire/Vermont.* Harpers Ferry, WV: Appalachian Trail Conference, 1985.

Fitzgerald, Brian T., ed. *Guidebook of the Long Trail.* Green Mountain Club, P.O. Box 889, Montpelier 05602. 1987.

HEADQUARTERS: Killington, VT 05751; (802) 775-5354.

GREEN MOUNTAIN NATIONAL FOREST

U.S. Forest Service   South
325,534 acres of Forest land; 629,019 acres within boundaries. (Now also administers the Finger Lakes National Forest in New York.)

Extends N from the MA border about half the length of VT. Two sections, N and S of Rutland. Numerous access routes from US 7 on the W, SR 100 on the E. (See Map 31 but note that map does not show park boundaries.)

The Green Mountains are VT's spine, N to S. The Long Trail, following the ridge, is America's oldest long-distance hiking route. It was conceived by the Green Mountain Club in 1910, built by its members, and completed, from MA to Canada, in 1930. The Club still maintains the trail, many side trails, and numerous shelters.

The Green Mountain National Forest was established in 1932, 20 years after the VT sections of the Long Trail came into use. It began with an acquisition of 1,842 acres. The authorized boundaries have since been expanded. Tracts have been acquired when owners were willing to sell and when purchase money was available. One of the most recent acquisitions was 12,000 acres of wooded wildlife habitat in Windham County, purchased by The Nature Conservancy and transferred to the Forest. Although other such choice tracts may be added, no large increase in Forest acreage is contemplated. In general, the Forest has high, rocky, sloping woodlands. Other lands within the boundaries include farms, a few towns, ski areas, resorts, and private woodlands. The Forest's 325,534 acres is half of all the publicly owned land in VT.

Thanks to the pioneering work of the Green Mountain Club, the patchwork of public and private land doesn't inhibit enjoyment of these scenic mountains. From Canada to MA, private owners have approved public use of the Long Trail and side trails crossing their lands.

Mt. Ellen, at the upper end of the N half is the Forest's highest point: 4,083 ft. (VT's highest is 4,393-ft. Mt. Mansfield.) Although this doesn't rival Colorado's towering Fourteeners, the Green Mountains are steep and rugged enough to challenge any hiker, with views from high points well worth the ascent. Rugged and diverse, with lakes, ponds, streams, and waterfalls, cliffs and rocky peaks, all in deep green forest.

Plants: 90% of the area is forested. Hardwoods predominate—maples, birches, beech, and oaks—with hemlock and white pine interspersed at lower elevations, spruce and fir on higher slopes. Much of the understory is dense, with witch hazel, hophornbeam, striped and mountain maples, shadbush, hobblebush, blueberry, and viburnum. Common wildflowers include Canada mayflower, red and painted trilliums, sessile bellwort, asters, goldenrods, bunchberry, clintonia, Indian cucumber-root, foamflower, goldthread, orange and yellow hawkweeds, jewelweed, jack-in-the-pulpit.

The pattern of vegetation is far from uniform, for the Forest is made up of tracts with a variety of histories of past uses and abuses. The long-range Forest Plan identifies 15 types of Management Areas. Included are 59,598 acres of wilderness, 12,100 acres of roadless primitive areas, and 77,600 acres of semiprimitive areas with few roads. Semiprimitive areas may be managed for timber production; the objective is large sawtimber, trees allowed to grow for years longer than most private woodland owners can afford. An additional 48,000 acres of roaded natural areas will be managed for high-quality sawtimber and wildlife habitats.

Birds: No checklist is available, but DeGraaf and Rudis's *New England Wildlife: Habitat, Natural History, and Distribution* (1986) is used by HQ for the purpose. Recorded species include woodcock, black-billed cuckoo, ruby-throated hummingbird, wild turkey, ruffed grouse, great blue heron. Hawks: sharp-shinned, Cooper's, red-tailed, red-shouldered, broad-winged, peregrine falcon. Owls: great horned, barred, long-eared, saw-whet. Woodpeckers: pileated, hairy, downy, yellow-bellied sapsucker, common flicker. Whip-poor-will, great crested flycatcher, eastern kingbird, eastern wood-pewee, American crow, black-capped chickadee, American robin, white-breasted and red-breasted nuthatches, brown creeper; wood, hermit, and Swainson's thrushes; veery, red-eyed and solitary vireos. Warblers: black-and-white, black-throated blue, yellow-rumped, Nashville, magnolia, black-throated green, blackburnian, ovenbird, mourning, yellow-throated, chestnut-sided, American redstart, Canada. Scarlet tanager, rose-breasted grosbeak, rufous-sided towhee, slate-colored junco, white-throated sparrow.

Mammals: Reported species include deer, moose, black bear, raccoon, porcupine, red and gray squirrels, red and gray foxes, skunk, beaver, otter. Bobcat, fisher, and coyote are present but seldom seen.

FEATURES

Six *Wilderness Areas* encompass 59,598 acres.

In the N half, Bread Loaf Wilderness, 21,480 acres, straddles the ridge and includes about 11 mi. of the Long Trail. Bread Loaf Mountain, 3,823 ft., is its highest point. Mt. Grant, Mt. Cleveland, Mt. Roosevelt, and Mt. Wilson are over 3,500 ft. Bristol Cliffs, 3,738 acres, is near the town of Bristol, just S of the scenic New Haven River Gorge. Steep slopes, cliffs, remote ponds, vistas.

In the S half, Big Branch Wilderness and Peru Peak Wilderness (6,720 and 6,920 acres) are parallel, separated by a narrow corridor, both crossed by the Long Trail. Lye Brook Wilderness, 15,680 acres, is on the W slope of the mountains, the Long Trail skirting its NE boundary. It has ponds, streams, meadows, including the attractive Trestle Cascade on a branch of Lye Brook. George D. Aiken Wilderness, 5,060 acres, is just S of Woodford State Park, on a plateau between two ski areas.

White Rocks National Recreation Area, 22,760 acres, is in the S half, just N of the Big Branch and Peru Peak wildernesses. Several Forest roads provide access. Limited timber management is practiced here with the objectives of improved wildlife habitat, recreation opportunities, and scenic values. The Long Trail is near its W boundary.

INTERPRETATION

Robert Frost Wayside and Trail, on SR 125 E of Ripton. The trail has exhibits with excerpts from the poet's works. His farmhouse is nearby.

Nature trail at the Hapgood Pond campground in the S sector.

The National Forest has no visitor center or nature center. Wildlife biologists and other specialists are available at the Rutland HQ to answer questions. Nature centers are nearby at Branbury and Emerald Lake State Parks (see entries) and Merck State Forest.

ACTIVITIES

Camping: 5 campgrounds; 94 sites. May to mid-Oct. About four times as many sites are available in nearby State Parks, 3 on the W side of the Forest, 3 on the E. Dispersed camping is allowed throughout the Forest. Popular hike-in sites are at Silver Lake, Grout Pond, Little Rock Pond, Stratton Pond, Bourn Pond, and Little Pond.

Hiking, backpacking: Of the Long Trail's 265 mi., 130 are within the Forest. Together with many side trails, this is part of a statewide network of 440 mi. Trailside camping is permitted in almost any suitable place, and there are also shelters maintained by the Green Mountain Club at intervals. Trampling has caused damage around some of the popular ponds, and hikers are asked to walk softly and observe rules.

Hunting: Deer, bear, rabbit, snowshoe hare, grouse, wild turkey, woodcock.

Fishing: 440 mi. of streams and 2,800 acres of ponds offer some good fishing for native brook, brown, and rainbow trout. Angler access is good where Forest lands abut waterways. A fisheries management program with professional staff was initiated in 1987. The Forest is making major efforts to restore the Atlantic salmon. The headwaters of the White and West rivers are important spawning and rearing habitat.

Canoeing: Limited opportunities on ponds and streams; some whitewater in spring runoff.

Skiing, ski touring: 7 ski touring centers are within the Forest boundaries. Downhill ski areas are nearby.

Snowmobiling: Permitted on designated, marked trails. One trial trail in Woodford has been designated for ATVs (all-terrain vehicles); winter only.

PUBLICATIONS

Forest Recreation Map, with contours. $1.

Forest maps, N and S units. $1 each.

Forest Service topographic quadrangles. $2.50 each.

REFERENCES

Appalachian Trail Conference. *Appalachian Trail Guide to New Hampshire/Vermont.* Harpers Ferry, WV: Appalachian Trail Conference, 1985.

Day Hiker's Guide to Vermont. Green Mountain Club, P.O. Box 889, Montpelier 05602. 1987.

DeGraaf, Richard M., and Deborah D. Rudis. *New England Wildlife: Habitat, Natural History, and Distribution.* General Technical Report NE-108. Broomwall, PA: U.S. Department of Agriculture, Forest Service, Northeastern Forest Experiment Station, 1986.

Fitzgerald, Brian T., ed. *Guidebook of the Long Trail.* Green Mountain Club, P.O. Box 889, Montpelier 05602. 1987.

Kulik, Stephen, Pete Salmansohn, Matthew Schmidt, and Heidi Welch. *The Audubon Society Field Guide to the Natural Places of the Northeast: Inland.* New York: Pantheon Books, 1984.

Sadlier, Heather and Hugh. *Fifty Hikes in Vermont.* Woodstock, VT: Backcountry Publications, 1985.

Shea, Peter. *Topo Maps of Vermont's Long Trail.* Burlington: Northern Cartographic, 1984.

Van Diver, Bradford B. *Roadside Geology of Vermont and New Hampshire.* Woodstock, VT: Backcountry Publications, 1986.

HEADQUARTERS: 151 West St., Rutland, VT 05701; (802) 773-0300.

RANGER DISTRICTS: Manchester RD, Manchester Center, VT 05255; (802) 362-2307. Middlebury RD, Middlebury, VT 05753; (802) 388-4362. Rochester RD, Rochester, VT 05767; (802) 767-4777. Finger Lakes National Forest, Mountour Falls, NY 14865; (607) 594-2750.

GROTON STATE FOREST
Department of Forests, Parks & Recreation   North
26,000 acres.

From I-91, Exit 17. NW 9 mi. on US 302, then N on SR 232. In about 2 mi., this road enters the Forest. Major entrance on right in 5 mi. (Map 34.)

This is VT's largest state recreation area. The terrain is rolling to steep. Signal Mountain's elevation is 3,348 ft. Several mountains are over 2,500 ft. There are many glacial boulders, ledges, rock outcrops. The area is almost entirely forested.

The Forest sprawls, with irregular boundaries, but this hardly matters as most of the surrounding area is undeveloped forest. Indeed, the Forest's trail map doesn't show boundaries, and a number of trails cross neighboring land. Lake Groton, the largest water body, is about 3 mi. long. There are several large and small ponds as well as swamps, bogs, and streams.

About half of the visitors come from nearby, to swim and fish in summer, hunt in the fall, snowmobile and ski tour in winter. Hiking is popular. Trailside camping is permitted, but few hikers camp.

Most campers are from out of state, often stopping here for a day or two en route to other destinations. The main season is from Labor Day to the end of Sept. Recreation areas are popular but seldom crowded; only rarely are all campsites occupied. One campground remains open all year.

Plants: Like many forests of this region, Groton reflects a history of abuse. It was heavily logged before 1900. Then great fires destroyed much of the soil's fertility. Recovery is slow. What is seen from the road is young mixed hardwood forest—maple, beech, birch—with an understory of shrubs and saplings and a carpet of herbaceous plants, ferns, mosses, lichens, and grasses. The forest on higher ground is mostly spruce/fir with considerably less understory.

The available plant list includes trees, shrubs, ferns, club mosses, and horsetails. The extensive list of herbaceous flowering plants is coded for season and habitat.

Birds: Over 100 species have been reported. The bird list is annotated for season, abundance, and habitat. Nesting species include red-tailed and broadwinged hawks, barred owl, grouse, woodcock, 5 woodpecker species, kingfisher, ruby-throated hummingbird, 5 flycatchers, wood and hermit thrushes, veery, many wood warblers, northern oriole, rose-breasted grosbeak, scarlet tanager, various finches and sparrows. Loons visit occasionally.

Mammals: Reported species include deer, red fox, porcupine, black bear, red squirrel, flying squirrel, chipmunk, beaver. A few moose frequent the Forest.

INTERPRETATION
The *Groton Nature Center,* near Big Deer Campground, is a large building with exhibits and films. An amphitheater is just outside.
Field trips and other special programs are conducted by naturalists.
A 1/2-mi. *nature trail* starts at the Nature Center.

ACTIVITIES
Camping: 4 campgrounds. 223 sites, including 54 lean-tos. Most are open Memorial Day weekend through Labor Day weekend; Seyon may be open earlier, closed later. Reservations are available.
Hiking, backpacking: 40 mi. of developed trails lead to various mountains, ponds, bogs. An abandoned railroad bed has been converted to a trail; one section is open to vehicle use. Trailside camping is permitted except in certain prohibited areas.
Hunting: Regulated by the Department of Fish and Wildlife. No hunting near developed areas.
Fishing: Trout in streams, warmwater species in lakes and ponds.
Swimming: Lake Groton and Ricker Pond.
Boating: Lake Groton and Ricker Pond. Ramps, rentals.
Canoeing: Access also at Kettle, Levi, and Osmore ponds.
Ski touring, snowmobiling: 12 mi. of marked roads and trails.

PUBLICATIONS
Fact sheet.
Trail map.
Campground maps.
Nature trail guide.
Plants of the Groton State Forest.
Birds of the Groton State Forest.

REFERENCE: *Day Hiker's Guide to Vermont.* Green Mountain Club, P.O. Box 889, Montpelier 05602. 1987.

HEADQUARTERS: Marshfield, VT 05658; (802) 584-3820.

JAY PEAK AREA

Mixed ownerships   North

Near the Canadian border, W of SRs 100 and 101. (Map 55.)

The Long Trail follows a chain of peaks northward to its terminus. Jay Peak, 3,861 ft., highest in this area, is within a small State Forest best known for its ski resort. Trail hikers enjoy a sweeping view from the top. Several other peaks along the route exceed or approach the 3,000-ft. elevation. Most of the area is privately owned forest land, available to visitors for hiking. The Green Mountain Club maintains shelters along the Long Trail.

From the S slope of the mountain, Jay Brook flows SW through terrain favored by cross-country skiers. Good trout fishing. On the E side, Jay Branch flows E to the Missisquoi River. Near North Troy, it passes through Jay Branch Gorge, rough and rocky, with a 15-ft. waterfall.

The Missisquoi is one of VT's longest rivers, flowing N past North Troy into Canada, turning W and SW back into VT, then W to Lake Champlain. (See entry, Missisquoi National Wildlife Refuge.) S of North Troy it drops over Big Falls, one of VT's largest and most spectacular. The 68 mi. from North Troy to Champlain are canoeable, with some rapids and portages.

REFERENCES

Fitzgerald, Brian T., ed. *Guidebook of the Long Trail.* Green Mountain Club, P.O. Box 889, Montpelier 05602. 1987.

Sadlier, Heather and Hugh. *Fifty Hikes in Vermont.* Woodstock, VT: Backcountry Publications, 1985.

Schweiker, Roioli, ed. *AMC River Guide: New Hampshire, Vermont.* Boston: Appalachian Mountain Club, 1983.

LAKE CHAMPLAIN

100 mi. long; 278,400 acres   North

NY-VT boundary.

For most of its length, the lake's deep-water channel is VT's W boundary. In the S, the lake is as broad as a respectable river. It widens in the N, the boundary swinging toward the W shore, so that the Alburg peninsula, Isle La Motte, Grand Isle, and the Hero Islands are in VT. On Isle LaMotte, on private land, are outcrops of what is said to be the world's oldest coral reef.

VT State Parks on the lake include North Hero, Knight Point, Burton Island, Grand Isle, Sand Bar, Kingsland Bay, Button Bay, and D.A.R. We have entries for Burton Island and Button Bay. The others, while not chosen as natural areas, provide lake access.

The lake's drainage basin is about 8,000 sq. mi. On the VT side are numerous rivers, often with extensive associated wetlands. We have entries for several wetland Wildlife Management Areas. A number of the rivers, such as the Missisquoi, Lamoille, Winooski, Lewis Creek, Otter Creek, Poultney, Mettawee, and tributaries are canoeable. These are usually mentioned in entries for sites such as Dead Creek Wildlife Management Area, which provide access.

Few sections of shoreline are roadless.

ACTIVITIES

Camping: At most of the State Parks.

Hunting: Chiefly waterfowl in bordering wetlands.

Fishing: Lake trout, steelhead, landlocked salmon, smelt, sauger, walleye, largemouth and smallmouth bass, northern pike, pickerel, muskellunge, yellow perch, channel catfish. A highly productive ice fishery.

Boating: Many access points, marinas, rentals.

LEWIS CREEK WILDLIFE MANAGEMENT AREA
Department of Fish and Wildlife   North
1,796 acres.

From Starksboro, S about 2 1/2 mi. on SR 116, then E on Ireland Rd. to parking areas. (Map 31.)

The site is on the W slopes of the Green Mountains. Terrain is gentle to moderately steep, rising from 1,000 ft. elevation at Lewis Creek to 2,560 ft. atop Hillsboro Mountain. In the past the area was logged, farmed, grazed, and abandoned. Now it is 95% forested, chiefly with sugar maple/beech/yellow birch, with one tract of hemlock/yellow birch. Logging is now managed for wildlife habitat improvement.

Except in hunting season, few visitors come here. It offers an opportunity for quiet day hiking on about 6 mi. of old logging roads. There has been some off-road vehicle (ORV) activity that the department hopes to control.

Lewis Creek is canoeable below Prindle Corners, not here.

Wildlife: Includes 3 beaver colonies, red fox, snowshoe hare, coyote, ruffed grouse, occasional black bear. It's a deer wintering area.

Fishing, we were told, is "not significant."

HEADQUARTERS: District Wildlife Biologist, III West St., Essex Junction, VT 05452; (802) 878-1564.

LITTLE OTTER CREEK WILDLIFE MANAGEMENT AREA
Department of Fish and Wildlife   North
1,048 acres.

From US 7 at Ferrisburg, W about 1 mi. Turn right on first paved road and go N 2 mi. Parking area is across the creek. (Map 30.)

The creek is broad, attractive, fringed by marsh and trees, with many water lilies. From the road, which carries little traffic, one can overlook open water and marsh. We saw two outboard craft motoring toward Lake Champlain, about a mile downstream. Upstream is a quiet wetland area with good birding.

ACTIVITIES
Fishing: Northern pike, largemouth bass.
Boating, canoeing: A good launching ramp is at the parking area.

HEADQUARTERS: District Wildlife Biologist, III West St., Essex, VT 05452; (802) 878-1564.

LITTLE RIVER STATE PARK
Department of Forests, Parks, & Recreation   North
12,000 acres.

From Waterbury, 1 1/2 mi. W on US 2, then right under the overpass and 3 1/2 mi. N. (Map 38.)

Open Memorial Day weekend to Columbus Day weekend.

The developed area of the park is near the dam of Waterbury Reservoir, an impoundment about 6 mi. long between steep-sided forested hills. It is part of the Mount Mansfield State Forest (see entry). Indeed, in the State's informal if somewhat confusing way, it is also called the Little River Block of the Forest (a part of which is also called the Woodward Hill Block).

Whatever the name, it's delightful. Many of the campsites are across a cove from the busier day-use beach and ramp. The sites are well spaced on the forested hillside. We swam from the rocky shore just below our camp. Elevation at the shore is about 550 ft.

Some private development has occurred, chiefly on the E side of the lake, but it seems unobtrusive. Canoeing for several hours, we were passed by less than a dozen motor craft. The water was clear, the swimming fine. The fishermen we talked with were less enthusiastic.

INTERPRETATION

Nature trail along Stevenson Brook, self-guiding.

The *"History Hike"* is fascinating if the printed guide is available. The center spread is an historical map of the Little River area, where the first settler arrived in 1790.

ACTIVITIES

Camping: 101 sites, including 20 lean-tos. Reservations accepted.

Hiking, backpacking: Several trails from the campground offer opportunities for day or overnight hikes. Trails extend through the Mount Mansfield State Forest, to the Long Trail, and to Camel's Hump Forest Reserve (see entries). Maps carry the State Forest name but are available at the Park office.

Hunting: In the State Forest.

Fishing: The *Vermont Guide to Fishing* (available from the Department of Fish and Wildlife) provides much useful information about VT lakes and rivers, but the copy we acquired in 1987 says of Waterbury Reservoir only "Temporarily Drained." It was at full pool when we saw it. No doubt it takes some time to restore the fishery.

Boating, canoeing: Ramp. Rentals.

PUBLICATIONS

Trail maps.

Nature and history trail guides.

HEADQUARTERS: RFD 1, Waterbury, VT 05676; (802) 244-7103.

LONG TRAIL
Green Mountain Club   North/South
265 miles.

From Canada to Massachusetts.

What a magnificent achievement! In 1910 a small group with a large vision founded the Green Mountain Club. By 1917 GMC volunteers had surveyed, cleared, and marked a trail from Killington to Massachusetts and published the first guidebook. (Our 1987 copy is the 23rd edition.) By 1930 the Trail had been completed from border to border, 265 miles.

Of this distance, about 30% is on privately owned land. It was more before the Green Mountain National Forest was assembled, and acquisitions by government and the Green Mountain Club may add to the publicly owned sections. The GMC had to persuade landowners to grant easements for routes acceptable to them. GMC volunteers maintain the trail and its shelters, relocate trail sections when necessary.

In addition to the Trail itself, the system includes almost a hundred side trails, totaling 175 mi. Volunteers have built and now maintain 70 primitive shelters and tenting areas.

The southern portion of the trail is also the Appalachian Trail. The AT turns E at Sherburne Pass.

It is not the aim of the GMC to make this route a smooth path for Sunday walks. We've hiked sections that were wet, muddy, steep, and rocky, sometimes encountering deadfalls and windfalls not yet cleared. As trail use has increased, more work has been required to control erosion and to prevent detours through fragile plant communities.

For much of the trail, the hiking season begins at the end of May. The spring mud season is no time to be on it, and better winter routes are available for ski touring and snowshoeing. GMC's Montpelier office will respond to letters or telephone calls asking about trail conditions and can suggest sections suitable for winter and spring hikes.

For anything more than a short day hike, the guidebook is essential. Having it adds much to the enjoyment of any outing. The Green Mountain Club invites all hikers to membership, even those who can't volunteer to help.

PUBLICATIONS
Day Hiker's Guide to Vermont. Green Mountain Club, P.O. Box 889, Montpelier 05602. 1987.

Fitzgerald, Brian T., ed. *Guidebook of the Long Trail.* Green Mountain Club, P.O. Box 889, Montpelier 05602. 1987.

Shea, Peter. *Topo maps of Vermont's Long Trail.* (Out of print in spring 1988, but a new set of maps will be published soon.)

HEADQUARTERS: The Green Mountain Club, Inc., P.O. Box 889, Montpelier, VT 05602; (802) 223-3463.

LOWER OTTER CREEK WILDLIFE MANAGEMENT AREA

Department of Fish and Wildlife   North
492 acres.

From Vergennes, W and N on local roads toward Fort Cassin. (Map 30.)

Canoeing is by far the best way to see this site. Topography is flat. Most of the area is flooded in spring and in a wet fall. The creek is canoeable from the public landing at Vergennes to Lake Champlain. A take-out is at Fort Cassin. The WMA is in several parcels, but boundaries aren't apparent.

The biologist who prepared the management plan said the site has "tremendous" fish and wildlife resources, high praise for a relatively small area. The Vermont Natural Heritage Program has also taken note of the wildlife, especially the least bittern, common moorhen, and black tern.

Plants: About 43% of the site is forested. Plants include silver and red maples, American elm, black ash, swamp white oak, one area of eastern hemlock. Also buttonbush, dogwood, cattail, water-lily, bulrush.

Birds: Numerous nesting species, including Canada goose, black duck, mallard, green-winged teal, grouse, wild turkey.

Mammals: Include beaver, muskrat, cottontail, mink, raccoon, gray squirrel, deer.

ACTIVITIES
   Camping: At Button Bay State Park (see entry).
   Hunting: Waterfowl, upland game.
   Fishing: Bass, bullhead, carp. Northern pike and chain pickerel spawn here.
   Canoeing: Otter Creek offers the longest canoe trip in VT, 100 mi. from Dorset at high water.

REFERENCES
   Schweiker, Roioli, ed. *AMC River Guide: New Hampshire, Vermont.* Boston: Appalachian Mountain Club, 1983.

Schweiker, Roioli. *Canoe Camping Vermont and New Hampshire Rivers.* Woodstock, VT: Backcountry Publications, 1985.

HEADQUARTERS: District Wildlife Biologist, 111 West St., Essex Jct., VT 05452; (802) 878-1564.

MAIDSTONE STATE PARK

Department of Forests, Parks & Recreation   North
469 acres.

NE VT. From Bloomfield, 5 mi. S on SR 102, then 5 mi. SW on State Forest road. (Map 51.)

Maidstone Lake covers 796 acres, a rough oval about 2 1/2 mi. long. Both shores have roads and seasonal residences. The Park, at the S end isn't large, but the country for miles around is wild, largely roadless, with clear streams, beaver flowages, ponds, small wetlands, and scattered hills up to about 2,100 ft. elevation. Away from the lake, there's ample solitude.

The forest has mixed northern hardwoods. Bird life includes warblers, finches, woodpeckers, loon. Mammals include deer, black bear, raccoon, moose, bobcat, snowshoe hare, porcupine, fisher.

There's a nature trail. A park naturalist offers programs in summer.

ACTIVITIES

Camping: 83 sites including 37 lean-tos. Season is Memorial Day weekend through Labor Day weekend. Reservations available.

Fishing: Rainbow and lake trout, yellow perch.

Boating: Ramp. Rentals.

HEADQUARTERS: RD 1, Box 185, Guildhall, VT 05905; (802) 676-3930.

MISSISQUOI NATIONAL WILDLIFE REFUGE

U.S. Fish and Wildlife Service   North
5,839 acres.

Near the Canadian border on the E shore of Lake Champlain. HQ is on SR 78, 2 mi. NW of Swanton. (Map 52.)

Open in daylight hours.

The Refuge occupies part of the delta of the Missisquoi River, on both sides of the channel. The delta is low-lying, marshy, cut by numerous winding creeks, with open water and wooded swamp. Narrow strips of cropland are on ridges. It was established to maintain and enhance feeding and resting areas for migrating waterfowl.

From HQ, a 1 1/2-mi. nature trail makes a loop beside two of the creeks. The trail is often flooded in spring and early summer. The first half of the trail is just a pleasant walk in the woods. After that it's close to the creeks, but thickets usually block the view. Ask at HQ what other parts of the Refuge can be visited on foot. At the boat ramp, we saw a jeep track behind a gate marked "Area Closed." In most federal refuges, this means "Keep Out," but at HQ we were told only vehicles are prohibited.

Much more can be seen from a canoe. At HQ we were told there's no nearby place to rent canoes.

The Refuge doesn't have a great number of visitors. Of those, many stop by in summer, as we did, when waterfowl numbers are low. It's a pleasant stop, but we don't recommend making a long detour.

Birds: A checklist of 199 species is available. The largest concentrations of waterfowl occur in Apr., Sept., and Oct. The most numerous nesting species are black duck, mallard, wood duck, and common goldeneye, with a few blue-winged teal and hooded merganser. Other nesting species include great blue heron, American bittern, common moorhen, many songbirds.

Seasonally abundant or common waterfowl and shorebirds include pied-billed grebe, green heron, black-crowned night-heron, Canada goose, green-winged teal, northern pintail, northern shoveler, gadwall, American wigeon, canvasback, ring-necked duck, lesser scaup, common merganser, Virginia rail, American coot, killdeer, greater yellowlegs, spotted sandpiper.

Mammals: Checklist of 34 species available. Deer are common, as are otter, red fox, meadow vole, white-footed mouse, beaver, red and gray squirrels, cottontail. During high water in Apr.–May, deer may be forced onto higher ground, as many as 30 in a group.

ACTIVITIES

Hunting: Special regulations. Waterfowl, deer, upland game.

Fishing: River and lake. Walleye, catfish, bullhead, muskellunge, pumpkinseed, crappie, salmon, northern pike, carp, smallmouth and largemouth bass, yellow perch.

Boating, canoeing: Ramp on SR 78, 2 mi. below junction with Dead Creek. The Missisquoi is canoeable for almost 70 mi., from North Troy to Lake Champlain, an upper section passing through Canada. Some rapids, dams, unrunnable drops.

PUBLICATIONS

Refuge leaflet with map.

Refuge map.
Black Creek and Maquam Creek Trail.
Bird checklist.
Mammal checklist.
Fishing.

REFERENCES

Schweiker, Roioli, ed. *AMC River Guide: New Hampshire, Vermont.* Boston: Appalachian Mountain Club, 1983.

Schweiker, Roioli. *Canoe Camping Vermont and New Hampshire Rivers.* Woodstock, VT: Backcountry Publications, 1985.

HEADQUARTERS: P.O. Box 163, Swanton, VT 05488; (802) 868-4781.

MOUNT MANSFIELD STATE FOREST
Department of Forests, Parks & Recreation   North
27,499 acres.

Two principal areas: From Stowe on SR 100, NW on SR 108; from Waterbury, 1 1/2 mi. W on US 2, then right under overpass and 3 1/2 mi. to Little River State Park. (Maps 37–38.)

The Forest has two principal blocks, the northern featuring Mt. Mansfield, the southern the Waterbury Reservoir. It includes 3 State Parks: Little River (see entry), Smugglers Notch, and Underhill. The entire area is in the Green Mountains. Mt. Mansfield, 4,393 ft., is the state's highest.

This is VT's best-known ski country. The famous mountain has been nastily scarred by the clear-cut slopes, more conspicuous in summer than winter. People look up from the valley to see the profile of a reclining giant's face, its features labeled on maps: Adam's Apple, The Chin, The Nose, The Forehead. In the warm months, many hike or drive to the top for the splendid views. Some features can be seen only by walking: Smugglers Cave, Lake of the Clouds, Bear Pond, Cave of the Winds.

It's great hiking country. More than 40,000 visitors per year walk around the Mt. Mansfield summit, a considerable threat to its delicate plant life. No such crowds are on the Long Trail as it follows the peaks southward through the N sector of the Forest. It then veers to the W, passing the Bolton Valley Ski Area. Side trails link it to the trail complex in the Little River sector. Portions of the trail are steep, rough, difficult.

Plants: As one ascends the mountain, a northern hardwood forest is gradually replaced by spruce/fir. Mt. Mansfield rises several hundred feet above timberline, and the summit has a complex of fragile alpine plant communities: sedge tundra, peat bogs supporting leatherleaf, bog laurel, and black crowberry; heath, with alpine bilberry and mountain cranberry; and rare species usually found miles to the N.

Birds: No species record has been kept. Species noted at lower elevations include yellow-bellied sapsucker, veery, Swainson's and hermit thrushes, solitary vireo, black-throated blue and black-throated green warblers, red-breasted nuthatch, brown creeper, winter wren, golden-crowned kinglet, scarlet tanager, ruffed grouse, American woodcock. Near timberline: gray-cheeked thrush, blackpoll warbler, slate-colored junco, white-throated sparrow, common raven. Hawks aloft in migration.

Mammals: Hunting is prohibited on the E side of the northern sector. Species reported include snowshoe hare, porcupine, gray fox, squirrel, cottontail, black bear, bobcat, deer.

FEATURES

The *summit ridge* is owned by the University of Vermont and state protected as a Natural Area. Green Mountain Club ranger-naturalists are stationed on the summit to provide information and protect the rare flora.

Smugglers Notch, between Mt. Mansfield and Sterling Peak, has spectacular cliffs, ledges, boulders, arctic flora.

Sterling Pond is on the Long Trail not far from *Elephant's Head.* A Green Mountain Club shelter is at the pond, with a resident caretaker in hiking season.

Waterbury Reservoir; Little River sector. See entry for Little River State Park. Ricker Mountain, 3,401 ft., is the highest peak in this sector, which is generally mountainous, with two principal streams, Cotton Brook and Stevenson Brook, flowing to the reservoir. The sector has many trails.

ACTIVITIES

Camping: Smugglers Notch State Park, on the road from Stowe, has 38 sites, 14 lean-tos. Underhill State Park, reached from Essex Junction (9 mi. E on SR 15, 8 mi. E on local roads too steep for trailers, including 4 mi. of gravel) has 14 sites, 11 lean-tos. Little River State Park (see entry) has 101 sites, 20 lean-tos. Season: Memorial Day weekend through Columbus Day weekend.

Hiking, backpacking: One of the most attractive segments of the Long Trail. Many trails for day hikes. Trailside camping is permitted except in the Smugglers Notch Ski Area and Moscow Tree Seed Orchard.

Fishing: Chiefly in Waterbury Reservoir, recently drained and refilled.

Boating: Reservoir.

Ski touring: Many trails, some maintained, in Mt. Mansfield sector.

Skiing: Chiefly Mt. Mansfield ski area in Stowe.

PUBLICATION: Trail maps.

REFERENCES

Day Hiker's Guide to Vermont. Green Mountain Club, P.O. Box 889, Montpelier 05602. 1987.

Mt. Mansfield Trail Map. Green Mountain Club, P.O. Box 889, Montpelier 05602. 1987.

Fitzgerald, Brian T., ed. *Guidebook of the Long Trail.* Green Mountain Club, P.O. Box 889, Montpelier 05602. 1987.

Kulik, Stephen, Pete Salmansohn, Matthew Schmidt, and Heidi Welch. *The Audubon Society Field Guide to the Natural Places of the Northeast: Inland.* New York: Pantheon Books, 1984.

Sadlier, Heather and Hugh. *Fifty Hikes in Vermont.* Woodstock, VT: Backcountry Publications, 1985.

HEADQUARTERS: RFD, Stowe, VT 05672; (802) 253-4014.

MUD CREEK WILDLIFE MANAGEMENT AREA
Department of Fish and Wildlife   North
1,019 acres.

On SR 78 0.7 mi. NE of its intersection with US 2. (Map 52.)

If you've just visited the Missisquoi National Wildlife Refuge (see entry) and are traveling W on SR 78, this site is worth a stop. Look for a small parking area on the right where the road crosses Mud Creek. A not-too-visible sign says this is a Fishing Access site. Across a small bridge are jeep trails, easy hiking. It seemed possible to launch a canoe and paddle up Mud Creek, how far we don't know. The wetlands along the creek attract waterfowl.

PINE MOUNTAIN WILDLIFE MANAGEMENT AREA
Department of Fish and Wildlife   North
2,274 acres.

S of US 302, about 4 mi. E of West Groton. Most acreage is in the NE corner of town of Topsham. Site's NE corner is in SE Groton and SW Ryegate, on the Wells River. Includes Melvin Hill in town of Newbury. Access by old railroad bed. (Map 34.)

Pine Mountain, 1,492 ft., is at the WMA's center. Highest point is 1,632-ft. Burnham Mountain, near the S boundary. Lowest elevation is 900 ft. on Keenan Brook. Terrain is moderately rolling with some steep slopes, several streams flowing to the Wells River, a portion of Scotts Brook Swamp in the SW.

The site is almost entirely forested with a mixture of mature northern hardwoods and softwood species. Timber harvesting is planned largely for wildlife habitat management.

Wells River is a scenic stream with numerous ledges, falls, cascades, and pools. For some miles it flows close to US 302. A few short stretches are canoeable if one doesn't mind frequent portages.

The site map shows no trails, but bushwhacking is feasible, and the 1 1/2 mi. walk from the highway to the top of Pine Mountain is a quiet, pleasant day hike.

Wildlife: Includes deer, bear, bobcat, fisher, snowshoe hare, grouse, wood duck, woodcock, occasional moose, one active beaver colony.

HEADQUARTERS: District Wildlife Biologist, 254 N. Main St., Barre, VT 05641; (802) 828-2454.

PLYMSBURY WILDLIFE MANAGEMENT AREA
Department of Fish and Wildlife   South
1,792 acres.

About 1 mi. NE of North Shrewsbury. Town Highway 20 crosses the S portion. Access to N sector by Northam Rd. and Grouse Hill Rd. (Map 15.)

The WMA adjoins a block of Calvin Coolidge State Forest on the N. The area is between the two portions of the Green Mountain & Finger Lakes National Forest, on the W slope of the mountains. Terrain is hilly, gentle to moderate slopes, with several crests near 2,400 ft. elevation. It has two principal watercourses. Great Roaring Brook crosses the S third, Tinker Brook the NE corner. Neither is canoeable, nor is either rated high as a fishery, although there are trout in Great Roaring Brook.

The site is almost entirely forested with trees of pole to sawlog size. About 1,000 acres are northern hardwoods, primarily beech, birch, and maple. Softwoods predominate in about 450 acres, chiefly spruce/fir. A 40-acre wooded swamp is in the N central sector.

Wildlife: Includes deer, bear, fisher, red fox, coyote, bobcat, raccoon. Beaver impoundments are along Great Roaring Brook. Moose have been seen. Small numbers of waterfowl visit the area: black duck, wood duck, mallard, common and hooded mergansers.

Because of easy access, the WMA and adjacent Forest have considerable recreational use, chiefly by local residents: primitive camping, hiking, hunting, fishing, birding. Annual snowfall is about 120 in., snow cover lasting about 100 days, and this attracts cross-country skiers and snowmobilers.

HEADQUARTERS: District Wildlife Biologist, Pittsford Academy, RD #1, Pittsford, VT 05763; (802) 483-2300.

PUTNAM STATE FOREST

Department of Forests, Parks & Recreation   North
8,661 acres.

From Waterbury Center on SR 100, turn E at Post Office sign. Local roads E and N about 3 1/2 mi to Mt. Hunger trailhead. (Map 38.)

The Forest has several separate blocks. The one of chief interest has the trail to Mt. Hunger, a 3,620-ft. peak in the Worcester Range. The trail extends S to White Rock Mountain and N along the crest of the range.

Trailside camping is permitted. Nearby is the Little River State Park campground in Mount Mansfield State Forest (see entry).

REFERENCE: Sadlier, Heather and Hugh. *Fifty Hikes in Vermont.* Woodstock, VT: Backcountry Publications, 1985.

QUECHEE GORGE STATE PARK

Department of Forests, Parks & Recreation   South
612 acres.

On US 4, 3 mi. W of I-89. (Map 16.)

When we first saw it in 1978, the Park had only 76 acres. From an overlook near the highway bridge, one looks down into the 155-ft.-deep rocky gorge of the of the Ottauquechee River. One could also hike a short trail. Since then the State has become the manager of land on both sides of the highway, on both sides of the gorge. On the S it extends for about a mile. On the N it includes Deweys Mills Ponds.

The walls of the gorge, steep to almost vertical, have plants from grasses to stunted trees clinging to ledges and crevices. Surrounding the gorge is northern hardwood forest with intermixed conifers: hemlock, beech, sugar and red maple, red spruce, white and red pines, yellow birch. In the understory are mountain maple, hobblebush, beaked willow, bush honeysuckle, witch hazel. Seasonal wildflowers include columbine, bishop's cap, harebell, flowering raspberry, little cinquefoil, fringed loosestrife, blunt-leaved sandwort, ground ivy, purple nightshade, violets, asters.

ACTIVITIES

Camping: 30 sites, including 4 lean-tos. Season is Memorial Day weekend to Columbus Day weekend. Reservations available.

Hiking: A 1-mi. loop trail provides fine views of the gorge from above and below, passing through forest, crossing streams.

Fishing: Brook, rainbow, and brown trout.

PUBLICATION: Geology brochure.

REFERENCES

Day Hiker's Guide to Vermont. Green Mountain Club, P.O. Box 889, Montpelier 05602. 1987.

Sadlier, Heather and Hugh. *Fifty Hikes in Vermont.* Woodstock, VT: Backcountry Publications, 1985.

HEADQUARTERS: RD, White River Jct., VT 05001; (802) 295-2990.

SOUTH BAY WILDLIFE MANAGEMENT AREA

Department of Fish and Wildlife   North
1,545 acres.

S end of Lake Memphremagog. From Coventry on US 5, E 4 mi. on local road. (Map 56.)

Lake Memphremagog, partly in Canada, is the second largest VT lake and one of its best fishing waters. Newport, at the S end of the main lake, is a popular resort. South Bay extends for about 2 mi. S of Newport. Beyond is the WMA, largely marshland on the Barton River, with some frontage on the bay.

Birds: The WMA is primarily for waterfowl. Seasonally common species include common moorhen, Canada goose, black tern, black duck, wood duck, blue-winged teal, American bittern, Virginia rail, killdeer, woodcock, osprey, common snipe, spotted sandpiper, snow goose, lesser scaup, common merganser.

Boating: Ramp on South Bay.

HEADQUARTERS: District Wildlife Biologist, 180 Portland St., St. Johnsbury, VT 05819; (802) 748-8787.

TOWNSHEND STATE PARK
Department of Forests, Parks & Recreation   South
856 acres.

From Brattleboro, about 17 mi. N on SR 30; then Town Rd. (Map 7.)

The U.S. Army Corps of Engineers has dammed the West River, backing up a long, narrow pool. The State Park is below the dam. The Corps' Recreation Area offers swimming, boating, and fishing; the Park has camping and hiking.

Elevation at the reservoir is about 478 ft. From the campground, the land rises to the S, to a high point of 1,680 ft. on Bald Mountain. On a contour map it looks like an easy ascent, but the trail to the top, at times steep and rocky, gains over 1,100 ft. in less than a mile. The trail passes an alder swamp, pine grove, an ancient white birch. Much of the forest has young beech, with maples and hemlock.

ACTIVITIES
Camping: 34 sites. Approximate season May 6–Oct. 12. Reservations available.
Hiking, backpacking: Although the site isn't large, trailside camping is permitted. We saw no trail extensions into adjoining areas.
Fishing: Rainbow and brown trout.
Swimming: Beach at Corps Recreation area.
Boating: Ramp at Corps Recreation Area.
Canoeing: West River.

REFERENCES
Day Hiker's Guide to Vermont. Green Mountain Club, P.O. Box 889, Montpelier 05602. 1987.
Sadlier, Heather and Hugh. *Fifty Hikes in Vermont.* Woodstock, VT: Backcountry Publications, 1985.

HEADQUARTERS: Rt. 1, Box 299, Newfane, VT 05345; (802) 365-7500.

VICTORY BASIN WILDLIFE MANAGEMENT AREA

Department of Fish and Wildlife   North

4,970 acres.

From St. Johnsbury, E on US 2 to North Concord, then NE on local road. Beyond Victory the road crosses the WMA. There are 3 parking areas. (Map 42.)

The WMA is part of one of the largest wetland-wilderness areas in the Northeast Kingdom (the local name of the Northeast Highlands). The land is generally flat and wet, with occasional ridges and hills. Elevations range from 1,100 to 1,400 ft.

The Moose River parallels the road through the site, which includes 1,800 acres of wetlands, from cedar swamp to cattail marshes. Also within the site are over 1,000 acres of northern hardwood forest and almost 2,000 acres of spruce/fir, interspersed with old fields and other openings. Flora include rhodora azalea, Labrador tea, leatherleaf, pitcher-plant.

Birds: Waterfowl populations are generally low. Nesting species include mallard, black duck, wood duck, hooded merganser. Upland species include several rather uncommon in VT, such as Canada jay, olive-sided flycatcher, black-backed three-toed woodpecker, rusty blackbird, pileated woodpecker, spotted sandpiper, common snipe.

Mammals: Many beaver ponds. An important deer wintering area. Moose are resident. Other species noted include black bear, coyote, red fox, bobcat, snowshoe hare.

ACTIVITIES

Hiking: Unmaintained logging road and bushwhacking.

Hunting: Deer, snowshoe hare, grouse, woodcock.

Fishing: Brook trout. Moderate fishing pressure.

Canoeing: Canoe access. A management document says Moose River is canoeable only at high water to Damon's Crossing, below that all year, with whitewater below Mitchell's Landing.

HEADQUARTERS: District Wildlife Biologist, 180 Portland St., St. Johnsbury, VT 05819; (802) 748-8787.

WENLOCK WILDLIFE MANAGEMENT AREA

Department of Fish and Wildlife   North

1,993 acres.

NE VT. Generally S of SR 105 between Island Pond and Bloomfield. From Island Pond, just under 8 mi. E on SR 105, then right on dirt road toward South America Pond. (Map 50.)

Boundaries don't matter much here, in this least populous part of VT. Essex County, in the NE corner, is mostly between SR 114 and the Connecticut River, the NH boundary. The Nulhegan River, paralleled by SR 105, crosses its middle, W–E. This is the Northeast Highlands (also locally called the Northeast Kingdom). Most of the land is owned by timber companies that permit recreational use of their lands. The map shows few roads, but there's a network of old logging roads that may not be suitable for a car but serve as hiking trails.

Elevations along the Nulhegan River are about 1,000 ft. Most of the county is hilly to mountainous, several peaks rising above 3,000 ft. The WMA occupies lowlands along the river and its tributaries, including bogs and beaver ponds, with a few knolls and ridges about 1,400 ft. elevation. Much of the site is spruce/fir forest, with a few hardwood knolls. Annual snowfall is 80 to 100 in., winter snow depth usually about 2 ft.

Moose Bog, a fascinating natural feature, is W of the dirt access road, reached by a track to the right about 0.2 mi. from the highway; in about half a mile look left for a trail. Sphagnum moss has formed a floating mat thick and strong enough to support shrubs. chiefly heath species such as leatherleaf, Labrador tea, bog rosemary, bog laurel, and cranberry. Pitcher plant and sundew are also seen.

Birds: This is a birding hot-spot, frequented by local birding societies, chiefly in spring and early summer. A Christmas bird count is made here. Some boreal forest species are seen here that are uncommon to rare elsewhere in VT. Nesting and migratory waterfowl include mallard, black duck, goldeneye, ring-necked duck. Breeding species include spruce grouse, three-toed black-backed woodpecker, Canada jay, Cape May warbler. Other notable species include boreal chickadee, rusty blackbird, yellow-bellied flycatcher, Swainson's thrush, Tennessee and blackpoll warblers, Lincoln's sparrow, white-winged crossbill.

Mammals: Deer population is high, especially in winter. Moose are present most of the year. Black bear are often here. Snowshoe hare are abundant. Other species include beaver, fisher, red fox, coyote, bobcat.

ACTIVITIES

Camping: At nearby Brighton State Park: 84 sites. Season is Memorial Day weekend through Columbus Day weekend. Reservations available: Island Pond, VT 05846; (802) 723-4360. No pets.

Hunting: Chiefly for upland game.

Fishing: Low to moderate trout populations in the river and beaver ponds.

Canoeing: The river is canoeable from Nulhegan Pond to its end, but the portion just below the pond is narrow, and one Class IV section is often portaged.

Ski touring, snowshoeing: Good opportunities.

HEADQUARTERS: District Wildlife Biologist, 180 Portland St., St. Johnsbury, VT 05819; (802) 748-8787.

WILLOUGHBY STATE FOREST

Department of Forests, Parks & Recreation   North
7,422 acres.

On both sides of the S end of Lake Willoughby, extending almost to US 5. From I-91, exit at Barton, then S on US 5. (Map 49.)

If you plan to hike here, get a trail map first. Because of VT's strange sign rules, trailheads aren't easy to find. Indeed, we saw no signs identifying the Forest itself or marking its boundaries, and local roads aren't well signed. The trails are blazed.

The Forest has two parts. The smaller, on the E side of the lake, includes 2,751-ft. Mt. Pisgah. Route 5A follows the lake shore. From here the mountain's flank rises steeply to vertical rock cliffs. We saw two attractive cascades beside the road. The Mt. Pisgah Trail begins at an inconspicuous trailhead on the highway, where there's no parking, and ends S of the lake. It's an energetic hike, rewarded with some fine vistas.

The larger part of the Forest is W of the lake. Until 1969 this was a patchwork, much of it open farmland on which the CCC (Civilian Conservation Corps) planted trees in the 1930s. Then the State acquired 5,000 acres to unify the tract, giving it control of the forest around Mt. Pisgah and its twin peak across the lake, Mt. Hor. Two other prominent peaks in this portion are Bartlett Mountain, SE of Mt. Hor, and Wheeler Mountain at the N tip of the site. Facing the cliffs of Mt. Pisgah are the cliffs below Mt. Hor. Arctic flora are said to grow on these cliffs.

Elsewhere the slopes are generally moderate to steep. This portion has a network of trails, including loops around a cluster of ponds: Marl, Duck, Blake, Vail, and Bean.

Plants: Generally young forest, mixed hardwoods at lower elevations, red spruce and balsam fir on upper slopes. Blueberry and blackberry are common. Many wildflowers and ferns.

Birds: Species observed include boreal chickadee, brown creeper, American goldfinch, red crossbill, great crested flycatcher, ruffed grouse, cedar waxwing, various raptors, warblers.

Mammals: Deer, bear, porcupine, fisher, bobcat, beaver, snowshoe hare, cottontail, red and gray squirrels, chipmunk.

ACTIVITIES

Hiking, backpacking: Trailside camping is permitted except in the cliff area and on the W shore of the lake. A good trail system, plus old roads in various conditions.

Fishing: Salmon, rainbow and lake trout, yellow perch in the lake; some trout fishing in ponds.

Boating: State ramp on Lake Willoughby.

Ski touring, snowmobiling: Said to have some of the best snowmobiling on state land.

PUBLICATIONS

Public use map (trails).

Snowmobile trail map.

REFERENCE: *Day Hiker's Guide to Vermont.* Green Mountain Club, P.O. Box 889, Montpelier 05602. 1987.

HEADQUARTERS: District Forester, Department of Forests, Parks & Recreation, 180 Portland St., St. Johnsbury, VT 05819; (802) 748-4890.

WOODFORD STATE PARK

Department of Forests, Parks & Recreation   South
400 acres.

From Bennington, 10 mi. E on SR 9. (Map 2.)

This park on a small reservoir is within the Green Mountain National Forest, at an elevation of 2,400 ft. Although we saw no trails leading from the site, it is surrounded by a network of National Forest trails, with trailheads on SR

9 both E and W of the site. The Long Trail crosses the highway between Bennington and the Park. The Prospect Mountain ski area is nearby.

Camping: 103 sites, including 16 lean-tos. Approximate season June 24–Oct. 12. Reservations available.

HEADQUARTERS: RFD, Bennington, VT 05201; (802) 447-7169.

NEW HAMPSHIRE

New Hampshire is magnificent, a state of high mountains and green forests, 1,300 lakes and ponds, with waterfalls and cascades, fine rivers, scenic highways, and long trails.

From the Canadian border to the Massachusetts line is almost 200 miles. The northern tip is less than 20 miles wide, the base almost 100 miles. The Connecticut River is most of the western boundary; on the east is Maine and an 18-mile seacoast with 131 mi. of shoreline.

Terrain is dominated by the White Mountains. Elevations below 500 ft. are found only near the coast and in central and southern river valleys. Elsewhere the base elevation is 500 to 1,500 ft., except in the extreme north, where elevations reach 2,500 ft. Rising above the base are numerous hills and mountains. Many White Mountain peaks exceed 4,000 ft. Eight peaks in the Presidential Range exceed 5,000 ft. The highest is 6,288-ft. Mt. Washington.

Logging the New Hampshire forests began in the 1600s, much earlier than in states to the south and west. By 1865 half of the land area had been cleared, and some farmers were abandoning their land. Much of it came back in white pine; browsing cattle kept down competitive deciduous species. Today 85 percent of the land is again forested.

Southern New Hampshire is experiencing severe environmental problems. Although the state had little more than a million residents in the last U.S. Census, its growth rate is double that of the next highest New England state. Almost all the explosive growth is in the south.

The numerous lakes and ponds have become almost a liability. By law, any water body of 10 acres or more is a Great Pond and State property, but the early lawmakers failed to assure public access. Today the State has legal access to only a third of its Great Ponds. On the state's largest lake, Winnepesaukee, a famous resort for 200 years, the State owns only one 600-ft. bit of shore.

In the past, one could always find a lakeside campsite or launch a boat. Today more and more lakes in the south are ringed by houses, condominiums, motels, marinas, and fishing camps.

For years the character of New Hampshire communities and the pristine quality of the lakes were maintained by consensus, the popular will. Hostile to government regulation, New Hampshire citizens scorned zoning and other land use ordinances. When the wave of development rolled outward from Boston, money overwhelmed consensus. Developers swarmed, buying whatever acreage they could, especially around lakes. Once they had titles, few rules limited what they could do.

Citizen hostility to government is written into the tax structure: no income tax, no sales tax. Per capita taxes are the nation's lowest. Agencies such as the Division of Parks and Recreation have pathetically small budgets. When we visited in early June several years ago, State Park entrances were barricaded; funds were so limited park officials couldn't say when they'd open.

One reason for past legislative indifference to parks is the great mass of the White Mountain National Forest, 11.5% of the state's area, far above the eastern average for public land. Also, most private forest land was open to recreation. In the forested northern two-thirds of New Hampshire, it still is.

The State and citizen organizations are seeking more green space in the fast-growing south. The park system now includes 41 recreation areas with almost 30,000 acres, most of them in the southern half of the state. The largest State landholding, 13,000-acre Pisgah State Park, is in the south. So are most of the woodlands of the Society for the Protection of New Hampshire Forests.

Information on parks and recreation can be obtained from

New Hampshire Division of Parks and Recreation
105 Loudon Rd.
Concord, NH 03301
(603) 271-3254

PUBLICATION:
New Hampshire Parklands. (Guide to State Parks, Beaches, etc.) 1986.

CLIMATE

New Hampshire's weather is influenced by elevations, prevailing westerlies, and the sea. It's highly changeable, with wide daily and annual temperature swings, great differences between the same seasons in different years. The north is cooler than the south. Some of the nation's wildest weather is recorded atop Mt. Washington. Summer temperatures throughout the state are called "delightfully comfortable" by the National Climatic Center. Snowfall is heavier in the north, but snow cover is continuous throughout the winter except, at times, near the coast and the Massachusetts border.

MAPS AND PATHFINDING

This atlas is indispensable to travelers and trip planners:
The New Hampshire Atlas and Gazetteer. Freeport, ME: DeLorme Publishing, 1986.
In addition to its 60 large maps, it has information on campgrounds, canoe trips, fishing, hiking, ski touring, and much more.

It shows the boundaries of State Parks but not those of State Forests or Wildlife Management Areas. Finding route numbers and town names isn't easy. The maps show the names of many rural roads; few of these roads have street signs at intersections. The official state highway map shows State Forest boundaries but not those of WMAs. The Fish and Game Department's *Wildlife Management Area Guide* has no site maps but does provide routings.

Even with these aids, we often had difficulty finding a State Forest or Wildlife Management Area. Many aren't identified by signs or boundary markers.

FLORA AND FAUNA

With habitats ranging from ocean beaches to New England's highest peak, summaries would have little meaning. Where information was available, we've included it in entries. For example, the entry for Fox Forest relates bird species to habitats. Such data are generally applicable to similar sites.

These regional references have much information relevant to New Hampshire:

DeGraaf, Richard M., and Deborah D. Rudis. *New England Wildlife: Habitat, Natural History, and Distribution.* General Technical Report NE-108. Broomwall, PA: U.S. Department of Agriculture, Forest Service, Northeastern Forest Experiment Station, 1986.

Harris, Stuart, and others. *AMC Field Guide to Mountain Flowers of New England.* Boston: Appalachian Mountain Club, 1982.

Kulik, Stephen, Pete Salmansohn, Matthew Schmidt, and Heidi Welch. *The Audubon Society Field Guide to the Natural Places of the Northeast: Inland.* New York: Pantheon Books, 1984.

TRAILS

Most backpacking and much day hiking is on the 250 trails in the White Mountain National Forest (see entry), a 1,200-mi. network. Most of the Appalachian Trail mileage in NH is within the Forest. Information sources include the following:

Appalachian Trail Conference. *Appalachian Trail Guide to New Hampshire/Vermont.* Harpers Ferry, WV: Appalachian Trail Conference, 1985.

Daniell, Eugene S., III, ed. *AMC White Mountain Guide.* Boston: Appalachian Mountain Club, 1987.

Doan, Daniel. *Fifty Hikes in the White Mountains.* Woodstock, VT: Backcountry Publications, 1983.

Doan, Daniel. *Fifty More Hikes in New Hampshire.* Woodstock, VT: Backcountry Publications, 1986.

Trail Map and Guide to the White Mountain National Forest. Freeport, ME: DeLorme Publishing, 1987.

The *AMC White Mountain Guide* and *Fifty More Hikes* also describe hikes in the southern region. One of the most popular hiking areas here is Mt. Monadnock (see entry), northern terminus of the Metacomet-Monadnock Trail, which begins in Connecticut, and the E end of the Monadnock-Sunapee Greenway.

Trailside camping is permitted in the National Forest. It is prohibited on State lands except at designated sites. (To our surprise, we learned that the Society for Protection of New Hampshire Forests permits trailside camping at some of its sites.)

Most of the northern third of NH is timber company land. We asked a few timber companies about their public use policies and got no official answers. As we understand it, visitors won't be challenged unless they ignore postings, interfere with timber operations, or misbehave as by building fires or littering. Landowners have the right to close any road or area to visitors. Most hiking in these forests is on used and unused woods roads rather than trails.

CAMPING

The National Forest has 20 campgrounds. Informal camping is permitted anywhere except in restricted areas. The season is generally mid-May to mid-Oct. Several are open all year but with no services or road plowing.

The State has 12 campgrounds in parks and recreation areas, with almost 1,000 sites. Season is generally mid-May through mid-Oct. No reservations. Dogs and cats are prohibited. (At Greenfield and Bear Brook, dogs are permitted on certain loops but must not be left unattended. We saw dogs in two other campgrounds and were told the rule is sometimes waived unless a dog or its owner misbehaves.)

We found campgrounds with water-based recreation crowded in fine weather. Otherwise we almost always found an open site.

CANOEING

New Hampshire has many splendid canoe runs, from easy floating to challenging whitewater, including canoe-camping trips of several days. The DeLorme *Atlas* gives brief descriptions of many. More detail is provided by

Schweiker, Roioli, ed. *AMC River Guide: New Hampshire/Vermont.* Boston: Appalachian Mountain Club, 1983.

Schweiker, Roioli. *Canoe Camping Vermont and New Hampshire Rivers.* Woodstock, VT: Backcountry Publications, 1986.

BOATING, FISHING

We found no comprehensive list of public boat-launching sites. However, the volume of fishing maps shows launch sites on 81 lakes, 16 rivers, and Great Bay.

New Hampshire fishing is excellent, from rushing mountain trout streams to saltwater bays, estuaries, and open sea. The fishing maps volume tells what species can be caught, not only in the mapped waters but in several hundred other ponds and streams.

Swasey, Charlton J., and Donald A. Wilson. *New Hampshire Fishing Maps.* Freeport, ME: DeLorme Publishing, 1986.

HUNTING

New Hampshire mammals include black bear and moose as well as deer and small mammals. Moose, once near the vanishing point, have increased enough to warrant a short hunting season. Game bird species include water-fowl, grouse, woodcock, turkey, pheasant. Information can be obtained from

New Hampshire Fish and Game Department
34 Bridge St.
Concord, NH 03301
(603) 271-3421

PRIVATE ORGANIZATIONS

Society for the Protection of New Hampshire Forests
54 Portsmouth St.
Concord, NH 03301
(603) 224-9945

Since 1901 SPNHF has led the effort to restore and preserve forests. The White Mountain National Forest was established through its efforts, as well as several State Parks and State Forests. SPNHF has a number of preserves, some of them model woodlands. Its unique headquarters building is well worth a visit. On a wooded hill overlooking the Merrimack River and Concord, it uses innovative means to minimize the energy required for heating or cooling in any season. A cassette tour is offered, and a nature trail is on the site.

PUBLICATIONS: Include *Lands Map and Guide,* describing 57 of the society's preserves.

Audubon Society of New Hampshire
P.O. Box 528-B

Concord, NH 03301
(603) 224-9909

As part of a comprehensive program of nature education and preservation, the society maintains 21 preserves, most of them in the southern third of NH. Some, like Paradise Point, have nature centers with many activities. Others, like Deering, are isolated and quiet refuges. Many publications.

MAP NOTES IN TEXT

All map references (e.g., Map 26) are to the DeLorme Publishing Company's *The New Hampshire Atlas and Gazetteer* (Freeport, ME: 1986). *South:* Maps 1–36. *North:* Maps 37–60.

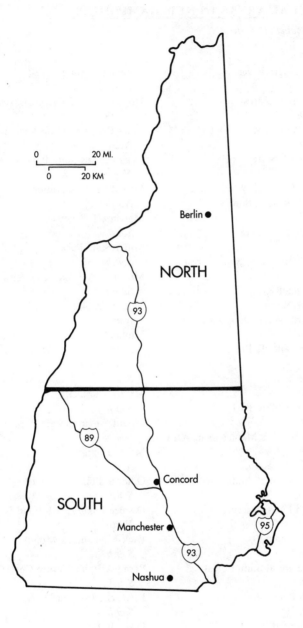

0   20 MI.

0   20 KM

Berlin ●

NORTH

93

89

Concord ●

SOUTH

Manchester ●

95

93

Nashua ●

NATURAL AREAS IN NEW HAMPSHIRE

An Alphabetical Listing

Androscoggin River
  North
Annett State Forest
  South
Appalachian Trail
  North
Bear Brook State Park
  South
Charles L. Peirce Wildlife and
  Forest Reservation
  South
Coleman State Park
  North
Connecticut Lakes State Forest
  North
Connecticut River
  North/South
Crawford Notch State Park
  North
Deering Wildlife Preserve
  South
Dixville Notch
  North
Echo Lake State Park
  North
Enfield Wildlife Management Area
  South
Fox Forest   *South*
Franconia Notch State Park
  North
Franklin Falls Reservoir
  South
Gap Mountain
  South
Gile Memorial State Forest
  South
Grafton Pond
  South
Hay Reservation
  South

Hemenway State Forest
  North
Hopkinton and Everett Lakes
  South
Jones Brook Wildlife Management
  Area   *South*
Lake Francis State Park
  North
Lost River Reservation
  North
Merrimack River
  South
Miller State Park
  South
Monadnock-Sunapee Greenway
  South
Moose Brook State Park
  North
Mount Cardigan State Park and
  State Forest   *North*
Mt. Kearsarge
  South
Mt. Monadnock
  South
Mount Sunapee State Park
  South
Mt. Washington
  North
Odiorne Point State Park
  South
Ossipee Lake/Heath Pond Bog
  North
Pack-Monadnock Mountain
  South
Paradise Point Nature Center
  South
Pawtuckaway State Park
  South
Peabody Forest
  North

Pillsbury State Park
South
Pine River State Forest
North
Pisgah State Park
South
Pondicherry Wildlife Refuge
North
Rhododendron Natural Area
South
Squam Lakes Region
North

Taves Reservation
South
Umbagog Lake
North
Wapack National Wildlife Refuge
South
White Lake State Park
North
White Mountain National Forest
North
Willard Pond Preserve
South

NATURAL AREAS IN NEW HAMPSHIRE

by Zone

North Zone

Androscoggin River
Appalachian Trail
Coleman State Park
Connecticut Lakes State Forest
Connecticut River
Crawford Notch State Park
Dixville Notch
Echo Lake State Park
Franconia Notch State Park
Hemenway State Forest
Lake Francis State Park
Lost River Reservation
Moose Brook State Park
Mount Cardigan State Park and
    State Forest
Mt. Washington
Ossipee Lake/Heath Pond Bog
Peabody Forest
Pine River State Forest
Pondicherry Wildlife Refuge
Squam Lakes Region
Umbagog Lake
White Lake State Park

White Mountain National Forest

South Zone

Annett State Forest
Bear Brook State Park
Charles L. Peirce Wildlife and
    Forest Reservation
Connecticut River
Deering Wildlife Preserve
Enfield Wildlife Management Area
Fox Forest
Franklin Falls Reservoir
Gap Mountain
Gile Memorial State Forest
Grafton Pond
Hay Reservation
Hopkinton and Everett Lakes
Jones Brook Wildlife Management
    Area
Merrimack River
Miller State Park
Monadnock-Sunapee Greenway
Mt. Kearsarge
Mt. Monadnock

South Zone continued

Mount Sunapee State Park
Odiorne Point State Park
Pack-Monadnock Mountain
Paradise Point Nature Center
Pawtuckaway State Park

Pillsbury State Park
Pisgah State Park
Rhododendron Natural Area
Taves Reservation
Wapack National Wildlife Refuge
Willard Pond Preserve

ANDROSCOGGIN RIVER
35 river miles.   North

From Errol to Berlin, beside SR 16. (Maps 53, 51.)

With rapids to Class II and III and a relatively long season, this is one of NH's most popular canoe runs. The shoreline is relatively undeveloped, but there's little public land along the route.

REFERENCES
Schweiker, Roioli, ed. *AMC River Guide:* New Hampshire/Vermont. Boston: Appalachian Mountain Club, 1983.
Schweiker, Roioli. *Canoe Camping Vermont and New Hampshire Rivers.* Woodstock, VT: Backcountry Publications, 1986.
Swasey, Charlton J., and Donald A. Wilson. *New Hampshire Fishing Maps.* Freeport, ME: DeLorme Publishing, 1986.

ANNETT STATE FOREST
New Hampshire Division of Forests and Lands   South
1,336 acres.

From US 202 at Jaffrey, SE on local roads past Squantum. (Map 3.)

The Forest includes more than half of the shoreline of Hubbard Pond, an irregularly shaped water body about 1 1/4 mi. long. Hubbard Pond Road crosses the Forest, which is typical of southern NH: flat to rolling terrain, second-growth northern hardwoods with some pine and hemlock.

ACTIVITIES
Hiking on old woods roads.

Hunting: Deer, small game.

Fishing: Smallmouth bass, pickerel, bullhead, yellow perch.

ADJACENT: Perry Reservation (Society for the Protection of New Hampshire Forests, 509 acres). From Jaffrey, 4.5 mi. E on SR 124. Park at historical marker for Wilder Chair Factory.

The site has 2 mi. of frontage on SR 124. The central feature is Tophet Swamp. It can be explored by canoeing on the Gridley River, but with several beaver dam portages.

HEADQUARTERS: 105 Loudon Rd., Concord, NH 03301; (603) 271-2214.

APPALACHIAN TRAIL
Mixed ownerships   North

Maine to Vermont.

The Trail enters NH from ME in the Mahoosuc Range, N of the White Mountain National Forest. Most of its NH mileage is within the Forest, and most trail hiking is here. Between the Forest and the VT border, it is mostly on private land, with some sections on public roads.

REFERENCE: Appalachian Trail Conference. *Appalachian Trail Guide to New Hampshire/Vermont.* Harpers Ferry, WV: Appalachian Trail Conference, 1985.

BEAR BROOK STATE PARK
New Hampshire Division of Parks and Recreation/New   South
Hampshire Division of Forests and Lands
9,585 acres.

From Manchester, N on US 3, then NE on SR 28 to sign on right. (Maps 13–14.)

The principal recreation area on Catamount Pond can accommodate 1,500 visitors in the picnic area, more on the beach and in the play areas. It's crowded in good weather. However, the trail system is extensive, and relatively few visitors venture beyond the developed area.

It was originally a National Park Service site. Facilities were built by the Civilian Conservation Corps. It was leased to the State in 1941 and eventually transferred to State ownership.

Terrain is rolling to steep. Elevation of Bear Hill is 800 ft., about 400 ft. above its base; Hall Mountain, in the S of the Park, rises to 925 ft. The area is heavily wooded. Bear Brook flows N from Hall Mountain Marsh. There are 5 ponds in addition to Catamount and a number of small streams.

INTERPRETATION

Bear Brook Nature Center is operated cooperatively with the Audubon Society of New Hampshire. *Exhibits, nature trails, daily naturalist programs in summer.*

ACTIVITIES

Camping: 81 tent sites; mid-May to mid-Oct. The camping area is reserved for campers and has its own beach.

Hiking: Over 30 mi. of hiking trails.

Hunting: Deer and small game.

Fishing: Brook trout and panfish; ponds and streams. One pond is reserved for fly fishing.

Swimming: Supervised beach.

Canoeing: Catamount Pond, Beaver Pond. No motors.

Ski touring: On marked trails apart from those used by snowmobilers.

PUBLICATIONS: Information for campers.

HEADQUARTERS: Suncook, NH 03275; (603) 485-9874.

CHARLES L. PEIRCE WILDLIFE AND FOREST RESERVATION

Society for the Protection of New Hampshire Forests   South
3,461 acres.

From SR 9 in Stoddard, 2 mi. N on SR 123. Turn right at fire station. Cross bridge. At junction, go straight on dirt road about 1 mi. Park on left beyond woods road. Trailhead at small brook. (Map 10. The bridge is shown on the map at Mill Village.)

Although this is SPNHF's second largest property, we learned of it too late for a visit. The site extends about 4 mi. N from the trailhead. Terrain is hilly. Some areas are intensively managed for timber and wildlife. Others will remain wild. The site is noted for its wildflowers. Bacon Ledge is a fine overlook.

Trout Pond is near the center. Over 10 mi. of trails and woods roads ascend ridges, traverse deep forests, pass beaver dams. Many organizations have chosen this site for field trips.

ADJACENT: *Thurston V. William Family Forest,* 379 acres, another SPNHF property, adjoins on the NW. Features include old-growth forest with large birch, white pine, sugar and red maples, beech, hemlock, and white ash. Access is a bit complicated, so we recommend obtaining the society's *Lands Map and Guide,* which has map and directions. It is recommended that hikers have compasses.

HEADQUARTERS: Society for the Protection of New Hampshire Forests, 54 Portsmouth St., Concord, NH 03301; (603) 224-9945.

COLEMAN STATE PARK

New Hampshire Division of Parks and Recreation/New   North
Hampshire Division of Forests and Lands
1,685 acres.

From US 3 at Colebrook, 6 mi. E on SR 26 to Kidderville, then N about 6 mi. (Map 56.)

Northern NH is mountainous, rugged, largely roadless except for logging roads. Coleman is on Little Diamond Pond, in the spruce-fir country, surrounded by near-wilderness. SR 26 is a scenic route, crossing the White Mountains at Dixville Notch. The developed Park area is 33 acres, the rest managed as a State Forest.

In this area, the State has developed an extensive network of snowmobile trails on timber company land. The distances between roads or settlements are great, snows usually deep, winters cold. One section of the Androscoggin Trail crosses the Park, a 55-mi. hiking route. Hiking guides mention no trails in this north country, but the woods invite the adventurous.

ACTIVITIES
Camping: 30 tent sites. Mid-May to mid-Oct.
Fishing: Trout.
Boating: Speed restriction.

HEADQUARTERS: RFD 1, Colebrook, NH 03576; (603) 237-4520.

CONNECTICUT LAKES STATE FOREST

New Hampshire Division of Forests and Lands   North
1,548 acres.

Both sides of US 3 for about 10 mi. S of the Quebec boundary. (Map 59.)

The Forest is a narrow strip of land beside the highway. It would be called a parkway in more developed country. The country beyond the strip is rugged, wild, and densely forested, roadless except for logging roads. The strip provides access to First, Second, and Third Connecticut lakes, through which the Connecticut River flows.

The general elevation is 1,200–1,400 ft., with nearby ridges over 2,000 ft. Most surrounding land is privately owned. Timber companies generally tolerate visitors on their land, but keep away from areas being logged and don't get in the way of logging trucks. Unused logging roads soon revert to muskeg.

Birds: The Audubon Society of New Hampshire considers this a prime birding area, especially for Canadian Zone species, but we couldn't find a local list. Reported species include black-backed and northern three-toed woodpeckers, spruce grouse, woodcock, saw-whet owl, common raven, Philadelphia vireo, Traill's and yellow-bellied flycatchers, boreal chickadee, redbreasted nuthatch, crossbills, purple finch, goldfinch, pine siskin, evening grosbeak, Swainson's thrush, swamp sparrow, gray jay, ruby-crowned and golden-crowned kinglets. Warblers: Tennessee, Wilson's, yellow-rumped, parula, magnolia, bay-breasted, mourning. On the lakes: common loon, ring-necked duck, goldeneye, mergansers.

Mammals: All species common to the region, including moose, black bear, bobcat, fox, otter, raccoon, porcupine, whitetail deer.

FEATURES

First Connecticut Lake, 2,807 acres, has a 19-mi. undeveloped shoreline in near-wilderness. Some of the best trout and salmon fishing in NH. Ice-out about May 1. Unpaved ramp near the dam. Some adjoining marshes.

Second Connecticut Lake, 1,286 acres, 11 mi. of wooded shoreline. Also good trout and salmon fishing. Ice-out about mid-May. Launch on Idlewild Rd., off US 3.

Third Connecticut Lake, 278 acres, at the Quebec border, is a natural body, not dammed. Launch site but no ramp. Good fishing.

East Inlet Natural Area is managed by The Nature Conservancy. The access road is on the right, just N of Second Connecticut Lake. East Inlet Pond is about 2 mi. up this road. About 3 mi. beyond is a trail to a 143-acre tract of virgin red spruce and balsam fir at Norton Pool on East Inlet Stream. This area is open to the public but serviced by a private road.

Camping: At Lake Francis State Park (see entry). Also at Moose Falls, on W side of US 3, N of Second Lake.

REFERENCES

Kulik, Stephen, Pete Salmansohn, Matthew Schmidt, and Heidi Welch. *The Audubon Society Field Guide to the Natural Places of the Northeast: Inland.* New York: Pantheon Books, 1984.

Swasey, Charlton J., and Donald A. Wilson. *New Hampshire Fishing Maps.* Freeport, ME: DeLorme Publishing, 1986.

HEADQUARTERS: Division of Parks and Recreation, P.O. Box 856D, Concord, NH 03301; (603) 271-3254.

CONNECTICUT RIVER

Mixed ownerships   North / South
260 river miles.

From Pittsburg to Vernon Dam near the MA border. (Maps 58 to 1.)

New England's longest river forms most of the VT-NH boundary. From the Canadian border, it flows through the Connecticut Lakes (see entry). The first canoe trip begins at the upper end of First Connecticut Lake.

The river valley was settled early in the colonial period. The primeval forest was felled and huge logs floated down the river. Dams provided power for mills. Roads were built on both sides of the river. Along some sections, however, new forests on the floodplain shut out the sound and sight of road traffic, or farmland lies between river and road.

Most canoeists choose these quiet sections, but it's possible to canoe the entire 260 miles. Although river flow is controlled by dams, all but the segment just below Pittsburg can be floated at any time, and that segment most of the time. The several portages are not difficult. Long segments of flatwater and quickwater are punctuated by Class I and Class II rapids and some avoidable hazards.

Camping is a problem. Only a few public or private campgrounds are along the way, often more than a day's travel apart. One can usually find an informal site without attracting unfavorable attention.

Fishing: From the Connecticut Lakes to North Stratford, this is a blue-ribbon trout stream. Farther down, it becomes a warmwater bass fishery.

REFERENCES

Canoeing on the Connecticut River. Vermont Department of Forests, Parks, and Recreation, 103 South Main St., 10 South, Waterbury, VT 05676.

The Connecticut River Guide. Connecticut River Watershed Council, 125 Combs Rd., Easthampton, MA 01027.

Schweiker, Roioli. *Canoe Camping Vermont and New Hampshire Rivers.* Woodstock, VT: Backcountry Publications, 1986.

Schweiker, Roioli. ed. *AMC River Guide: New Hampshire Vermont.* Boston: Appalachian Mountain Club, 1983.

Swasey, Charlton J., and Donald A. Wilson. *New Hampshire Fishing Maps.* Freeport, ME: DeLorme Publishing, 1986.

CRAWFORD NOTCH STATE PARK

New Hampshire Division of Parks and Recreation   North
5,950 acres.

On US 302, 12 mi. N of Bartlett. (Maps 45, 46.)

This 6-mi. mountain pass through some of the most rugged terrain of the White Mountains has been a well-traveled route since stagecoach days. The scenic 1 1/2-mi.-wide strip is surrounded by the White Mountain National Forest. The Notch is at 1,773-ft. elevation. Several nearby peaks are well above 3,700 ft., still higher ones not far off. The Appalachian Trail crosses the Park, and other trails lead to points of interest.

When loggers were felling white pines all around, the then owner of the Notch kept his forest intact. In 1911 the Society for the Protection of New Hampshire Forests persuaded the state legislature to buy it, before the National Forest was established.

FEATURES

Arethusa Falls, one of NH's highest, is reached by a moderately steep 1 1/2-mi. trail. When we last visited, the trail was badly eroded.

Silver Cascade can be seen from the road.

Frankenstein Cliff is W of the highway, across from the campground.

A *nature trail* is near the Park office.

ACTIVITIES

Camping: 30 tent sites.

Fishing: Nearby trout streams.

HEADQUARTERS: Star Route, Bartlett, NH 03812; (603) 374-2272.

DEERING WILDLIFE PRESERVE

Audubon Society of New Hampshire   South
500 acres.

W of Manchester. SR 149 through Deering. Right on Clement Hill Rd. Look for small Preserve sign marking right turn on a narrow dirt road. Site is near top of hill. (Maps 11–12.)

For a quiet hike in an out-of-the-way forest, this is the place. The parking area is large enough for half a dozen cars, but the weeds stood tall and we saw no signs of recent use, there or on the white-blazed trail. Yet the trail was deeply worn, evidence of much use in years gone by. The forest now is mostly a mixture of northern hardwoods, trees 4 to 6 inches in diameter, but we saw a few ancient white pines, so gnarled and twisted the loggers had let them be. A few hundred yards into the woods we came to a massive stone wall, once the boundary of a field. We didn't find the end of the trail. Chances are it continues beyond the Audubon property line.

Although southern NH is the fastest-growing part of New England, this area is developing slowly. Most of the nearby roads are unpaved, and some are rough and narrow.

HEADQUARTERS: Audubon Society of New Hampshire, P.O. Box 528B, Concord, NH 03301; (603) 224-9909.

DIXVILLE NOTCH

New Hampshire Division of Parks and Recreation   North
137 acres.

On SR 26 between Colebrook and Errol. (Map 56.)

SR 26 is a fine scenic highway. The Notch is a rocky cleft in the mountains through which the highway squeezes. Waterfalls and cascades are on Flume Brook and Cascade Brook. A trail leads up to Table Rock. Other trails and woods roads lead into the surrounding near-wilderness region.

ECHO LAKE STATE PARK

New Hampshire Division of Parks and Recreation   North
396 acres.

From North Conway on US 302, W on River Rd. (Map 42.)

This day use park is open weekends beginning on Memorial Day, daily from late June to Labor Day. Most visitors come to picnic and swim, but there are attractive hiking trails around the lake and up to Cathedral and White Horse ledges. Cathedral Ledge can also be reached by an auto road.

ENFIELD WILDLIFE MANAGEMENT AREA

New Hampshire Fish and Game Department   South
2,600 acres.

From Enfield Center, S on SR 4 A. Right on Bog Road about 2 mi. Sign and parking on right. (Map 25.)

When we visited, a rough washboard on Bog Road helped cars churn up clouds of dust. At other times, birders would enjoy walking the road, which offers brook, ponds, marsh, fields, and woods.

The sign and small parking area are the trailhead for Cole Pond. It's a mile-plus hike on a pleasant trail, ascending gradually from swamp forest to a 17-acre pond in a scenic setting. Fly fishing only. The couple we met on the trail had been swimming. "Delightful!" they said.

The forest is mostly mixed northern hardwoods with a few scattered large white pines, the understory generally light enough to permit bushwhacking.

No site map is available, and we saw no boundary signs. Along Bog Road are unmarked gates that may indicate State land. The WMA includes frontage on George Pond, at the 4A-Bog Rd. intersection, which attracts many waterfowl in season. The WMA borders 96-acre Smith Pond (which is closed to fishing) and 7-acre Halfmile Pond, both shown on Map 25. Prospect Hill, 2,100 ft., seems to be the highest point. On the upper slopes, the mixed hardwoods merge into spruce-fir.

ACTIVITIES

Hunting: Deer, upland game.

Fishing: Brook trout in Cole Pond. Brook trout, largemouth bass, pickerel, bullhead, and yellow perch in George Pond.

NEARBY: Grafton Pond (see entry).

HEADQUARTERS: 34 Bridge St., Concord, NH 03301; (603) 271-3421.

FOX FOREST
New Hampshire Division of Forests and Lands   South
1,445 acres.

From US 202 at Hillsborough, NW on SR 107. (Map 11.)

In 1922 Caroline A. Fox donated the original 348 acres and established a trust fund that has supported a continuing program of research and education. Far more information about flora and fauna is offered here than at other State sites, in publications, exhibits, classes, and nature trails.

The area is hilly, moderately rugged. Much of it was open farmland in the 1930s. The resident research forester undertook comparative studies, letting some sections revert naturally, planting others with larch, scotch pine, jack pine, spruce, and Douglas-fir. Most of the site is again forested. Some portions of the original forest remain, never logged so far as is known.

The site has over 20 mi. of trails.

Plants: Lists of trees, flowering plants, and ferns are available. Native trees include white, red, and pitch pine; red and black spruce, balsam fir, eastern redcedar, tamarack, eastern hemlock; and hardwoods: black willow, trembling and large-toothed aspen, butternut, shagbark hickory; black, yellow, paper, and gray birch; speckled alder, red and white oak; sugar, red, and striped maple. Also identified are the numerous introduced species, American and exotic. The extensive shrub list includes American yew, sweet gale, spice bush, witch hazel, shadbush, wild plum, dogwoods, blueberries, snowberry, withe-rod.

Birds: The summer checklist suggests where to look for various species. *Around buildings, shade trees, and orchards:* rock and mourning doves, ruby-throated hummingbird, yellow-bellied sapsucker, hairy and downy woodpeckers, eastern phoebe, eastern wood-pewee, tree and barn swallows, black-capped chickadee, tufted titmouse, white-breasted nuthatch, house wren, American robin, eastern bluebird, red-eyed and warbling vireos, house sparrow, northern oriole, rose-breasted grosbeak, purple finch, chipping sparrow. *Freshwater marshes, swamps, and bogs:* pied-billed grebe, great blue heron,

American bittern, black duck, wood duck, mallard, hooded merganser, American woodcock, spotted sandpiper, belted kingfisher, eastern kingbird, alder and olive-sided flycatchers, tree swallow, long-billed marsh wren, northern and Louisiana waterthrushes, yellow warbler, common yellowthroat, red-winged blackbird, swamp sparrow. *Fields, meadows, and brush borders:* turkey vulture; red-tailed, red-shouldered, and broad-winged hawks; kestrel, ring-necked pheasant, whip-poor-will, common nighthawk, eastern phoebe, eastern kingbird, great crested flycatcher, chimney swift; tree, bank, barn, and cliff swallows; common crow, blue jay, gray catbird, brown thrasher, American robin, cedar waxwing, European starling, chestnut-sided and yellow warblers, common yellowthroat, indigo bunting, rufous-sided towhee, American goldfinch; field, song, vesper, and savannah sparrows; northern flicker, killdeer, mourning and rock doves. *Birds of mixed woods:* Hawks—goshawk, sharp-shinned, red-tailed, red-shouldered, broad-winged. Ruffed grouse; great horned, barred, and saw-whet owls; pileated, hairy, and downy woodpeckers; yellow-bellied sapsucker, least flycatcher, eastern wood-pewee, black-capped chickadee, white-breasted and red-breasted nuthatches, brown creeper, wood and hermit thrushes, veery, solitary and red-eyed vireos. Warblers: black-and-white, magnolia, yellow-rumped, black-throated green, black-throated blue, blackburnian, ovenbird, Canada, American redstart, Nashville, parula, pine. Scarlet tanager, rose-breasted grosbeak, purple finch, slate-colored junco, white-throated sparrow.

Mammals: Include snowshoe hare, red and gray squirrels, chipmunk, fox, porcupine, raccoon, beaver, skunk, otter, muskrat, mink, whitetail deer, occasional bobcat.

INTERPRETATION

Forestry museum.

Environmental Center is used chiefly for classes, groups.

Mud Pond Natural Area, reached by 1-mi. trail, has a quaking bog with insectivorous plants, beaver lodge.

Hemlock Ravine Natural Area, along Gerry Brook, has an old-growth stand of beech and hemlock.

Black Gum Swamp Natural Area: a glacial kettle that has evolved into a forest growing on a deep bed of peat.

Nature trails include Mushroom Trail, Tree Identification Loop Trail.

PUBLICATIONS

Fox Forest Notes, a bulletin series.

Trail guide, leaflet with map.

HEADQUARTERS: Hillsboro, NH 03244; (603) 464-3453.

FRANCONIA NOTCH STATE PARK

New Hampshire Division of Parks and Recreation   North

6,786 acres.

On I-93 S of Franconia. (Map 44.)

The 8-mi.-long pass between the peaks of the Franconia and Kinsman ranges is one of the most spectacular areas in the White Mountains. It is also one of the busiest. The current park leaflet says; "Interstate 93 through Franconia Notch has resulted in over $20 million dollars in new visitor facilities . . . ." (and considerably more traffic and congestion!) It is surrounded by the White Mountain National Forest, however, and numerous trails offer routes to places of quiet beauty.

Elevations in the Park range from 1,200 to 2,000 ft. Nearby peaks include 5,249-ft. Mt. Lafayette, 4,040-ft. Cannon Mountain. The Pemigewasset River flows through the Notch. Profile Lake and Echo Lake are beside the highway.

Since I-93 is now the only road through the Notch, it's advisable to have the Park leaflet or other detailed map at hand, so as to choose the right exit. To drive from Park Headquarters to the campground or the Flume Visitor Center, one must get back on the Interstate.

Plants: Trees of the valley floor are mostly northern hardwoods, uncut since the late 1800s: yellow birch, beech, sugar maple. Above 2,000 ft. on the hillsides are mature red spruce and balsam fir with some white birch, the less accessible areas never logged. Flowers of the valley include dutchman's-breeches, spring beauty, violets, trilliums, Solomon's-seal. On slopes up to 4,500-ft. elevation are subalpine flowers, many blooming in May and early June. Above the timberline, some arctic species occur.

Birds: Large flocks of Canada and snow geese often migrate through the valley. Other waterfowl are sometimes seen on the lakes. Many hawks come through, as well as golden and bald eagles and common raven. About 100 species have been recorded.

Mammals: Severe winters and deep snow limit resident mammal populations. Bear and moose are occasional visitors. Deer are present, not abundant. More common species include red fox, weasel, snowshoe hare, porcupine, mink, fisher, raccoon, bobcat. chipmunk, mole, woodchuck. Most streams are too rapid for beaver.

FEATURES

The Flume is a unique geological area with an 800-ft. gorge, walls 70 to 90 ft. high, width as narrow as 12 ft. Other features include Avalanche Falls, Liberty Gorge and Cascade, water-washed Table Rock, glacier-deposited boulders. The area has a network of trails.

Old Man of the Mountains, a 40-ft. profile in granite 1,200 ft. above Profile Lake.

Cannon Mountain, a ski area, has North America's first aerial passenger tram, which transports summer visitors to the top for fine vistas. An observation tower is near the tram station. One can also hike to the top.

The Basin, beside the highway, is a 20-ft. granite pothole at the base of a waterfall.

INTERPRETATION

Flume Visitor Center has film introduction to the Park's natural and cultural history.

Interpretive panels, about 40, are throughout the Park.

ACTIVITIES

Camping: 98 sites. Late May to mid.-Oct.

Hiking, backpacking: The Appalachian Trail crosses the Park. Several Appalachian Mountain Club huts are within hiking range. Local trails to Artist Bluff, Bald Mountain, Lonesome Lake, Mt. Pemigewasset, other points of interest.

Fishing: Brook trout stocked in Echo and Profile Lakes.

Swimming: In Echo Lake.

Skiing, ski touring: Cannon Mountain has 26 mi. of trails and slopes.

PUBLICATIONS

Folder with map.

The Flume Guide.

Roaring River Nature Trail Guide.

REFERENCES

Doan, Daniel. *Fifty Hikes in the White Mountains.* Woodstock, VT: Backcountry Publications, 1983.

Kostecke, Diane M., ed. *Franconia Notch.* Concord: Society for the Protection of New Hampshire Forests, 1975.

Kulik, Stephen, Pete Salmansohn, Matthew Schmidt, and Heidi Welch. *The Audubon Society Field Guide to the Natural Places of the Northeast: Inland.* New York: Pantheon Books, 1984.

HEADQUARTERS: Franconia, NH 03580; (603) 823-5563.

FRANKLIN FALLS RESERVOIR

New Hampshire Fish and Game Department/New Hampshire   South
  Division of Forests and Lands
3,704 acres.

Along the Pemigewasset River between Bristol and Franklin. Access from SR 3A and SR 127. (Map 27.)

The Franklin Falls Dam near Franklin was built by the U.S. Army Corps of Engineers for flood control. The reservoir, on the long, narrow floodplain, is normally empty, and the Pemigewasset River flows through. As recently as the late 1960s, the river was heavily polluted. Now it's clean enough for fishing and pleasant canoeing. Perhaps for swimming, although we wouldn't try it after a rainstorm. The area is managed by the New Hampshire Division of Forests and Lands, whose first task was forest improvement.

ACTIVITIES

Hunting: Pheasants have been stocked.

Fishing: Brook and rainbow trout. Sections near the road are heavily fished, remote sections lightly.

Canoeing: The run from Bristol to Franklin, 15 mi., depends in part on water releases from a hydroelectric dam. Rapids to Class II, with stretches of flatwater.

REFERENCES

Schweiker, Roioli, ed. *AMC River Guide: New Hampshire, Vermont.* Boston: Appalachian Mountain Club, 1983.

Swasey, Charlton J., and Donald A. Wilson. *New Hampshire Fishing Maps.* Freeport, ME: DeLorme Publishing, 1986.

HEADQUARTERS: 34 Bridge St., Concord, NH 03301; (603) 271-3421.

GAP MOUNTAIN

Society for the Protection of New Hampshire Forests   South
1,107 acres.

From Troy, take SR 12 0.4 mi. S. Turn left on Quarry Rd. At a sharp left, a woods road continues straight, uphill. Park, hike up hill, look for trail markers on left. (Map 2.)

Many fine natural areas in New England have been saved from development by concerned citizens and landowners. The story of Gap Mountain is more complex than most, acquisitions being made over more than a decade. The *Monadnock Guide* tells how it was done.

SW of the more imposing Mt. Monadnock, Gap has three main peaks, the highest 1,862 ft. It's an easier climb. The northern and middle peaks are open. The wooded southern peak is a protected natural area. The site includes two bogs and a rich variety of flora and fauna. The Metacomet-Monadnock Trail crosses the site.

PUBLICATION: *Monadnock Guide.*

HEADQUARTERS: Society for the Protection of New Hampshire Forests, 54 Portsmouth St., Concord, NH 03301; (603) 224-9945.

GILE MEMORIAL STATE FOREST
New Hampshire Division of Forests and Lands   South
6,681 acres.

Crossed by SR 4 A, near Springfield. (Map 26.)

The DeLorme *Atlas* map shows the boundaries of the Forest but not the private inholdings, of which there are many along 4 A. We saw one Forest sign where the highway leaves the Forest on the SE side; also a parking area and trailhead at Mud Pond. Several old woods roads along the highway looked promising for hiking but not for vehicles without 4-wheel drive.

The terrain is flat to rolling, with a few hills and scattered small wetlands. The land, once cleared, is now heavily forested with mixed northern hardwoods, pine, and hemlock.

Except in hunting season, the site has few visitors.

HEADQUARTERS: 105 Loudon Rd., Concord, NH 03301; (603) 271-2214.

GRAFTON POND
Society for the Protection of New Hampshire Forests   South
935 acres/235-acre lake.

From Enfield, SE on SR 4A. Left on Bluejay Rd. (Map 26.)

A natural pond was raised by a dam. The Society acquired the surrounding land in 1984, assuring that the lake would remain undeveloped. With depths to 66 ft., a rocky shoreline, and many small islands, it's a lightly fished, highly regarded smallmouth bass fishery. The 7-mi. shoreline provides many nesting sites for loons. Many anglers fly-fish from canoes. Motors are limited to 6 hp. Camping is prohibited.

NEARBY: Enfield Wildlife Management Area (see entry).

REFERENCE: Swasey, Charlton J., and Donald A. Wilson. *New Hampshire Fishing Maps.* Freeport, ME: DeLorme Publishing, 1986.

HAY RESERVATION
Society for the Protection of New Hampshire Forests   South
675 acres.

> From the S end of Lake Sunapee, take SR 103 A (E shore) 2.9 mi., then right on Chalk Pond Rd. to abandoned Old County Rd. and walk in. (Map 19.)

Old County Road bisects the site. Adjoining, with lake frontage, is a 144-acre undeveloped National Wildlife Refuge. Sunset Hill, shown on the DeLorme *Atlas* map, is a pleasant hiking destination. Most of the site is managed as a productive woodlot, but a natural area is preserved along Beech Brook.

HEMENWAY STATE FOREST
New Hampshire Division of Forests and Lands   North
1,958 acres.

> From Conway, 9 mi. SW on SR 16 to Chocorua; W 2 mi. on SR 113, then NW on SR 113A. (Map 41.)

About 6 mi. from Conway, look for *Lovejoy Marsh Wildlife Preserve,* a beaver marsh with good birding. A dirt road crosses the marsh. 3 mi. beyond is picturesque *Chocorua Lake,* 222 acres, at the base of Mt. Chocorua. Fishing for brook trout, smallmouth bass, pickerel, hornpout, best from mid-Apr. to early June. Hand-carried boats can be launched; no motors.

The Forest, just S of the White Mountain National Forest, is rolling to hilly, mostly in conifers, chiefly white pine. The *Big Pines Natural Area,* 125 acres, is a 150-year-old coniferous forest on a wild river. The largest white pine has a 42-in. diameter.

Hiking: On old woods roads and local trails. Trail to lookout tower. Nearby, off SR 16, are trails to Mt. Chocorua and other destinations. (Mt. Chocorua has been called the State's most-climbed mountain, but the most popular hiking routes are from the Kancamagus Highway on the N.)

NEARBY: White Lake State Park. Camping. (See entry.)

HEADQUARTERS: New Hampshire Division of Forests and Lands, 105 Loudon Rd., Concord, NH 03301; (603) 271-2214.

HOPKINTON AND EVERETT LAKES

U.S. Army Corps of Engineers/New Hampshire Division of   South
    Department of Parks and Recreation/New Hampshire Fish and Game
7,342 acres of land; 650 acres of permanent water.

W of Concord. From I-89, Exit 5, then N and E on US 202. (Maps 20 and 12.)

The Hopkinton Dam on the Contocook River and the Everett Dam on the Piscataquog River, some miles to the S, were built in 1962–1963 for flood control. They formed relatively small permanent pools connected by a canal and Drew Lake, with far more extensive storage areas branching along the floodplains of the two rivers and tributary streams. The project required relocation or abandonment of State and local roads, a railroad line, power and telephone lines.

The maps suggest a cluttered area. It isn't. Driving along the secondary roads we saw some private homes, but most of the land above the floodplain is heavily wooded, young northern hardwoods with scattered white pines, spruce and fir intermixed on upper hillsides.

No trail map is available, and we saw no marked trails. Hiking opportunities aren't hard to find, however. We saw several old woods roads, and bushwhacking on the floodplain is no problem. The area is closed to off-road vehicles.

Birds: No checklist or species record is available, but the variety of habitats indicates a diversity of species, including waterfowl and shorebirds in season.

Mammals: New Hampshire Fish and Game Department says all upland species except moose and bear.

FEATURES
The federal land is available for public use. Most of it has been leased to the State agencies for recreation management. The principal features are

shown on the *Atlas* maps, but the map available from the Corps is easier to read. Sites of special interest include

Elm Brook Pool Park, near Hopkinton Dam and Information Center. Boat launch, swimming, picnicking, nature trail.

Clough State Park, map 12. Swimming, picnicking.

Drew Lake and Canal, on Map 12 but not labeled. Launch.

Stark Pond, Map 12. 60-acre open water marsh. Fishing.

Stumpfield Marsh, Map 20. 95-acre open marsh. Boat launch, fishing.

The sites with swimming and picnicking are crowded on warm summer weekends.

ACTIVITIES

Hiking: Possible short day hikes on unmarked routes.

Hunting: Good waterfowl hunting. Pheasant stocked.

Fishing: We saw a few people fishing. However, Charlton Swasey and Donald Wilson's comprehensive *New Hampshire Fishing Maps* (Freeport, ME: DeLorme, 1986) makes no mention of these waters.

NEARBY: *Smith Pond Bog,* 55 acres, a New Hampshire Audubon Society Preserve, has a kettlehole pond surrounded by a bog with a red maple swamp. Boardwalk. Great botanical diversity.

Access by SR 9, 1/2 mi. W of Hopkinton Village. Trail is opposite Gage Hill Rd.

PUBLICATION: Folder with site map.

HEADQUARTERS: U.S. Army Corps of Engineers, Franklin Falls Dam, P.O. Box 351, Franklin, NH 03235.

JONES BROOK WILDLIFE MANAGEMENT AREA

New Hampshire Fish and Game Department   South
863 acres.

NW of Rochester. From Middleton Corners, N 2 1/2 mi. on Wolfeboro Road ("Kings Highway" on the DeLorme *Atlas* map). The next 3/4 mi., on the right, is WMA frontage. Walk-in dirt road in 1/2 mi. (Map 30.)

Varied habitat. Steep, rocky, burned-over terrain in the N. Flat with good softwood cover in the S. A 25-acre, fly-fishing only, trout pond is in the center. All upland game, including moose. A major deer wintering area.

HEADQUARTERS: New Hampshire Fish and Game Department, 34 Bridge St., Concord, NH 03301; (603) 271-3421.

LAKE FRANCIS STATE PARK
Division of Parks and Recreation   North
38 acres.

Far N. From Pittsburg, about 6 mi. NE on US 3, then S to entrance. (Map 59; doesn't show the Park.)

It's just a small campground but it's on a 2,051-acre lake in gorgeous country at the gateway to the Connecticut Lakes. The lake is artificial, supplying water for hydropower. The shore is heavily forested and undeveloped. The park attendant knew of no hiking trails nearby. The DeLorme *Atlas* map shows a few, and we saw many little-used woods roads.

ACTIVITIES
Camping: 36 sites.
Fishing: Maximum lake depth is 85 ft. Excellent trout and salmon fishing. Also large pickerel.
Boating: Ramp.

Swimming is prohibited.

HEADQUARTERS: Division of Parks and Recreation, P.O. Box 856D, Concord, NH 03301; (603) 271-3254.

LOST RIVER RESERVATION
Society for the Protection of New Hampshire Forests   North
146 acres.

From North Woodstock on I-93, W on SR 112 to Kinsman Notch. (Map 39.)

Open June–Aug.: 9 A.M.–6 P.M.; May, Sept., Oct.: 9 A.M.–5:30 P.M.

The Reservation, the society's first, was acquired in 1912, the year the society persuaded Congress to establish the White Mountain National Forest. In scenic Kinsman Notch, surrounded by the Forest, the Reservation includes a dramatic rocky gorge with waterfalls, great tumbled boulders, caves, giant potholes with crystal-clear water, a nature garden with 300 varieties of native wildflowers, a small natural history museum, a nature center, and several trails. When we visited in 1987, guided walks were being offered daily at 1 P.M.

The Lost River vanishes beneath the jumble of boulders. Visitors can explore the natural caves and passages underneath these huge rocks.

The Reservation is managed by the White Mountains Attraction Association, which operates its gift shop and cafeteria.

ACTIVITIES

Camping: The Wildwood Campground of the Forest Service is about 2 1/2 mi. N on SR 112.

Hiking: The Dilley Trail, maintained by the SPNHF, is a scenic route up the Kinsman Notch Cliffs to the Appalachian Trail. Some of the spruce trees on the upper cliffs are more than 400 years old. The Kinsman Notch Ecology Trail passes a beaver pond.

PUBLICATION: Tour leaflet.

HEADQUARTERS: Society for the Protection of New Hampshire Forests, 54 Portsmouth St., Concord, NH 03301; (603) 224-9945.

MERRIMACK RIVER

60 river miles.   South

From Franklin to the MA border.

The Merrimack River has friends: the Merrimack River Watershed Council. Flowing through the state's most heavily populated region, the river became heavily polluted. Today it's clean enough to support fish populations. Efforts are being made to restore the anadromous Atlantic salmon and shad.

The upstream watershed has several flood-control dams. Along the river are dams built for water power. The Council identified a 33-mi. segment of the river, S from the confluence of the Pemmy and the Winnepesaukee, as free-flowing and worthy of inclusion in the national Wild and Scenic River system. The council has successfully opposed construction of a hydro dam at Sewall's Falls.

The 60 mi. in NH are canoeable, with portages around dams. Stretches of flatwater are punctuated with some Class I and Class II rapids. In general, the upstream segments are the most attractive.

REFERENCES
   Schweiker, Roioli, ed. *AMC River Guide: New Hampshire, Vermont.* Boston: Appalachian Mountain Club, 1983.
   Schweiker, Roioli. *Canoe Camping Vermont and New Hampshire Rivers.* Woodstock, VT: Backcountry Publications, 1986.
   Swasey, Charlton J., and Donald A. Wilson. *New Hampshire Fishing Maps.* Freeport, ME: DeLorme Publishing, 1986.

INFORMATION: Merrimack River Watershed Council, 694 Main St., West Newbury, MA 01958.

MILLER STATE PARK
New Hampshire Division of Parks and Recreation   South
83 acres.

On SR 101, 3 mi. W of Peterborough. (Map 3.)

NH's oldest park sits atop South Pack Monadnock Mountain. A paved road ascends to the 2,288-ft. summit. Most visitors come for the view or to picnic. The vista includes Mt. Monadnock (see entry) 12 mi. away.

Hiking: The Wapack Trail is a 21-mi. route from Ashburnham, MA, to and across the Pack Monadnocks.

ADJACENT: The Wapack National Wildlife Refuge (see entry) can be reached by the Wapack Trail.

REFERENCE: Daniell, Eugene S., III, ed. *AMC White Mountain Guide.* Boston: Appalachian Mountain Club, 1987. (See "Wapack Trail.")

MONADNOCK-SUNAPEE GREENWAY
Society for the Protection of New Hampshire   South
   Forests/Appalachian Mountain Club
51 trail miles.

From Mount Sunapee State Park through Pillsbury State Park to Mt. Monadnock (see entries). (Map 2 to map 19.)

In 1976 the SPNHF and AMC completed initial clearing of this remarkable footpath. The route follows highlands wherever possible, dropping down into meadows and streams, on the divide between the Connecticut and Merrimack River watersheds. Although the trail is anchored in State land at each end, what lies between are private holdings. The sponsoring organizations had to seek easements or permissions from landowners to cross their properties.

Our last information indicates the trail is still open. Keeping the goodwill of landowners is essential if it is to remain open; one owner offended by litter, vandalism, or other nuisance could block it.

Obtaining and keeping permission to maintain wayside campsites is touchy. Don't plan an overnight hike without getting the latest information from SPNHF or AMC.

PUBLICATION: *The Monadnock-Sunapee Greenway Trail Guide.*

HEADQUARTERS: Society for the Protection of New Hampshire Forests, 54 Portsmouth St., Concord, NH 03301. Appalachian Mountain Club, 5 Joy St., Boston, MA 02108.

MOOSE BROOK STATE PARK

New Hampshire Division of Parks and Recreation   North
755 acres.

Off US 2, 2 mi. W of Gorham. (Map 50.)

This is a good base for sightseeing, hiking, and fishing. The Park, at the foot of the Crescent Range, lies between and close to two portions of the White Mountain National Forest. The Presidential Range is to the S. Moose Brook, a trout stream, is tributary to the nearby Androscoggin River.

Camping: 42 sites. Late June to Labor Day; weekends from mid-May.

HEADQUARTERS: RFD 1, Berlin, NH 03570; (603) 466-3860.

MOUNT CARDIGAN STATE PARK AND STATE FOREST

New Hampshire Division of Parks and Recreation/New   North
   Hampshire Division of Forests and Lands
5,655 acres.

Off US 4 and SR 118, about 4 1/2 mi. from Canaan. (Map 32.)

Mt. Cardigan, 3,121 ft., is popular with hikers. A network of trails surrounds the mountain, offering several routes to the top. More than a century ago, vegetation on the upper slope was destroyed by fire. Consequent erosion stripped the dome to bare rock. A fire tower is at the top, and the vistas are fine. Erosion is now a problem on the more heavily used trails.

Hiking: The shortest and easiest route to the summit is West Ridge Trail, 1.3 mi. High trails lead to nearby peaks including Firescrew, 3,040 ft., and South, 2,920 ft. More than 30 mi. of trails in the network.

NEARBY

Cardigan Reservation, 1,000 acres. The Appalachian Mountain Club maintains a lodge here for hikers and backpackers. From Bristol, N on SR 3 A to S end of Newfound Lake, then 9.3 mi. W. (AMC Cardigan Lodge, RFD, Bristol, NH 03222.)

Wellington State Beach, on Newfound Lake.

Paradise Point Nature Center (see entry).

HEADQUARTERS: Division of Parks and Recreation, P.O. Box 856D, Concord, NH 03301; (603) 271-3254.

MT. KEARSARGE

New Hampshire Division of Parks and Recreation/New   South
Hampshire Division of Forests and Lands
4,460 acres.

NW of Concord. S side: From I-89, exit 8; SR 103 to Warner, then N. N side: I-89 Exit 10; N on local road toward Wilmot Flat. (Maps 19, 20, 26.)

Not to be confused with Kearsarge North Mountain near North Conway, Mt. Kearsarge is a complex including Rollins and Winslow State Parks, a State Forest, and Fish and Game lands. At 2,937 ft., it's the highest point for some miles around and provides fine vistas. The top is bare rock showing glacial striae. Upper slopes have stunted, wind-torn spruce. Lower are mixed conifers and northern hardwoods.

On the N side, a scenic drive in Winslow State Park ends in a parking area and viewpoint. From here, it's a steep mile-long trail to the summit and a fire tower. On the S side, a drive in Rollins State Park leads to an easy 1/2-mi. trail.

REFERENCES

Daniell, Eugene S., III, ed. *AMC White Mountain Guide.* Boston: Appalachian Mountain Club, 1987.

Doan, Daniel. *Fifty More Hikes in New Hampshire.* Woodstock, VT: Backcountry Publications, 1986.

MT. MONADNOCK

New Hampshire Division of Parks and Recreation/Society   South
for the Protection of New Hampshire Forests
5,000 acres.

Off SR 124, 4 mi. N of Jaffrey. (Map 2.)

Is it a natural area? Some say only Mt. Fuji attracts more climbers. Here several thousand come on pleasant weekends, over 100,000 in a year. Once one could drive a toll road to the summit. That road is now a hikers' route. Halfway House, a resort built in 1861, is gone. Once there were about 80 trails to the summit. Most of them are now closed and revegetating. Of the presently open routes, about a dozen, not all are maintained.

The 3,165-ft. peak is by no means the state's highest, and it rises less than 2,000 ft. from its base. But it is a monadnock, an isolated mountain on a plain, and thus conspicuous.

The original forest was much abused. After logging came sheep grazing, and what forest remained was burned, they say, to drive off wolves. By 1820 the upper 300 to 500 ft. were stripped of soil. The top is now bare rock. On the lower slopes, a regenerated forest is a healthy mix of conifers and hardwoods.

The townspeople of Jaffrey led the preservation movement, buying some of the land in 1884. State acquisition began in 1905. In 1913 the Society for Protection of New Hampshire Forests began purchases. Most of the mountain and lower slopes are now owned by the society and leased to the State. Monadnock State Park now occupies 1,009 acres.

Monadnock Visitor Center has exhibits, slide programs, publications, nature trails, guided hikes. Several summit trails begin here.

ACTIVITIES

Camping: 21 sites at the State Park.

Hiking: 30 mi. of trails. This is the E end of the 51-mi. Monadnock-Sunapee Greenway (see entry). It is also the northern terminus of the Metacomet-Monadnock Trail that extends from Connecticut across Massachusetts.

PUBLICATIONS
   Leaflet.
   Forest Nature Trail Guide.
   Monadnock Guide. (SPNHF.)

REFERENCES
   AMC White Mountain Guidebook Committee, *AMC White Mountain Guide.* Boston: Appalachian Mountain Club, 1987.
   Doan, Daniel. *Fifty More Hikes in New Hampshire.* Woodstock, VT: Backcountry Publications, 1986.
   Kulik, Stephen, Pete Salmansohn, Matthew Schmidt, and Heidi Welch. *The Audubon Society Field Guide to the Natural Places of the Northeast: Inland.* New York: Pantheon Books, 1984.

HEADQUARTERS: Monadnock State Park, Jaffrey Center, NH 03454; (603) 532-8862.

MOUNT SUNAPEE STATE PARK
New Hampshire Division of Parks and Recreation   South
2,763 acres.

On SR 103, 3 mi. W of Newbury. (Map 19.)

Mt. Sunapee, 2,720 ft., was fast being stripped of trees when the Society for the Protection of New Hampshire Forests bought its first 600 acres in 1911, including a 256-acre remnant of virgin timber and Lake Solitude, a small glacial lake. Holdings were increased until the State bought the land in 1948.

It's a busy place. In winter it's a ski area. In summer the main chair lift takes visitors to the top, where the lodge offers meals and views. Across the road is Sunapee State Beach, with bathhouse, refreshment stand, picnic area, and launching ramp on 4,085-acre Sunapee Lake.

For those who seek the quiet places, there are fine hiking trails, notably the 51-mi. Monadnock-Sunapee Greenway, which links Mt. Sunapee and Mt. Monadnock (see entry).

Camping is available at Pillsbury State Park (see entry).

HEADQUARTERS: Division of Parks and Recreation, P.O. Box 856D, Concord, NH 03301; (603) 271-3254.

MT. WASHINGTON
U.S. Forest Service   North
Within the White Mountain National Forest.

From SR 16 N of Pinkham Notch. (Map 46.)

The toll road is open mid-May to Oct., weather permitting.

The highest peak in the Northeast, 6,288 ft., is one of 11 in the Presidential Range, 6 of the others towering over 5,000 ft. Visitors can drive to the top on a toll road, ride up on the cog railway, or hike on any of several trails. In doing so, they cross the timberline more than 1,000 ft. below the summit and enter into a region of near-arctic conditions.

The mountain is broad and massive, with three major ridges, secondary ridges, numerous valleys and ravines. Slopes range from gentle to steep. Down the slopes many streams rush over falls and cataracts.

Mt. Washington has long attracted attention and visitors. The Summit House was built in 1852. The toll road to the summit was completed in 1861, the cog railway in 1869. In 1867 the State sold 2,000 acres, including the summit. Later Dartmouth College bought 60 acres surrounding the summit. Still later the State repurchased the summit. This is now Mount Washington State Park, but the State's title is subject to easements and leases pertaining to the toll road, cog railway, weather station, and television broadcasting facilities.

The first weather observatory was built in 1870. There is much weather to observe, considered by some to be the world's worst. On the summit was recorded the highest wind velocity ever known on Earth's surface: 231 mph. Combine this with subzero temperatures and the wind-chill factor rivals anything Antarctica can offer. More than once hikers who set out on fine, sunny days have been caught in sudden, blinding blizzards and perished.

Plants: Vegetation below timberline is typical of the White Mountain National Forest (see entry). At that elevation, the forest becomes krummholz, a low tangle of spruce and fir, stunted and twisted by fierce wind and cold. Above is the largest alpine zone in the eastern United States, extending to neighboring mountaintops. Here are low-growing sedges and heaths, carpeting mosses, and wildflowers that bloom even as they poke up through melting snow in June.

FEATURES
The summit has visitor information, rest rooms, post office, snack shop, souvenir shop—and shelter from high winds.

Great Gulf and *Tuckerman Ravine* are large glacial cirques, dramatic features attractive to hikers and mountain skiers.

Alpine Garden, a natural feature noted for its wildflowers, is on a trail between the auto road and Tuckerman Ravine.

Glen Ellis Falls is one of several impressive falls and cataracts.

ACTIVITIES

Hiking, backpacking: Several trails ascend the mountain. The Appalachian Trail crosses it. Trails link with the trail network of the National Forest. Many people hike the mountain, but all should be warned: It's dangerous at any season.

The climb is steep and strenuous: about 4,000 ft. in 4 miles. 100-mph winds can occur in any season, along with rain, snow, or cold to threaten hypothermia. Weather, including clouds and fog, can blind the hiker, and this is a grave threat above timberline where the trails are marked only by stone cairns. Many hikers, leaving one cairn before they can see the next, have become hopelessly lost.

Even if it's a sunny July day, be prepared. First and foremost that means understanding the hazards and how to meet them. It requires trail maps and knowing how to read them, a compass, proper clothing, and survival gear. Know in advance what to do if bad weather strikes.

Trailside camping is not permitted above timberline between May 1 and Nov. 1. We'd think it inadvisable at other times.

REFERENCES

AMC Maine Mountain Guidebook Committee. *AMC Guide to Mt. Washington and the Presidential Range.* Boston: Appalachian Mountain Club, 1983.

—*AMC White Mountain Guide.* Boston: Appalachian Mountain Club, 1987.

Harris, Stuart K., and others. *AMC Field Guide to Mountain Flowers of New England.* Boston: Appalachian Mountain Club, 1982.

Kulik, Stephen, Pete Salmansohn, Matthew Schmidt, and Heidi Welch. *The Audubon Society Field Guide to the Natural Places of the Northeast: Inland.* New York: Pantheon Books, 1984.

HEADQUARTERS: White Mountain National Forest, P.O. Box 638, Laconia, NH 03247; (603) 524-6450. New Hampshire Division of Parks and Recreation, P.O. Box 856D, Concord, NH 03301; (603) 271-3254.

ODIORNE POINT STATE PARK

New Hampshire Division of Parks and Recreation   South
137 acres.

On SR 1A, S of Portsmouth. (Map 16.)

This fragment of undeveloped seaside and tidal marsh is a war relic. After Pearl Harbor, the Army commandeered the site and evicted residents to install coastal defenses. It became a park in 1961. It has both sandy and rocky shores, with stands of scotch pine and oak, wild rose thickets.

Its special distinction is a visitor center maintained cooperatively by the Division of Parks and Recreation, Audubon Society of New Hampshire, Friends of Odiorne Point, and the University of New Hampshire Cooperative Extension Service Sea Grant Marine Program. Open in summer, it includes exhibits, illustrated talks, guided walks. Available pamphlets describe the area's geology, archeology, and ecosystems.

HEADQUARTERS: Division of Parks and Recreation, P.O. Box 856D, Concord, NH 03301; (603) 271-3254.

OSSIPEE LAKE/HEATH POND BOG

New Hampshire Division of Parks and Recreation   North
Lake: 3,092 acres. Bog: 744 acres.

The lake is at Center Ossipee, NE of the intersection of SRs 16 and 25. The Bog parking area is about 2 mi. E, on the S side of SR 25. (Map 36.)

The State owns most of the sandy S lakeshore, but there is no developed access. Most of the shore has escaped residential development thus far, although there are clusters. The lake is best known for fishing.

Heath Pond Bog is a National Natural Landmark, a wild area, fragile, left undeveloped and little publicized. A floating mat of peat covered with sphagnum moss supports a unique plant community, including insectivorous plants, orchids, heaths. Trees around the pond are chiefly spruce and tamarack. Visitors are asked to stay on the trail.

ACTIVITIES

Fishing: Salmon, lake and brook trout, pickerel, smallmouth bass, cusk, yellow perch, suckers, hornpout, smelt.

Boating: Fishing map shows a launch site on E shore.

NEARBY: Pine River State Forest (see entry).

REFERENCES

Kulik, Stephen, Pete Salmansohn, Matthew Schmidt, and Heidi Welch. *The Audubon Society Field Guide to the Natural Places of the Northeast: Inland.* New York: Pantheon Books, 1984.

Swasey, Charlton J., and Donald A. Wilson. *New Hampshire Fishing Maps.* Freeport, ME: DeLorme Publishing, 1986.

HEADQUARTERS: Division of Parks and Recreation, P.O. Box 856D, Concord, NH 03301; (603) 271-3254.

PACK MONADNOCK MOUNTAIN

See Miller State Park; Wapack National Wildlife Refuge.   South

PARADISE POINT NATURE CENTER

Audubon Society of New Hampshire   South
43 acres.

> From Plymouth, 4 mi. W on SR 35, then 6 mi. S on SR 3A. W 1 mi. toward Hebron. Center is on left. (Map 33.)

> *Open daily, 10 A.M.–5 P.M., late June until Labor Day.*

This small site has much of interest. From the parking lot one walks up a trail through a fine old forest, chiefly hemlocks, many of them large. At the top is the Nature Center, which has good wildlife exhibits, a library and study area, literature, and room for talks and film showings. The hill overlooks 3,000 ft. of unspoiled shoreline on Newfound Lake, a precious asset where almost every other inch has been developed. Near the shore is a small swamp.

The site has five self-guiding nature trails: Loop, Swamp, Ridge, Point, and Lakeshore, each with a guide.

The rapid development around Newfound Lake has brought a new constituency to the Nature Center, which now offers evening programs.

NEARBY

Hebron Marsh is operated by the Audubon Society in conjunction with the town of Hebron. It's another mile W, toward Hebron. When we visited, there was no sign; we were told to look for the red cottage with a white picket fence and take the dirt road just to the S. Audubon owns about 36 acres. The site has a marsh and pastures on the river. An observation tower overlooks the marsh, a good place to look for waterfowl beginning in Sept.

Quincy Bog is a small private preserve on the N side of the road, between SR 3A and the Nature Center. It's well marked. Ask about it at the center.

PUBLICATIONS
Leaflet.
Nature trail guides.

HEADQUARTERS: East Hebron, NH 03232; (603) 744-3516.

PAWTUCKAWAY STATE PARK

New Hampshire Division of Parks and Recreation/New Hampshire Division of Forests and Lands   South
5,535 acres.

At Raymond, 3 1/2 mi. N of the intersection of SRs 101 and 156. (Maps 14, 15.)

When we looked in 1987, Pawtuckaway Lake had thus far escaped the development that has captured most lakes in southern NH. The 903-acre lake is about 3 mi. long, narrow, with many arms, coves, and bays. The park occupies most of the W shore, plus two islands accessible by bridges.

In summer the 900-ft. beach, 25-acre picnic ground, camping areas, and boating facilities attract crowds from nearby population centers. However, almost 5,000 park acres are undeveloped, and hikers can find quiet trails. To the W are the Pawtuckaway Mountains, three low ridges; the highest is 1,011-ft. North Peak. Fine views are seen from the fire tower on South Peak. The forest is mostly oak-hickory. A stream flows through a hemlock ravine.

Burnham's Marshes lie between Fundy Cove and Neal Cove, northern and southern arms of the lake.

ACTIVITIES
Camping: 170 sites. Mid-May to mid-Oct.
Fishing: A bass tournament is held here each spring. Smallmouth and largemouth bass, pickerel, yellow perch, hornpout.
Boating: Ramps at the Park and at the dam.

REFERENCE: Swasey, Charlton J., and Donald A. Wilson. *New Hampshire Fishing Maps.* Freeport, ME: DeLorme Publishing, 1986.

HEADQUARTERS: Raymond, NH 03077; (603) 895-3031.

PEABODY FOREST

Society for the Protection of New Hampshire Forests   North
83 acres.

> From Gorham, 3 1/2 mi. E on US 2. Left across the river. E 1 mi. on
> North Rd. to trailhead on left. (Map 51.)

The trail passes among large white pines and hemlocks in the S, then northern hardwoods. The Peabody Trail continues beyond the site along Peabody Brook toward Giant Falls and the Mahoosuc Range.

PILLSBURY STATE PARK

New Hampshire Division of Parks and Recreation/New   South
    Hampshire Division of Forests and Lands
5,250 acres.

> On SR 31, 3 1/2 mi. N of Washington. (Map 18.)

Open weekends from Memorial Day, daily mid-June to Labor Day.

The last of several sawmill owners here was one of the founders of the Society for the Protection of New Hampshire Forests. In 1920 he deeded 2,400 acres to the State as a forest reservation. In the 1930s the Civilian Conservation Corps restored ponds once choked with sawdust, and rebuilt dams. The site was opened as a State Park in 1952, but only 151 acres have been developed; the rest remains a near-wilderness, the regenerated forest healing past wounds. Recently a corridor has been acquired linking Pillsbury with Mount Sunapee State Park (see entry).

Base elevation is about 1,200 ft., with hills rising to over 2,000 ft. Seven ponds, the largest over 1/2 mi. long, are scattered through the site.

ACTIVITIES

Camping: 20 primitive sites on 150-acre May Pond.

Hiking: 20 mi. of trails. The 51-mi. Monadnock-Sunapee Greenway crosses the Park. (See entry.)

Fishing: Largemouth bass, pickerel, hornpout, yellow perch.

Canoeing: Hand-carried craft can be used.

HEADQUARTERS: Division of Parks and Recreation, P.O. Box 856D, Concord, NH 03301; (603) 271-3254.

PINE RIVER STATE FOREST
New Hampshire Division of Forests and Lands   North
3,084 acres.

Pine River flows N from Pine River Pond, crossing SR 16 about 7 1/2 mi. S of Center Ossipee, 2.7 mi. S of SR 28. It flows N to Lake Ossipee, crossing SR 25 about 1/2 mi. E of SR 16. (Map 36.)

The Forest doesn't appear on the *Atlas* map. It is noteworthy for a remarkable esker, some exceptionally large white pines, and the river. The esker, a ridge 7 mi. long, 120 ft. high, formed in the last Ice Age, is reached by an old road off SR 16, site of an abandoned hatchery. The pines are here, too.

Pine River is canoeable for 20 mi., usually all year. Class II rapids are in the 5 mi. from Pine River Pond to Granite Road. From there the river flows gently through unspoiled forest, with stretches of sandy bottom, deep pools. Many wildflowers in season. Some canoeists camp on the way. It's a little-known stream, with good fishing for brook trout.

NEARBY: Ossipee Lake/Heath Pond Bog (see entry).

REFERENCES
Kulik, Stephen, Pete Salmansohn, Matthew Schmidt, and Heidi Welch. *The Audubon Society Field Guide to the Natural Places of the Northeast: Inland.* New York: Pantheon Books, 1984.
Schweiker, Roioli, ed. *AMC River Guide: New Hampshire, Vermont.* Boston: Appalachian Mountain Club, 1983.

HEADQUARTERS: 105 Loudon Rd., Concord, NH 03301; (603) 271-2214.

PISGAH STATE PARK
New Hampshire Division of Parks and Recreation/New   South
   Hampshire Division of Forests and Lands
13,066 acres.

Off SR 63, 2 mi. E of Chesterfield. (Map 1.)

A 20-square-mile wilderness in fast-growing southern NH may seem improbable, but a management plan adopted in 1987 by the State's park, forest, and wildlife agencies would maintain Pisgah as a place "where visitors can experience a sense of relative solitude and remoteness from 'civilization.' " The site was acquired in 1968. Since then several studies have defined its natural and cultural resources. The evolving management plan was influenced by an opinion survey showing that most respondents want no further development.

Just leaving it alone won't preserve it, however. For almost 20 years the land was looked after by one part-time custodian who had two other parks to oversee. The multiple entrances were uncontrolled. If there were rules, no one gave them much heed. Off-road vehicles roamed the area, damaging vegetation, soil cover, and foot bridges.

It was called "the Pisgah wilderness" before the State bought it. Terrain is mostly a series of low ridges dividing valleys that have streams, ponds, and marshes. The highest point is 1,416-ft. Davis Hill. Mt. Pisgah is 1,303 ft. Pisgah Pond, the largest water body, is about 1 1/2 mi. long, Fullam Pond about half that length.

Plants: 95% forested: mixed hardwoods with white pine and hemlock. Prominent species are beech, yellow birch, red oak. Flowering plants include azalea, rhodora, mountain laurel, hobblebush.

Birds: No list has yet been prepared. Observed: waterfowl, herons, many hawks, owls. Fall roosting of grackles at Fullam Pond. Many warblers in season.

Mammals: Include beaver, bobcat, fisher, coyote, red fox, porcupine, raccoon, deer.

ACTIVITIES

The management plan lists activities judged "generally appropriate": hiking, nature study, cross-country skiing, picnicking, fishing, hunting, nonmotorized boating, and berry picking. "Only in designated zones": snowmobiling, ATV use, motorized boating, horseback riding, and sled dog training. "Only under applicable permit": primitive camping, archeology digs, large group outings, trapping, and field dog trials. "Generally inappropriate": camping in vehicles, swimming, sailing, speed boating and water skiing, using off-road vehicles, and target shooting.

These recommendations were made in 1987. They may not take effect for some time. To make them work, some present entrances must be closed and remaining entrances controlled. Some roads must be closed, others improved. Proposals include a perimeter trail, based in part on existing old roads.

In view of the chronic underfunding of NH's resource agencies, full realization of plans may be years away, but it's a promising beginning.

Hiking: At least 30 mi. of old logging roads.

Hunting: Probably the chief activity now. Deer, grouse.

Fishing: In several ponds. Trout, bass.

HEADQUARTERS: Division of Parks and Recreation, P.O. Box 856D, Concord, NH 03301; (603) 271-3254.

PONDICHERRY WILDLIFE REFUGE
Audubon Society of New Hampshire/New Hampshire Fish   North
and Game Department
310 acres.

From Whitefield on US 3, follow signs E to airport. Drive along the old railroad right-of-way as far as you can, then walk. Beyond Cherry Pond is a trail, often wet, to Little Cherry Pond. (Map 49.)

The ponds are State property; Audubon owns the land. The area is relatively flat, poorly drained, densely forested with northern conifers and a few hardwoods. Big Cherry Pond, about 100 acres, is adjoined by two large sphagnum bogs, partly open, sparsely covered with tamarack and black spruce. Little Cherry Pond, 25 acres, is surrounded by an extensive bog forest with a narrow ring of open bog. Both ponds have cattails and other emergent plants. Little Cherry Pond has many yellow water-lilies.

Birds: Green-winged teal and ring-necked duck nest; both are rare summer residents in NH. Also black and wood ducks, occasional hooded merganser. Other summer residents include pied-billed grebe, great blue heron, American bittern, Virginia and sora rails, woodcock, common snipe; other waterfowl in migration. Upland species include yellow-bellied flycatcher, Canada jay, common raven, boreal chickadee, ruby-crowned kinglet, Tennessee and Wilson's warblers, rusty blackbird.

Mammals: Include moose, black bear, deer, beaver, snowshoe hare, raccoon, skunk, coyote.

Fishing: Pickerel, hornpout, yellow perch. No motorized craft.

HEADQUARTERS: Audubon Society of New Hampshire, P.O. Box 528B, Concord, NH 03301; (603) 224-9909.

RHODODENDRON NATURAL AREA
New Hampshire Division of Parks and Recreation   South
292 acres.

Off SR 12, 2 1/2 mi. N of Fitzwilliam. (Map 2.)

The park, donated to the State by the Appalachian Mountain Club, was named for the exceptional 15-acre colony of rhododendron, the largest such assemblage in New England, a National Natural Landmark. They bloom in July. The site has many other wildflowers. From Apr. through Sept. some are always in bloom.

Many species of rhododendron are native to Asia and eastern North America. Exotics have been introduced, and many hybrids have been developed. Common in the North Carolina mountains, rhododendrons are at the northern limit of their range in New Hampshire, and thus unusual.

. Wildflowers seen along the 1-mi. Wildflower Trail include

- *Apr.–May:* bloodroot, dutchman's breeches, hepatica, mayflower, bellwort, blue flag, bunchberry, clintonia, columbine, fringed polygala, foamflower, goldthread, jack-in-the-pulpit, painted trillium, shadbush, Solomon's-seal, starflower, wake robin, wild oats.
- *June–July:* checkerberry, dewdrop, heart-leaved aster, mountain laurel, partridgeberry, pink lady's-slipper, pipsissewa, red baneberry, rhododendron, shin-leaf, twinflower, white baneberry, wood azalea, wood sorrel.
- *Aug.–Sept.:* Indian-pipe, wild lettuce, wood aster, woodland aster.

Hiking: The 160-mi. Metacomet Trail (see entry) crosses the park.

PUBLICATIONS: Leaflet with map and Wildflower Trail guide.

HEADQUARTERS: Division of Parks and Recreation, P.O. Box 856D, Concord, NH 03301; (603) 271-3254.

SQUAM LAKES REGION
Squam Lakes Association and others   North

At Holderness on US 3. (Maps 33, 34.)

Squam Lake, 6,765 acres, is a natural water body whose level was raised by a dam. It has a 61-mi. rocky, wooded shoreline. Linked to it by a narrow waterway is 408-acre Little Squam Lake. Both are long-established fishing and summer vacation sites with moderate shoreline development. *On Golden Pond* was filmed here.

The Squam Lakes Association was organized in 1905, with the primary mission of protecting the lake's water quality. Its current publication admonishes residents to keep soap, detergent, and human waste out of the lake, to use fertilizer sparingly and not at all within 150 ft. of the water, to have septic tanks pumped every 3 years, and not to use lumber treated with creosote or pentachlorophenol for docks or decks.

It also manages shorefront property for public use, maintains trails on the surrounding mountains, and offers a summer program for children. The Association owns Moon Island, available for low-impact recreation. It promotes conservation and good land use practices. Would that other NH lakes had such protectors!

ACTIVITIES

Camping: The SLA maintain 3 primitive lakeside campsites, two of which require boat access. Reservations required.

Hiking: More than 40 mi. of trails extend N into the Squam Mountains and beyond to the trails of the White Mountain National Forest.

Fishing: Squam Lake is well known for its salmon and lake trout. Also smallmouth bass, pickerel, white and yellow perch, hornpout, whitefish, cusk, smelt.

Boating: Ramps at Holderness and elsewhere.

PUBLICATIONS

Squam Lakes Trail Guide. $3.25.

Lake charts and Range map.

Birds of the Squam Lakes Region. (In press.)

REFERENCE: Swasey, Charlton J., and Donald A. Wilson. *New Hampshire Fishing Maps.* Freeport, ME: DeLorme Publishing, 1986.

HEADQUARTERS: P.O. Box 204, Holderness, NH 03245; (603) 968-7336.

TAVES RESERVATION

Society for the Protection of New Hampshire Forests   South

539 acres.

From Keene, E on SR 101, then N on road to Otter Dam (Branch Rd. on *Atlas* map). Turn right at crossroads by Roxbury town hall. In 4 mi., at old Roxbury center, bear left, to parking. (Map 10.)

In 1973 the Taves family bought the land to protect a small town from development; ten years later they gave it to the Society, which manages it for forest

products and wildlife. The terrain is rough, with steep hillsides and ravines. It includes the watershed of Wheeler Brook. From the entrance a dirt road extends N along Otter Brook, the W boundary. A compass is recommended for off-trail hiking.

It can be seen from SR 9, across Otter Brook.

HEADQUARTERS: Society for the Protection of New Hampshire Forests, 54 Portsmouth St., Concord, NH 03301; (603) 224-9945.

UMBAGOG LAKE

Private land ownerships   North
8,000 acre lake.

On the NH-ME border. Near Errol on SRs 16 and 26. (Maps 54, 57.)

Here is a quiet wilderness for canoeists to explore. Except for the two put-ins and unmapped logging roads the shoreline is roadless, and some of the extensive wetlands can't be reached on foot. The lake is 10 mi. long, but the irregular shoreline measures—by our rough calculation—more than 60 mi. The lake is shallow but clear, with good fishing.

The Magalloway and Androscoggin rivers join at the NW corner of the lake. Both are canoeable, and a put-in on the Magalloway off SR 16 is good access to rivers and lake.

Big Island, 156 acres, is at the narrow dividing point between the lake's sparsely developed lower third and the undeveloped upper two-thirds. A recent acquisition of the Society for the Protection of New Hampshire Forests, it's available for hiking and, by permit, primitive camping. For permits, write to Umbagog Lake Camps, P.O. Box 181, Errol, NH 03579. *In May–July, take care not to disturb loons nesting on the shore.*

Flora and Fauna: This region is a splendid mix of habitats: river oxbows, heath bog, swamp forest, ponds, marshes. Trees include both northern conifer species, notably the jack pine, as well as hardwoods such as the red oak.

We could find no wildlife inventory of the area, but fishermen say it's abundant. Moose are frequently seen, bear somewhat less often. The loon is common, as are many ducks, songbirds, and raptors. Birders told us this area has more species than any other NH site in breeding season. Waterfowl include wood duck, hooded merganser, goldeneye. Upland species include great crested flycatcher, phoebe, bank swallow, white-breasted nuthatch, marsh wren, catbird, wood and gray-cheeked thrushes, veery, evening grosbeak, many warblers.

When we visited in midsummer, the water was too warm for good brook trout fishing, which may be why we saw no boat trailers at the ramp. However, we doubt that it's ever a crowded place.

We have a 1985 map of the New Hampshire's Department of Resources and Economic Development, which shows a 262-acre Umbagog State Park near Errol. The 1986 *New Hampshire Parklands* (Division of Parks and Recreation—see State Preface) doesn't mention it, nor do other sources. The reference may be to an easement the State acquired along SR 16 to preserve the scenic qualities of the Androscoggin Valley.

ACTIVITIES

Camping: Commercial campgrounds at Errol. Although we have had no direct communication from landowners, we understand that boat camping in suitable sites is permitted.

Fishing: Maximum depth is 48 ft., for most of the lake 10 to 22 ft. Salmon, brook trout, brown trout, pickerel, yellow perch, hornpout, smelt.

Boating: Ramp on SR 26 SE of Errol.

Canoeing: The Magalloway is canoeable from Wilsons Mills, ME, on SR 16, the Androscoggin for about 30 mi. below the Errol dam. Get information before trying either.

REFERENCES

Kulik, Stephen, Pete Salmansohn, Matthew Schmidt, and Heidi Welch. *The Audubon Society Field Guide to the Natural Places of the Northeast: Inland.* New York: Pantheon Books, 1984.

Schweiker, Roioli. *Canoe Camping Vermont and New Hampshire Rivers.* Woodstock, VT: Backcountry Publications, 1986.

Swasey, Charlton J., and Donald A. Wilson. *New Hampshire Fishing Maps.* Freeport, ME: DeLorme Publishing, 1986.

WAPACK NATIONAL WILDLIFE REFUGE
U.S. Fish and Wildlife Service   South
1,672 acres.

By trail from Miller State Park (see entry) or by Old Mountain Road E from Peterborough. (Map 3.)

We're not sure why this is a federal refuge, but we're glad it's there. The land was acquired by gift, not purchase. On 2,288-ft. North Pack Monadnock Mountain, 1,200 ft. above the valley floor, the site is rugged, unspoiled, forested, with bogs and swamps, ledges, cliffs, open alpine flats, streams. Visitors are few.

Birds: It's a good place to watch the migration of hawks. Nesting species include tree sparrow, winter wren, Swainson's thrush, magnolia warbler, white-throated sparrow. Also noted: belted kingfisher, green heron, pine siskin, crossbill, pine grosbeak, ruffed grouse, woodcock.

Mammals: Include deer, fisher, mink, squirrel, porcupine, chipmunk, mice, voles, weasel, raccoon, fox, bobcat, snowshoe hare.

Hiking: The Wapack Trail crosses the site, a 3-mi. segment.

HEADQUARTERS: c/o Great Meadows National Wildlife Refuge, Weir Hill Rd., Sudbury, MA 01776; (617) 443-4661.

WHITE LAKE STATE PARK
New Hampshire Division of Parks and Recreation   North
624 acres.

From West Ossipee, 1/2 mi. N on SR 16. (Map 35.)

The lake is a bit over 1/2 mi. long with a good natural beach. The Division calls it one of NH's most popular camping spots, and it's crowded in the swimming season. However, the site includes some forest, a black spruce bog, and two small bog ponds. It's near Hemenway State Forest (see entry).
   White Lake Pitch Pines is a 72-acre National Natural Landmark, a grove of exceptionally tall and straight old trees.
   Tamworth Black Spruce Ponds Preserve, 35 acres, a property of the town of Tamworth, adjoins the Park and is linked by trails.

Camping: 173 sites. Late May to mid-Oct.

PUBLICATION: White Lake Pitch Pines folder.

HEADQUARTERS: West Ossipee, NH 03890; (603) 323-7350.

WHITE MOUNTAIN NATIONAL FOREST
U.S. Forest Service   North
In NH: 798,305 acres within boundaries; 714,336 acres of federal land. Additional 49,166 acres in ME.

Between Plymouth on the S and SR 110 on the N; from the ME border almost to VT. Crossed by US 2, I-93, US 302, and other routes. (Maps 33 to 53.)

The Forest occupies over 11% of NH's land area, the highest percentage of federal land for any eastern State. It wasn't federal land when the Society for the Protection of New Hampshire Forests was organized in 1901. Much of it had been cut over. Only the N slope of the Presidential Range and a few tracts such as Crawford Notch remained intact. The SPNHF urged Congress to act, but it was 10 years before legislation passed and 2 more before the first land was bought for the new National Forest. Acquisition has continued. Several thousand more acres have been identified as suitable additions. Almost all these tracts are on present boundaries or along road corridors.

The White Mountains dominate northern NH and extend into ME. Their most striking feature is the Presidential Range, a chain of peaks named for American Presidents, a number of them more than a mile high. Mt. Washington, at 6,288 ft., is highest of all. Along the ridges is an alpine zone about 8 mi. long and 2 mi. wide, treeless and windswept, with species of shrubs, wildflowers, mosses, and lichens typical of arctic regions, left here on these lofty islands, many think, when the last ice sheet receded.

Although the Forest produces timber, about 95% of it is natural in appearance, showing no conspicuous signs of human alteration. On the average, 3,400 acres are logged each year, only 1,900 acres in conspicuous openings. The 5% also includes ski areas, campgrounds, roads, and service areas.

Recreation use of the Forest totals about 2 3/4 million visitor-days per year. On days when traffic is heavy at Pinkham, Crawford, and Franconia notches, motorized sightseeing appears to be the chief visitor activity, but it accounts for only one-fifth of the visitor-days. Camping and picnicking make up a quarter of the total, downhill skiing about one-twelfth. Almost half of the visitor-days are spent in the backcountry: hiking, hunting, fishing, and so on.

Forests that are extensively logged have networks of logging roads. Here the entire road system, including the public highways, totals only 761 mi. Less than half are National Forest roads, and only 150 mi. are open to visitor traffic.

By contrast, there are 1,167 mi. of hiking trails and 100 mi. of cross-country ski trails. About 43% of the Forest is open to winter off-road vehicle travel, chiefly on 362 mi. of winter ORV trails. When snow is off the ground, however, ORVs are restricted to a few trails, no off-trail driving.

The Forest offers opportunities for extensive backpacking, demanding mountain hikes, or easy day walks in scenic valleys. The hiking season in the mountains is generally from June to mid-Oct., but weather on the mountains can be severe in any season, windier, colder, and wetter than in the valleys. Clouds often shroud the peaks, sometimes reducing visibility to a few feet. Above timberline, where trails are marked by stone cairns, many hikers have lost their way, some their lives. Proper clothing and gear, and knowing what to do in case of trouble, are essential to full enjoyment of these lofty places.

Although most of the Forest is accessible only to those who travel on foot, other travelers can see its most spectacular features. A toll road and a cog railway ascend to the top of Mt. Washington; an aerial tram carries passengers to the top of Cannon Mountain; and other high viewpoints are no less accessible. Scenic highways pass waterfalls, cataracts, and ponds. Along the way are parking areas with short, easy trails to places of interest and beauty.

Great cirques in the mountainsides mark the action of past glaciers. Rivers have cut down through faults, forming steep-sided ravines, here called "notches," of which Franconia Notch and Crawford Notch are best known.

FEATURES

Throughout the Forest are attractive cirques, waterfalls, cascades, pools, ponds, vistas, and other natural attractions, among them:

Presidential Range—Dry River Wilderness, 27,380 acres, includes the 4,930-acre Alpine Area, treeless, along the ridge tops, with many alpine plants. Wildflowers blooming in the brief summer include alpine azalea, bearberry, bluet, goldenrod, speedwell, black crowberry, bluebell, dwarf cinquefoil, dwarf willow, eyebright, Labrador tea, Lapland rose bay, mountain cranberry, pale laurel.

Great Gulf Wilderness, 5,552 acres, on the N slope of Mt. Washington adjoining the Alpine Area. The largest cirque in the White Mountains, walls rising up to 1,600 ft., with old-growth red spruce and balsam fir. Many trails.

Pemigewasset Wilderness, 45,000 acres, between Franconia Notch and Crawford Notch. Mountainous, forested, bounded by the Appalachian Trail; also internal trails.

Pemigewasset Extension, 16,000 acres, bordering the E side of the Pemigewasset Wilderness. Steep, heavily forested, no trails.

Sandwich Range Wilderness, 25,000 acres, lies between the Kancamagus Highway, SR 112, and the S boundary of the Forest. It includes the *Bowl Natural Area,* which has a virgin climax spruce/fir forest and virgin climax northern hardwood forest within a large cirque.

Franconia Notch and *Crawford Notch.* See entries.

Pinkham Notch Scenic Area includes a cluster of features on both sides of SR 16, with Mt. Washington on the W, Wildcat Mountain on the E: Tuckerman and Huntington ravines, Alpine Gardens, Crystal Cascades, Glen Ellis Falls.

Snyder Brook Scenic Area, just W of Randolph on US 2. Old-growth trees, cascades.

Gibbs Brook Scenic Area, on the slopes of Mt. Pierce, E of US 302. One of the few extensive stands of virgin spruce in New England.

Sawyer Ponds Scenic Area, via Sawyer Ponds Trail from US 2 or the Kancamagus Highway. Secluded glacial ponds.

Rocky Gorge Scenic Area on the Kancamagus Highway. A narrow gorge cut by the Swift River bordering tall red spruce.

Nancy Brook Scenic Area, W of US 302, S of Crawford Notch. Cascades and ponds.

Greeley Ponds Scenic Area, S of the Kancamagus Highway. Trail through Mad River Notch. Isolated ponds below rugged slopes.

Mount Chocorua Scenic Area, 5,700 acres at the SE corner of the Forest. One of the most-climbed NH mountains. Numerous trails, fine views from the bare summit.

Scenic drives include

- *Kancamagus Highway,* between Lincoln and Conway. Lower Falls, Greeley Ponds, and Rocky Gorge Scenic Areas, Sabbaday Falls, campgrounds, and trailheads.
- *Jefferson Notch Road,* N from Crawford Notch, highest road in NH, narrow and steep.
- *Evans Notch,* from Chatham N on SR 113 into ME. The ME portion of the Forest (see entry in ME) is the Evans Notch Ranger District.

Aerial tramways are on Cannon, Black, Wildcat, and Loon mountains.

Birds: A checklist of 194 species is available. Only 21 of these are generally present in winter. Well over half of those listed are species that breed here but migrate. Species common in summer include great blue heron, mallard, black duck, wood duck, rock and mourning doves, black-billed cuckoo, chimney swift, ruby-throated hummingbird, belted kingfisher, northern flicker, yellow-bellied sapsucker, hairy and downy woodpeckers, eastern kingbird, eastern phoebe, yellow-bellied and least flycatcher, eastern wood-pewee; tree, bank, and barn swallows; blue jay, common raven, American crow, black-capped and boreal chickadees, white-breasted and red-breasted nuthatches, brown creeper, winter wren, gray catbird, brown thrasher, American robin; wood, hermit, Swainson's and gray-cheeked thrushes; golden-crowned and ruby-crowned kinglets, cedar waxwing, European starling, solitary and red-eyed vireos.

Warblers: black-and-white, Nashville, parula, magnolia, black-throated blue, yellow-rumped, black-throated green, blackburnian, chestnut-sided, blackpoll, ovenbird, northern waterthrush, yellowthroat, Canada, American redstart. House sparrow, bobolink, eastern meadowlark, red-winged blackbird, common grackle, brown-headed cowbird, scarlet tanager, rose-breasted grosbeak, purple finch, American goldfinch. Sparrows: savannah, chipping, white-throated, song. Slate-colored junco.

Mammals: In 1978, moose were gradually moving into NH from ME. The NH population then was thought to be around 100, presumed present but uncommon in the National Forest. Now the Forest has over 750, and they are seen more often than deer. Other common species include moles, shrews, bats, snowshoe hare, black bear, raccoon, woodchuck, chipmunk, red and flying squirrels, red fox, skunk, porcupine, beaver, muskrat, fisher, otter, bobcat. Uncommon: lynx, pine marten.

INTERPRETATION

Visitor center at the Saco Ranger Station in Conway, at the E end of the Kancamagus Highway, SR 112.

Nature trails at the Russell Colbath Historic Site and near the Covered Bridge campground on the Kancamagus Highway. Also the Patte Brook Auto Tour near Crocker Pond campground in ME.

Campfire programs at Dolly Copp campground, July–Aug.

ACTIVITIES

Camping: 22 campgrounds; 844 sites. Campgrounds usually open May 15–Oct. 15. Several are open in winter but roads aren't plowed. Most campgrounds are filled during summer and fall peaks. No reservations.

Informal camping elsewhere is permitted except in zones bordering main roads.

Hiking, backpacking: With over a thousand miles of trails to choose among, it's advisable to study one of the hiking guides before setting forth. The *AMC White Mountain Guide* is the most complete and includes advice on equipment and safety. *Fifty Hikes in the White Mountains* describes a number of short day hikes and a few longer trips. Trailside facilities include 43 shelters, 8 Appalachian Mountain Club huts, and 8 cabins.

The first hut was built a century ago. The huts, open to the public, are more than their name implies. Madison Hut, for example, can accommodate 50 hikers in three-high bunks. Hut crews provide dinners and breakfasts. Huts are reached only by hiking at least 1 1/2 mi. Some visitors hike hut-to-hut along the mountains; others make a one-night stand.

Hunting is a significant activity, but we found little reference to it in Forest documents. Game species include deer, bear, raccoon, rabbit, ruffed grouse, woodcock, duck.

Fishing: The best trout fishing waters are the Saco and Swift rivers and their tributaries. The Pemigewasset, once heavily polluted, now has good fishing again; it's in the I-93 corridor bordered by Forest land.

Canoeing: The Pemigewasset has Class I and II rapids below North Woodstock, canoeable except at low water. Its East Branch, draining the Pemigewasset Wilderness, has rapids to Class IV Apr.–May and after heavy rains. Another tributary, the Mad River, also has rapids to Class IV but for a short season. So does the upper Saco River.

Skiing: Four downhill ski areas are wholly or partly on Forest land. Tuckerman Ravine has been called "the only true alpine ski area east of the Rockies." The season may last until mid-June.

Ski touring: Opportunities are unlimited, with several hundred miles of marked trails for skiing and snowshoeing.

Snowmobiling: Restricted to designated areas and corridors and to times when the minimum snow cover is 6 in. Operators should obtain map and regulations.

PUBLICATIONS
Forest map. $1.
Campground schedule.
Camping and Hiking. Information page.
Off-Road Vehicle Conditions of Use.
Checklists: birds, mammals, reptiles, and amphibians.
The Alpine Garden. Leaflet.
Trout Fishing.

REFERENCES
AMC Maine Mountain Guide Committee. *AMC Guide to Mt. Washington and the Presidential Range.* Boston: Appalachian Mountain Club, 1983.
Daniell, Eugene S., III, ed. *AMC White Mountain Guide.* Boston: Appalachian Mountain Club, 1987.
Doan, Daniel. *Fifty Hikes in the White Mountains.* Woodstock, VT: Backcountry Publications, 1983.
Harris, Stuart K., and others. *AMC Field Guide to the Mountain Flowers of New England.* Boston: Appalachian Mountain Club, 1987.
Kulik, Stephen, Pete Salmansohn, Matthew Schmidt, and Heidi Welch. *The Audubon Society Field Guide to the Natural Places of the Northeast: Inland.* New York: Pantheon Books, 1984.
Schweiker, Roioli, ed. *AMC River Guide: New Hampshire, Vermont.* Boston: Appalachian Mountain Club, 1983.
Swasey, Charlton J., and Donald A. Wilson. *New Hampshire Fishing Maps.* Freeport, ME: DeLorme Publishing, 1986.
Trail Map and Guide to the White Mountain National Forest. Freeport, ME: DeLorme Publishing, 1986.

HEADQUARTERS: 719 Main St., Laconia, NH 03247; (603) 524-6450.

RANGER DISTRICTS: Ammonoosuc RD, Trudeau Rd., Box 239, Bethlehem, NH 03574; (603) 869-2626. Androscoggin RD, 80 Glen Rd., Gorham, NH 03581; (603) 466-2713. Saco RD, Kancamagus Highway, Box 94, Rt. 1, Conway, NH 03818; (603) 447-5448. Pemigewasset RD, RFD #3, Box 15, Rt. 175, Plymouth, NH 03264; (603) 536-1310. Evans Notch RD, Bridge St., Bethel, ME 04217; (207) 824-2134.

WILLARD POND PRESERVE
(also known as DePierrefeu Willard Pond Sanctuary)
Audubon Society of New Hampshire   South
642 acres.

> From Hancock, 3 mi. NW on SR 123, then 1 1/2 mi. N on dirt road.
> (Map 11.)

The Preserve has about one-third of the shoreline of the 100-acre pond. The rest is largely undeveloped. Much of the site is reverting pasture, but it also has good stands of white pine and hardwoods and a large patch of mountain laurel. The lake is at 1,100-ft. elevation. Bald Mountain rises on the W to 2,037 ft. Three hiking trails, a canoe landing, and good birding, here and at nearby marshes.

HEADQUARTERS: Audubon Society of New Hampshire, P.O. Box 528B, Concord, NH 03301; (603) 224-9909.

MASSACHUSETTS

E very resident of Massachusetts lives within 10 miles of a public park, forest, or wildlife area. The State has over 200 sites open to public recreation. This is remarkable in a state where growth and development often seem out of control.

With only one-eighth of New England's land area, Massachusetts has almost half of its population. More than three-fourths of the people live within commuting range of Boston, whose metropolitan area now extends onto Cape Cod and into southern New Hampshire.

We had known Massachusetts for many years. Returning after a 10-year absence, we were shocked by the changes along the coast and Cape. After two days of fighting heavy traffic and seeking almost any overnight parking for our motor home, we considered recommending that readers stay west of I-495. Choked highways, polluted air, water shortages, and politicians unable to say no to developers mark the east an environmental casualty.

Still, we couldn't ignore the east's delightful natural areas: the National Seashore, attractive State Parks and State Forests, numerous private preserves. We have entries for them, but those who dislike crowds should plan their visits. Beaches are best enjoyed out of season. When beaches are crowded, upland areas aren't. Even in winter, don't head toward Cape Cod on a Friday afternoon.

State Forests have fewer visitors than State Parks, Parks without campgrounds fewer than those with camping. Except in hunting season, Wildlife Management Areas have the least visitors.

You can find quiet natural areas in the east, but there's no way to avoid the traffic. It's easier to find quiet places in the western part of the state, and the forested mountain trails are cool in summer.

We have divided the state into three zones. *East* has the coast and the most congestion. *Central* is hilly, forested, with many streams and rivers. *West* has mountain ranges and river valleys.

GEOGRAPHY AND CLIMATE

Excluding the Cape, Massachusetts measures about 50 mi. N–S, about 150 mi. W–E. The terrain is mountainous along the western border, generally above 1,000-ft. elevation W of the Connecticut River. At 3,491 ft., Mt. Greylock is the state's highest. Most of the central region is between 500 and

1,000 ft. The Connecticut River Valley and the coastal region are below 500 ft. The Cape and some coastal areas are flat with many wetlands.

Average Jan. temperatures are in the low 20s in the west, near 30° along the coast. Summers are warm, with less regional variation. Total annual precipitation is 40 to 50 in., with no wet or dry seasons and little regional difference, but the west receives much more snow than the east.

The Connecticut River drains most of the western half of the state, the Merrimack the NE portion. Other rivers are small.

STATE LANDS

Massachusetts has no National Park or National Forest. (The National Seashore is part of the National Park Service system.) It has a few small National Wildlife Refuges. The State has 300,000 acres of public lands, well distributed: 56 State Parks, 71 State Forests, 12 State Reservations, 3 State Recreation Areas, more than 50 Wildlife Management Areas, 13 Wildlife Sanctuaries. Of these, 45 have 2,000 or more acres, 13 have 5,000 or more. (That's not all. The State has title to other areas that are not yet ready for public access.)

Gathering information about State lands was difficult. We had the most help from the Division of Fisheries and Wildlife: maps of the WMAs, site descriptions they were preparing for a forthcoming guide, and talks with staff members who know the areas. Our file of information from the Division of Forests and Parks is the thinnest we've had for any state: site maps, a few site descriptions, almost nothing on flora and fauna. The DFP *Massachusetts Forests and Parks* folder has a chart showing acreages and activities, an outline map, and such directions as "Rte. 47, Hadley." Requests for more data were unproductive. However, most of our entries were thoughtfully reviewed in draft, with many helpful corrections and additions.

In the end, however, these seven entries had not been reviewed, and we were told no staff was available to check them for accuracy:

- Clarksburg State Forest
- D.A.R. State Forest
- Harold Parker State Forest
- Mt. Washington State Forest
- October Mountain State Forest
- Sandisfield State Forest
- Walden Pond State Reservation

We have marked each site "Not checked by HQ." Judging from those that were reviewed, corrections would be minor.

Our field work was hampered by sparse signing. Campgrounds and developed recreations sites usually have entrance signs. So do many Wildlife Management Areas. Often, however, we couldn't tell whether forested land was public or private. Perseverance was rewarding. Unsigned areas are rarely crowded; we seldom met anyone there.

We visited sites that seemed to be candidates for entries. Sites planned for intensive use are omitted unless they include significant natural areas.

MAPS

Massachusetts has no road atlas comparable to those available in Maine, New Hampshire, and Vermont. Nothing, indeed, other than the Official Transportation Map. This map marks Parks and Forests with names and symbols in their general locations. It doesn't show their boundaries and sometimes doesn't show the secondary roads leading to them. Wildlife Management Areas are not marked.

The scale of the Official Transportation Map is about 5.8 miles per inch. Tourist offices sometimes hand out a smaller version, at the scale of 8.3 miles per inch. Neither served our needs well, but the larger is certainly preferable.

State headquarters supplied maps of almost all the Wildlife Management Areas and of many State Parks and Forests (the latter sometimes showing only developed areas). We found them valuable.

FLORA AND FAUNA

Little published information about plants and animals is available from State agencies. More is available at private preserves, notably those of the Massachusetts Audubon Society and especially the Felix Neck sanctuary (see entry, Martha's Vineyard). These references were most helpful:

DeGraaf, Richard M., and Deborah D. Rudis. *New England Wildlife: Habitat, Natural History, and Distribution.* General Technical Report NE-108. Broomwall, PA: U.S. Department of Agriculture, Forest Service, Northeastern Forest Experiment Station, 1986.

Jorgensen, Neil. *A Sierra Club Naturalist's Guide to Southern New England.* San Francisco: Sierra Club Books, 1978.

Kulik, Stephen, Pete Salmansohn, Matthew Schmidt, and Heidi Welch. *The Audubon Society Field Guide to the Natural Places of the Northeast: Coastal.* New York: Pantheon Books, 1984.

Kulik, Stephen, Pete Salmansohn, Matthew Schmidt, and Heidi Welch. *The Audubon Society Field Guide to the Natural Places of the Northeast: Inland.* New York, Pantheon Books, 1984.

Sammartino, Claudia F. *The Northfield Mountain Interpreter.* Berlin, CT: Northeast Utilities, 1981.

TRAILS

Massachusetts has several long trails. In the west are 83 mi. of the Appalachian Trail and extensive trails on the Taconic Range. The Metacomet-Monadnock Trail crosses from NH to CT, with sections on both sides of the Connecticut River. In the east are trails linked to Rhode Island trails.

Opportunities for overnight hikes are limited, however. Even on the Appalachian Trail, there is no chain of shelters spaced at convenient intervals, and informal trailside camping is forbidden everywhere.

Opportunities for day hiking are almost unlimited. Thanks largely to the Appalachian Mountain Club and New England Trail Conference, trails have been established on public and private land throughout the state. The AMC's comprehensive trail guide includes descriptions of trails as short as 1 mi.

AMC Massachusetts and Rhode Island Trail Guide. Boston: Appalachian Mountain Club, 1988.

For the Appalachian Trail:

Appalachian Trail Guide to Massachusetts/Connecticut. Harpers Ferry, WV: Appalachian Trail Conference, 1985.

Other guides describe trails to or through places of special interest:

Brady, John, and Brian White. *Fifty Hikes in Massachusetts.* Woodstock, VT: Backcountry Publications, 1983.

Fisher, Alan. *Country Walks Near Boston.* Boston: Appalachian Mountain Club, 1985.

Griswold, Whit. *Berkshire Trails for Walking and Ski Touring.* Charlotte, NC: East Woods Press, 1983.

Ryan, Christopher J. *Western Massachusetts Trail Map Kit.* Athol: Millers River Publishing, 1987.

Sadlier, Hugh and Heather. *Short Walks on Cape Cod and the Vineyard.* Chester, CT: Globe Pequot Press, 1987.

Scheller, William G. *More Country Walks Near Boston.* Boston: Appalachian Mountain Club, 1986.

With minor exceptions, these guides don't describe trails in Wildlife Management Areas. Most hiking in WMAs is on woods roads and informal trails. We found the WMA site maps adequate. We rarely saw another hiker in a WMA.

CAMPING

Camping has had low priority in development of the MA parks and forests. Only 32 of them have campgrounds. At the extremes are 4 with more than two hundred campsites, others with as few as three. Most of the large campgrounds and more than half of the sites are in the east. They are much in demand in summer.

In the west, we camped several nights in State Parks and State Forests. We were lucky, twice getting the last available site. You might be lucky, too, but don't count on it. The campgrounds are popular. We saw few out-of-state vehicles in them. There's no reservation system.

Reservations can be made at private campgrounds. During the busy season, it's wise to make them.

CANOEING

Except on the Connecticut River, Massachusett's longest river canoe run is about 10 mi. Most runs are seasonal, and canoeists should inquire about water conditions. There are a few stretches of whitewater.

Borton, Mark C., ed. *The Complete Boating Guide to the Connecticut River.* Woodstock, VT: Backcountry Publications, 1985.

Schweiker, Roioli, ed. *AMC River Guide: Massachusetts, Connecticut, Rhode Island.* Boston: Appalachian Mountain Club, 1985.

Weber, Ken. *Canoeing Massachusetts, Rhode Island, and Connecticut.* Woodstock, VT: Backcountry Publications, 1980.

BOATING

Public access is available at points on nine rivers and about 80 ponds, most of the latter small. A 1974 publication, *Public Access to Waters of Massachusetts,* was out of print when we inquired but may become available again from:

Public Access Board
Department of Fisheries, Wildlife, and Recreational Vehicles
100 Nashua St.
Boston, MA 02114
(617) 727-1843

The state's 1,519-mi. shoreline provides unlimited opportunities for saltwater boating.

FISHING

Freshwater game species include brook, rainbow, and brown trout; landlocked salmon, smallmouth and largemouth bass, chain pickerel, northern pike, tiger muskie, walleye. Trout are stocked in several hundred streams and ponds. Fishing regulations and a list of stocked waters are available from the Division of Fisheries and Wildlife.

The *Massachusetts Saltwater Fishing and Weather Guide* is available from the Division of Marine Fisheries, 100 Cambridge St., Boston, MA 02202.

HUNTING

Game species include deer, black bear, small mammals, waterfowl, turkey, grouse, pheasant, and quail. Seasons, bag limits, and regulations differ in various counties. The *Abstracts of the Fish & Wildlife Laws* is available from the Division of Fisheries and Wildlife.

STATE AGENCIES

Responsibility for State Parks and State Forests lies with:

Massachusetts Division of Forests and Parks
100 Cambridge St.
Boston, MA 02202
(617) 727-3180

Responsibility for wildlife management, including Wildlife Management Areas, lies with:

Division of Fisheries and Wildlife
100 Cambridge St.
Boston, MA 02202
(617) 727-3151

PRIVATE ORGANIZATIONS

As part of its many activities in nature education and conservation, the Massachusetts Audubon Society owns and protects more than 13,000 acres of wildlife habitat in more than 18 sanctuaries and several interpretive centers.

South Great Road
Lincoln, MA 01773
(617) 259-9500

The Trustees of Reservations was established in 1891 to hold and protect "beautiful and historical places and tracts of land." It owns 68 properties, totaling more than 16,500 acres.

224 Adams St.
Milton, MA 02186
(617) 698-2066

Both organizations provided information about their sites. We visited many and have entries for a number. (We usually don't include sites that limit public access or that are so small and fragile as to be damaged by too many visitors.)

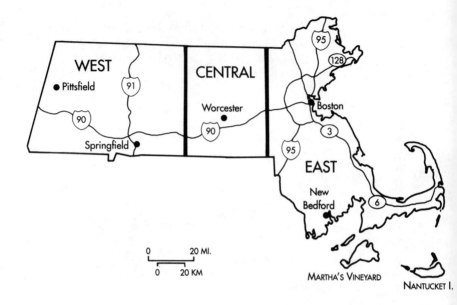

NATURAL AREAS IN MASSACHUSETTS

An Alphabetical Listing

Appalachian Trail
  West
Arcadia Nature Center and
  Wildlife Sanctuary
  West
Ashumet Holly Reservation and
  Wildlife Sanctuary
  East
Bartholomew's Cobble
  West
Beartown State Forest
  West
Birch Hill Wildlife Management
  Area *Central*
Blue Hills State Reservation
  East
Bolton Flats Wildlife Management
  Area *Central*
Borderland State Park
  East
Brimfield State Forest
  Central
Broadmoor Wildlife Sanctuary
  East
Campbell Falls State Park
  West
Canoe Meadows Wildlife Sanctuary
  West
Cape Cod *East*
Cape Cod National Seashore
  East
Cape Cod Rail Trail
  East
Catamount State Forest
  West
Charles H. Ward Reservation
  East
Chester-Blandford State Forest
  West
Clarksburg State Forest
  West

Connecticut River
  West
Crane Pond Wildlife Management
  Area *East*
Crane Wildlife Management Area
  East
D.A.R. State Forest
  East
Daniel Webster Wildlife Sanctuary
  East
Dorothy F. Rice Sanctuary for
  Wildlife *West*
Erving State Forest
  West
Eugene D. Moran Wildlife
  Management Area (see entry,
  Windsor State Forest)
  West
Garden in the Woods
  Central
Granville State Forest
  West
Great Meadows National Wildlife
  Refuge *East*
H. O. Cook State Forest
  East
Harold Parker State Forest
  East
High Ridge Wildlife Management
  Area *Central*
Hinsdale Flats Wildlife
  Management Area
  West
Hiram H. Fox Wildlife
  Management Area
  West
Hockomock Swamp Wildlife
  Management Area
  East
Hopkinton State Park
  East

Hubbardston Wildlife Management Area *Central*

Ipswich River Sanctuary *East*

John C. Phillips Wildlife Sanctuary/Boxford State Forest *East*

Kenneth Dubuque Memorial State Forest (formerly Hawley State Forest) *West*

Lake Dennison Recreation Area (see entry, Birch Hill Wildlife Management Area) *Central*

Laughing Brook Education and Wildlife Sanctuary *Central*

Leominster State Forest *Central*

Martha's Vineyard *East*

Martin Burns Wildlife Management Area *East*

Metacomet-Monadnock Trail *West*

Midstate Trail *Central*

Millers River Wildlife Management Area *West*

Mohawk Trail State Forest *West*

Monomoy National Wildlife Refuge *East*

Monroe State Forest *West*

Moose Hill Wildlife Sanctuary *East*

Mount Grace State Forest/Northfield State Forest/Warwick State Forest *West*

Mount Greylock State Reservation *West*

Mount Tom Reservation *West*

Mt. Washington State Forest *West*

Myles Standish State Forest *East*

Nickerson State Park *East*

Norcross Wildlife Sanctuary *West*

North Hill Marsh Wildlife Sanctuary *East*

Northfield Mountain Recreation and Environmental Center *West*

Notchview Reservation (see entry, Windsor State Forest) *West*

October Mountain State Forest *West*

Old Town Hill Reservation *East*

Otter River State Forest (see entry, Birch Hill Wildlife Management Area) *Central*

Oxbow National Wildlife Refuge *Central*

Parker River National Wildlife Refuge *East*

Peru Wildlife Management Area *West*

Phillipston Wildlife Management Area *West*

Pittsfield State Forest *West*

Pleasant Valley Wildlife Sanctuary *West*

Quabbin Reservoir *West*

Quaboag Wildlife Management Area *Central*

Richard T. Crane, Jr., Memorial Reservation *East*

Sandisfield State Forest
West
Savoy Mountain State Forest
West
Stony Brook Nature Center and
Wildlife Sanctuary
East
Taconic Skyline Trail
West
Tolland State Forest
West
Upton State Forest
Central
Wachusett Meadow Wildlife
Sanctuary *Central*
Wachusett Mountain State
Reservation *Central*

Walden Pond State Reservation
East
Wampanoag Commemorative
Canoe Passage
East
Wellfleet Bay Wildlife Sanctuary
East
Wendell State Forest
West
Willard Brook State Forest
Central
Willowdale State Forest
East
Windsor State Forest
West
Wompatuck State Park
East

NATURAL AREAS IN MASSACHUSETTS

by Zone

West Zone

Appalachian Trail
Arcadia Nature Center and
Wildlife Sanctuary
Bartholomew's Cobble
Beartown State Forest
Campbell Falls State Park
Canoe Meadows Wildlife Sanctuary
Catamount State Forest
Chester-Blandford State Forest
Clarksburg State Forest
Connecticut River
Dorothy F. Rice Sanctuary for
Wildlife
Erving State Forest
Eugene D. Moran Wildlife
Management Area (see entry,
Windsor State Forest)
Granville State Forest

Hinsdale Flats Wildlife
Management Area
Hiram H. Fox Wildlife
Management Area
Kenneth Dubuque Memorial State
Forest (formerly Hawley State
Forest)
Metacomet-Monadnock Trail
Millers River Wildlife Management
Area
Mohawk Trail State Forest
Monroe State Forest
Mount Grace State
Forest/Northfield State
Forest/Warwick State Forest
Mount Greylock State Reservation
Mount Tom Reservation
Mt. Washington State Forest
Norcross Wildlife Sanctuary

Northfield Mountain Recreation
and Environmental Center
Notchview Reservation (see entry,
Windsor State Forest)
October Mountain State Forest
Peru Wildlife Management Area
Phillipston Wildlife Management
Area
Pittsfield State Forest
Pleasant Valley Wildlife Sanctuary
Quabbin Reservoir
Sandisfield State Forest
Savoy Mountain State Forest
Taconic Skyline Trail
Tolland State Forest
Wendell State Forest
Windsor State Forest

Central Zone

Birch Hill Wildlife Management
Area
Bolton Flats Wildlife Management
Area
Brimfield State Forest
Garden in the Woods
High Ridge Wildlife Management
Area
Hubbardston Wildlife Management
Area
Lake Dennison Recreation Area
(see entry, Birch Hill Wildlife
Management Area)
Laughing Brook Education and
Wildlife Sanctuary
Leominster State Forest
Midstate Trail
Otter River State Forest (see entry,
Birch Hill Wildlife Management
Area)
Oxbow National Wildlife Refuge
Quaboag Wildlife Management
Area
Upton State Forest

Wachusett Meadow Wildlife
Sanctuary
Wachusett Mountain State
Reservation
Willard Brook State Forest

East Zone

Ashumet Holly Reservation and
Wildlife Sanctuary
Blue Hills State Reservation
Borderland State Park
Broadmoor Wildlife Sanctuary
Cape Cod
Cape Cod National Seashore
Cape Cod Rail Trail
Charles H. Ward Reservation
Crane Pond Wildlife Management
Area
Crane Wildlife Management Area
D.A.R. State Forest
Daniel Webster Wildlife Sanctuary
Great Meadows National Wildlife
Refuge
H. O. Cook State Forest
Harold Parker State Forest
Hockomock Swamp Wildlife
Management Area
Hopkinton State Park
Ipswich River Sanctuary
John C. Phillips Wildlife
Sanctuary/Boxford State Forest
Martha's Vineyard
Martin Burns Wildlife Management
Area
Monomoy National Wildlife Refuge
Moose Hill Wildlife Sanctuary
Myles Standish State Forest
Nickerson State Park
North Hill Marsh Wildlife
Sanctuary
Old Town Hill Reservation
Parker River National Wildlife
Refuge

Richard T. Crane, Jr., Memorial Reservation
Stony Brook Nature Center and Wildlife Sanctuary
Walden Pond State Reservation

Wampanoag Commemorative Canoe Passage
Wellfleet Bay Wildlife Sanctuary
Willowdale State Forest
Wompatuck State Park

APPALACHIAN TRAIL
Mixed ownerships   West
83 trail miles.

From the VT line near North Adams to the CT line in Mount Washington State Forest (see entry).

Western MA is mountainous, the Berkshire Valley framed by the Taconic Range on the W, the Hoosac Range on the E. Two principles guided trail planning: to keep to the highest ground, following ridges between peaks, and to stay on public land wherever possible.

Western MA has the mountains and many State Forests and Parks, but there were and are difficulties. The mountains don't have continuous ridges, and much of the Trail must be on private land. The Appalachian Trail Club and its allies have had admirable success in obtaining permissions from landowners, but some Trail sections had to use public roads. Occasionally a change of ownership or mind requires rerouting.

Massachusetts prohibits trailside camping on its public lands, and most of its many parks and forests don't have campgrounds. AT hikers find a few shelters, but intervals are too long for hut-to-hut trips. Hikers must spend some nights off the Trail.

We have entries for most of the Parks and Forests along the way. Trail guides are essential, whether one is planning a long AT hike or seeking a local access trail for a day trip.

REFERENCES
AMC Massachusetts and Rhode Island Trail Guide. Boston: Appalachian Mountain Club, 1988.
Appalachian Trail Guide to Massachusetts/Connecticut. Harpers Ferry, WV: Appalachian Trail Conference, 1985.

ARCADIA NATURE CENTER AND WILDLIFE SANCTUARY

Massachusetts Audubon Society   West
518 acres.

> From I-91, exit 18. S 1.3 mi. on US 5 (not easily seen on the State map). Right on East St.; 1.2 mi. to Fort Hill Rd., and turn right.
>
> *Open daily except Mon., dawn to dusk.*

The Sanctuary is on the W side of an oxbow in the Connecticut River. Almost half of the site is floodplain forest, woody swamp, and marsh. Wild rice was planted some years ago. The site is at the crossroads of two bird migration routes. The upland half of the site is forested with mixed hardwoods and conifers planted in the early 1900s. These factors add up to fine birding.

An observation tower overlooks the marsh.

This is also the headquarters of the Connecticut River Watershed Council.

INTERPRETATION

Nature center is the base for a lively educational program.

Guided tours and canoe trips.

ACTIVITIES

Hiking: More than 4 mi. of trails.

Canoeing: Access to the Oxbow and Connecticut River.

Pets are prohibited.

PUBLICATIONS

Site map.

Four bird lists, one for each season.

HEADQUARTERS: Easthampton, MA 01027; (413) 584-3009.

ASHUMET HOLLY RESERVATION AND WILDLIFE SANCTUARY

Massachusetts Audubon Society   East
45 acres.

> On Cape Cod in East Falmouth. From the intersection of SRs 28 and 151, E on 151 4 mi. Left on Currier Rd. to entrance.
>
> *Open Tues.–Sun., dawn to dusk.*

In this small space one can see eight species and 65 varieties of holly trees. On the S side of the Cape, the site's highest point is 18 ft. above sea level. It includes 27 acres of mixed woodland, 10 agricultural acres, and an 8-acre pond. Also present is the unusual fall-flowering Franklinia tree.

Two *nature trails* offer tours of the hollies and other site features. The Society maintains an active program including a holly sale at Christmas, spring open house, Lotus Festival in summer, Franklinia Festival in the fall, day camp, and seasonal boat tours to Cuttyhunk, the Elizabeth Islands, and Gay Head.

Pets are prohibited.

PUBLICATIONS
Ashumet Discovery Guide. $1.
The Hollies of Ashumet. $1.

REFERENCE: Brady, John, and Brian White. *Fifty Hikes in Massachusetts.* Woodstock, VT: Backcountry Publications, 1983.

HEADQUARTERS: 286 Ashumet Rd., East Falmouth, MA 02536; (508) 563-6390.

BARTHOLOMEW'S COBBLE
The Trustees of Reservations   West
277 acres.

W of US 7 in Ashley Falls, near CT. Take Rannapo Rd. S to Weatogue Rd. and entrance.

Open dawn to dusk.

A National Natural Landmark, this scenic site is on the Housatonic River. The Cobble is a natural limestone rock garden, elevations from 600 to 1,050 ft., with an extraordinary diversity of plants: nearly 500 species of wildflowers; 100 of trees, shrubs, and vines; 40 species of ferns. Best wildflower blooming seasons are Apr.–June and Sept.

A small museum has displays of wildflowers, birds' nests, Indian artifacts, geology.

Birds: Checklist available. 236 species have been recorded, an extraordinary number for any site, especially one so small.

PUBLICATIONS
Information page.
Map. $0.35.
Ledges Interpretive Trail Guide. $2.
Birds at Bartholomew's Cobble. $1.

REFERENCE: Kulik, Stephen, Pete Salmansohn, Matthew Schmidt, and Heidi Welch. *The Audubon Society Field Guide to the Natural Places of the Northeast: Inland.* New York: Pantheon Books, 1984.

HEADQUARTERS: P.O. Box 233, Ashley Falls, MA 01222; (413) 298-8600.

BEARTOWN STATE FOREST

Massachusetts Division of Forests and Parks   West
10,852 acres.

From Great Barrington, about 5 mi. E on SR 23 to Blue Hill Road and Forest sign. HQ is 1/2 mi. N, Forest boundary another 1 1/2 mi.

This is handsome country, a high plateau with hilltops of the Hoosac Range. Mt. Wilcox, at the Forest center, is 2,150 ft.; Beartown Mountain is 1,865. The area has many streams and ponds. Lookout points offer fine views. The site extends N almost to the Housatonic River and SR 102. It is crossed by several roads, woods roads, and trails, including the Appalachian Trail.

It's surprising that one of the State's largest Forests has a campground with only 12 sites, not surprising that they are usually occupied in season. Even when weekend campers leave on Sunday, others are waiting to take their places.

The area is 90% forested with mixed hardwoods, some spruce plantations. Many wildflowers in season.

Birds: Include wild turkey, grouse, woodcock, hawks, owls, woodpeckers, flycatchers, vireos, finches, crossbills, thrushes, warblers.

Mammals: Include deer, black bear, bobcat, coyote, snowshoe hare, cottontail, red and gray foxes, red and gray squirrels, porcupine, fisher.

ACTIVITIES
Camping: 12 sites. May 1–Columbus Day. All year for self-contained units.
Hiking, backpacking: 5 mi. of the Appalachian Trail, including 2 shelters.

Fishing: Trout stocked in streams. Bass in ponds.
Swimming: 36-acre Benedict Pond.
Ski touring: 11 mi. of marked trails.

PUBLICATION: Site map.

REFERENCES

AMC Massachusetts and Rhode Island Trail Guide. Boston: Appalachian
  Mountain Club, 1988.
Appalachian Trail Guide to Massachusetts/Connecticut. Harpers Ferry,
  WV: Appalachian Trail Conference, 1985.
Brady, John, and Brian White. *Fifty Hikes in Massachusetts.* Woodstock,
  VT: Backcountry Publications, 1983.

HEADQUARTERS: Monterey, MA 01245; (413) 528-0904.

BIRCH HILL WILDLIFE MANAGEMENT AREA
Massachusetts Division of Fisheries and Wildlife
OTTER RIVER STATE FOREST/LAKE DENNISON
RECREATION AREA
Massachusetts Division of Forests and Parks   Central
9,000 acres.

From US 202 at Baldwinville, left on Old US 202 (Dennison St.) For Lake
Dennison, continue NE on US 202 about 6 mi. to entrance on left.

This complex includes the largest Wildlife Management Area in central MA,
a State Forest, and a State Recreation Area, all based in part on land made
available by the U.S. Army Corps of Engineers. The site map shows the three
elements, but on the ground we couldn't tell one from the other. A State Forest employee said he'd never heard of a Birch Hill WMA. For the visitor, it
doesn't matter.

The Corps is involved because of Birch Hill Dam, which impounds water
only during floods. At other times the lands on the floodplain are available
for recreation. Terrain is flat to gently rolling. Millers River, Otter River, and
Priest Brook drain most of the site. Brushy fields are interspersed with hardwood and coniferous forest, swampy areas, and wetlands. Forest understory
includes dogwood, mountain laurel, viburnum, azalea, blueberry, raspberry.

Paved and dirt roads crisscross the site, and we saw many trails. We chose
one at random that gave us easy hiking through quiet woods, passing a lily
pond and marsh. The next trail, however, showed that trail bikers are a nasty
problem for management. A steel gate blocked the trailhead, but bikers had

cut the steel cable on one side and worn a track around the gate. Down the trail we came to a little valley whose bottom and sides were ripped raw. The trail was littered with motor oil and beer cans.

Lake Dennison, 82 acres, a natural lake, is the activity center of the Recreation Area.

Birds: Pheasants are stocked. Wild turkey, introduced in 1982, are seen occasionally. Common species include woodcock, grouse, waterfowl, flycatchers, woodpeckers, warblers.

Mammals: Stocked with snowshoe hare. Common species include deer, raccoon, cottontail, beaver, mink, muskrat.

ACTIVITIES

Camping: 150 campsites at Lake Dennison. All year, but self-contained units only after Oct. 15. 118 sites at Otter River SF, seasonal. Lake Dennison CG is usually full on summer weekends; Otter River usually has sites.

Hiking: More than 30 mi. of back roads and trails.

Hunting: Waterfowl, deer, small upland game.

Fishing: Excellent trout fishing in Millers River and Priest Brook. Trout stocked. Warmwater species in the lake.

Canoeing: Both streams can be canoed, but watch for rocks and fallen trees. Boats with electric motors only on the lake.

PUBLICATION: Birch Hill WMA map shows the entire area.

HEADQUARTERS: WMA, Birch Hill WMA Headquarters, Area Supervisor, Dennison St., Baldwinville, MA 01436; (617) 939-8977. Recreation Area and State Forest, New Winchendon Rd., Baldwinville, MA 01436; (508) 939-8962.

BLUE HILLS STATE RESERVATION

Metropolitan District Commission   East
6,000 acres.

Bisected by SR 28 S of Boston. I-93/SR 128 crosses its S portion. See the "Boston and Vicinity" inset of the official highway map.

The Metropolitan District Commission was the nation's first regional park commission. Established in 1893, it acted with remarkable foresight and speed, acquiring within a decade most of the parkland now in the Boston system. Blue Hills was its first large acquisition.

The Blue Hills are monadnocks, massive granite domes thrust up by volcanism, exposed by erosion of glacial till and slate. This part of MA has numerous domes less than 100 ft. high. The Blue Hills rise over 635 ft., affording fine views. Habitats of the Reservation include forest, ledges, rock outcrops, grassy meadows, bog, streams, and ponds. Ponkapog, the largest pond, is bordered by a quaking peat bog. The developed recreation sites and some trails are often crowded in good weather. The more challenging trails have fewer hikers.

Plants: Wooded areas include scrub pitch pine and redcedar near windswept summits; white pine, sumac, poplar, oaks, hickories, and red maple at midelevations; white-cedar, red maple, ash, and elm in swamps and bogs. Bog species include pitcher plant and sundew.

Birds and Mammals: No checklists available but the Trailside Museum has information.

INTERPRETATION: *The Trailside Museum* is operated by the Massachusetts Audubon Society. Live native animals, nature walks, talks. Open 10 A.M.– 5 P.M. Tues.–Sun.; also Mon. on State holidays.

ACTIVITIES
Hiking: The extensive trail network is well described in the REFERENCES. The longest trail is about 8 mi. Several trails begin at the museum. Principal trails are blazed.
Fishing: Streams, pond.
Swimming: Houghton's Pond.
Ski touring: On trails and unplowed roads.

REFERENCES
AMC Massachusetts and Rhode Island Trail Guide. Boston: Appalachian Mountain Club, 1988.
Brady, John, and Brian White. *Fifty Hikes in Massachusetts.* Woodstock, VT: Backcountry Publications, 1983.
Fisher, Alan. *Country Walks Near Boston.* Boston: Appalachian Mountain Club, 1985.

HEADQUARTERS: 20 Somerset St., Boston, MA 02108; (617) 727-5114. Trailside Museum: 1905 Canton Ave., Milton, MA 02186; (617) 333-0690.

BOLTON FLATS WILDLIFE MANAGEMENT AREA
Massachusetts Division of Fisheries and Wildlife   Central
1,040 acres.

From I-495, Exit 27. NW on SR 117. Site is on both sides of SR 117 beyond SR 110. Parking areas on SR 110 and SR 117.

This river flood plain doesn't get high marks for scenery or hiking opportunities, but it's great for birding. The Still River is close to SR 100, the larger Nashua River on the W boundary of the site. Most of the area is open agricultural fields and brushfields, with marshy wetlands, maple swamps, and brushy river banks.

Birds: Said to be one of the best inland spots for egrets, glossy ibis, herons. In migration, the site is said to "teem" with black duck, mallard, pintail, snow goose, blue goose. Also reported: ruff, purple gallinule. American and least bitterns, Virginia and sora rails, hooded merganser, wood duck.

ACTIVITIES
Hunting: Pheasant stocked in season.
Canoeing: Nashua River.

PUBLICATIONS
Site map.
Birds of Bolton Flats Wildlife Management Area.

ADJACENT: Oxbow National Wildlife Refuge (see entry).

HEADQUARTERS: Wildlife District Manager, Temple St., West Boylston, MA 01583; (508) 835-3607.

BORDERLAND STATE PARK

Massachusetts Division of Forests and Parks   East
1,600 acres.

On Massapoag Ave. in North Easton, E of Foxborough.

This was a country estate. The owners maintained the property as a game and forest preserve, clearing sections, building dams to form new ponds and fire roads that now serve as trails. Habitats range from low swamp forest in the S to granite hills in the N.

Hiking: On woods roads and trails, hilly on the N.

HEADQUARTERS: Massapoag Ave., North Easton, MA 02356; (508) 238-6566.

BRIMFIELD STATE FOREST
Massachusetts Division of Forests and Parks   Central
4,033 acres.

S central MA, between Sturbridge and Palmer. From US 20, S on local
road W of SR 19.

The area is hilly, the highest elevation 1,150 ft. Just N of the Forest, Steerage
Rock on the ridge of Mt. Waddaquadduck was a landmark on the trail from
Boston to villages on the Connecticut River. There's a fire tower on the moun-
tain.

The area is forested with mixed northern hardwoods, the understory including azalea, laurel. Many wildflowers in season. Several fast-flowing
streams. Dean Pond is the largest of several small ponds. (No boats are permitted on Dean Pond.)

No lists of fauna are available, but the area seems promising for birds.

ACTIVITIES
Hiking: 24 mi. of forest roads.
Hunting: Deer, bobcat, rabbit, raccoon, ruffed grouse, woodcock.
Fishing: Trout in streams.

HEADQUARTERS: Brimfield, MA 01010; (413) 245-9966.

BROADMOOR WILDLIFE SANCTUARY
Massachusetts Audubon Society   East
608 acres.

Between Boston and Framingham. From South Natick, 1.8 mi. W on SR
16.

With frontage on the Charles River, the Sanctuary has woodland, fields,
marsh, and pond. It's a quiet natural island in a heavily settled region. It's
open all year, with activities. Apr.–May and Sept.–Oct. are the periods with
the most visitors. It has a built-in safeguard against crowding: the capacity
of its parking lot. There is no nearby street parking.

Plants: About half of the site is forested with mixed hardwoods and softwoods. An extensive plant list includes among trees: white and Norway

spruces, hemlock, Douglas-fir, larch; white, red, and pitch pines; eastern red-cedar, pussy willow, bigtooth aspen, hickories, American hazel, hophornbeam, birches, alder, American beech, American chestnut, oaks, American elm, mulberries.

The diverse habitats produce many seasonal wildflowers. A checklist is available, including arrowhead, jack-in-the-pulpit, arrow arum, skunk cabbage, spiderwort, pickerelweed, day-lily, Canada lily, clintonia, false Solomon's-seal, Solomon's-seal, white trillium, greenbrier, stargrass, blue-eyed grass, yellow iris, blue flag, lady's-slipper, rattlesnake plantain, coralroot orchid, campions, yellow pond-lily, water-lily, buttercups, hepatica, marsh marigold, goldthread, columbine, pitcher-plant, sundew, cinquefoils, clovers, jewelweed, St. Johnswort, violets, evening primrose, Queen Anne's lace, pipsissewa, Indian-pipe, loosestrife, starflower, forget-me-not, speedwell, asters, many more.

Birds: Instead of a checklist, the Sanctuary has a list of species observed here with a paragraph of information about each. Some of those mentioned are uncommon. The list includes mallard, black duck, blue-winged teal, wood duck, ring-necked duck, red-tailed and broad-winged hawks, osprey, American kestrel, ruffed grouse, yellow-billed and black-billed cuckoos, belted kingfisher, common flicker, hairy and downy woodpeckers, eastern kingbird, great crested flycatcher, eastern phoebe, eastern wood-pewee, tree and barn swallows, blue jay, black-capped chickadee, tufted titmouse, white-breasted nuthatch, house wren, brown creeper, brown thrasher, gray catbird, mockingbird, American robin, veery, wood thrush, red-eyed vireo, red-winged blackbird. In the study period, 18 wood warblers were observed, 12 of them only once or twice. Those seen more often include black-and-white, yellow, yellow-rumped, blackpoll, palm, common yellowthroat.

Nature center is open 9 A.M.–5 P.M. Tues.–Fri.; 10 A.M.–5 P.M. weekends and holidays. Information, exhibits, occasional films, talks, workshops, special events. Announcements in newsletter.

Hiking: 9 mi. of trails feature historic mill sites, foot bridge over Indian Brook, riverside.

Pets are prohibited.

PUBLICATIONS
Newsletter.
Trail map. $1.
"World of Water." $0.35.
"Welcome to Broadmoor." $0.30.
Reading Ancient Landscapes. $4.20.
"Mills at Broadmoor." $1.

HEADQUARTERS: 280 Eliot St., South Natick, MA 01760; (508) 655-2296.

CAMPBELL FALLS STATE PARK
Massachusetts Division of Forests and Parks   West
4.6 acres.

From New Marlboro on SR 57, turn S and follow signs.

Signs along the way point to "Campbell Falls State Park" and "Campbell Falls State Forest." The last turn is onto a single-lane dirt road that leads to a small, rough parking area. The sign here calls it "State Forest." Nearby is a boundary marker indicating that one has crossed into Connecticut!

We followed the well-marked trail for less than half a mile and emerged into a much larger parking and picnic area where a sign said we were in Campbell Falls State Park, Connecticut (see entry). Had we continued to drive S on SR 272 and turned right on Spalding Rd. just over the state line, we would have come to this other parking area, by a better road.

The short trail between the two parking areas passes through mixed forest with some unusually large white pines and hemlocks. It crosses what would be a modest cascade when the stream is flowing.

No waterfall? We didn't find it at first, but it's there, on a stub trail W of the concrete post: a 50-ft. drop in a narrow ravine, better seen when there's more water.

If you want to hike and 1/2 mi. isn't enough, Sandisfield State Forest is nearby. See entry.

REFERENCE: Kulik, Stephen, Pete Salmansohn, Matthew Schmidt, and Heidi Welch. *The Audubon Society Field Guide to the Natural Places of the Northeast: Inland.* New York: Pantheon Books, 1984.

CANOE MEADOWS WILDLIFE SANCTUARY
Massachusetts Audubon Society   West
254 acres.

From Massachusetts Turnpike, Exit 2. Follow US 7 N to Holmes Rd., then right 2 mi.

Open daily except Mon., 9 A.M. to dusk.

The site's W boundary is the Housatonic River. From river, floodplain, swamps, brooks, and ponds, the land slopes up to hemlock forest. Fields comprise most of the northern, western, and southeastern portions, and here are many seasonal wildflowers.

Visits to these relatively small sanctuaries are rewarding because they have been studied more systematically than most of the larger State landholdings. The resources here include descriptions of each of the eight habitats: fields, coniferous woods, upland deciduous woods, riverbank, lowland deciduous woods, cattail marsh, sedge meadows, and fencerows and planted areas, noting the plant species typical of each.

Our file has no bird list, although over 100 species have been recorded here. There is an extensive plant list with common as well as Latin names, and lists of mammals, reptiles, and amphibians. It also includes a fascinating discussion of local invertebrates, noting that "few or no preserved areas in the country are being managed to conserve habitat for rare or specialized invertebrates" and that Canoe Meadows is "an ideal area for invertebrate, particularly butterfly, conservation."

INTERPRETATION

Canoe Meadows and the Pleasant Valley Wildlife Sanctuary (see entry) are managed as the Berkshire Sanctuaries. Their seasonal publication includes a calendar of events: nature hikes, canoe tours, nature ski hikes, talks, slide shows, workshops, and others.

ACTIVITIES

Hiking: 5 mi. of trails. The Wolf Pine Trail passes an unusually large white pine, the Sacred Way Trail, and the reconstruction of an Indian wigwam.
Canoeing: Access to the Housatonic River.

Pets are prohibited.

PUBLICATIONS

Trail map.
Quarterly newsletter.
Self-guiding trail leaflets.

HEADQUARTERS: Berkshire Sanctuaries, 472 West Mountain Rd., Lenox, MA 01240; (413) 637-0320.

CAPE COD
Mixed ownerships.   East

Traversed by US 6, SR 28.

Early one New Year's Day we drove the length of the Cape and walked the beach at Race Point, its outer tip. Few people were about that morning, none on the beach, although the day was bright and warm.

Back then, a string of small towns were threaded along US 6. Many un-marked, unpaved roads led to broad, sandy beaches. Small crowds gathered in summer where these roads ended, but those who wanted solitude had only to walk along the shore until they found it. We never knew whether it was forbidden to camp on the beach; no one seemed to care.

We had planned to visit the Cape during our summer fact-finding tour. Then we saw the traffic inching along the route from Boston and turned back. Summer wasn't our time.

The Cape is a disaster area today, overwhelmed by growth the part-time town governments couldn't manage. They had loose zoning laws, if any, no comprehensive plans for roads, water, waste disposal, fire protection, or other needs. Developers could do as they pleased.

Population on the Cape has grown explosively. From what was a summer resort, thousands of all-year residents commute daily to Boston. More than 15,000 wells tap the Cape's only aquifer, and no one seems to know whether this can continue. More and more wells are polluted. A lot bought for $25,000 last year sold for $60,000 this spring, and the seller now asks $95,000.

With land speculators, builders, and a billion-dollar tourist industry de-manding more, those who loved the Cape struggle to preserve remaining frag-ments. By far their greatest victory came in 1961, when Congress authorized the National Seashore. Towns are now seeking funds to preserve green space.

We have entries for the National Seashore and for:

Nickerson State Park
Wellfleet Bay Wildlife Sanctuary
Ashumet Holly Reservation
Lowell Holly Reservation
Mashpee River Reservation
Martha's Vineyard

REFERENCE: Clayton, Barbara, and Kathleen Whitley. *Exploring Coastal Massachusetts: New Bedford to Salem.* New York: Dodd Mead, 1983.

CAPE COD NATIONAL SEASHORE

National Park Service   East
25,930 acres; 27,004 acres within boundaries.
(The boundaries enclose 44,596 acres of land and water.)

On Cape Cod between Chatham and Provincetown. Access points along US 6.

Thoreau called Cape Cod "the bared and bended arm of Massachusetts." In this image, the National Seashore occupies most of the hand and forearm. It extends for 40 mi. along the Atlantic Ocean with additional frontage on Cape Cod Bay and Provincetown Harbor.

It was established just in time. Developers coveted the land even then, and heavy lobbying opposed the proposal. Surely Congress would not have approved purchasing at today's land prices, often well over $50,000 an acre and going higher by tomorrow. But it was possible in 1961, a magnificent acquisition for the people.

The land didn't qualify as a National Park. The National Park Service had to reconcile conflicting interests in deciding what facilities should be developed and where. No campground was provided. Conservationists urged that off-road vehicles be barred, while beach buggy users and vendors wanted no restrictions; the decision allows oversand vehicles to use designated routes in one area. One of the superintendent's many tribulations was deciding what to do about nude sunbathing, traditional on isolated beaches long before 1961.

Historic structures were to be preserved, and the interpretive program would recall the Cape's history. Modest rules would minimize conflicts among fishermen, surfers, and sunbathers.

No one knows how many visitors come here. The Seashore records about 5 million *visits.* If you have a week's vacation and go to the beach twice a day, that's 14 visits. You won't find an isolated beach next to your parked car, but walking can provide escape from crowds.

Cape Cod is the product of glaciers. Its beaches, dunes, and cliffs were shaped by wind and wave over centuries. Within the Seashore, banks and cliffs of sand, gravel, and clay rise as much as 175 ft. The diverse habitats include migrating dunes, tidal flats, salt and freshwater marshes, swamps, kettlehole ponds, and woodlands.

Climate on the Cape is milder than on the mainland because of the moderating influence of the ocean. Spring is cooler, fall warmer. Less snow falls on the Cape, and it remains for shorter periods; occasional winters are snow-free. But the low-lying Cape is exposed to maritime winds and storms. Birds have occasionally been swept here all the way from Yucatan.

FEATURES

Nauset. At the S end of the Seashore, long barrier beaches shelter the extensive Nauset Marsh, a major gathering place for shorebirds and waterfowl. Theme of the Salt Pond Visitor Center is the human and natural history of the Cape. There are 3 *nature trails:* Nauset Marsh, Fort Hill, and Buttonbush Trail for the Blind. *Evening programs* at the amphitheater in summer, and on occasional weekends in spring and fall. *Guided walks* in summer; weekends in spring and fall. Activity notices are posted at the visitor center.

Marconi Station. So named because the first U.S. wireless station was here. Wayside shelters tell the story. Seashore HQ is in this area, as are extensive beaches and a *nature trail.* The Wellfleet Bay Wildlife Sanctuary (see entry) is adjacent.

Pilgrim Heights. In North Truro. People from the Mayflower landed here. An interpretive trail traces a part of their adventure. Nearby are beaches, sand dunes, *Small's Swamp Trail.*

Province Lands. At the tip of the Cape. *Visitor center, Beech Forest Trail,* beaches, dunes, salt marshes.

The Beaches. Side roads extend from US 6 to all the principal beaches. Most are on the Atlantic Ocean, but Duck Harbor Beach at Wellfleet and Herring Cove Beach at Provincetown are on Cape Cod Bay. Duck Harbor and several of the ocean beaches are town-owned and managed. Access to some is restricted to cars with stickers that are available only to town residents and tenants.

Plants: Dune vegetation includes beach plum, cranberry, American beach grass, salt spray rose. Some bay shallows have eelgrass. Back of the dunes are low-lying areas with numerous shallow ponds, freshwater marsh, scrub, and woodland patches. Pond-lilies and cattails abound in ponds, cinnamon and wood fern in woodlands. Pitch pine is the predominant tree species, with Atlantic white-cedar and red maple in wetter areas. Some fine beech trees, remnants of the original oak/beech forest, remain in the Province Lands area.

Birds: Checklist available. Over 300 species have been recorded. Long, narrow Cape Cod forms a funnel along the Atlantic Flyway. Large numbers of migrating shorebirds, gulls, terns, sea and freshwater ducks pass through, as well as geese, swans, and pelagic birds. Winter residents include Canada goose, brant, black duck, mallard, goldeneye, bufflehead, eider, red-breasted merganser, great black-backed gull, sanderling. Prominent upland species include red-tailed hawk, crested flycatcher, pine warbler, yellowthroat, catbird, towhee, vesper sparrow, horned lark. Often seen in winter: pheasant, yellow-rumped warbler, goldfinch, song sparrow, dark-eyed junco.

Mammals: Checklist available includes raccoon, cottontail, woodchuck, chipmunk; red, gray, and flying squirrels; muskrat, weasel, red fox, deer, harbor seal. Whales, dolphins, and porpoises are often seen offshore, occasionally beached.

Other Fauna: Checklists of reptiles, amphibians, and mollusks are available.

ACTIVITIES

Camping: The Seashore has no campground. HQ has a list of commercial campgrounds. Reservations are essential in summer. Many of the campgrounds prohibit pets.

Hiking: Nature trails offer opportunities for short walks. The principal hiking route is the ocean beach. Experienced beachcombers know that hiking conditions can change from day to day, although low tides generally offer the best footing. According to the Seashore map, the longest distance between access roads is about 8 mi.

Hunting: Upland game and migratory waterfowl may be hunted in designated areas, subject to federal, state, and local rules. Consult HQ.

Fishing: Surf, outside swimming areas. State license is required for fishing in freshwater ponds.

Horse riding: On three bridle paths only. Stables nearby.

Swimming: Lifeguards are provided at the principal beaches in season. The water is cold.

Bicycling: Three trails, 1.6 to 7.3 mi.

Pets are prohibited in public buildings and picnic areas and on protected beaches and interpretive trails. They must be kept under restraint in developed areas and wherever visitors concentrate.

Oversand vehicles are restricted to designated routes and must have permits. Driving on the dunes is prohibited.

PUBLICATIONS

Seashore leaflet with map.
Schedules of ranger-guided activities.
Leaflets:
General information: health, safety, etc.
Nauset Marsh Trail.
Atlantic White Cedar Swamp Trail.
Beech Forest Trail.
Marconi and His South Wellfleet Wireless.
The Lifesavers of Cape Cod.
Fort Hill Trail.
Great Island Trail.
Cranberries on Cape Cod.
Small's Swamp Trail.
Pilgrim Spring Trail.
Camping information.

REFERENCES

AMC Massachusetts and Rhode Island Trail Guide. Boston: Appalachian Mountain Club, 1988.

Brady, John, and Brian White. *Fifty Hikes in Massachusetts.* Woodstock, VT: Backcountry Publications, 1983.

Jorgensen, Neil. *A Sierra Club Naturalist's Guide: Southern New England.* San Francisco: Sierra Club Books, 1978.

HEADQUARTERS: South Wellfleet, MA 02663; (508) 349-3785.

CAPE COD RAIL TRAIL
Massachusetts Division of Forests and Parks   East
19 miles.

On Cape Cod, from SR 134 in Dennis to the Cape Cod National Seashore
in Eastham.

The route was abandoned by a railroad in 1965. It now provides one of the
longest trails in eastern New England, open to hikers, horseriders, and cyclists, closed to motor vehicles. It passes forests, ponds, cranberry bogs, salt
marshes, beaches.

PUBLICATION: Leaflet with map.

HEADQUARTERS: c/o Nickerson State Park, Route 6A, Brewster, MA 02631;
    (508) 896-3491.

CATAMOUNT STATE FOREST
Massachusetts Division of Forests and Parks   West
1,125 acres.

From Shelburne Falls, 1 mi. W on SR 2, turn on Four Mile Square Rd.

Here is an opportunity for quiet day hiking in moderately interesting country:
rolling to hilly, somewhat rugged, with kettleholes, potholes, marsh, streams,
a 47-acre pond, mixed forest. Elevations are from 1,000 to 1,250 ft. Cata-
mounts—mountain lions—no longer den under the ledges, but there may be
porcupine.

Hiking: 5 mi. of foot trails; 3 mi. of woods roads.

HEADQUARTERS: c/o Mohawk Trail State Forest, P.O. Box 7, Charlemont,
    MA 01339; (413) 339-5504.

CHARLES W. WARD RESERVATION
The Trustees of Reservations   East
640 acres.

From I-93, Exit 15. N 5 mi. on SR 125; right on Prospect Rd. at Reservation
sign.

The site's principal features are a northern bog and 420-ft. Holt Hill, a drum-lin, highest point in Essex County. Most of the area is natural woodland, mixed species including some large white pine. The entrance is on a quiet residential street. A site map with contours is on the bulletin board at the parking lot. Elevations appear to range from 180 ft. to the hilltop. On a July weekday, we saw no other visitors.

A self-guiding nature trail through the bog includes a boardwalk, from which we saw a great variety of plant life, including a wild orchid. It dead-ends at a small pond fringed with shrubs. There are several miles of hiking and skiing trails.

PUBLICATIONS

By mail; $0.50 for postage and handling:
Leaflet. $0.50.
Map. $0.50
Bog Nature Trail Guide. $2.

HEADQUARTERS: Supt. Bob Murray, 5 Wood Lane, Andover, MA 01845.

CHESTER-BLANDFORD STATE FOREST

Massachusetts Division of Forests and Parks   West
2,308 acres.

From Springfield, 20 mi. W on US 20.

The highest point is only 1,501 ft., but that's more than 1,000 ft. above the lowest. The forested slopes are steep, with many brooks and streams. The mixed forest is dominated by oaks with many substantial hemlocks.

Sanderson Brook has a 100-ft. cascade. The road to the falls and brookside trail has been closed to vehicles, but it's an attractive quarter-mile walk from the parking area.

ACTIVITIES

Camping: 12 sites.
Hiking: Trails and forest roads.
Hunting: Deer, bobcat, snowshoe hare, cottontail, raccoon, woodcock, ruffed grouse.
Fishing: Trout in streams.

REFERENCE: *AMC Massachusetts and Rhode Island Trail Guide.* Boston: Appalachian Mountain Club, 1988.

HEADQUARTERS: Chester, MA 01050; (413) 354-6347.

CLARKSBURG STATE FOREST
Massachusetts Division of Forests and Parks   West
3,250 acres.

NW corner of MA. From North Adams, about 2 mi. N on M Rd.

A heavily forested site overlooking the Hoosic River. Elevations from about 900 to over 2,200 ft. Rock outcrops and ledges. Trees are mixed hardwoods with white and red pine, spruces. Fine display of fall colors.

ACTIVITIES
Camping: 47 sites.
Hiking: The Appalachian Trail crosses the Forest. Other trails and woods roads.

REFERENCES
AMC Massachusetts and Rhode Island Trail Guide. Boston: Appalachian Mountain Club, 1988.
Brady, John, and Brian White. *Fifty Hikes in Massachusetts.* Woodstock, VT: Backcountry Publications, 1983.

HEADQUARTERS: Middle Road, Clarksburg, MA 01247; (413) 442-8928.

CONNECTICUT RIVER
69 river miles.   West

From VT to CT.

I-91 and US 5 parallel the river from border to border, but they aren't always within sight or earshot of canoeists. Most of the shore is heavily developed in the S, but N of Northampton much of the course is through farmland. There's almost no riverside State land.

One of the first public access points S of the NH border is where SR 2 crosses and the river turns sharply W. At Barton Cove, just E of Turners Falls, the Northeast Utilities Company has a camping, picnicking, and swimming area, with boat ramp.

Several dams impede the river flow. Most canoeing and boating is within their impoundments. The longest unimpeded run is the 36 mi. from Turners Falls to Holyoke. Anyone contemplating a border-to-border cruise should study the route first. Low water can be a problem in some stretches. Portages must be arranged around dams. Some rapids and hazards will be encountered. Even informal campsites are scarce.

REFERENCES

Kulik, Stephen, Pete Salmansohn, Matthew Schmidt, and Heidi Welch. *The Audubon Society Field Guide to the Natural Places of the Northeast: Inland.* New York: Pantheon Books, 1984.

Schweiker, Roioli, ed. *AMC River Guide: Massachusetts, Connecticut, Rhode Island.* Boston: Appalachian Mountain Club, 1985.

CRANE POND WILDLIFE MANAGEMENT AREA

Massachusetts Division of Fisheries and Wildlife   East
2,600 acres.

From I-95, Exit 54. W on SR 133 to center of Georgetown. Turn right on North St. 1.8 mi. Left on Thurlow. In about 1.5 mi. look for gated entrances.

This site is W of I-95, lying across the town lines of Georgetown, Groveland, Newbury, and West Newbury. The site map is confusing because the road shown crossing the site appears to change names: Pond Street becomes Star Road, which becomes Little Road, the latter two intersecting Seven Star Road, Bear Hill Road, and Byfield Road. Look for the steel gates typical of Department of Environmental Management (DEM) sites.

We parked at one of the gates and hiked for a while, picking blackberries. Most of the area is abandoned farmland now reverting to brush and forest. About one-fifth is marsh, bog, and open water. We didn't see the Parker River; it's not shown on the site map but the accompanying text says it flows through.

Parking areas aren't shown on the site map, but we saw several along perimeter roads. Motor vehicles, including trail bikes and snowmobiles, aren't allowed inside. The text mentions "a large network of walking trails." Some are overgrown, but we found enough for pleasant hiking. We met no other visitors.

ACTIVITIES
Hunting: Most native game species are present. Pheasant and snowshoe hare are stocked.
Fishing: Trout are stocked in the Parker River Apr.–May. Bass and pickerel in Crane Pond and Little Crane Pond.

PUBLICATIONS: Site map and description.

HEADQUARTERS: Wildlife District Manager, Harris St., Box 86, Acton, MA 01720; (508) 263-4647.

CRANE WILDLIFE MANAGEMENT AREA
Massachusetts Division of Fisheries and Wildlife   East
1,615 acres.

At the W end of Cape Cod, near Falmouth. From SR 28, E on SR 151 about 3 mi., to entrance and parking.

Terrain is flat to gently rolling, with a few low ridges. Most of it is open and reverting farmlands, with some scrub forest. The site has a few small streams and ponds, a small marsh in the SW corner. A separate 53-acre parcel is managed for quail. A large open area was once an airport.

A network of trails is often used by hikers and horse riders in spring and summer, and on Sundays in hunting season. Common wildlife species include pheasant, quail, woodcock, grouse, deer, fox, rabbit, woodchuck, squirrel.

PUBLICATION: Map.

HEADQUARTERS: Wildlife District Manager, Massachusetts Division of Fisheries and Wildlife, 195 Bournedale Rd., Buzzards Bay, MA 02532; (508) 759-3406.

D.A.R. STATE FOREST
Massachusetts Division of Forests and Parks   West
1,517 acres.

From Goshen on SR 9, 1 mi. N on SR 112.

This seems to be the most popular State Forest in western MA. In summer the campground begins filling on Thursday evening, and by Friday evening there are no available sites. At times long lines of cars form early in the morning, waiting for a vacancy.

Visitors come because there's swimming, an attractive campground, an unusually active naturalist program, and pleasant scenery. Terrain is rolling to hilly, with rock outcrops. Moor's Hill, 1,713 ft., is the highest point, offering a four-state view from its fire tower. Devil's Den is a craggy cleft on Rogers Brook. Upper and Lower Highland lakes are each a bit less than a mile long. One side of Lower Highland has private homes.

About two-thirds of the site is undeveloped except for hiking trails. In this portion are streams, ponds, swamps, and a waterfall. The area is forested with northern hardwoods, white pine, and hemlock. The understory includes mountain laurel, azalea, blueberry. Many wildflowers, including lady's-slipper, trillium, swamp pink.

The *Nature Center* is the base for an active and innovative naturalist program, which includes *evening programs, night walks, pond walks,* a 3-mi. *nature trail,* and *special events.*

ACTIVITIES
Camping: 58 sites, mid-May to mid-Oct.
Hiking: 9 mi. of trails and forest roads.
Fishing: Bass, perch, trout.
Canoeing: On both lakes. No boats with motors.
Swimming: In Upper Lake.

PUBLICATION: Trail map.

HEADQUARTERS: Goshen, MA 01032; (413) 268-7098.

DANIEL WEBSTER WILDLIFE SANCTUARY
Massachusetts Audubon Society   East
444 acres.

From SR 3 N of Plymouth, Exit 11. Go E about 5 mi. on SR 139 to Marshfield Center. Pass 2 stoplights and turn right on Webster St. In 1 mi., turn left on Winslow Cemetery Rd.

Once owned by Daniel Webster, the site was acquired by Massachusetts Audubon in 1983. On Cape Cod Bay, mostly grassland and riparian land, it drains to Green Harbor Basin, a shallow river controlled by tidal gates.

About 150 bird species have been recorded. The site attracts migratory waterfowl, shorebirds, and raptors. As many as a thousand ducks may be present at one time. Mammals include red fox, opossum, raccoon, rabbit, field rodents, mink, muskrat, weasel. This site and two other Audubon sanctuaries are managed as the South Shore Regional Center.

Pets are prohibited.

PUBLICATIONS
Leaflet.
South Shore calendar of events: nature hikes, slide shows, etc.

HEADQUARTERS: South Shore Regional Center, 2000 Main St., Marshfield, MA 02050; (617) 837-9400.

DOROTHY F. RICE SANCTUARY FOR WILDLIFE
New England Forestry Foundation   West
273 acres.

E of Pittsfield. From SR 8 in Hinsdale, E on SR 143 to South St. in Peru Center (a crossroads). 0.9 mi. S on South St. to Sanctuary sign.

A visitor center is at the parking area about 1/4 mi. past the gate. It's open daily except Tues. May–Aug,; weekends only Sept.–Oct.; closed in winter. A bulletin board provides information when the center is closed. Guided hikes can be arranged when the supervisor is available in summer.

From the parking area, 6 trails lead out through the diverse habitats of the Sanctuary: forest, grassland, reverting fields, swamp, beaver pond. Elevations range from 1,810 to 2,140 ft.

The site is 90% forested. Tree species include red spruce, eastern hemlock, red maple, yellow birch, white ash, sugar maple, white and gray birches, beech, balsam fir, larch, red oak, mountain and striped maples. Wildflowers include lady's-slipper, swamp pink, asters, many more.

Birds: List of 68 species available includes 16 warblers, hawks, osprey, owls, woodpeckers, grouse, woodcock, ducks. Peak season is spring.

Mammals include deer, raccoon, porcupine, beaver, skunk, red fox, red and gray squirrels, weasel, chipmunk, bobcat, bear, cottontail.

Hiking: More than 12 mi. of trails, mostly easy.

PUBLICATIONS
Trail guide.
Lists of birds, mammals, etc. may be available.

REFERENCE: Brady, John, and Brian White. *Fifty Hikes in Massachusetts.*
Woodstock, VT: Backcountry Publications, 1983.

HEADQUARTERS: Rice Road, Peru, MA 01050. Boston office: (617) 437-1441.

ERVING STATE FOREST
Massachusetts Division of Forests and Parks   West
4,479 acres.

From Athol, 8 mi. W on SR 2A, then N 2 mi. on Wendell Depot Rd.

The camping area is on a steep, forested hillside above a small lake. The opposite shore has private cottages. We were told the campground is often full on weekends.

In the morning we hiked up a steep forest road from the campground. Trees are mostly oak, white pine, and hemlock, with mountain laurel, azalea, blueberry, and honeysuckle in the understory. Seasonal wildflowers include painted trillium, Solomon's-seal, bunchberry, clintonia, mayflower.

Birds: Mostly upland forest species: whip-poor-will, flycatchers, wrens, hawks, owls, grouse, woodcock, scarlet tanager, bluebird, thrushes, warblers, chickadee, titmouse. We saw no waterfowl but assume some migrants come through.

Mammals: Include raccoon, snowshoe hare, chipmunk, weasel, cottontail, muskrat, beaver, fox, red and gray squirrels, bobcat.

Nature trail, 1 mi.

ACTIVITIES
Camping: 32 sites. May to mid-Oct.
Hiking: 2-mi. trail; 12 mi. of forest roads.
Hunting: Deer, upland small game.
Fishing: Trout in Laurel Lake and streams.

HEADQUARTERS: Erving, MA 01364; (413) 544-3939.

GARDEN IN THE WOODS
New England Wild Flower Society   Central
45 acres.

From SR 128, west 8 mi. on SR 20. Left on Raymond Rd. 1.3 mi. to Hemenway Rd.

Open Apr. 15–Oct. 31, except Mondays. 9 A.M.–4 P.M.

From early spring through late fall, this remarkable site displays 1,500 varieties of plants, including many rare and endangered native species. Plants and books on sale.

Pets, picnicking, smoking, and baby strollers are prohibited.

Children under 16 must be accompanied by an adult.

INTERPRETATION
Guided walks, Tuesdays at 10 A.M., Apr. 15–Oct. 11.
Horticultural and botanical library.
Special events.

PUBLICATIONS
Site leaflet.
Site map.
Plant sales list.
Calendar of special events.
Curtis Trail Guide, self-guiding booklet.
Wildflower Cultivation, Propagation, and Sources.

HEADQUARTERS: Hemenway Rd., Framingham, MA 01701; (508) 877-6574.

GRANVILLE STATE FOREST
Massachusetts Division of Forests and Parks   West
2,376 acres.

From SR 57 just E of Granville town line, S at sign.

The entrance road passes a campground, swimming area, and many scattered picnic sites. On the slopes above the river, the forest is largely mature hemlocks with almost no ground cover. Elsewhere is a fine spring display of moun-

tain laurel. Terrain is steep with many ridges and ravines draining to the
Hubbard River. Elevations range from 400 to 1,400 ft. The river, dropping
over a waterfall and cascade, descends 450 ft. in 2 1/2 mi.

ACTIVITIES
Camping: 2 campgrounds, 40 sites. May to mid-Oct.
Hiking: 3 mi. of trails. The AMC guide describes several trails extending
along the river and beyond the Forest.
Hunting: Deer, snowshoe hare, grouse, woodcock.
Fishing: Trout stocked.
Swimming: Stream and small pond.
Ski touring, snowmobiling: 11 mi. of unplowed roads.

REFERENCE: AMC Massachusetts and Rhode Island Trail Guide. Boston: Appalachian Mountain Club, 1988.

PUBLICATION: Map.

HEADQUARTERS: Granville, MA 01034; (413) 357-6611.

GREAT MEADOWS NATIONAL WILDLIFE REFUGE
U.S. Fish and Wildlife Service   East
2,883 acres.

About 20 mi. W of Boston. Two sections. To Sudbury Visitor Center: From
I-95, Exit 26; W on US 20 to SR 27; W on SR 27 to Water Row Rd.; N
to Lincoln Rd.; E to Weir Hill Rd. To Concord Unit: From I-95, Exit 29B;
W on SR 2 to Cambridge Turnpike; N to SR 62 (Bedford St.); NE on SR
62 to Monsen Rd.

This is one of the best inland birding sites in MA, whether one travels on foot
or by boat. Both units are clearly shown on the "Boston and Vicinity" section
of the official highway map. The Sudbury Unit, larger of the two, lies along
the Sudbury River. The Concord Unit lies along the Concord River. Together
they occupy about 12 mi. of river bottomland and marsh. Walden Pond (see
entry) lies between them; Thoreau explored the area and made field notes
about its flora and fauna. The State's 411-acre Pantry Brook Wildlife Management Area adjoins the Sudbury Unit on the NW, at the end of Weir Hill Rd.;
hunting is permitted there.
      The Refuge was established and is managed for migratory birds, chiefly wa-
terfowl. The floodplain has marshes and impoundments. A fringe of trees
grows on the narrow strip of upland, but the range of elevations within the

Refuge is only 8 ft. Many waterfowl stop here during the fall migration. The best viewing is from the Dike Trail in the Concord Unit.

Plants: Wetland species include water-lilies, American lotus, wild iris, duckweed, cattail, pickerelweed, arrowhead, loosestrife, wild oats, wild cucumber, buttonbush, sparganium, jack-in-the-pulpit, skunk cabbage, touch-me-not.

Birds: Despite the limited upland habitat, 221 birds species have been recorded in recent years. A checklist is available, prepared in cooperation with the Massachusetts Audubon Society.

Seasonally abundant or common water and shore birds include great blue heron, black-crowned night-heron, Canada goose, wood duck, American black duck, mallard, green-winged and blue-winged teal, American wigeon, ring-necked duck, sora, American coot, killdeer, spotted and least sandpipers.

INTERPRETATION
Visitor Center in Sudbury Unit has displays, auditorium, information. Open daily except winter weekends and holidays.
Nature trails include 3 in Concord, 1 in Sudbury:
- *Dike Trail* along impoundment with view of marsh pools has an observation tower and photo blind. The parking area is small, often full; best to walk from Concord or come by canoe.
- *Black Duck Trail* follows the edge of the marsh upper pool.
- *Timber Trail* enters a wooded area off the Dike Trail.
- *Weir Hill Trail* in Sudbury traverses 4 habitats.

ACTIVITIES
Fishing: Both rivers; bass, perch, bullhead.
Canoeing: Both rivers are canoeable to their confluence, traversing both Refuge units. Both are passable at all water levels, with no rapids. Especially at higher water, paddling against a headwind is difficult.

PUBLICATIONS
Refuge leaflet with map.
Bird checklist.

REFERENCES
Brady, John, and Brian White. *Fifty Hikes in Massachusetts.* Woodstock, VT: Backcountry Publications, 1983.
Fisher, Alan. *Country Walks Near Boston.* Boston: Appalachian Mountain Club, 1985.
Schweiker, Roioli, ed. *AMC River Guide: Massachusetts, Connecticut, Rhode Island.* Boston: Appalachian Mountain Club, 1985.

HEADQUARTERS: Weir Hill Rd., Sudbury, MA 01776; (508) 443-4661.

H. O. COOK STATE FOREST

Massachusetts Division of Forests and Parks   East
1,620 acres.

On the VT border. From SR 2 at Charlemont, N 8 mi. on SR 8A.

Rugged, forested terrain is sharply dissected by several large streams. Highest elevation is 1,740 ft. Of interest are several hundred acres of Norway spruce and white pine planted in the early 1900s and now reaching maturity. Elsewhere the pattern is familiar: northern hardwoods with red spruce. Azalea and hobblebush are prominent in the understory. Numerous wildflowers in openings.

Hiking: 6 mi. of little-used forest roads.

HEADQUARTERS: c/o Mohawk Trail State Forest, P.O. Box 7, Charlemont, MA 01339; (413) 339-5504.

HAROLD PARKER STATE FOREST

Massachusetts Division of Forests and Parks   East
3,014 acres.

SE of Andover, between SRs 125 and 114. Several entrances, well signed.

We were told most visitors come from nearby, chiefly for fishing and camping. Most other campers are transients staying for one night, as we did.

The original forest was cut or burned long ago, followed by farming and pasturing. Now there is again a mature forest cover, some developing through succession, but we also saw extensive plantations. The site includes 10 ponds and wooded swamp.

Although the site is relatively large, a number of paved and unpaved roads divide it into blocks, none of which seems larger than about 400 acres. The map shows no point more than 1/2 mi. from a road.

The site is considered poor to fair for birding.

We didn't rate the site highly as an attractive natural area, because of road traffic and relatively heavy use. It is an entry because it has one of the few public campgrounds in the region, a base for visits to other sites.

ACTIVITIES

Camping: 134 sites.

Hiking: Trails and woods roads throughout the site.

Hunting: Limited seasonal releases of pheasant and snowshoe hare. Hunting restricted to section E of Jenkins Rd.

Fishing: Berry Pond is stocked with trout but is rated marginal. Fair to good warmwater fishing for bass and pickerel in other ponds.

PUBLICATION: Site map showing trails and roads.

REFERENCE: *AMC Massachusetts and Rhode Island Trail Guide.* Boston: Appalachian Mountain Club, 1988.

HEADQUARTERS: Middleton Rd., North Andover, MA 01845; (508) 686-3391.

HIGH RIDGE WILDLIFE MANAGEMENT AREA

Massachusetts Division of Fisheries and Wildlife   Central
1,800 acres.

N central MA, near Gardner. From the intersection of SRs 101 and 140, go SE on 140, left on Smith St., see WMA sign and proceed to parking.

This was once a mental hospital surrounded by productive farm fields. The buildings, across the railroad tracks, are now a minimum security prison. The land is a recent WMA acquisition. Only foot travel is permitted beyond the parking area.

Terrain is rolling, from a base elevation of about 900 ft. to the open ridge at 1,200 ft. that gives the site its name. A mix of agricultural fields, brushy fields, and hardwood forest provides the habitat edges favored by many wildlife species. An arm of Whitman Reservoir penetrates the NE corner. Two small streams with native trout supply several marshy areas.

Wildlife includes deer, waterfowl, grouse, woodcock, rabbit.

The site's attractions are modest, but it's easy hiking and except in hunting season you're not likely to have company. The view from the ridge includes Mt. Wachusett and Mt. Monadnock.

PUBLICATION: Site map.

HEADQUARTERS: Wildlife District Manager, Temple St., West Boylston, MA 01583; (508) 835-3607.

HINSDALE FLATS WILDLIFE MANAGEMENT AREA
Massachusetts Division of Fisheries and Wildlife   West
1,226 acres.

> E of Pittsfield. From its junction with SR 143, 0.8 mi. S on SR 8. Left on Middlefield Rd. (Skyline Trail) 0.7 mi. to WMA sign. Park on roadside.

Middlefield Rd. is at the N end of the WMA, whose N–S length is about 4 times its width. From here, the highest part of the site, one overlooks a large area of rolling old fields, dropping down to the forest edge and seasonally flooded stream bottoms. The East Branch of the Housatonic River is near the W boundary. Bilodeau Brook bisects the area. The site has two small artificial ponds and a beaver pond.

ACTIVITIES
   Hunting: Stocked pheasant, woodcock, grouse, waterfowl, raccoon, gray squirrel, cottontail, deer. Other mammals present include beaver, otter, mink, muskrat, black bear.
   Fishing: Trout in the East Branch and several brooks.

HEADQUARTERS: Wildlife District Manager, 400 Hubbard Ave., Pittsfield, MA 01201; (413) 447-9789.

HIRAM H. FOX WILDLIFE MANAGEMENT AREA
Massachusetts Division of Fisheries and Wildlife   West
2,424 acres.

> From SR 9 near Cummington, drive S on SR 112 through Ringville and angle right on Goss Hill Rd.

We couldn't find a Goss Hill Road sign and had to ask. The parking area is on the right a little over 1 mi. from 112. From this point, a trail runs SW.
   The site is rolling with some steep ledges and gullies, elevations from 700 ft. to 1,200 ft., forested with a mixture of hardwoods and conifers. Meadow Brook crosses the site, as does Little River, close beside SR 112. There are two small marshy areas.
   Wildlife includes black bear, wild turkey, deer, grouse, deer, raccoon, snowshoe hare, gray squirrel, bobcat, some waterfowl.

HEADQUARTERS: Wildlife District Manager, 400 Hubbard Ave., Pittsfield, MA 01201; (413) 447-9789.

HOCKOMOCK SWAMP WILDLIFE MANAGEMENT AREA

Massachusetts Division of Fisheries and Wildlife   East
4,833 acres.

From SR 24, Exit 15 (just N of I-495). Take SR 104 W. Lake Nippenicket is on the right.

Lake Nippenicket is at the SE corner of the WMA, which extends N to SR 106 and W to Bay Rd. in Taunton. You'll need a map, because State land occupies only about half of this area, in one large but irregular and sprawling block plus numerous detached bits.

Much of the area is wooded, but the chief attractions are the wetlands: maple and cedar swamps, marshlands, open water, and flowing streams. With a map one can find trails and other foot routes, but the best way to explore the area is by canoe.

In the SW corner, Bay Road runs between the WMA and Winnecunnet Pond. About 0.6 mi. N, turn right on Toad Island Road to a parking area. From here unimproved roads cross and encircle a 450-acre tract on the N side of the Snake River, which is bordered by marshland. This tract was a turkey farm, and the open lands are under cultivation. Pheasants are stocked, and waterfowl frequent the area.

Lake Nippenicket, 368 acres, was formerly owned by a hunting club. About 1 1/2 mi. long, the lake has a boat ramp at the SE corner. Shore fishing, birding, and duck hunting opportunities along an unimproved road and foot trail on the W side.

The Division of Fisheries and Wildlife told us that about all of the wildlife species occurring in SE MA can be found here.

Birds: Of the waterfowl, black duck, mallard, wood duck, and teal are most abundant, but many others stop during migrations. Other bird species include pheasant, grouse, woodcock, quail, and many songbirds.

Mammals: Include deer, snowshoe hare, cottontail, squirrel, muskrat, fox, raccoon, mink, weasel, opossum, otter, skunk.

ACTIVITIES

Fishing: Lake has chain pickerel, largemouth bass, black crappie.

Canoeing, boating: The Town River flows N from the N end of Lake Nippenicket, being joined in about 1 mi. by the S-flowing Hockomock and continuing NE. These two rivers, the Snake, and the lake are canoeable, although the segment of the Town River just beyond the lake is often overgrown.

PUBLICATIONS: Maps of the WMA and the Erwin S. Wilder and Harry C. Darling tracts.

REFERENCE: Schweiker, Roioli, ed. *AMC River Guide: Massachusetts, Connecticut, Rhode Island.* Boston: Appalachian Mountain Club, 1985.

HEADQUARTERS: Wildlife District Manager, 195 Bournedale Rd., Buzzards Bay, MA 02532; (508) 759-3406.

HOPKINTON STATE PARK
Massachusetts Division of Forests and Parks   East
1,450 acres.

From I-495, Exit 21. E to Hopkinton; N on SR 85 to entrance.

Like most State Parks within the I-495 beltway, this one is for day use only. Like most parks with water-based recreation, it is heavily used in warm weather, at least on weekends. We visited about 9 A.M. on a July weekday and saw few visitors.

Hopkinton doesn't fit our definition of "natural area" because it has been developed for intensive use, with recreation field, pavilion, boathouse, bathhouse, 5 launching ramps, and a dozen parking areas. Development is on the N side of mile-long Hopkinton Reservoir. The lake is largely surrounded by hardwood forest.

We include it as an example of sites we generally omit: attractive, popular, but not a quiet place.

Hiking: A trail about 1 mi. long skirts the N boundary of the site. We were told there is undeveloped acreage on the other side of SR 85, near Park HQ, but the site map shows only the developed area.

PUBLICATION: Site map.

HEADQUARTERS: Cedar St., Hopkinton, MA 01748; (508) 435-4303.

HUBBARDSTON WILDLIFE MANAGEMENT AREA
Massachusetts Division of Fisheries and Wildlife   Central
1,000 acres.

N central MA. From Hubbardston on SR 68, E on Westminster Rd. At the fork of Westminster and New Westminster, take your choice; the former crosses the N portion of the site, the latter the S portion.

The Metropolitan District Commission owns about 8,000 acres in this watershed, of which 1,000 are managed for wildlife. This area is dotted with many low hills, mostly surrounded by wetlands, most drained by Joslin Brook. Uplands are open fields, brushy fields, and young forest.

Nothing dramatic, but it's a quiet and pleasant area for a day hike with good birding, not in hunting season. Warmwater fish in the ponds.

PUBLICATION: Map.

HEADQUARTERS: Wildlife District Manager, Temple St., West Boylston, MA 01583; (508) 835-3607.

IPSWICH RIVER SANCTUARY
Massachusetts Audubon Society   East
2,217 acres.

About 20 mi. N of Boston, in Topsfield. From US 1, E on SR 97 at traffic light. Left on Perkins Row. 1 mi. to entrance.

Open Tues.–Sun., dawn to dusk.

The site, a former estate, has many exceptional qualities, not the least of which is the information describing its flora and fauna. Few sites in this region with similar characteristics can provide such data.

Its numerous habitats include coniferous and deciduous woods, fields, shrublands, wooded swamp, marsh, bog, and meadow.

Plants: 445 species have been recorded. A list with common and scientific names is available for inspection.

The wooded upland overlooks the Ipswich River. In the early 1900s, the then owner developed an impressive arboretum. At The Rockery, great boulders were arranged in a setting for both endemic and exotic flora. Included are Douglas-fir; Korean, mugho, and Jeffrey pines; dwarf Alberta spruce, sawara cypress, as well as sourwood, mountain laurel, azaleas, and rhododendrons. Exotic species include winged euonymus, Frazier and sweet bay magnolias, mountain and Japanese andromedas, Amur corktree, Oriental photinia, red-veined enkainthus, and many more.

Arboretum Road, circling Bradstreet Hill, is bordered with azaleas, rhododendrons, and many exotics.

The Wildflower Garden, SE of Bradstreet Hill, was begun in 1951, with the aim of assembling all the spring wildflower species occuring in Essex County.

Birds: 221 species have been recorded. A list is available for inspection. 98 of the species are reported as nesting here. The inventory gathered data on abundance, seasonality, and habitat preference.

An observation tower overlooks the Bunker Meadows Waterfowl Management Area.

Prominent species include black and wood duck, greater scaup, hooded merganser, Canada goose, bald eagle, osprey; Cooper's, red-tailed, red-shouldered, and broad-winged hawks; kestrel, merlin, northern and loggerhead shrikes, brown thrasher, veery, white-breasted nuthatch, goldfinch, Philadelphia vireo, Henslow's sparrow. Warblers include black-and-white, golden-winged, yellow, black-throated green, blackburnian, chestnut-sided, Canada, yellowthroat, ovenbird, redstart.

Mammals: 26 species have been recorded. The list is available for inspection.

Reptiles and Amphibians: 18 species have been recorded. The list is available for inspection.

ACTIVITIES
Hiking: 10 mi. of trails.
Canoeing: River ecology float trips on the Ipswich River. Canoe rentals.

Pets are prohibited.

NEARBY: Parker River National Wildlife Refuge; Richard T. Crane, Jr., Memorial Reservation; Willowdale State Forest. (See entries.)

PUBLICATION: Calendar of events.

REFERENCE: *AMC Massachusetts and Rhode Island Trail Guide.* Boston: Appalachian Mountain Club, 1982.

HEADQUARTERS: Topsfield, MA 01983; (508) 887-9264.

JOHN C. PHILLIPS WILDLIFE SANCTUARY/BOXFORD STATE FOREST

Massachusetts Division of Fisheries and Wildlife; Massachusetts   East
Division of Forests and Parks
335 acres; 780 acres.

From Exit 51 on I-95, turn W. Take first right turn (Middleton Road) 1.4 mi. to parking on left.

With no adequate map or directions, we wandered around roads that had no street signs. On what proved to be Middleton Road, we spotted a small sign identifying the Sanctuary but no parking place. Proceeding toward I-95, we came on a parking area at a steel gate, with a posting of the Department of Environmental Management. We would have done less wandering had we had the Division of Fisheries and Wildlife pamphlet *Wildlife Sanctuaries*. This was the first sanctuary donated to the Commonwealth of Massachusetts by a citizen.

Beyond the gate is a pleasant, quiet trail marked with red blazes. We assume this is the Bald Hill Trail described in the AMC guide. The portion we hiked is an old woods road. No recent traffic has worn it so deeply, and we imagined it might once have carried stagecoaches.

It's rolling terrain with some steep banks. The section we hiked has an open white pine forest, with some large trees. At a small pond we saw tracks of fishermen, but no one was fishing.

Now that we have the pamphlet, we see that the tract extends about 1 1/2 mi. S from the first sign. Most of the area is swampland. The site is noted among birders for barred owl, pileated woodpecker, and Louisiana waterthrush, as well as many more common nesting species.

Wildflowers include lily-of-the-valley, Solomon's-seal, Indian pipe, pipsissewa, pink lady's-slipper.

REFERENCE: *AMC Massachusetts and Rhode Island Trail Guide*. Boston: Appalachian Mountain Club, 1988.

KENNETH DUBUQUE MEMORIAL STATE FOREST

(formerly Hawley State Forest)
Massachusetts Division of Forests and Parks   West
7,822 acres.

NW MA. From Adams, 13 mi. SE on SR 116, then N 1 mi. on SR 8A. (The AMC trail guide has a more complicated route to the trail system.)

In the high northern Berkshires, this is part of the large block that includes Mohawk Trail and Savoy State Forests (see entries). However, we could find no trail links. This Forest has a well-developed trail system, with separate trails for hiking, horse riding, and recreation vehicles. It is one of the few where overnight stays are permitted. The terrain is heavily forested, rugged, elevations from 1,200 to 2,000 ft. The site has several brooks and beaver dams. Two ponds, the largest about 1/2 mi. long. The forest is typical of the region: northern hardwoods with some white pine, hemlock, and spruce; azalea and hobblebush in the understory. Seasonal wildflowers include violets, adder's-tongue, orchids, trillium, touch-me-not, trout lily, spring beauty, gentians.

Birds: Include ruffed grouse, woodcock, hawks, owls, bluebird, scarlet tanager, thrushes, brown thrasher, flycatcher, black-capped chickadee, tufted titmouse, brown creeper, warblers, some waterfowl.

Mammals: Include snowshoe hare, cottontail, red and gray squirrels, fox, raccoon, skunk, muskrat, beaver, otter, mink, weasel, bobcat, deer. Occasional black bear and coyote.

INTERPRETATION: *Nature trail* around Hallockville Pond, near HQ on SR 8A.

ACTIVITIES
Hiking, backpacking: 8 mi. of designated hiking trails; 35 mi. of little-used woods roads, some overgrown. 3 Adirondack shelters are along the hiking trails E of SR 8A.
Fishing: Ponds and streams. Trout, perch, pickerel.

REFERENCE: *AMC Massachusetts and Rhode Island Trail Guide.* Boston: Appalachian Mountain Club, 1988.

HEADQUARTERS: Hawley, MA 01070; (413) 339-6631.

LAUGHING BROOK EDUCATION AND WILDLIFE SANCTUARY
Massachusetts Audubon Society   Central
259 acres.

From I-91 near Springfield, Exit 4. Take SR 83 S to Sumner Ave. E 3.6 mi. on Sumner, then bear right on Allen St. for 4.7 mi. into Hampden. Left 2 mi. on Main St.

With some 250 people enlisted as volunteers, this is one of Audubon's liveliest sanctuaries. The site map shows the way to the Environmental Center, Storyteller's House, goose and deer pen, wildflower garden, nature center, land use ethic exhibit, Smiling Pool, dinosaur tracks, live animal loop, and more. This was the estate of Thornton W. Burgess; his house is now the Storyteller's House.

The buildings and other developments occupy 5 acres. Around them are 200 acres of woodland, 37 of swampland, 8 in open fields, Laughing Brook, the Scantic River.

Plants: The wildflower list notes seasonal abundance.

Birds: The bird list is divided into winter and summer residents, with notes on migrants.

Mammals: Although the site is near Springfield and just off a main commuter route, it has deer, porcupine, red and gray foxes, and bobcat, as well as opossum, shrews, little brown bat, river otter, mink, shorttail weasel, woodchuck, chipmunk; gray, red, and flying squirrels, beaver, deer and white-footed mice, meadow jumping mouse, and cottontail.

Pets are prohibited.

INTERPRETATION
The Education Center is a fine, 2-story, modern building with library, auditorium, exhibits, program room, solar greenhouse, shop, and offices. Open Tues.–Sun., 10 A.M.–5 P.M.; also open holiday Mondays.

Program brochure lists many special events for children and adults, continuing throughout the year. They include classes, films, guided hikes, day camps.

Five nature trails, 0.5 to 1.6 mi. Trails visit a glacial esker, red pine forest, boardwalk near the river, hemlock grove.

PUBLICATIONS
Seasonal program brochure.
Sanctuary newsletter, published seasonally.
Introductory guide.
Trail map.
Composting Toilets.
Volunteer Opportunities.

HEADQUARTERS: 789 Main St., Hampden, MA 01036; (413) 566-8034.

LEOMINSTER STATE FOREST
Massachusetts Division of Forests and Parks   Central
4,265 acres.

Near Fitchburg and Leominster. From SR 2, about 2 1/2 mi. on SR 31.

SR 31 cuts N–S across the W side of the Forest. Its highest point, 1,234-ft. Crow Hill, and the Mid-State Trail, are in the narrow strip between SR 31 and the W boundary. Park HQ is on SR 31. Rocky Pond Road runs W–E across the middle.

Terrain is rolling to steep, from a base elevation of about 800 ft. Most of it is forested with a mixture of hardwoods, most of them 6- to 8-inch diameter, and white pine. We saw much mountain laurel and were told there are 1,000 acres of it, plus 75 to 100 acres of azalea. Many blueberries and wildflowers.

We stopped at a picnic area parking lot and began walking down what looked like an attractive woodland trail. At once we saw red arrows nailed to trees, bearing the legend:

> This arrow marks the route of a cross-country motorcycle endurance run, to be held within the next two weeks. It will be removed in the week following the event. Please do not remove.
>   New England Trail Rider Association

The run had been held. We were shocked by its destructiveness. The trail was deeply rutted, muddy, and eroding. Many cyclists had ridden as much as 30 ft. off the trail, cutting raw gouges into the forest duff. It was a nasty mess we didn't care to hike through.

ACTIVITIES

Hiking: 28 mi. of trails, some steep. The Mid-State Trail links Leominster with the Wachusett Reservation (see entry). A popular trail ascends Crow Hill, which has a 165-ft. open face and ledge used by rock climbers.

Hunting: Deer and small upland game, in undeveloped areas.

Fishing: Trout stocked in Crow Pond.

Swimming: Pond and stream.

PUBLICATION: Site map, showing trails.

REFERENCES

AMC Massachusetts and Rhode Island Trail Guide. Boston: Appalachian Mountain Club, 1988.

Brady, John. *Fifty Hikes in Massachusetts.* Woodstock, MA: Backcountry Publications, 1983.

HEADQUARTERS: P.O. Box 32, East Princeton, MA 01517; (508) 874-2303.

MARTHA'S VINEYARD

Mixed ownerships   East
25 mi. W–E, 10 mi. N–S.

Car ferry from Woods Hole. Summer passenger service from Falmouth, Hyannis, and New Bedford. Also air service.

This triangular island lies 7 mi. S of Cape Cod. Vineyard Sound and the Elizabeth Island are on the NE, Nantucket Sound on the NW, the Atlantic Ocean along its S base. Of the 3 principal towns, Vineyard Haven and Oak Bluffs are on the N, Edgartown on the SE.

We spent enough time there in the 1940s to enjoy some of its traditions and folkways. Development has changed it. Devoted islanders have helped preserve some significant natural areas, including a State Forest and several private sanctuaries. Magnificent South Beach is still there, but the access routes we used are now marked "No Trespassing." Traffic has come to the dirt roads where we cycled.

It's still attractive. Being an island gives it some insulation. If we do go back, it will be after the summer crowds have gone.

Birds: The Felix Neck Wildlife Sanctuary has a *Birds of Martha's Vineyard Checklist.* Of the 359 species, 247 are called "regulars": recorded yearly 1979–1983.

Pets are prohibited at the private sanctuaries.

MARTHA'S VINEYARD STATE FOREST

Massachusetts Division of Forests and Parks
4,000 acres.

From Vineyard Haven, 4 mi. SE on the Edgartown road; turn right toward airport; in 1 mi. see Forest sign.

At the center of the island, this site is furthest removed from summer activity. The Chamber of Commerce leaflet doesn't mention it. We remember woodlands, brushy fields, windswept hilltops, and fine views; it hadn't become a State Forest then.

FELIX NECK WILDLIFE SANCTUARY

Massachusetts Audubon Society
350 acres.

From Vineyard Haven, 4 mi. SE on the Edgartown road.

Open dawn to 7 P.M., except Mon.

On the S and E coasts of the Island are a complex of barrier beaches, salt ponds, marshes, open fields, and pine woods. The Sanctuary is a terminal moraine with a good representation of these habitats. About half of the site is forested with oak and pitch pine.

Flora and Fauna: Responding to our request for information, the Sanctuary sent us *Lists of Felix Neck Plants and Animals.* This is the most comprehensive inventory of living organisms we received from any site. Under "Plants," for example, the headings include "Seaweeds," "Lichens," "Fungi," "Mosses," "Ferns and Horsetails," and "Seed-Bearing Plants," with numerous subheads, giving the Latin name for each species and, where there is such, the common name. The compiler is careful to note that, for the seed-bearing plants, only species conspicuous in mid-summer have been listed; observation in other seasons remains to be done.

Headings under "Invertebrates" include "Sponges," "Coelenterates," "Annelids," and "Echinoderms"; "Arthropods"—with 6 single-spaced pages of listings—and "Mollusks." Under "Vertebrates" are the "Fishes," "Reptiles and Amphibians," "Birds," and "Mammals."

Under "Mammals," the compiler observes,

> Mammals have not enjoyed a happy history on Martha's Vineyard. Early settlers (both red and white) did their best to eradicate all of them and in some cases (Striped Skunk is cited by Keith, 1969) may have extirpated endemic island races. . . .

INTERPRETATION

Visitor center has exhibits, films, talks, literature. Open 8 A.M.–4:30 P.M.
Nature trails: Four main trails and shorter trails.
Waterfowl pond with observation building.
Raptor barn and rehabilitation building are for treatment of injured, oiled, and orphaned birds.
Photography blind on Sengekontacket Pond is also used for observation.

PUBLICATIONS

Information page with map.
Bird checklist.

HEADQUARTERS: Box 494, Vineyard Haven, MA 02568.

LONG POINT WILDLIFE REFUGE

The Trustees of Reservations
580 acres.

From Edgartown-West Tisbury Road, left on Deep Bottom Road (at gravel pit) 1 mi. past airport entrance. Proceed 3 mi. to entrance on left.

The glacial outwash plain has pitch pine and oak forest, fields, salt and freshwater ponds, salt marshes, sandy beaches on the ocean. A fine birding area.

CAPE POGE WILDLIFE REFUGE, 501 acres.
MYTOI, 14 acres.
WASQUE RESERVATION, 200 acres.

The Trustees of Reservations

On Chappaquiddick Island, by ferry from Edgartown.

Chappaquiddick is the SE corner of Martha's Vineyard, separated from it by a narrow channel and Katama Bay. On its N, a barrier beach, with Cape Poge at its N tip, encircles Cape Poge Bay.

The Cape Poge refuge is well known to birders. Low sand dunes, cedar thickets, salt ponds, tidal flats, and more than 6 mi. of beach provide habitat for thousands of sea and shore birds. This is a nesting area for oyster catcher, snowy egret, black-crowned night-heron, Canada goose, least tern.

REFERENCE: *AMC Massachusetts and Rhode Island Trail Guide.* Boston: Appalachian Mountain Club, 1988.

HEADQUARTERS: The Trustees of Reservations, 572 Essex St., Beverly, MA 01915; (508) 921-1944.

MARTIN BURNS WILDLIFE MANAGEMENT AREA

Massachusetts Division of Fisheries and Wildlife   East
1,500 acres.

S of Newburyport, between I-95 and US 1. From US 1, SW on Middle St. Bear right on Orchard St., about 1 mi. to entrance on right.

This is an attractive area for day hiking. On the last day of July we were the only visitors. The gravel entrance road passes the HQ building. Several parking areas are beyond. A network of trails spans the site. Trail bikes and all-terrain vehicles are prohibited.

The land is gently rolling with many rock outcrops. Primary habitats are brush and young hardwood forest with small clearings, but there are also large areas of marsh and wooded swamp. We saw many wildflowers, including large patches of loosestrife.

Wildlife: Most native species are present, including many songbirds. Pheasant and snowshoe hare are stocked, and these seem to be the chief hunting interest.

Hunting: Special rules are posted.

PUBLICATION: Map with text.

HEADQUARTERS: Wildlife District Manager, Harris St., Box 86, Acton, MA 01720; (508) 263-4347.

METACOMET-MONADNOCK TRAIL
Mixed ownership   West

Connecticut to New Hampshire

The Trail extends from the Hanging Hills of Meridan, CT. to Mt. Monadnock in New Hampshire. It enters MA just W of SR 187, near Agawam, and enters NH from the Warwick State Forest (see entry). That the Trail even exists is remarkable. It has had far less publicity, official support, and volunteer work than the Appalachian Trail, and the route presented even greater difficulties.

Like the AT, it links a series of State Parks and State Forests, and wherever possible it keeps to high ground. But the mountains framing the Connecticut River Valley aren't as high as those of the Berkshires, and much of the route had to be over lowlands. Many sections of the Trail follow roads, but the planners have been ingenious in piecing together back roads, abandoned rights-of-way, and other lightly traveled routes.

Trailside camping is prohibited in MA, and few of the State Parks and Forests have campgrounds. Those who hike from border to border must spend most nights off the Trail.

REFERENCE: *AMC Massachusetts and Rhode Island Trail Guide.* Boston: Appalachian Mountain Club, 1988.

MIDSTATE TRAIL
Midstate Trail Committee   Central
85 trail miles.

From Ashburnham, near the NH border, to Douglas State Forest on the RI border.

The Trail travels the length of Worcester County, linking a chain of State Parks, State Forests, and Wildlife Management Areas. An earlier footpath from Mt. Watatic to Wachusett Mountain fell into disrepair by the 1950s. In 1972 the County Commissioners formed an advisory committee to rejuvenate and extend the Trail. Planning and clearing the route required permission from landowners in sections between public landholdings. It was dedicated in 1985. The Trail, blazed with yellow triangles, is maintained by volunteers.
Five Adirondack shelters are available for backpackers.
At the N end, the Trail connects with the 20-mi. Wapack Trail.

PUBLICATIONS
Leaflet.
19-page trail guide on U.S. Geological Survey maps.

REFERENCE: *AMC Massachusetts and Rhode Island Trail Guide.* Boston: Appalachian Mountain Club, 1988.

INFORMATION: The Midstate Trail Committee, P.O. Box 155, Clinton, MA 01510.

MILLERS RIVER WILDLIFE MANAGEMENT AREA
Massachusetts Division of Fisheries and Wildlife   West
2,067 acres.

From Athol, Millers River Rd.

Millers River flows W to meet the Connecticut River at Greenfield. The S part of the WMA is a narrow strip along the river, which offers good trout fishing and part of a whitewater canoe run. The larger portion of the WMA extends N, a little E of the Athol-Royalston Road. Here the terrain is steep and rocky, forested, good habitat for upland wildlife.

Although the road follows the river, access points are limited. Fishermen willing to walk and scramble can find good trout waters where fishing pressure is light.

The Birch Hill Flood Control Dam regulates river flow. Whitewater canoeists are attracted by Class III rapids during spring high water.

PUBLICATION: Map.

REFERENCE: Schweiker, Roioli, ed. *AMC River Guide: Massachusetts, Connecticut, Rhode Island.* Boston: Appalachian Mountain Club, 1985.

HEADQUARTERS: District Wildlife Manager, Temple St., West Boylston, MA 01583; (508) 835-3607.

MOHAWK TRAIL STATE FOREST

Massachusetts Division of Forests and Parks   West
6,457 acres.

On both sides of SR 2 about 18 mi. E of North Adams; 25 mi. W of the Greenfield/I-91 rotary.

At the N end of the Hoosac Range, the Forest straddles SR 2, the Mohawk Trail. One of the larger State Forests, it has a common boundary on the W with the 10,500-acre Savoy State Forest (see entry), making this the largest block of undeveloped land in MA. The Kenneth Dubuque Memorial State Forest (see entry) is on the S. The terrain is hilly to mountainous, with ridges, deep gorges, rock outcrops, and ledges. Principal streams are the Cold and Deerfield rivers. Elevations range from 700 ft. at the rivers to 1,961 ft. at Indian Lookout.

This is a hiker's forest. The adjacent Savoy has a more extensive trail system, but here there are also woods roads, some used, others abandoned, and paths worn by hunters and fishermen. Or one can bushwhack. Except in hunting season, few people are in the backcountry.

Plants: 95% forested, chiefly with beech, birches, and maples; oaks on S slopes; scattered stands of hemlock, white pine, and spruce. What we saw of the forest seemed more mature than most others in MA, with more trees about 100 ft. tall, diameters over 3 ft. Abundant mountain laurel, azalea, blue-berries, raspberry, wild rose. Seasonal wildflowers include bloodroot, dutch-man's-breeches, trout lily, violets, orchids, trillium, gentians, lily-of-the-valley.

Birds: No checklist is available. Many grouse, woodcock, hawks, owls, song-birds.

Mammals: Deer, black bear, bobcat, raccoon, skunk, red and gray squirrels, red and gray foxes, otter, snowshoe hare, cottontail, coyote, porcupine, fisher.

ACTIVITIES
   Camping: 56 sites on the Cold River.
   Hiking: Trails to Clark Mountain, Todd Mountain, other destinations.
   Fishing: Good trout fishing in both rivers.
   Canoeing: Whitewater on some sections of the Deerfield River. Conditions change seasonally and daily, depending on releases from the power dam up-stream.
   Swimming: Beach near campground.

REFERENCES
   AMC Massachusetts and Rhode Island Trail Guide. Boston: Appalachian
      Mountain Club, 1988.
   Schweiker, Roioli, ed. *AMC River Guide: Massachusetts, Connecticut,*
      Rhode Island. Boston: Appalachian Mountain Club, 1985.

HEADQUARTERS: P.O. Box 7, Charlemont, MA 01339; (413) 339-5504.

MONOMOY NATIONAL WILDLIFE REFUGE
U.S. Fish and Wildlife Service   East
2,702 acres.

   An island at the bend of Cape Cod, S of Chatham. Accessible only by pri-vate or commercial boat across a mile-wide channel. There is road access to HQ on Morris Island in Chatham.

Monomoy, a 10-mile-long barrier beach between Nantucket Sound and the Atlantic Ocean, is a National Wilderness Area, roadless and undeveloped, with no visitor facilities. Most of its visitors are birders. The island is famous for its spring shorebirds.
   The long, narrow island has sand beaches, dunes over 100 ft. high, salt and freshwater marshes, freshwater ponds and kettleholes, dense thickets of scrub oak, pitch pine, black alder, and willow. The beach often offers good shelling.

Birds: Checklist available. 252 species have been reported, 75 of them considered rare. Species nesting here include Canada goose, black duck, piping plover, horned lark, savannah and sharp-tailed sparrows; common, arctic, roseate, and least terns. Migrants include semipalmated and black-bellied plovers, ruddy turnstone, whimbrel, greater and lesser yellowlegs, red knot; pectoral, least, and semipalmated sandpipers; dunlin, sanderling, harlequin duck, king eider, hooded merganser, bald eagle, osprey, peregrine falcon, hudsonian godwit, Wilson's phalarope. Thousands of common eider and white-winged scoter lie just off the beach, along with common loon, goldeneye, bufflehead, red-breasted merganser. Offshore oceanic birds often include shearwater, gannet, jaeger, black-legged kittiwake, razorbill, thick-billed murre, dovekie.

Mammals: Include muskrat, mink, river otter, raccoon, longtail weasel, deer, occasional harbor seal.

Other Fauna: Include Fowler's toad, diamondback terrapin, Atlantic Ridley turtle, leatherback sea turtle.

ACTIVITIES
Hiking: Beach on Monomoy. Short trails on Morris.
Fishing: Striped bass, bluefish, flounder. Best season is May–Oct.
Swimming: Surf, unsupervised.

Pets are not permitted on Monomoy.

Permit is required for group visit.

Winds and rip tides often make the crossing to Monomoy dangerous, especially Nov.–Mar. Safe landings can be made only on the W shore. It is recommended that visitors hire a commercial fishing boat at Chatham.

PUBLICATIONS
Refuge leaflet with map.
Bird checklist.

HEADQUARTERS: *June–Sept.:* Morris Island, MA 02633; (617) 945-0594. *All year:* Parker River National Wildlife Refuge, Northern Blvd., Plum Island, Newburyport, MA 01950; (508) 465-5753.

MONROE STATE FOREST
Massachusetts Division of Forests and Parks   West
4,321 acres.

From North Adams, about 4 mi. E on SR 2; 2 mi. E on Tilda Hill Rd.

In the high northern Berkshires, the terrain is mountainous, with steep slopes, rock ledges and outcrops, elevations from 1,700 to 2,730 ft. The SE boundary is a road following the Deerfield River. The Forest has no river frontage but Raycroft Lookout overlooks the scenic river gorge. Dunbar Brook, which runs across the Forest NW–SE, has numerous small falls and rapids.

The area is 95% forested, chiefly with northern hardwoods, red spruce increasing on upper slopes. Wildlife is typical of the area: deer, bear, upland small game, many birds.

ACTIVITIES

Camping: 3 hike-in sites.

Hiking: 9 mi. of designated foot trails, plus 6 mi. of woods roads.

Hunting: Deer, snowshoe hare, bobcat, raccoon, cottontail, squirrels, grouse, woodcock.

Fishing: Trout streams.

HEADQUARTERS: c/o Mohawk Trail State Forest, P.O. Box 7, Charlemont, MA 01339; (413) 339-5504.

MOOSE HILL WILDLIFE SANCTUARY
Massachusetts Audubon Society   East
929 acres.

From US 1 at Sharon, turn E on SR 27. First right turn on Moose Hill St. and go 1.5 mi.

Open 8 A.M.–6 P.M., Tues.–Sun.

This became the society's first sanctuary in 1916 when a board member offered use of his estate. Terrain is rolling. From a granite bluff at 600-ft. elevation, where there's a fine view, the land drops down through open deciduous forest to open fields and a red maple swamp traversed by a boardwalk.

Several trails lead through the site's several habitats. The Fern Trail has an exceptional number of fern species.

An active program includes school tours, maple sugaring, crafts, day camp, adult classes.

Pets are prohibited.

Birds: No checklist is available. Migrating waterfowl pause at the swamp. Species often seen include hooded merganser, Canada goose, teal. Also goshawk, northern harrier, green heron, bluebird, woodpeckers, grackles, blue jay, tufted titmouse, red-eyed vireo, northern oriole, scarlet tanager, grouse, warblers.

Mammals: Include deer mouse, chipmunk, squirrel, skunk, opossum, raccoon, deer.

PUBLICATION: Brochure.

REFERENCE: *AMC Massachusetts and Rhode Island Trail Guide.* Boston: Appalachian Mountain Club, 1982.

HEADQUARTERS: 300 Moose Hill St., Sharon, MA 02067; (617) 784-5691.

MOUNT GRACE STATE FOREST/NORTHFIELD STATE FOREST/WARWICK STATE FOREST

Massachusetts Division of Forests and Parks   West
11,012 acres.

From Athol, W on SR 2 A; N on SR 78. Northfield is W of SR 78; Mt. Grace is further N; Warwick is on the road E from Warwick.

These Forests have a common HQ. At 7,100 acres, Warwick might seem to be the largest, but the map shows it to be a number of separate blocks. Without maps it would be difficult to know where Forest land begins and ends, but this is sparsely settled country and boundaries seldom matter.

The pattern is common to N central MA: rolling, forested, elevations generally between 700 and 1,200 ft., a few hills rising higher. Trees are northern hardwoods with some white pine and hemlock; mountain laurel and azalea are prominent in the understory; trillium, lady's-slipper, mayflower, Solomon's-seal, and clintonia are common wildflowers. Birds and mammals are also typical of the region.

Northfield has several streams and small swamps. It is crossed by several gravel roads. The map shows no trails, but woods roads offer hiking opportunities. Snowmobilers use the area in winter.

Mt. Grace, on the VT border, attracts more hikers, chiefly because the Metacomet-Monadnock Trail (see entry) crosses the 1,617-ft. summit of Mt. Grace. There's a shelter for backpackers on the Trail. Several brooks and springs. This area, too, is used by snowmobiles and trail bikes.

Warwick is also crossed by gravel and woods roads. Sheomet Lake, almost a mile long, has a boat ramp. Numerous brooks. Snowmobiling in winter.

PUBLICATIONS: Maps.

REFERENCE: (Metacomet-Monadnock Trail): *AMC Massachusetts and Rhode Island Trail Guide.* Boston: Appalachian Mountain Club, 1988.

HEADQUARTERS: Warwick, MA 01264; (508) 544-7474.

MOUNT GREYLOCK STATE RESERVATION
Massachusetts Division of Forests and Parks   West
11,500 acres.

From Pittsfield, about 5 mi. N on SR 7, then right following signs.

The state's highest mountain, 3,491 ft., is also one of its most accessible, with auto roads and several trails to the top. At the top a 100-ft. tower gives an even wider sweep to the 360-degree view. Even when there's a crowd at the top, however, hiking a mile or two will provide a sense of isolation.

Greylock is an isolated peak on a spur of the Taconic range, at the S end of VT's Green Mountains. Because of its height and exposure, its climate is cooler and more severe than is usually encountered in MA. Fog, enshrouding clouds, and storms are common. Terrain is generally steep, with rock outcrops and ledges. Roaring Brook is the largest of several streams, "roaring" because of its impressive cascade.

Plants: The lower and middle slopes are forested with species typical of the region: northern hardwoods with scattered hemlock and white pine. Mountain ash, spruce, red-berried elder, hobblebush, mountain maple, and beech become more common above 3,000-ft. elevation. At the top is a boreal zone with such species as creeping snowberry, mountain wood fern, large-leafed goldenrod, club moss, wood asters, balsam, yellow birch.

Birds: No checklist, but an illustrated folder shows many species and where to look for them. Some species seen here are rare elsewhere in MA. Some more common here than further S are olive-sided flycatcher, red-breasted nuthatch, brown creeper, winter wren, Swainson's thrush, golden-crowned kinglet. Summer visitors that may breed here include yellow-bellied flycatcher, Tennessee warbler, pine siskin, red-and white-winged crossbills.

Mammals: No checklist. Species observed include deer, black bear, coyote, bobcat, red and gray foxes, porcupine, longtail weasel, snowshoe hare, beaver.

INTERPRETATION: *Visitor center* is open daily, 8 A.M. to 4:30 P.M. weekdays, 9 A.M. to 5:30 P.M. weekends.

ACTIVITIES

Camping: 35 sites. Mid-May to mid-Oct.

Hiking, backpacking: This is one of the few sites on the Appalachian Trail with overnight shelters. 35 mi. of hiking trails include 11 mi. of the AT. Most trails to the summit are steep.

Fishing: Trout streams.

PUBLICATION: *Birds of Mount Greylock.*

REFERENCES

AMC Massachusetts and Rhode Island Trail Guide. Boston: Appalachian Mountain Club, 1988.

Appalachian Trail Guide to Massachusetts/Connecticut. Harpers Ferry, WV: Appalachian Trail Conference, 1985.

Brady, John, and Brian White. *Fifty Hikes in Massachusetts.* Woodstock, VT: Backcountry Publications, 1983.

HEADQUARTERS: Box 138, Lanesboro, MA 01237; (413) 499-4262.

MT. TOM RESERVATION

Mt. Tom Reservation Trustees   West
1,800 acres.

From I-91 N, Exit 17 B. N on SR 141; see signs.

It's State land, managed by the Trustees, who are the Commissioners from Hampden and Hampshire counties.

The mountain rises to 1,202 ft., offering fine views of the Connecticut River Valley and beyond. The geological record is interesting, providing evidence of ancient crystalline rock, marine deposits, volcanism, stream action, and glaciation. The site has streams and a pond; Lake Bray is about 1/3 mi. long.

It's a popular hiking area. The climb to the top is moderate to fairly difficult, through woods and over ledges to numerous viewpoints.

The Mt. Tom Ski Area is privately owned, not part of the Reservation.

INTERPRETATION

Robert Cole Museum of Natural History, on Reservation Road, has exhibits on geology, geography, butterflies, insects, birds. Usually open Memorial Day–Labor Day.

Nature trail.

ACTIVITIES
Hiking: The Metacomet-Monadnock Trail (see entry) crosses the site. Within the site are 20 mi. of trails.
Fishing: Bass and panfish in Lake Bray.

PUBLICATIONS
Brochure with map.
Nature trail pamphlet.

REFERENCE: Kulik, Stephen, Pete Salmansohn, Matthew Schmidt, and Heidi Welch. *The Audubon Society Field Guide to the Natural Places of the Northeast: Inland.* New York: Pantheon Books, 1984.

HEADQUARTERS: P.O. Box 985, Northampton, MA 01061; (413) 527-4805.

MT. WASHINGTON STATE FOREST
Massachusetts Division of Forests and Parks   West
3,289 acres.

SW corner of MA. From S Egremont on SR 41, S on Mt. Washington Rd. (Or E from Copake, NY.)

The Southern Taconic Highland straddles the NY–MA border at the S ends of the Berkshires. On the MA side are some of the state's highest mountains. Mt. Everett, 2,623 ft., is the highest. The area is rugged, scenic, heavily forested, with steep slopes, rock outcrops, and ledges. Some of the nearby mountains are privately owned and inaccessible, but there's plenty of backcountry for hikers.
The principal attraction for visitors here is Bash-Bish Falls, set in a spectacular gorge. The falls are most impressive during the spring runoff but always scenic. The Forest has other falls, too, as well as streams and cascades, mostly away from the road.

ACTIVITIES
Camping: 15 hike-in sites.
Hiking, Backpacking: The Appalachian Trail crosses Mt. Everett, heading S into CT. On the W is the South Taconic Trail, partially in NY's Taconic State Park. A trailhead for Mt. Everett is at the Berkshire School off SR 41. Total of 15 mi. of trails within the Forest.

REFERENCES
AMC Massachusetts and Rhode Island Trail Guide. Boston: Appalachian Mountain Club, 1988.

Brady, John, and Brian White. *Fifty Hikes in Massachusetts.* Woodstock, VT: Backcountry Publications, 1983.

HEADQUARTERS: Mt. Washington, MA 01258; (413) 528-0330.

MYLES STANDISH STATE FOREST
Massachusetts Division of Forests and Parks   East
14,635 acres.

Near Plymouth. From I-495, Exit 2, then N on SR 58 to South Carver; then follow signs.

About 40 mi. S of Boston, near major highways, and with the State's largest public campground, this site is heavily used in summer, during hunting season, and when under snow cover. It is also the second largest area of State land.

A glacial moraine and outwash plain, it has sandy flat lowlands broken by a few small, steep-sided knobs. Elevations range from 50 to 240 ft. Of its many kettle ponds, the largest covers 53 acres. The site has a few marshy areas.

Plants: The Forest supports one of the largest assemblages of rare plant species occurring in MA. They are found throughout the Forest in two rare natural communities: coastal plain pondshore, and pitch pine/scrub oak barrens.

95% of the area is forested, chiefly with dense growth. Ground cover includes blueberry, ferns, mushrooms, wildflowers. Open fields have been planted with seed crops for birds.

Birds: No checklist is available. Species mentioned include hawks, owls, whippoor-will, nighthawk, chickadee, junco, titmouse, nuthatch, sparrows, scarlet tanager, bluebird, northern oriole, cedar waxwing, woodpeckers, warblers, grosbeaks, marsh birds, waterfowl.

Mammals: No checklist is available. Species mentioned include red and gray foxes, red and gray squirrels, raccoon, cottontail, opossum, muskrat, mice, occasional deer.

Reptiles and amphibians: Garter, black, grass, and hog-nosed snakes; box tortoise.

INTERPRETATION: Naturalist programs, June–Aug.

ACTIVITIES
Camping: 475 sites in several campgrounds. Some are open all year.

Hiking: Despite its size, this isn't a hiker's forest. Roads crosshatch the area at intervals of about a half mile, and these roads are used by horses, bicycles, and motorcycles. There are many paths, used mostly by hunters and fishermen.

Hunting: Pheasant and quail are stocked. Grouse, rabbit, deer.

Fishing: Bass, perch, pickerel, trout, in the ponds.

Swimming: Two sand-bottom ponds. Supervised in season.

INCLUDES: Myles Standish Wildlife Management Area (Massachusetts Division of Fisheries and Wildlife, 1,870 acres). Two areas within the Forest. The larger lies W of Upper College Pond Rd., S of College Pond. The smaller is a quail area about 1 mi. SE. Both areas are managed for game birds, with clearings and plantings.

PUBLICATIONS
State Forest map.
Wildlife Management Area map

HEADQUARTERS: P.O. Box 66, South Carver, MA 02366; (508) 866-2526.

NICKERSON STATE PARK
Massachusetts Division of Forests and Parks   East
1,779 acres.

Off SR 6A in East Brewster.

Don't expect to find room here in midsummer. At the bend in Cape Cod, the Park is near but not on Cape Cod Bay, near the S end of Cape Cod National Seashore, a few minutes away from ocean beaches. Many use this as a base for visiting the National Seashore, which has no campground.

Cliff Pond, at its center, is the largest of four ponds within the boundaries that offer swimming, boating, and fishing. The Park has an interpretive program, including an amphitheater.

ACTIVITIES
Camping: The 420 well-spaced sites are in great demand during the summer season.

Hiking: 8 mi. of trails link with the Cape Cod Rail Trail (see entry).

HEADQUARTERS: Route 6A, Brewster, MA 02631; (508) 896-3491.

NORCROSS WILDLIFE SANCTUARY

Norcross Wildlife Foundation   West
3,000 acres.

From Springfield, E on US 20; S on SR 32; E on Monson-Wales Rd.

Open daily except Sundays and holidays. Pets prohibited.

Beyond the reception and museum area, visitors must stay on designated trails. The area of wooded hills, fields, and streams is managed to conserve wildlife, land, and water, with emphasis on research, education, and conservation training. The diverse plant life includes some exotics. Feed crops attract a large bird population.

The museum has natural history exhibits.

PUBLICATIONS
Leaflet with map.
Bird checklist.

HEADQUARTERS: R.D. 2, Monson, MA 01057; (413) 267-9654.

NORTH HILL MARSH WILDLIFE SANCTUARY

Massachusetts Audubon Society   East
137 acres of land.

N of Plymouth. From SR 3A, E 1.3 mi. on Mayflower St. (Duxbury).

Open dawn to dusk, Tues.–Sun.

Freshwater marshes and an oak/pine forest surround a 90-acre pond. Near the coast; elevations range from 16 ft. to 140 ft. The site has over 3 mi. of trails.

It's a small natural oasis in a heavily developed area. 122 bird species have been observed here. The South Shore Regional office has lists of the flora and fauna.

Pets are prohibited.

HEADQUARTERS: South Shore Regional Center, 2000 Main St., Marshfield, MA 02050; (617) 837-9400.

NORTHFIELD MOUNTAIN RECREATION AND ENVIRONMENTAL CENTER

Northeast Utilities   West
2,000 acres.

From I-91, Exit 27. E on SR 2, across the Connecticut River, then 2 mi. N on SR 63.

Open Wed.–Sun., 9 A.M.–5 P.M. Trails are open daily.

Information about the natural history of Massachusetts is hard to find. With so little available from government and academic sources, it was astonishing and refreshing to see what a power company has done.

The centerpiece is a splendid 160-page book: *The Northfield Mountain Interpreter.* It has everything you want to know about the region, well written, excellently organized and illustrated. It begins with the origins of Earth, continues through plate tectonics, traces the geologic history of the Connecticut Valley and the beginnings of life. It has a wonderful section on the flora and fauna of the region, not just identifying species but explaining their functions and relationships. For example, one spread shows the diets of animal species, from black bear to turtles, while another lists plants and tells what animals eat them. It recounts the history of the land from Indians through early settlers to modern times. Anyone from age 12 up can read and enjoy.

The center is at the site of the company's pumped storage hydroelectric station. Recreation facilities include hiking and nature trails, camping and picnic grounds, a pavilion where a variety of performances are scheduled in summer, cross-country ski trails. Activities include riverboat tours, canoe instruction, orienteering instruction, star gazing, and more. It's not all nature-oriented; other activities include jazz cruises, bicycle tours, sing-alongs, and foot races.

ACTIVITIES

Camping: 20 sites. Reservations needed.

Canoeing, boating: Ramp, rentals. No hp limit. Canoe-camping opportunities.

Ski touring: 25 mi. of maintained trails.

PUBLICATIONS

Seasonal newsletter with program schedules.

Site map.

Leaflets:

Interpretive riverboat ride.

Barton Cove Nature and Camping Area.

Hidden Quarry Nature Trail.

Northfield Mountain Cross-Country Ski Area.

Sammartino, Claudia F. *The Northfield Mountain Interpreter.* Berlin, CT: Northeast Utilities, 1981.

HEADQUARTERS: RR 2, Box 117, Route 63, Northfield, MA 01360; (413) 659-3714; information recording: (413) 659-3713.

Not checked by HQ.

OCTOBER MOUNTAIN STATE FOREST
Massachusetts Division of Forests and Parks   West
15,710 acres.

From US 20 at Lenox or Lee, E to Forest entrance.

One of the largest MA State Forests lies across the Hoosac Range, E of the Berkshire Valley. This portion of the range is a high plateau, elevations generally between 1,800 and 2,000 ft., with a few peaks rising higher. The region is rugged, scenic, heavily forested, with many rock outcrops and ledges. The numerous streams draining the area drop over many falls and cataracts. The largest of several ponds are 212-acre Lake Felton and 200-acre Finerty Pond. From Lake Felton, a swift brook rushes through Schermerhorn Gorge, emptying into the Housatonic River.

The Appalachian Trail crosses the Forest. Adjoining the Forest on the W is the 613-acre Housatonic Valley Wildlife Management Area, spread along the oxbows and backwaters of the Housatonic River. Access is from October Mountain Rd.

Plants: 90% of the area is forested with mixed hardwoods, maples, oaks, and birches, with hemlock and spruce. Many flowering shrubs in the understory. Seasonal wildflowers include bloodroot, hepatica, jack-in-the-pulpit, wood and trout lilies, may-apple, lady's-slipper, trillium, rhodora, blue flag, trailing arbutus.

Birds: No checklist. Abundant populations of woodland species.

Mammals: include deer, black bear, bobcat, coyote, red fox; red, gray, and flying squirrels; shorttail weasel, cottontail, snowshoe hare, muskrat, porcupine, beaver, fisher, raccoon, skunk, otter, deer and white-footed mice.

ACTIVITIES
  Camping: 50 sites. All year.
  Hiking: 12 mi. of trails, including the Appalachian.
  Fishing: Bass, pickerel, bullhead.
  Boating: Pond. Ramp.

REFERENCES

AMC Massachusetts and Rhode Island Trail Guide. Boston: Appalachian Mountain Club, 1988.

Appalachian Trail Guide to Massachusetts/Connecticut. Harpers Ferry, WV: Appalachian Trail Conference, 1985.

HEADQUARTERS: Woodlawn Rd., Lee, MA 01238; (413) 243-1778.

OLD TOWN HILL RESERVATION
The Trustees of Reservations   East
373 acres.

> From SR 128, Exit 20N, proceed N 16.2 mi. on SR 1A. Left on Newman Rd. (200 yds. N of Parker River) to entrance on right: sign and brown wood stile.

The trail ascends a hill. At the top one has a sweeping view of Parker River, Plum Island River, Parker River National Wildlife Refuge, and Isles of Shoals. Much of the trail is in forest, but there are also open areas. On the hill are several side trails, and it's easy to make a wrong turn, as we did on the way down, but then one sees more of the site.

Farther on Newman Road is another entrance, not as clearly marked, to the floodplain of the river. This open area is less scenic but offers better birding.

REFERENCE: Brady, John, and Brian White. *Fifty Hikes in Massachusetts.* Woodstock, VT: Backcountry Publications, 1983.

HEADQUARTERS: The Trustees of Reservations, 572 Essex St., Beverly, MA 01915; (508) 921-1944.

OXBOW NATIONAL WILDLIFE REFUGE
U.S. Fish and Wildlife Service   Central
711 acres.

> From I-495, Exit 29. W on SR 2 to SR 110; S to Still River. W on Still River Depot Rd. to dirt parking area.

The Department of Defense transferred this former bombing range to the Fish and Wildlife Service in 1974. Visitors are warned not to touch "unusual metallic objects." We saw none. The site is largely open water, marsh, and swamp, bounded by the Nashua River on the W, SR 2 on the N, railroad right-of-way on the E. It adjoins the Fort Devens Military Reservation. Uplands include a few pine-covered knolls. Several primitive trails cross the Refuge, one beside the river. The range of elevations is 210 to 250 ft.

Birds: The Refuge is maintained primarily for migratory birds, notably black and wood ducks. No checklist is available. Other waterfowl can be seen, as well as bittern, herons, snipe, sandpipers, woodcock, osprey, pheasant, grouse.

Mammals: Species reported include woodchuck, snowshoe hare, red and gray squirrels, cottontail, raccoon. Seen occasionally: skunk, opossum, river otter, red fox, muskrat, deer.

ACTIVITIES
  Hunting: Special regulations define season, number of hunters, species. Inquire.
  Fishing: Some chain pickerel and bullhead in the river. It was heavily polluted but improvements have been made.
  Canoeing: Nashua River.
  Ski touring: Trail map available from Fort Devens, Ayer, MA 01433.

ADJACENT: Bolton Flats Wildlife Management Area (see entry).

PUBLICATION: Leaflet with map.

REFERENCE: *The Nashua River Canoe Guide.* Nashua River Watershed Association, 484 Main St., Fitchburg, MA 01420. $5 plus postage.

HEADQUARTERS: Great Meadows National Wildlife Refuge, Weir Hill, Sudbury, MA 01776; (508) 443-4661.

PARKER RIVER NATIONAL WILDLIFE REFUGE
U.S. Fish and Wildlife Service   East
4,662 acres.

  On Plum Island. From Newburyport on SR 1A, E on Water Street and Plum Island Turnpike, following signs.

  During summer, capacity is often reached and gates are closed by 9 A.M. Gates usually reopen about 3 P.M.

We've never seen a Refuge quite like it. It includes 6 mi. of splendid barrier beach, and crowds of visitors come just to enjoy the beach. When we arrived on a weekday midmorning, cars were queued at the gatehouse. A pleasant woman was greeting each party, handing out maps and leaflets, explaining rules, and suggesting which parking area was least crowded. Another hundred cars, she told us, and the gate would be closed. 400,000 people visit the Refuge annually, most of them in summer.

A comprehensive planning process was initiated in 1980. Of the six alternatives considered, none would have curtailed public access, although two would limit vehicular travel. The chief question was visitor facilities: add more buildings and services or not? Admission fee? Shortly after our visit a fee was adopted: $5 per car or an annual pass.

The gate is at the N end of the Refuge. At the S tip of the island is a small tract called Sandy Point State Park, administered as part of the Refuge. 7 parking areas are spaced along the road. Beach access is by boardwalk from 6 of them. 4-wheel-drive and off-road vehicles are allowed on the beach, by permit.

Beach and fore-dunes are barren. Rear dunes, up to 50 ft. high, are heavily vegetated. On the inland side of the road, dikes have created several freshwater marshes and pools. Beyond are 3,200 acres of salt marsh and tidewater. These wetlands can be observed from dikes and a nature trail. Other habitats include glaciated uplands with goose pasture and wooded patches, and small glacial drumlins.

Natural Events. The Refuge leaflet includes an unusual summary of seasonal highlights:

- *January–February.* Snowy owls, rough-legged hawks, northern harriers present and frequently seen flying over marshes or roosting in trees at marsh edge; heavy storms may block Refuge roads for extended periods.
- *March–April.* Marshes thaw; northbound migrations of waterfowl, raptors and early shorebird and wading birds; courtship activity of waterfowl around April 1; serviceberry flowers in late April.
- *May–June.* Geese hatch and broods feed in roadside fields; warbler migration peaks in May; beach plums, false heather, and honeysuckle flower; striped bass migration reaches refuge.
- *July–August.* Ducks hatch and feed in pools; fox kits play near dens; mosquitoes and greenhead flies in strength; purple loosestrife flowers; concentration of snowy egrets; large flocks of shorebirds and swallows seen in late August.
- *September–October.* Plum and cranberry picking (check regulations); waterfowl migration underway; hunting permits available September 1; Youth Waterfowl Training Program ends late September; glasswort in salt marshes very colorful; peregrine falcons seen occasionally.
- *November–December.* Migrating Canada and snow geese present; American black duck numbers peak; sea ducks rafting in large numbers

offshore; snow buntings, horned larks, and Lapland longspurs seen in large flocks; seals sunning on Emerson's Rocks; marshes freeze.

Plants: Species seen along the nature trail include blueberry, greenbrier, grape, chokecherry, blackberry, pin and black cherry, woodbine, raspberry, honeysuckle, bayberry, poison ivy, beach plum, cranberry, spirea, speckled alder, willow, trembling aspen, dune grass, serviceberry, arrowwood, winter berry, cedar, staghorn sumac, wild rose, honeysuckle.

Birds: Checklist records 301 species plus 33 accidentals. The Refuge is along major bird migration routes. Salt marshes are important feeding and resting areas. Peak concentrations of up to 25,000 ducks and 6,000 geese occur in spring and fall. Other habitats attract large flocks of warblers and shorebirds.

Mammals: Species often seen include cottontail, fox, skunk, weasel, muskrat, harbor seal, woodchuck, deer. Woodchucks emerge from hibernation Mar.–Apr. Red fox kits are sometimes seen on roads at dawn or dusk in Jun.–July.

Other Fauna: Monarch butterflies migrate through the Refuge in Sept.

INTERPRETATION

Visitor contact station at HQ, N tip of Plum Island. (Instead of turning right for Refuge gate, continue on, then left.) Plans call for a new visitor center next to the airport and Plum Island Turnpike.

Hellcat Swamp Wildlife Trail, begins at parking lot 4 (where there is no beach access). About 2 mi., with spurs and boardwalk, visits dunes, freshwater swamp, freshwater marsh, salt marsh. Observation tower. Trail guide available.

ACTIVITIES

Hiking: When the crowds have gone, 6 mi. of fine beach. Back of the beach, 2 mi. of nature trail, 2 mi. of dike. At the S end, trails around the goose browse fields.

Hunting: In designated area. Special regulations. Inquire at HQ.

Fishing: Ocean beach, daylight hours, except a N portion that is closed to fishing May through mid-Oct. HQ has fishing leaflet with information on night access and vehicle permits.

Swimming: No lifeguards. Relatively cold water, rough surf, strong tides, undertow.

Boating: Launching or landing on the Refuge is prohibited except as specified in waterfowl hunting regulations. Boating in tidewater is governed by State and local regulations.

Pets are prohibited Apr.–Oct. Permitted Nov.–Mar. on leash.

PUBLICATIONS

Refuge leaflet with map.

Bird checklist.
Hellcat Swamp Nature Trail guide.
Refuge rules.
Hunting and fishing rules.

REFERENCE: Kulik, Stephen, Pete Salmansohn, Matthew Schmidt, and Heidi Welch. *The Audubon Society Field Guide to the Natural Places of the Northeast: Coastal.* New York: Pantheon Books, 1984.

HEADQUARTERS: Northern Blvd., Plum Island, Newburyport, MA 01950; (508) 465-5753.

PERU WILDLIFE MANAGEMENT AREA
Massachusetts Division of Fisheries and Wildlife   West
2,638 acres.

From SR 143 E of Peru, turn N on North Road. The next paved road to the right is East Windsor Rd. In about 1 1/4 mi, look for an abandoned road on the right. This bisects the site. There is no parking area.

The site lies between SR 143 and Pierce Road, E of North Road. Trout Brook crosses it NW to SE. From the brook at about 1,500 ft. elevation, hills rise to 2,000 ft. in the SW, 2,050 ft. in the NW. The site is almost totally forested with a mix of northern hardwoods and conifers. The unused woods road crosses N to S.
Wildlife includes grouse, woodcock, snowshoe hare, raccoon, beaver, black bear, bobcat, deer. The brook has trout.

HEADQUARTERS: Wildlife District Manager, 400 Hubbard Ave., Pittsfield, MA 01201; (413) 447-9789.

PHILLIPSTON WILDLIFE MANAGEMENT AREA
Massachusetts Division of Fisheries and Wildlife   West
3,230 acres.

From Athol, S on SR 32 to SR 101, N of Petersham. NE on Popple Camp Rd. WMA is on both sides, before coming to Queens Lake.

The S unit is the larger, extending S about 3 mi. to East Petersham Rd. Bakers Lane, first turn beyond SR 101, leads to a parking area. Narrow Lane, turn at Queens Lake, leads to parking near the S end. It runs along a low ridge, from which the land slopes gradually down on both sides to marshes and streams 200 ft. below. Moccasin Brook, on the W side, has a great blue heron rookery. The upland is forested but recently logged; skid roads now serve as trails.

The N unit lies along the East Branch Swift River, from which the land rises on both sides. Here the upland has both forest and old fields.

ACTIVITIES

Hunting: Stocked with snowshoe hare. Game species include deer, turkey, grouse, cottontail, woodcock, pheasant. Some waterfowl use the marshy areas.

Fishing: Trout in several streams.

PUBLICATIONS: Site maps.

HEADQUARTERS: Wildlife District Manager, Temple St., West Boylston, MA 01583; (508) 835-3607.

PITTSFIELD STATE FOREST
Massachusetts Division of Forests and Parks   West
9,695 acres.

From Pittsfield, W on West St., N on Churchill St., W on Cascade St.

The Forest lies W of Onota Lake, near the NY border, extending from near Hancock almost to US 20 along the ridge of the Taconic Range. Peaks along the Range include 2,314-ft. Honwee Mountain, 2,170-ft. Smith Mountain. The slopes are drained by numerous streams with waterfalls and cascades. 9-acre Berry Pond, at 2,150 ft., is the highest in the state. A road leads to the campground there from near Forest HQ.

It's a hiker's forest. The Taconic Skyline Trail (see entry) runs the length of the ridge, passing Berry Pond. More than a dozen trails ascend from the E side, offering opportunities for circuit hikes of 3 mi. or more.

Slopes are moderate to steep, with rock outcrops, ledges, and caves. Most of the area is forested with mixed hardwoods and hemlock. June brings an attractive azalea display.

Wildlife is typical of the region, including deer and black bear. Hawks follow the ridge in migration. One observer said to look for red-spotted newts along the trail after a spring or summer shower.

ACTIVITIES
Camping: 31 sites. Mid-May to mid-Oct.
Hiking: 30 mi. of fair trails.
Fishing: Berry Pond is stocked.

PUBLICATION: Map prepared by Appalachian Mountain Club.

REFERENCES
AMC Massachusetts and Rhode Island Trail Guide. Boston: Appalachian
Mountain Club, 1988.
Brady, John, and Brian White. *Fifty Hikes in Massachusetts.* Woodstock,
VT: Backcountry Publications, 1983.

HEADQUARTERS: Cascade St., Pittsfield, MA 01201; (413) 442-8992.

PLEASANT VALLEY WILDLIFE SANCTUARY
Massachusetts Audubon Society   West
1,117 acres.

From the intersection of US 7 and US 20 at Lenox, N 3 mi. on US 7; W
on W Dugway Rd.; left on West Mountain Rd. to entrance.

Open Tues.–Sun. all year; Mon. on holidays.

Yokun Brook, fed by numerous small streams, flows through a series of many
ponds, including beaver ponds, along West Mountain Road. From here, at
an elevation of about 1,250 ft., the land slopes up to a fire tower on Lenox
Mountain at 2,124 ft. About 800 acres of the site are forested with northern
hardwoods, hemlock, and white pine. 65 acres are open fields, 30 acres alder
swamp. Many shrubs and wildflowers.

Pets are prohibited.

Birds: More than 60 species nest here. Twice that number have been observed
in migrations. A list is available. Houses and feeding stations attract many
for close observation.

Mammals: Many beaver ponds and lodges, with muskrat sometimes sharing
space. Mink, otter, cottontail, fox, deer.

INTERPRETATION
Canoe Meadows Wildlife Sanctuary (see entry) and Pleasant Valley are
managed as the Berkshire Sanctuaries. Their seasonal publication includes a
calendar of year-round events: nature hikes, canoe tours, nature ski hikes,
talks, slide shows, workshops, and others.

Trailside Museum has wildlife exhibits, observation beehive, nature games. Open in summer.

Nature trails begin at the museum.

Hiking: 7 mi. of trails.

PUBLICATION: Berkshire Sanctuaries quarterly newsletter.

HEADQUARTERS: 472 West Mountain Rd., Lenox, MA 01240; (413) 637-0320.

QUABBIN RESERVOIR
Metropolitan District Commission   West
55,000 land acres, including 3,500 acres on 60 islands; 25,000 water acres.

W central MA. From I-90, Exit 8; N 10 mi. on Sr 32 to Ware; then 6 mi. W on SR 9 to three entrances to Quabbin Park area.

It's called the world's largest man-made domestic water supply, providing water to 2 1/2 million people in 46 towns and cities. The dam on the Swift River was completed by 1939. Submerged were towns, villages, and farms whose beginnings were in the early 1700s. To protect the water supply, 120 sq. mi. of the watershed are maintained in near-wilderness condition. The area is open to passive recreation, with conditions: no swimming is allowed, for example, no horses or dogs, no fires, camping, skiing, hunting, littering.

The principal public area is Quabbin Park at the S end. Here there are a visitor center, hiking trails, a picnic area, scenic vistas, an observation tower.

The reservoir is surrounded by wooded hills, with wet meadows, marshes, shrubby areas, and reverting fields.

Birds: Checklist is available. 250 species have been recorded. Both golden and bald eagles are seen, chiefly in winter. Other raptors include osprey, northern harrier, goshawk, kestrel; red-tailed, red-shouldered, broad-winged, and rough-legged hawks. Owls: great horned, barred, saw-whet, screech. Loons and Canada geese have nested. Red-headed and pileated woodpeckers, black-billed cuckoo, northern shrike, black-billed cuckoo, bluebird, blue-gray gnat-catcher, many warblers. Many others in migration.

Mammals: Many beaver, deer, raccoon, porcupine, muskrat, mink. Also chipmunk, red and gray squirrels, red and gray foxes, coyote, snowshoe hare, cottontail. Increasing populations of otter and fisher.

ACTIVITIES

Hiking: All areas are open to hiking except Prescott Peninsula and the islands.

Fishing: The fishing guide has map showing areas of lake and shoreline where fishing is permitted. Also regulations. Coldwater species include lake, rainbow, and brown trout; salmon, smelt. Warmwater species include largemouth and smallmouth bass, pickerel, white and yellow perch, bullhead.

Boating: Permitted for fishing purposes only. Three launch areas. 20 hp limit. Rentals.

PUBLICATIONS
Brochure with map.
Trail map.
Watershed map.
Fishing guide.
History and data sheet.
Friends of Quabbin leaflet.

QUABBIN VISITOR INFORMATION CENTER: 485 Ware Rd., Belchertown, MA 01007; (413) 323-7221.

QUABOAG WILDLIFE MANAGEMENT AREA

Massachusetts Division of Fisheries and Wildlife   Central
1,101 acres.

From Worcester, W about 20 mi. on SR 9 to West Brookfield; S on Davis Rd. to Hill Rd. and parking.

Much of the site is freshwater marsh along the Quaboag River. From here the land slopes up about 250 ft. on the W side of the tract. The river and wetlands attract osprey, American bittern, long-billed marsh wren, sandpipers, egrets, and herons.

The site is about 1/2 mi. downstream from Quaboag Pond, the river's source. Pond and wetlands are stopovers for many waterfowl in migration.

From the pond downstream 9 mi. to Warren, the river is canoeable, usually all year, slow-moving flatwater. There is no established put-in or take-out in the WMA, but we saw one or two places where it might be managed. In any case it would be no great task to paddle down from the pond and return, and this would be the best way to see the marsh. Downstream is a 10-mi. stretch of rapids from Class II to Class IV.

ACTIVITIES
Hiking: 3 mi. of roads and trails.
Hunting: Deer, squirrel, cottontail, raccoon, fox, pheasant (stocked), woodcock, waterfowl.

Fishing: Pike, largemouth bass, panfish.

PUBLICATION: Map.

REFERENCE: Schweiker, Roioli, ed. *AMC River Guide: Massachusetts, Connecticut, Rhode Island.* Boston: Appalachian Mountain Club, 1985.

HEADQUARTERS: District Wildlife Manager, Temple St., West Boylston, MA 01583; (508) 835-3607.

RICHARD T. CRANE, JR., MEMORIAL RESERVATION
The Trustees of Reservations   East
1,399 acres.

From I-95 N of Boston, Exit E on SR 128 to Beverly. N on SR 1A; E on SR 133; right on Argilla Rd. Direction signs say "Crane's Beach."

Any New England beach open to the public attracts crowds in warm weather. The Trustees of Reservations have a handsome array of quiet preserves, but this one is far from quiet in summer. We couldn't pass through the gate because of our dog but were quite willing to turn back. The guard told us that as many as 2,000 cars may park before the gates must be closed. From fall to spring, however, this is well worth a visit.

It's a fine ocean beach, more than 4 mi. on Ipswich Bay according to one publication, 6 mi. according to the guard. Back of the beach are dunes, salt marsh, and steep uplands. The several habitats attract sea, shore, and upland birds. Mammals seen in quiet times include deer, red fox, striped skunk, otter, muskrat, opossum.

The site includes Great House on Castle Hill, used for cultural events and occasionally open for tours.

Nature trail explores the dunes and red maple swamp.

Pets are prohibited May to mid-Oct., must be under control at other times.

PUBLICATION: Pine Hollow trail guide, available at Beach office or from ranger.

ADJACENT: Cornelius and Mine S. Crane Wildlife Refuge (The Trustees of Reservations, 753 acres). There's no public transportation to this cluster of 5 islands and salt marsh in the estuary of the Essex River. Private boats may land only at a dock on Long Island, Memorial Day weekend to Columbus Day weekend.

HEADQUARTERS: Argilla Rd., Ipswich, MA 01938; (508) 356-4354.

SANDISFIELD STATE FOREST

Massachusetts Division of Forests and Parks   West
7,785 acres.

> From New Marlborough on SR 57, S and bear right on Sandisfield Rd. Sign
> points to State Forest. In 3 mi., turn left.

The entrance leads to 36-acre York Lake, apparently the center of visitor activity. On an August morning no visitors were there, but an attendant was
prepared to sell tickets. The area includes a bathhouse, beach, and launching
ramp. The lake is fringed with trees.

State HQ couldn't provide a Forest map, and we saw no signs along the
road beyond the lake. We assume it's Forest land. Here the terrain is flat to
gently rolling. The surrounding forest is young, interspersed with pine plantations. The road ends at SR 57.

Here we turned right, looking for Forest HQ, its address listed as
"West St." The street sign was so bent and rusted as to be almost unreadable.
Soon we came to a small building labeled "West Lake Headquarters." It was
closed and appeared to be a utility shed rather than an office. Nearby, a jeep
trail goes a short distance to West Lake, a small pond with no shore development. A small parking area seemed to be used by hunters and fishermen.

The official description of the Forest says the terrain is hilly, with brook,
streams, and swamps, and a diverse wildlife population. There are said to be
20 mi. of hiking trails and 10 "wilderness" campsites. Local residents doubt-
less know where to go. Without a map or signs, a visitor from elsewhere is
unlikely to go beyond York Lake.

The Forest and Parks folder lists Cookson State Forest, 2,385 acres, on the
CT border immediately S of Sandisfield SF. The symbols say there's fishing
and hiking but, oddly, no hunting. The HQ address is that same little building
on West St. You might inquire, if anyone's there.

HEADQUARTERS: West St., Sandisfield, MA 01255; (413) 258-4774.

SAVOY MOUNTAIN STATE FOREST

Massachusetts Division of Forests and Parks   West
10,500 acres.

> From North Adams, about 5 mi. E on SR 2, then 3 mi. S on Central Shaft
> Rd.

This is one of the numerous State Forests in northwestern MA. Combined with the adjacent Mohawk Trail State Forest (see entry), it is the largest block of State Forest land. Terrain is rugged to mountainous, elevations from 1,800 ft. to 2,566-ft. Spruce Hill and 2,506-ft. Borden Mountain. A fire tower atop Borden Mountain offers sweeping views. The area has many streams and waterfalls, several ponds, the largest 40 acres. Scenic trails ascend the two peaks and lead to such points of interest as North Pond, Balanced Rocks, Crooked Forest, and 80-ft. Tannery Falls.

Plants: About 80% forested with mixed hardwoods, increasing amounts of spruce, fir, and pine at high elevations. Understory of striped maple, mountain laurel, raspberry, blackberry, fireweed. Some reverting fields. Spring wildflower displays. Some boggy areas have typical wetland species. Crooked Forest has trees presumably deformed by an ice storm years back.

Birds: No checklist or reports of observations, other than hawks migrating through in the fall.

Mammals: Deer, bear, snowshoe hare, cottontail, porcupine, fisher, red and gray squirrels, red and gray foxes, woodchuck.

ACTIVITIES
Camping: 45 sites. May 15–Oct. 15.
Hiking: 24 mi. of trails, some rugged. Also woods roads. The Appalachian Trail is several miles W.
Fishing: Trout streams, ponds.
Swimming: South Pond and North Pond.

HEADQUARTERS: RFD #2, North Adams, MA 01247; (413) 663-8469.

STONY BROOK NATURE CENTER AND WILDLIFE SANCTUARY
(Includes Blake State Reservation, 200 acres, managed cooperatively.)
Massachusetts Audubon Society   East
301 acres.

SW of Boston. From Norfolk, S 1 mi. on SR 115 to North St. Turn right.

All the Massachusetts Audubon sanctuaries attract birds and birders. One sanctuary specializes in butterflies, another in ferns. At Stony Brook a specialty is the Odonata—dragonflies and damselflies.

About half of the site is forested with mixed hardwoods and white pine. The land slopes down to about 80 acres of wetlands: wet meadow, red maple swamp, Kingfisher Pond, and stream.

Birds: A checklist of 147 species is available, annotated to show seasonal abundance. 23 other species have been recorded once or twice. Spring and fall are the peak seasons.

Pets are prohibited.

INTERPRETATION

Nature center has exhibits, literature.

Nature trail, 1.3 mi., passes through the several habitats to the swamp boardwalk.

Guided hikes and *special events* are scheduled all year, as well as educational programs for children and adults.

PUBLICATIONS

Newsletter and program list.

Trail guide and map. $0.50.

Bird checklist. $0.25.

Dragonflies. $0.25.

Stony Brook's Past. $1.

REFERENCES

AMC Massachusetts and Rhode Island Trail Guide. Boston: Appalachian Mountain Club, 1982.

Brady, John, and Brian White. *Fifty Hikes in Massachusetts.* Woodstock, VT: Backcountry Publications, 1983.

HEADQUARTERS: North St., Norfolk, MA 02056; (508) 528-3140.

TACONIC SKYLINE TRAIL

About 23 mi. West

From US 20 to Mt. Greylock, near the NY border.

Much of this trail is in the Pittsfield State Forest and Mt. Greylock State Reservation (see entries). AMC says it is well blazed but poorly maintained.

Many access trails, chiefly on the E side, especially in Pittsfield SF. Campground in Pittsfield SF.

REFERENCE: *AMC Massachusetts and Rhode Island Trail Guide.* Boston: Appalachian Mountain Club, 1988.

TOLLAND STATE FOREST
Massachusetts Division of Forests and Parks   West
3,286 acres.

From SR 8 S of Otis, turn E on Reservoir Rd. Cross the dam and continue 1.6 mi. to marked campground entrance.

The Forest lies between SR 8 and the S end of Otis Reservoir. The campground, beach, and boat ramp are at the N end of the Forest on a peninsula that divides Southwest Bay from the main water body. Between the dam and the campground entrance, a paved road runs S to the Forest boundary.

We saw no signs identifying Forest land. We inquired at the campground ticket booth, but the attendant didn't know of any area but the campground. We asked for directions to Forest headquarters. "This is it," she said, pointing at her booth.

The area covered by the map is rolling to hilly, forested, with a moderate understory. State HQ provided a description that mentions 310-acre Big Pond, evidently beyond the map's scope, and rivers, streams, a waterfall.

Birds: We obtained an interesting bird list, including hawks: Cooper's, red-tailed, goshawk, sharp-shinned. Owls: barred, great horned, long-eared, short-eared, screech, saw-whet. Great blue heron, American bittern, common loon, gulls, black skimmer, osprey, belted kingfisher, northern oriole, brown creeper, cedar waxwing, cardinal, purple finch, American goldfinch; evening, pine, and rose-breasted grosbeaks; bank, barn, and cliff swallows; woodpeckers, ruby-throated hummingbird, many warblers and sparrows, chimney swift. The list includes no waterfowl, but mallard and Canada goose have been reported.

Mammals: Include red and gray foxes, beaver, bobcat, muskrat, otter, weasel, mink, skunk, snowshoe hare, cottontail, chipmunk; red, gray, and flying squirrels; deer.

ACTIVITIES

Camping: 90 sites, 35 on the shore. Mid-May to mid-Oct.

Hiking: State HQ said "10 mi. of multi-purpose trails bordering reservoir." The map shows some of these trails, but there must also be woods roads.

Hunting: Deer, small game, turkey.

Fishing: Trout stock in streams. Reservoir: largemouth and smallmouth bass, bluegill, white and yellow perch, pickerel, trout.

Swimming: Beach near camping area.

Boating: Ramp near camping area. No horsepower limit, but a 24-ft. length limit except for pontoon craft.

PUBLICATION: Map.

HEADQUARTERS: Otis, MA 01008; (413) 269-7268.

UPTON STATE FOREST

Massachusetts Division of Forests and Parks   Central

2,660 acres.

From I-495, Exit 21. NE to SR 135 in Hopkinton, then NW on SR 135. Just past Whitehall Reservoir, turn left on Spring St., 2 mi. to Westboro Rd.

We saw nothing extraordinary here, but the site offers an opportunity for pleasantly quiet woodland hiking when most sites near Boston are crowded. Off-road vehicles are permitted, but we heard none during our visit.

Hiking: About 6 mi. of trails in 2 loops. Some trail markings.

WACHUSETT MEADOW WILDLIFE SANCTUARY

Massachusetts Audubon Society   Central

1,000 acres.

N of Worcester. From Princeton on SR 31, 3/4 mi. W on SR 62 to Sanctuary sign.

Open Tues.–Sun., dawn to dusk.

One of the Society's larger sanctuaries, this adjoins the 1,950-acre Wachusett Mountain State Reservation and is linked to it and other State properties by the Mid-State Trail (see entries). On the S slope of the mountain, it was a

farm. From Brown Hill, its highest point, 1,312 ft., one looks out over upland meadows, woodland, red maple swamp, ponds, and distant mountains.

Plants: Most of the site is forested with red oak, white pine, hemlock, sugar maple, white ash, and black cherry, beech, birch, and basswood, with an understory including hophornbeam and blueberry. The Crocker Maple is one of the largest of its species in North America, over 300 years old. Woodlands include a hemlock ravine, a stand of shagbark hickory, dark groves of hemlock and beech.

As New England's farm acreage has declined, so have populations of bobolink, eastern meadowlark, and other open-meadow species. Here fields are kept open, mowed after the nesting season. Trails pass through or beside both young and old-growth forest, a hayfield, another hayfield allowed to revert, former pastures now growing small trees and shrubs, thick patches of ferns. A boardwalk crosses the red maple swamp that has many cinnamon and royal ferns.

May is the peak season for wildflowers. Prominent are foamflower, painted trillium, three-toothed cinquefoil, dwarf ginseng, wood anemone, marsh marigold.

Birds: No printed checklist is available, but we saw several records: a tally of 96 species recorded 1964–1973, another of early June sightings. (The best birding season is May to mid-June.) Over the period the top 10 species were rufous-sided towhee, ovenbird, red-eyed vireo, common yellowthroat, blue jay, American robin, tree swallow, black-capped chickadee, red-winged blackbird, cliff swallow. This is a good place to see the fall migration of hawks, peaking in mid-Sept.

Mammals: A preliminary list included a number of species as "potential" or "possible." Those confirmed as present included shorttail shrew, big brown bat, white-footed mouse, redback and meadow voles, porcupine, woodchuck, chipmunk, red and gray squirrels, snowshoe hare, cottontail, raccoon, weasel, skunk, red and gray foxes, deer.

INTERPRETATION

The Sanctuary has no visitor center. Maps and other orientation material are available at the trailhead, near the parking lot.

Guided hikes are offered on weekends, occasionally on weekdays.

Ten nature trails, 0.1 to 1.8 mi., have interpretive markers. Descriptions are provided with the site map.

Hiking: 11 mi. of trails. The Mid-State Trail, Rhode Island to New Hampshire, crosses the site. Mountain Trail leads to the State Reservation.

Pets are prohibited.

PUBLICATION: Trail map with descriptive text. $1.

HEADQUARTERS: P.O. Box 268, Princeton, MA 01541; (508) 464-2712.

WACHUSETT MOUNTAIN STATE RESERVATION

Massachusetts Division of Forests and Parks   Central
2,000 acres.

From Princeton on SR 31, N 3 mi. on Mountain Rd.

At 2,006 ft., Mt. Wachusett is the highest point in central and eastern MA. That's not breathtakingly high, but high enough to have some alpine flora at the summit, giving the mountain exceptional floral diversity. Although there's no camping, the Reservation attracts over 250,000 visitors per year. Many drive the road to the summit, especially in Oct. when the fall colors are bright. Some come to ski in winter, many to hike in the warmer months.

The Reservation was created by the Great and General Court of Massachusetts in 1899. The mountain's vertical rise is 1,119 ft. From the top on a clear day, one can see Mt. Washington, 150 miles away.

Information about the natural history of MA state lands is generally scanty, but here we have a 1978 management plan buttressed by extensive field studies.

Because of its steep slopes, the mountain kept its forest cover after most surrounding forest was cut. By 1900 most of its trees were gone, however, and the slopes were grazed. Forest regeneration began about 1930, so the present cover is rather young. About half the Reservation is now forested. With improved moisture retention, the Reservation now has four small ponds, six water holes, and several small streams.

Plants: Dominant species are red oak, shagbark hickory; red, sugar, and mountain maples; witch hazel, hophornbeam, and birches, with aspen and willow at lower elevations, white pine and spruce higher, juniper in dry, exposed locations, some hemlock in damp ravines. Shrubs include azalea, sheep laurel, blueberry, huckleberry. State-protected plants include pink azalea, pink lady's-slipper, trailing arbutus, swamp honeysuckle, rhodora, helleborine, rattlesnake-plantain, rose pogonia. May brings a display of azalea; June, of mountain laurel. April sees a profusion of bloodroot. Purple trillium appears in May, wood lily in July. Many other wildflowers.

Birds: Checklist of 84 species available. A few pairs of goshawk have nested. Also breeding here: mallard, black duck, ruffed grouse, woodcock, barred owl, whip-poor-will, northern flicker; downy, hairy, and pileated woodpeckers, 16 warbler species, many other songbirds. The annual New England

Hawk Watch held here each fall recorded over 10,000 raptors in the report we saw.

Mammals: Deer, an occasional bear, red and gray foxes, raccoon, porcupine, woodchuck, snowshoe hare, red and gray squirrels, cottontail, opossum, weasel, mink, skunk, chipmunk, mice, moles, shrews, bats. As the habitat improves, it is expected that beaver, marten, fisher, bobcat, shorttail weasel, and flying squirrel will return.

Reptiles and amphibians: Include snapping, spotted, and painted turtles; water, garter, milk, and smooth green snakes; timber rattlesnake; spotted, red-backed, spring, dusky, and two-lined salamanders; red-spotted newt; wood, bull, green, leopard, and pickerel frogs.

FEATURES
Visitor center is near the entrance. Information, exhibits, maps.

The summit is the chief attraction. Along the 4-mi. road to the top are several overlooks. At the top are several communications towers and buildings that have to stay, but no major buildings will be added. From the summit, an alpine ski trail goes to the ski area.

Wachusett Meadow Wildlife Sanctuary is on the S slope. (See entry.)

Minns Wildlife Sanctuary is a 200-acre preserve on Little Wachusett Mountain. It has some of the best forest cover and a number of rare plant species.

ACTIVITIES
Hiking: Trails from the base converge at the summit, about 13 1/2 mi. in all. The Mid-State Trail (see entry) crosses the Reservation.

Hunting: Restricted to an area on the W side of the mountain.

Ski touring: Designated trails on unplowed roads, beginning at the ski area.

Skiing: Chair lifts and rope tow.

PUBLICATIONS
We were given a sheaf of trail maps, ski trail maps, trail descriptions, etc. Most are currently available. We've seen no general leaflet nor printed checklists of flora and fauna.

REFERENCES
AMC Massachusetts and Rhode Island Trail Guide. Boston: Appalachian Mountain Club, 1988.

Brady, John, and Brian White. *Fifty Hikes in Massachusetts.* Woodstock, VT: Backcountry Publications, 1983.

HEADQUARTERS: Mountain Rd., Princeton, MA 01541; (508) 464-2987.

WALDEN POND STATE RESERVATION
Massachusetts Division of Forests and Parks   East
411 acres.

From SR 2 in Concord, S on SR 126.

To see where Henry David Thoreau found solitude, go out of season, mid-week, on a rainy day. Hiking the trails then, one can imagine what it was like. On fine weekends, parking for a thousand cars isn't sufficient.

WAMPANOAG COMMEMORATIVE CANOE PASSAGE
70 river miles.   East

From Scituate on Massachusetts Bay to Dighton Rock State Park on the Taunton River at the head of Narragansett Bay.

The route, a linked series of waterways, is within a few miles of Boston and passes under some of the state's busiest highways. However, if one is seeking quiet places in this bustling metropolis, there's no better way than by canoe. The route was used by the Wampanoag Indians, whose chief greeted the pilgrims.

Paddling the entire route would take 3 to 5 days and require several portages. We found no reliable information about camping. Some canoeists use informal, unsanctioned sites. One can scout the route by land to find accommodations near landings. Most canoeists travel one section at a time.

REFERENCES

Schweiker, Roioli, ed. *AMC River Guide: Massachusetts, Connecticut, Rhode Island.* Boston: Appalachian Mountain Club, 1985.

Wampanoag Commemorative Canoe Passage. Pamphlet with sketch map and route description. Plymouth County Development Council, Box 1620, Pembroke, MA 02359.

WELLFLEET BAY WILDLIFE SANCTUARY
Massachusetts Audubon Society   East
700 acres.

On Cape Cod. On the W side of US 6 just N of the Eastham-Wellfleet town line.

Open: Summer, 8 A.M.–8 P.M. Winter, dawn to dusk; closed Mondays.

The society has preserved an unspoiled area on Wellfleet Bay, which opens onto Cape Cod Bay. More than 430 acres are salt marsh. Other wetlands include a diked freshwater pond and brackish marsh and salt marsh tidepools. Uplands are pine woods, large open fields, and a moor overlooking the sea. The Sanctuary is near the Marconi Beach section of Cape Cod National Seashore.

Plants: Woods are chiefly pitch pine. Shrubs include sweet pepperbush, bayberry, beach plum, shadbush, tartarian honeysuckle, highbush blueberry, huckleberry, dwarf sumac. Flowering plants include bearberry, sea lavender, butterfly weed, asters, broom crowberry, heathers.

Birds: The Cape is an exceptional birding area, and the variety of habitats provides excellent opportunities here, especially for shorebirds (late May through early June, and mid-July to mid-Sept.) and sea ducks (winter). About 250 species have been recorded. A checklist is available. Nestings have been recorded for green heron, mallard, black duck, red-tailed hawk, kestrel, bobwhite, clapper rail, piping plover, woodcock, mourning dove, black-billed cuckoo, great horned owl, chimney swift, ruby-throated hummingbird, kingfisher, northern flicker, eastern kingbird, phoebe, wood-pewee, horned lark, tree and barn swallows, blue jay, chickadee, mockingbird, catbird, American robin, yellow warbler, pine warbler, yellowthroat, red-winged blackbird, orchard and northern orioles, boat-tailed grackle, cowbird, cardinal, purple and house finches, American goldfinch, towhee. Sparrows: savannah, sharp-tailed, chipping, field, swamp, song.

Mammals: Include red and gray squirrels, red fox, cottontail, muskrat, deer.

INTERPRETATION

Visitor center is planned, replacing a small information office.
Nature trail with 71 stations.
Guided walks daily in summer.
Guided tours of Nauset Marsh, Pleasant Bay, Monomoy Island.
Canoe trips; pelagic birding trips.

Hiking: 5 mi. of trails.

Pets are not permitted.

PUBLICATIONS
  Site map.
  Quarterly newsletter.
  Goose Pond Trail guide. $1.25.
  Checklist, *Birds of Cape Cod.* $0.50.

HEADQUARTERS: P.O. Box 236, South Wellfleet, MA 02663; (508) 349-2615.

WENDELL STATE FOREST
Massachusetts Division of Forests and Parks   West
7,557 acres.

  From Greenfield, 12 mi. E on SR 2 to Millers Falls, then 3 mi. SE on Dry
  Hill Rd.

The Forest lies immediately to the S of Millers River, with SR 2 across the
stream, but it has little or no river frontage. The Forest map shows an unusual
number of roads crisscrossing the area, plus three power lines, but this appearance seems to be a mapmaker's artifact. Most are woods roads, carrying little
or no traffic, suitable for hiking. Laurel and blueberries are abundant.
  The area is rolling to hilly, less mountainous than are nearby Forests. Forest cover is mostly oak and sugar maple with some hemlock and white pine.
Ruggles Pond and Wickett Pond are within the Forest, Bowens Pond just outside.

ACTIVITIES
  Hiking: On the Metacomet-Monadnock Trail (see entry), which has an Ad-
irondack shelter. About 30 mi. of trails and woods roads.
  Hunting: Deer, woodcock, turkey, grouse, rabbit, bobcat, raccoon.
  Fishing: Trout in streams. Bass, perch, pickerel in Wickett Pond.
  Swimming: Ruggles Pond.
  Canoeing: Millers River is canoeable in season from the NH border to the
Connecticut River. The section beside the Forest has rapids to Class II.

PUBLICATION: Map.

HEADQUARTERS: RFD 1, Wendell Rd., Millers Falls, MA 01349; (413) 659-
  3797.

WILLARD BROOK STATE FOREST

Massachusetts Division of Forests and Parks   Central
2,380 acres.

From Fitchburg, N about 6 mi. on SR 31; right on SR 119.

The entrance was well signed, but the road to the Damon Pond campground was marked "Road Closed." No matter; one could get there. We saw several unmarked trails; headquarters had a trail map. (The road is open again, and trail signs have been replaced.)

The site is hilly with rock ledges, forested with an understory of shrubs, ferns, and wildflowers. We saw large areas of mountain laurel, which blooms in June. Elevation is 350 ft. along Trap Falls Brook, which has a 15-ft. waterfall, 765 ft. on SR 119.

Many picnic sites are distributed along the brook. There and in the two camping areas the only auto tags we saw were Massachusetts, except for two from New Hampshire. Headquarters confirmed the observation: 80% of visitors come from within the state; most others are from New Hampshire or transients making an overnight stop.

The campground at Damon Pond is sometimes full, but we were told sites are usually available at Pearl Hill, on New Fitchburg Road S of SR 119.

ACTIVITIES

Camping: 21 sites at Damon Pond, 51 at Pearl Hill. Damon Pond season is mid-Apr. through Oct., Pearl Hill a bit shorter.

Hiking: 18 mi. of trails, chiefly in the roadless center of the Park. Also a brookside trail.

Hunting: Small upland game.

Fishing: Trout stocked.

Swimming: Pearl Hill Pond (5 acres) and Damon Pond (2 acres).

PUBLICATION: Site map.

REFERENCE: *AMC Massachusetts and Rhode Island Trail Guide.* Boston: Appalachian Mountain Club, 1988.

HEADQUARTERS: Townsend, MA 01469; (508) 597-8802.

WILLOWDALE STATE FOREST

Massachusetts Division of Forests and Parks   East
2,400 acres.

From US 1 in Ipswich, 3.6 mi. N of SR 97, right about 1 mi. on Linebrook Rd. to sign and gate.

The central feature is Willowdale Swamp. The surrounding higher ground is mixed conifer and deciduous forest with meadows and reverting fields. Several brooks drain to the Ipswich River on the S. Highest point is 194-ft. Bartholomew Hill.

Off-road vehicles are prohibited, which makes for quiet hiking. The diversity of habitats attracts a variety of wildlife. Birding is good.

Hiking: Chiefly on old woods roads, on upland surrounding the swamp. A 3 1/2-mi. circuit hike is described in the AMC guide.

REFERENCE: *AMC Massachusetts and Rhode Island Trail Guide.* Boston: Appalachian Mountain Club, 1988.

NEARBY: Ipswich River Wildlife Sanctuary (see entry).

HEADQUARTERS: Massachusetts Division of Forests and Parks, 100 Cambridge St., Boston, MA 02202; (617) 727-3180.

WINDSOR STATE FOREST
Massachusetts Division of Forests and Parks   West
1,626 acres.
EUGENE D. MORAN WILDLIFE MANAGEMENT AREA
Massachusetts Division of Fisheries and Wildlife
1,147 acres.
NOTCHVIEW RESERVATION
The Trustees of Reservations
3,000 acres.

From Pittsfield, E on SR 9. For the Forest: turn left 2 mi. beyond Windsor. For WMA, turn N at Windsor on SR 8 A. Reservation entrance is on SR 9 E of Savoy Hollow Rd.

The three contiguous sites are in one of the most scenic areas of the Berkshires. Elevations range from about 1,600 ft. to 2,297 ft. Although several roads cross the area, much of the upland is wild, rocky, heavily wooded. In the Forest, Windsor Jambs is a narrow, picturesque ravine cut by Windsor Jambs Brook.

The WMA surrounds two hills, each about 2,000 ft. high, and occupies the S slope of a third hill that is mostly within the Forest. Whereas the Forest is almost entirely woodland, the WMA has extensive open fields and fresh meadows. It includes Windsor Brook, a shallow marsh, and a beaver pond. The Reservation includes the area's highest point, 2,297-ft. Judges Hill. Three brooks drain to the Westfield River. A small marsh is at the foot of Judges Hill. The area N of SR 9 is mostly spruce and hardwood forest. The open fields and farm buildings S of the road are also part of the Reservation.

Birds: No checklist is available, but the Reservation visitor center can provide information. 175 species have been recorded, 99 of them known to breed here.

Mammals: Include deer, bear, bobcat, snowshoe hare, cottontail, porcupine, raccoon, squirrel, woodchuck, fisher, beaver, otter.

ACTIVITIES
Camping: In the Forest. 24 sites.
Hiking: The Reservation has the best-developed trail system: 25 mi. Trails interconnect with those on the Forest and WMA.
Fishing: Streams and the Westfield River.
Swimming: Pond in the Forest.

PUBLICATIONS
WMA map.
Reservation map.

REFERENCES
AMC Massachusetts and Rhode Island Trail Guide. Boston: Appalachian Mountain Club, 1988.
Brady, John, and Brian White. *Fifty Hikes in Massachusetts.* Woodstock, VT: Backcountry Publications, 1983.

HEADQUARTERS: *Forest:* Windsor, MA 01270; (413) 684-0948. *WMA:* Wildlife District Manager, Massachusetts Division of Fisheries and Wildlife, 400 Hubbard Ave., Pittsfield, MA 01201; (413) 447-9789. *Reservation:* The Trustees of Reservations, 572 Essex St., Beverly, MA 01915; (508) 921-1944.

WOMPATUCK STATE PARK
Massachusetts Division of Forests and Parks   East
2,877 acres.

About 20 mi. SE of Boston. From SR 3, exit 14, then N on SR 228.

It's near Boston, near the coast, and it has one of the State's largest camp-grounds. But because the Park has no swimming, the campground is almost never full. Its natural features make it well worth a visit.

The land slopes toward Massachusetts Bay, gently rolling, with some steep-sided knobs of rock and glacial debris 50 to 100 ft. high. It has a few streams and small ponds, not large enough for canoeing.

Plants: The site has 3 of the state's oldest forest groves. Forest Sanctuary Climax Grove has large white pine, hemlock, and American beech, some specimens more than 180 years old. Other tree species in the Park include red pine, elm, white oak, sweet birch, Norway maple, white ash. Understory species include holly, swamp azalea, sheep laurel. Many wildflowers.

Wildlife: No checklists are available. Bird species mentioned include pheasant, grouse, goshawk, owls, northern harrier, green heron, quail, many songbirds. Mammals mentioned include cottontail, raccoon, skunk, muskrat.

INTERPRETATION
  Visitor center at entrance.
  Nature trail, self-guiding, 1 mi.
  Naturalist programs, June–Aug.

ACTIVITIES
  Camping: 400 sites. Apr. 15–Oct. 15.
  Hiking: 10 mi. of trails.
  Hunting: Pheasant, grouse, cottontail.
  Ski touring: 10 mi. of trails. Warming room at visitor center.

PUBLICATIONS
  Information page.
  Trail map.

REFERENCE: *AMC Massachusetts and Rhode Island Trail Guide.* Boston: Appalachian Mountain Club, 1988.

HEADQUARTERS: Union St., Hingham, MA 02043; (617) 749-7160.

RHODE ISLAND

S mallest of the 50 states, Rhode Island measures less than 50 mi. from N to S, 30 mi. W-E. No place in the state is more than 25 mi. from the sea.

Its population density, 925 people per square mi., is exceeded only by New Jersey's. Almost nine-tenths of the people live in urban areas. The western half of the state is rural.

Only about 9 percent of the land is in publicly owned forests, wildlife management areas, and parks. Nevertheless, the landscape is green. Much land once cleared and farmed has reverted to forests, which cover more than half of the state. Well-kept fields, farmyards, and lawns, and the absence of signboards and litter, help make Rhode Island pleasing to the eye.

Many citizens want to keep it that way, but the losses today are to developers, not loggers, and are more permanent. The State is buying development rights to preserve some farmland and buying ecologically important sites for parks and wildlife areas.

There's no room for adventurous backpacking. The longest named trail is only 8 mi., although there are connections. The state's highest point is 812 ft., no challenge to mountaineers. We could find no dry-land point as much as a mile from a road. The State has only 5 publicly owned campgrounds, and campsites are in great demand between Memorial Day and Labor Day.

Yet we found quiet places to enjoy. In summer, when crowds gather wherever there's a beach, we hiked forest trails few people use except in hunting season. Coastal wetlands offer splendid birding. Canoeists, too, can enjoy the feeling of isolation. Rhode Island has an impressive array of flora and fauna.

The State has an attractive park system, but we don't include sites developed for intensive use. We have included several very small sites, such as those of the Rhode Island Audubon Society, because they are protected fragments of natural ecosystems, where one can see and learn.

TERRAIN AND WEATHER

Many outdoorsmen here look seaward. The state's 420-mi. coastline is a complex of bays, sounds, islands, estuaries, and barrier beaches. Boaters outnumber hikers. Saltwater anglers outnumber those who fish in streams and ponds.

Rhode Island has three topographic divisions. The narrow coastal plain along the S shore and around Narragansett Bay is below the 100-ft. contour. To the N and E of the Bay are gently rolling uplands rising to about 200 ft. The western two-thirds of the state has rolling hills, mostly between 200 and 600 ft. elevation, rising to about 800 ft. in the NW corner.

Temperature ranges are relatively wide daily, seasonally, and from year to year, less so on the coastal plain. Annual precipitation ranges from 42 to 46 in. over most of the state, rather evenly distributed from season to season. Average annual snowfall ranges from 10 to 35 in. along the coast and 25 to 60 in. over the western uplands. Around the Bay, snow seldom remains for more than a few days. The western interior is usually snow-covered from mid- or late Dec. to mid-Mar.

MAPS

Rhode Island's official highway map shows many street names, including most of those in our directions to sites. It shows all of the public recreation lands and many of the private preserves open to the public.

The Division of Fish and Wildlife issues 8 1/2 × 11-inch maps of the largest and least-developed public areas. We were told some of these are out of date, but we had no difficulty matching them with the official highway map.

PLANTS

More than 1,800 plant species have been recorded in RI. Oak/hickory is the dominant forest type; oak/pine, pitch pine, eastern redcedar, and white pine make up most of the remainder. Less than one-quarter of the stands have trees of sawtimber size.

We didn't find a convenient plant or wildflower checklist. Many site managers are good information sources, as are the Ninigret National Wildlife Refuge and Audubon Society of Rhode Island.

BIRDS

Birders have excellent opportunities here. Observers describe "waves of warblers" seen on Block Island in the fall. Many pelagic birds are seen from ferries. Coastal wetlands are lively during migrations. Wintering waterfowl make birding an all-season activity.

More than 300 species have been recorded in Rhode Island. In larger states, we list abundant and common species for typical sites, if we can get the information. Here one such list will serve for the state.

Species that are seasonally abundant or common in suitable habitats include common and red-throated loons, horned and pied-billed grebes, Cory's and greater shearwaters, Wilson's storm-petrel, great and double-crested cormorants; great blue, green, and little blue herons; cattle, great, and snowy egrets; black-crowned night-heron, mute swan, Canada goose, brant, mallard, black duck, gadwall, pintail, green-winged and blue-winged teals, American wigeon, wood duck, ring-necked duck, canvasback, greater and lesser scaups, common goldeneye, bufflehead, oldsquaw, common eider; white-winged, surf, and black scoters; ruddy duck, common and red-breasted mergansers.

Also turkey vulture. Hawks: sharp-shinned, red-tailed, red-shouldered, broad-winged, northern harrier, osprey, merlin, American kestrel. Ruffed grouse, bobwhite, ring-necked pheasant, Virginia rail, American coot. Plovers: semipalmated, piping, black-bellied, ruddy turnstone. Greater and lesser yellowlegs. Sandpipers: spotted, solitary, purple, pectoral, white-rumped, least, semipalmated, western. American woodcock, common snipe, whimbrel, willet, red knot, dunlin, short-billed dowitcher, sanderling.

Gulls: great black-backed, herring, ring-billed, laughing, Bonaparte's. Terns: Forster's, common, roseate, least. Mourning dove, yellow- and black-billed cuckoos, screech and great horned owls, whip-poor-will, common nighthawk, chimney swift, ruby-throated hummingbird, belted kingfisher.

Northern flicker, hairy and downy woodpeckers. Flycatchers: eastern kingbird, great crested, eastern phoebe, willow, least flycatcher, eastern woodpewee, horned lark. Swallows: tree, bank, rough-winged, barn, purple martin. Blue jay, American crow, black-capped chickadee, tufted titmouse, white-breasted and red-breasted nuthatches, brown creeper. Wrens: house, Carolina, long-billed marsh. Mockingbird, gray catbird, brown thrasher, American robin. Thrushes: wood, hermit, Swainson's. Eastern bluebird, blue-gray gnatcatcher, golden-crowned and ruby-crowned kinglets, water pipit, cedar waxwing, European starling. Vireos: white-eyed, yellow-throated, solitary, red-eyed, warbling.

Warblers: black-and-white, blue-winged, Tennessee, Nashville, northern parula, yellow, magnolia, Cape May, black-throated blue, yellow-rumped, black-throated green, blackburnian, chestnut-sided, bay-breasted, blackpoll, pine, prairie, palm, ovenbird, northern waterthrush, common yellowthroat, hooded, Wilson's, Canada, American redstart.

Bobolink, eastern meadowlark, red-winged blackbird, northern oriole, rusty blackbird, common grackle, brown-headed cowbird, rufous-sided towhead, scarlet tanager, cardinal, rose-breasted grosbeak, indigo bunting. Finches: evening grosbeak, purple, house, pine siskin, American goldfinch. Sparrows: savannah, sharp-tailed, seaside, dark-eyed junco, tree, chipping, field, white-throated, swamp, song. Snow bunting.

OTHER WILDLIFE

The following reference provides information on the abundance, ranges, habitats, seasonality, and food habits of the region's bird, mammals, reptiles, and amphibians:

DeGraaf, Richard M., and Deborah D. Rudis. *New England Wildlife: Habitat, Natural History, and Distribution.* General Technical Report NE-108. Broomwall, PA: U.S. Department of Agriculture, Forest Service, Northeastern Forest Experiment Station, 1986.

TRAILS

An excellent system of short but pleasant trails is maintained by the State, the Appalachian Mountain Club, and Sierra Club volunteers. Trailside camping is prohibited.

CAMPING

The State has 5 campgrounds with 1,134 sites, 755 of them at Burlingame State Park. The *Camping in Rhode Island* leaflet doesn't mention reservations. The leaflet also lists about two dozen commercial campgrounds with over 2,500 sites; these generally accept reservations.

Camping is permitted in campgrounds only, prohibited elsewhere in State Forests and Management Areas.

FISHING AND HUNTING

Some streams are stocked with trout, and there's action in some freshwater lakes and ponds. More fishermen head for salt water. The Division of Fish and Wildlife has hunting maps that name the principal game species. Hunting is not permitted in the federal refuges.

BOATING, CANOEING

Saltwater opportunities are unlimited. Several lakes are large enough for power boats. Canoeing waters include several rivers, lakes, and ponds, as well as wetlands and sheltered tidewater.

STATE AGENCIES

Department of Environmental Management
22 Hayes St.
Providence, RI 02908
(401) 277-6800, Office of Information and Education

All environmental matters, including wildlife, forests, and parks, are within this department. Sites that include forests, wildlife management areas, and parks are jointly managed. Sometimes it's not clear who has primary responsibility, but it doesn't matter; they work together.

Division of Fish and Wildlife
Washington County Government Center
Tower Hill Rd.
Wakefield, RI 02879
(401) 789-3094

PUBLICATIONS: Wildlife Area maps.

Division of Forest Environment
Rt. 101
N. Scituate, RI 02867
(401) 647-3367

Division of Parks and Recreation
22 Hayes St.
Providence, RI 02908
(401) 277-2632

Department of Economic Development
Tourism and Promotion Division
7 Jackson Walkway
Providence, RI 02903
(401) 277-2601. From ME to VA, WV, and northern OH (except RI):
(800) 556-2484, Mon.–Fri., 8:30 A.M.-4:30 P.M.

PUBLICATIONS
Boating and Fishing in Rhode Island.
Camping in Rhode Island. Information on both public and private campgrounds.
Official State Highway Map. Includes information on parks, beaches, local attractions, etc.

PRIVATE GROUPS

Appalachian Mountain Club
5 Joy St.
Boston, MA 02108
(617)523-0636

The Narragansett Chapter of AMC has major responsibility for maintaining the state's hiking trails.

PUBLICATION: *AMC Massachusetts and Rhode Island Trail Guide,* 1988.

Audubon Society of Rhode Island
12 Sanderson Rd.
Smithfield, RI 02917
(401) 231-6444

The society owns and operates several preserves, conducts conservation education programs in State Parks, and develops interpretive materials for State Parks.

PUBLICATIONS:
Conway, Robert A. *Field Checklist of Rhode Island Birds.* Bird checklist.

REFERENCES

AMC Massachusetts and Rhode Island Trail Guide. Boston: Appalachian Mountain Club, 1988.

Schweiker, Roioli, ed. *AMC River Guide: Massachusetts, Connecticut, Rhode Island.* Boston: Appalachian Mountain Club, 1978.

Weber, Ken. *Canoeing Massachusetts, Rhode Island and Connecticut.* Woodstock, VT: Backcountry Publications, 1980.

Weber, Ken. *Walks & Rambles in Rhode Island.* Woodstock, VT: Backcountry Publications, 1988.

Woonsocket

295

Providence

95

95

138

Newport

Westerly

1

0   10 MI.

0   10 KM.

NATURAL AREAS IN RHODE ISLAND

An Alphabetical Listing

Arcadia Complex
Bay Islands Park System
Black Hut Management Area
Block Island
Buck Hill Wildlife Management
Area
Burlingame Complex
Caratunk Wildlife Refuge
Carolina Game Management Area
Davis Memorial Wildlife Refuge
Ell Pond; Long Pond; Blue Pond
George B. Parker Woodland
George Washington Management
Area
Great Swamp Management Area

Ninigret National Wildlife
Refuge/Ninigret Conservation
Area
Powder Mill Ledges Wildlife
Refuge
Sachuest Point National Wildlife
Refuge/Norman Bird Sanctuary
Seapowet Marsh Management
Area/Emilie Ruecker Wildlife
Refuge
Snake Den State Park
Trestle Trail
Trustom Pond National Wildlife
Refuge
Wickaboxet Management Area

ARCADIA COMPLEX
Rhode Island Department of Environmental Management
13,000 acres.

On both sides of SR 165 between the CT border and I-95.

Largest of RI's public lands, the Complex sprawls over a 6- by 6-mi. area. It combines under integrated management what were 3 State Parks, 2 Management Areas, and a State Forest. The only campground has been eliminated.

Terrain is rolling to hilly with rock ledges and outcrops, some vertical rock walls, ponds, and streams with cascades. The two principal recreation areas, both at ponds, are often crowded in warm weather. Total visitation is about 120,000 a year.

This is the state's prime hiking area. Fifteen of the 40 trails described in Ken Weber's *Walks & Rambles in Rhode Island* are here, and there are links with the CT trail system. Hiking is most popular in spring and fall. On a hot summer day, we met no one during an hour's walk. About 5,000 visitors per year are hunters.

Entering from CT, we saw first the entrance to the Beach Pond Recreation Area. Its parking lot was near capacity. Next on SR 165, at an Arcadia sign, we turned onto a well-kept dirt road. Gated woods roads were on both sides.

We stopped at a bridge, and our Labrador plunged into the stream. We passed no cars.

Plants: Except in the developed area, the site is almost entirely forested, predominantly with mixed hardwoods, mostly oaks and hickories with smaller stands of maple and beech. White pine is the principal softwood. We saw some dense thickets of laurel and rhododendron. The understory includes pin cherry, dogwood, laurel, sassafras, witch hazel, hawthorn, greenbrier, grape. Blueberries grew along the roadside. On the trails we saw many ferns, club mosses, lichens, fungi, wildflowers.

Birds: No checklist here, but the Audubon publication is useful. It looks like a good birding area.

Mammals: Reported species include chipmunk, gray squirrel, fox, raccoon, otter, cottontail, snowshoe hare, beaver, coyote, deer.

FEATURES
  Browning Mill Recreation Area on Browning Mill Pond. Fishing, swimming, boating, picnicking.
  Beach Pond Recreation Area shares a 2-mi. beach with CT's Pachaug State Forest (see entry). Fishing, swimming, boating, picnicking.
  Stepstone Falls is a cascade on Falls River. A fire tower is nearby.

ACTIVITIES
  Hiking: Over 65 mi. of trails, gentle to moderately steep, through varied habitats. Many are part of RI's Inter-Park Trail System, maintained by the Narragansett Chapter of the Appalachian Mountain Club. Trail links with Pachaug State Forest. Trailside camping is prohibited except at AMC shelters.
  Hunting: In designated areas. Raccoon, gray squirrel, cottontail, snowshoe hare, deer, pheasant, quail, dove, grouse, woodcock, some waterfowl.
  Fishing: Trout in stocked streams. Ponds have pickerel, small- and largemouth bass.
  Boating, canoeing: On ponds.

PUBLICATIONS: Fish and wildlife maps.

REFERENCES
  AMC Massachusetts and Rhode Island Trail Guide. Boston: Appalachian
    Mountain Club, 1988.
  Weber, Ken. *Walks & Rambles in Rhode Island.* Woodstock, VT: Back-
    country Publication, 1988.

HEADQUARTERS: Arcadia Headquarters, Forest Environment Division, RFD
  #1, Box 55, Hope Valley, RI 02832.

BAY ISLANDS PARK SYSTEM
Rhode Island Department of Environmental Management
2,300 acres.

Bridge access to several islands. Ferry from Colt Park in Bristol to Prudence Island. Access to others by private boat.

When gales kept sailing ships from maneuvering into the seaports of Boston and New York, Narragansett Bay offered safe haven. The 25-mi.-long estuary offered abundant supplies of fish and shellfish. Trade and fishing made the colony prosper.

Such a harbor needed defenses. The first fort, on Goat Island, was built in 1702. As recently as World War II, big guns guarded the Bay's entrance. In 1973 the Navy began releasing some of its property to the State, and the Bay Island Parks system began to take shape.

The official State highway map shows a number of small State Parks in and around the Bay. South Prudence is the largest of the island parks. Camping is permitted on Prudence Island and the S end of Dutch Island. Little information has as yet been published about islands other than Prudence.

RI's 420-mi. shoreline and its sheltered waters offer great opportunities for sailing, crusing, fishing, and other water-based activities. The Bay Parks assure public access.

FEATURES
Prudence Island was settled in the 1600s. The central portion of the 7-mi.-long island has both permanent and seasonal residents. In 1980 the N end became the first National Estuarine Sanctuary, and the S end became a State Park. The island is said to have more deer per square mile than any other place in New England, a condition that seems likely to inflict damage on the island's vegetation and cause winter kill of deer.

Trees including red maple, gray birch, pitch pine, black oak, and redcedar grow here, but much of the island is in early stages of succession.

ACTIVITIES
Camping: 15 sites at South Prudence, 3 mi. from the ferry. 12 primitive sites on Dutch Island. Obtain permits at Colt State Park in Bristol. Telephone reservations can be made up to one week in advance: (401) 253-7482. 3-night limit. Season is May 15–Oct. 15.
Hiking: Nature trails, N and S ends of Prudence.

PUBLICATIONS
Information page.
Estuarine Sanctuary pamphlet.

South Prudence nature trail guide.

REFERENCE: Weber, Ken. *Walks & Rambles in Rhode Island.* Woodstock, VT: Backcountry Publications, 1988.

HEADQUARTERS: Division of Parks and Recreation, 22 Hayes St., Providence, RI 02908; (401) 277-2635.

BLACK HUT MANAGEMENT AREA
Rhode Island Division of Fish and Wildlife
1,290 acres.

N central RI. From Glendale on SR 102, left on Joslin Rd. and Spring Lake Rd., which crosses the site. Follow signs to Spring Lake.

It's "Spring Lake Road" on the official state highway map, "Pond Road" on the map supplied by the Division of Fish and Wildlife. The map shows the road ending at Herring Rd., with parking areas there and woods roads leading off. On the ground, we saw a few woods roads and overgrown trails leading into what we surmised was the Management Area, with little-used parking areas.

Turning back, we followed commercial signs to Spring Lake. A blacktop road passes through a shoreline resort community of modest cottages. Beyond, on the side away from the lake, is a Black Hut Management Area sign with little-used woods roads nearby. As the highway map shows, the Management Area has no lake frontage. However, a State Fishing Area is close by, providing lake access for canoes and small boats. The lake is about 3/4 mi. long, with a forested shoreline and many water lilies.

What we saw of the terrain is gently rolling hardwood forest with moderate to dense understory.

ACTIVITIES
Hiking: About 5 mi. of trails, plus woods roads.
Hunting: Pheasant, grouse, cottontail, snowshoe hare, woodcock, dove, waterfowl, deer.
Fishing: Trout, panfish.

PUBLICATION: Site map.

HEADQUARTERS: Rhode Island Division of Fish and Wildlife, Government Center, Tower Hill Rd., Wakefield, RI 02879; (401) 789-3094.

BLOCK ISLAND
Mixed ownerships
About 7,000 acres.

12 mi. offshore in Block Island Sound, SE of Westerly. Ferry service from Westerly and Point Judith; in summer from Providence, New London, Newport. Also air service.

Shaped somewhat like a pork chop, this quiet, rustic island is about 7 mi. long, 3 mi. wide. Although most of the land is privately owned, commercial development is modest. Overnight accommodations are limited, so it's unwise to come without a reservation. Reservations are needed for cars on the ferries, too, but why bother? Most people walk or rent bicycles.

Much of the coast has rocky bluffs up to 160 ft. high, but there are also fine sandy beaches. The landscape includes low hills, moors, and valleys. Great Salt Pond divides the island into two. North of the pond is a pine forest with hiking trails. The Chamber of Commerce says there are "hundreds" of freshwater ponds.

Birds: Birders come here to see such oceanic species as shearwater and storm petrel. Early Oct. is the season for migrants. An annual, organized bird count on an Oct. weekend often yields 150 species or more. Late fall and winter species include gulls, scoters, cormorant, loon, gannet, grebe.

FEATURES
Block Island National Wildlife Refuge, 47 acres, is at the NW tip of the island. It has a sandy beach and dunes with such coastal vegetation as rose, beach pea, and beachgrass. Visitors are welcome daily, dawn to dusk. A checklist of over 190 bird species can be obtained from HQ: Ninigret NWR Complex, Box 307, Charlestown, RI 02813; (401) 364-9124.

Mohegan Bluffs Overlook has a fine view, stairs down to the beach, naturalist programs in summer.

Clay Head, on the NE side, has 1 1/2 mi. of shore trail.

Other refuges, various ownerships, are shown on an inset of the state highway map. One of the most attractive, for hiking as well as birding, is *Rodman's Hollow,* on Blackrock Road at the S end of the island, where trails descend below sea level.

ACTIVITIES
Hiking: Walks and trails are mostly pastoral rather than wild, but many are quiet and delightful, through pine forests, across flower-dotted meadows, along seacoast bluffs.

Fishing: Commercial fishing has a long history here. Charter boats are available. Saltwater species include striped bass, bluefish, flounder. Ponds have bass, perch, pickerel.

REFERENCE: Weber, Ken. *25 Walks in Rhode Island.* Somersworth, NH: New Hampshire Publishing, 1978.

INFORMATION: Block Island Chamber of Commerce, Drawer D, Block Island, RI 02807; (401) 466-2436. Information packet, $4.

BUCK HILL WILDLIFE MANAGEMENT AREA
Rhode Island Division of Fish and Wildlife
2,090 acres.

In RI's NW corner. From SR 100, left on Buck Hill Rd. Look for unpaved entrance road in about 2 1/2 mi.

CT is the site's W boundary, MA the N. Trails lead into both neighboring states. The shore of Wallum Lake is about half of the E boundary. Most of the site is hardwood forest, growing on land once cleared. Just N of the parking area is a 35-acre marsh that attracts waterfowl and shorebirds.

Birds: No checklist. Species mentioned include woodcock, ruffed grouse, wild turkey, mourning dove, black duck, wood duck, northern harrier, herons, flycatchers, hawks, owls, swallows.

Mammals: No checklist. Mentioned: cottontail, snowshoe hare, deer, gray squirrel, fox, raccoon, mink.

Hiking: 4-mi. blazed trail loop in the W half of the site, not approaching the lake.

PUBLICATION: Division of Fish and Wildlife map.

REFERENCE: Weber, Ken. *Walks & Rambles in Rhode Island.* Woodstock, VT: Backcountry Publications, 1988.

HEADQUARTERS: Rhode Island Division of Fish and Wildlife, Government Center, Tower Hill Rd., Wakefield, RI 02879; (401) 789-3094.

BURLINGAME COMPLEX
Rhode Island Department of Environmental Management
2,666 acres.

SW RI. From US 1, N on Cookestown Rd. or Kings Factory Rd.

Driving the several roads that cross or penetrate this area, we found it less attractive than the Arcadia or George Washington sites. Along the roads are many private homes, summer camps, and other establishments. Seeing no boundary markers, we couldn't tell whether these are inholdings or neighbors. We saw no marked trailheads and few woods roads.

The Complex has a gigantic camping area with 755 sites. That and 600-acre Watchaug Pond seem to be its primary attractions. We saw the usual summer crowd at the lakeside recreation center.

The area is mostly forested with mixed hardwoods. Some open and marshy areas. Spring flowers and fall foliage are colorful.

The Kimball Wildlife Refuge, operated by the Rhode Island Audubon Society, is within the area. The society has a summer day camp here.

ACTIVITIES

Camping: 755 sites. All year. No reservations.

Hiking: About 10 mi. of trails.

Hunting: In designated areas. Snowshoe hare, woodcock, grouse, waterfowl, gray squirrel, cottontail, deer.

Fishing: Trout, warmwater species.

Swimming: Beach on Watchaug Pond.

Boating: Canoes and small craft. Ramp.

PUBLICATIONS: Division of Fish and Wildlife maps.

HEADQUARTERS: Rhode Island Department of Environmental Management, Division of Parks and Recreation, 22 Hayes St., Providence, RI 02908; (401) 277-2632.

CARATUNK WILDLIFE REFUGE

Audubon Society of Rhode Island

200 acres.

From I-195 in East Providence, exit to SR 114. N to SR 152 (Newman Ave.), continuing on SR 152 about 3 mi. to Brown Ave. in Seekonk, MA, then left 1 1/4 mi.

Open Tues.–Sun.

The Refuge is in MA, but access is from RI and the RI Audubon Society owns it. The site has ledgy hills, glacial boulders, glacial stream floodplain, small streams and ponds. An old farm, its past is seen in open and reverting fields. Seven mi. of trails for hiking and ski touring.

Plants: White, northern red, and black oaks; white pine, red cedar, hickories, red maple, hophornbeam, flowering dogwood. Field flora are well represented.

Birds: No checklist available. Spring courtship display of woodcock. Pheasant, ruffed grouse. Nesting species include meadowlark. Many songbirds.

Mammals: Red and gray foxes, skunk, raccoon, weasel, mink, red and gray squirrels, chipmunk, cottontail, woodchuck. Many mice, shrews, moles.

Pets are prohibited.

PUBLICATION: Site map.

HEADQUARTERS: 301 Brown Ave., Seekonk, MA 02771; (617) 761-8230 or (401) 231-6444.

CAROLINA GAME MANAGEMENT AREA
Rhode Island Division of Fish and Wildlife
1,563 acres.

SW RI. From I-95, Exit 3. E 2 mi. on SR 138, then S 2 1/2 mi on SR 112. Right on Pine Hill Rd., which crosses the middle of the site.

Carolina is in the chain of public lands in western RI, lying between Arcadia and Burlingame, W of Great Swamp (see entries), but there are no linking trails. The terrain is level to rolling with a few rock outcrops and ledges. The site has ponds, Meadow Brook, and tributaries of the Pawcatuck River, which forms part of the E boundary. The land's history is indicated by old fruit trees among the oaks, maples, hawthorn, and pines. Among the attractions for birds are milkweed, clover, thistle, ironweed, knotweed. Bird species noted include quail, grouse, catbird, thrasher, red-winged blackbird, swallows.

The site is crossed by a network of unpaved roads. The site map indicates a number of developed inholdings; we didn't see them.

Few visitors come here except in hunting season.

ACTIVITIES
Hiking: About 5 mi. of trails, plus lightly traveled roads.
Hunting: Deer, grouse, quail, cottontail, wild turkey, pheasant.

Fishing: Trout, warmwater fish; in small ponds, stream, and river. Meadowbrook and Carolina Trout Pond are stocked with trout.

Canoeing: On the Pawcatuck River. Two campsites for canoeists are at the put-in.

PUBLICATION: Division of Fish and Wildlife map.

REFERENCE: Weber, Ken. *Walks & Rambles in Rhode Island.* Woodstock, VT: Backcountry Publications, 1988.

HEADQUARTERS: Rhode Island Division of Fish and Wildlife, Government Center, Tower Hill Rd., Wakefield, RI 02879; (401) 789-3094.

DAVIS MEMORIAL WILDLIFE REFUGE
Audubon Society of Rhode Island
102 acres.

In East Greenwich. From SR 2 at Frenchtown, E on SR 402 (Frenchtown Rd.). S on Davisville Rd. (SR 403) to entrance at Hunt River.

This site was classified as a "Unique Natural Area" because of its woodland, freshwater wetland, and bog. Flat to rolling terrain adjoins the steep banks of the Hunt River. There is a self-guiding nature trail.

Plants: The woodland is mostly hardwoods: red, white, and black oaks; hickories, maples, beech, birches. Some white pine. Hemlock and Russian olive were planted for wildlife food and shelter. Understory includes sassafras, sweet pepperbush, huckleberry, shadbush, buttonbush, highbush blueberry. Swamp and bog vegetation includes red maple, sphagnum moss, pitcherplant, sundew, swamp azalea, sweet gale, leatherleaf. Flowering species include trailing arbutus, water-lilies, arrow-arum, Indian-pipe, starflower, rose pogonia, iris.

Birds: No checklist available. Site is said to have abundant populations of many species, including wood and black ducks, sora, catbird, wood thrush, cardinal, flycatchers, woodpeckers, scarlet tanager, towhee, chickadee, nuthatch, titmouse, swallows, sparrows, finches.

Mammals: Species reported include raccoon, beaver, red fox, opossum, muskrat, skunk, chipmunk, gray squirrel, occasional otter, deer.

Canoeing: Canoes and boats without motors are allowed on the river. We were told this offers "a nice half-day of naturalizing."

No pets are permitted.

PUBLICATION: Nature trail guide.

HEADQUARTERS: Audubon Society of Rhode Island, 12 Sanderson Rd., Smithfield, RI 02917; (401) 231-6444.

ELL POND/LONG POND/BLUE POND
Audubon Society of Rhode Island; The Nature Conservancy; Rhode Island Division of Fish and Wildlife
490 acres plus recent additions.

In SW RI, from I-95 Exit 2, NW a short distance to SR 3, SW a short distance to Canonchet Rd., then N about 2 mi. to parking.

The official State highway map shows two tracts of State land in green, one on Ell Pond, the other around Ashville Pond. The Division of Fish and Wildlife map shows the Audubon and TNC tracts, Audubon owning the land around Long Pond, TNC on the N side of Ell Pond. The State has acquired land around Blue Pond.

Although small, the area has exceptional natural qualities. It's a National Natural Landmark. Weber's *Walks & Rambles in Rhode Island* called the first section of the trail the "magnificent mile."

The trail ascends to rocky overlooks above two ponds, descends through a deep gorge. Along the way are forest groves and clearings, tall rhododendrons and hemlocks, carpets of sphagnum moss.

Ashville, largest of the ponds, is about 2,500 ft. long. Long Pond is longer but narrower. Ell, considerably smaller, is a glacial kettlehole lake surrounded on three sides by a red maple/Atlantic white-cedar swamp.

Plants: The upland forest is largely oak/hickory. Other woodland species include chestnut oak, gray and yellow birches, sassafras, rhododendron, mountain laurel, sarsaparilla, trailing arbutus, teaberry. In moist area, swamp azalea, sweet pepperbush. The sphagnum bog mat has cranberry, sundew, Virginia chain fern, pitcher plant.

Birds: No checklist available. Reported: hawks, owls, whip-poor-will, woodpeckers, flycatchers, chickadee, titmouse, wood thrush, vireos, northern oriole, scarlet tanager, rose-breasted grosbeak, numberous warblers.

Mammals: Snowshoe hare, gray squirrel, deer, occasional bobcat and otter.

ACTIVITIES
Hiking: The site is on the Narragansett Trail. 3 mi. of trails within the site.
Hunting: In the State-owned Rockville Management Area only.

Fishing: Ponds. Warmwater species.

PUBLICATION: Division of Fish and Wildlife map.

REFERENCE: Weber, Ken. *Walks & Rambles in Rhode Island.* Woodstock, VT: Backcountry Publications, 1988.

HEADQUARTERS: Audubon Society of Rhode Island, 12 Sanderson Rd., Smithfield RI 02917, (401) 231-6444. The Nature Conservancy, 294 Washington St., Boston, MA 02108; (617) 542-1908. Rhode Island Division of Fish and Wildlife, Government Center, Tower Hill Rd., Wakefield, RI 02879; (401) 789-3094.

GEORGE B. PARKER WOODLAND
Audubon Society of Rhode Island
550 acres.

From SR 102 near Greene, E on Maple Valley Rd. HQ is just off the highway on left. Parking is 1/2 mi. beyond. Site is shown on the official State highway map.

A sign and trail map at the parking area explain that this is a place for "historical archeology": studies of old foundations, ruins of mills, and other artifacts. We took the Yellow Trail through a pleasant woodland, rolling with some small, steep slopes and a deep gorge with pools and modest cataracts. The trees are mostly second-growth hardwoods with scattered large specimens including beech and oak. The site has a 15-acre nearly pure stand of chestnut oak.

We visited on a weekday. A nature study class was investigating stream fauna. We saw no one else.

There is a bird list, but HQ was closed and we couldn't get one. Mammals are said to include bobcat, fox, red and gray squirrels, cottontail, chipmunk, skunk, mink, raccoon, mice, shrews, deer.

Hiking: 9 mi. of trails. The Yellow Trail intersects the Blue Trail, which leads to the Foster Tract, a second portion of the site.

Pets are prohibited.

PUBLICATIONS
  Site map.
  Bird list.

REFERENCE: Weber, Ken. *Walks & Rambles in Rhode Island.* Woodstock, VT: Backcountry Publications, 1988.

HEADQUARTERS: Audubon Society of Rhode Island, 12 Sanderson Rd., Smithfield, RI 02917; (401) 231-6444.

GEORGE WASHINGTON MANAGEMENT AREA
Rhode Island Division of Forest Environment
3,200 acres.

Entrances on N side of US 44 near CT border.

Entering from CT on a summer weekend, we turned in at the first marked entrance, the Pulaski Recreation Area, saw a great mass of parked cars, and left. The next entrance was marked "George Washington Camping Area." We paid a $2 entrance fee and drove to the beach parking area, which was far less crowded. The two are on the W and E shores of Bowdish Reservoir, an irregularly shaped impoundment about 1 1/4 mi. long, with private homes on much of its shoreline.

The George Washington complex is the largest of a cluster of State lands in the NW corner of RI, one of the largest in the state. This is the state's highest land, with elevations to 770 ft. (RI's highest point is Jerimoth Hill, about 6 mi. S.) Terrain is rolling to hilly, with many rock outcrops and ledges. In addition to the reservoir, the site has streams, ponds, a white-cedar swamp, and a wildlife marsh.

The beach area where we stopped was only moderately crowded. A flock of Canada geese wandered about, accepting handouts. A sign at the boat-launching area announced a 10-hp limit, but this didn't apply to or was ignored by boaters launching from private land; we saw several boats towing skiers. The beach area is also a trailhead. The ranger told us camping and water-based recreation are heavy all summer, weekdays included. In spring and fall, the hiking trails are well used.

A few well-maintained unpaved roads cross the site. We drove them, seeing no other cars except at fishing ponds.

Who comes here? Cars in the parking lots were all from RI, CT, and MA. The ranger confirmed that well over 90% of the visitors come from nearby.

Plants: The site is heavily wooded, an attractive open forest with trees that looked 50 to 60 years old. A ranger told us the Civilian Conservation Corps did extensive reforestation in the late 1930s. Trees are being planted now to offset gypsy moth damage. Principal species include maple, birches, beech, ash, hickories. Some fine specimen trees, including a hemlock grove, remain from earlier times. Forest understory includes laurel, sassafras, and witch hazel, with some chestnut saplings. Wildflowers include partridgeberry, Indian pipe, wintergreen, goldthread. Many ferns, lichens, and fungi. Water-lilies in ponds.

Birds: No checklist available. Mentioned: herons, black and wood ducks, hawks, owls, swallows, flycatchers, thrushes, warblers, quail, grouse, woodcock, dove.

Mammals: No checklist available. Mentioned: snowshoe hare, rabbit, muskrat, deer, gray squirrel, raccoon.

ACTIVITIES

Camping: 55 sites. Early Apr.–Oct. 31. No reservations.

Hiking: 8, 6, and 2-mi. loops.

Hunting: In Management Areas. Pheasant, grouse, dove, snowshoe hare, deer, waterfowl, woodcock, rabbit, squirrel.

Fishing: Warmwater species; reservoir and ponds.

Swimming: Reservoir, Peck Pond, Wilbur Pond.

Boating: Ramps on reservoir and Clarkeville Pond; no motors on Clarkeville.

Ski touring: Loops begin at Peck Pond in Pulaski Memorial Park.

PUBLICATIONS

Trail and campground maps.

Division of Fish and Wildlife site map.

REFERENCES

AMC Massachusetts and Rhode Island Trail Guide. Boston: Appalachian Mountain Club, 1988.

Weber, Ken. *Walks & Rambles in Rhode Island.* Woodstock, VT: Backcountry Publications, 1988.

HEADQUARTERS: Forestry Headquarters, RR 2, Box 2185, Chepachet, RI 02814; (401) 568-2013.

GREAT SWAMP MANAGEMENT AREA
Rhode Island Division of Fish and Wildlife
3,011 acres.

From Kingston, W on SR 138 through West Kingston to Liberty Lane. W to entrance.

The route is well signed. We drove on an unpaved road past HQ to a large parking area at a closed gate. Beyond is a jeep track bordering the swamp. To the S is a large wetland around shallow, 1,000-acre Worden Pond. Canoe access is on the S.

Plants: Upland forest of young mixed hardwoods. In better-drained areas are black and white oaks, some white pine. Understory includes dogwood, choke-cherry, blackberry, huckleberry, pepperbush, blueberry. Dense moist wooded areas with red maple, tupelo, pin and swamp white oaks. Nearby are black cherry and holly, the latter rare in RI. Habitats include some dry and sandy areas, open grasslands, sphagnum bogs. Ferns include cinnamon, bracken, sweet, hay-scented, lady.

Birds: Migrating waterfowl include lesser and greater scaups, ruddy duck, common merganser, goldeneye, bufflehead, teal, Canada goose. Gamebirds include pheasant, quail, ruffed grouse, woodcock, snipe. Breeding species include black and wood ducks, bittern, red-tailed and broad-winged hawks, osprey, owls, woodpeckers, tree swallow, chickadee, white-breasted nuthatch, wrens, vireos, catbird, wood thrush, veery, ovenbird, water-thrust, red-winged blackbird, towhee, warblers, sparrows.

Mammals: Deer, cottontail, gray squirrel, fox, muskrat, mink, raccoon, snowshoe hare, otter.

ACTIVITIES

Hiking: The road we entered on the N is part of a 5-mi. loop, part of it on a dike. Miles of unimproved dirt roads and trails are shown on the site map, some penetrating the swamp. The observation tower shown on the map is gone.

Hunting: All legal species. This is one of RI's most popular hunting areas, best avoided by nonhunters in hunting season.

Fishing: Trout stocked in Chickasheen Brook, on the W side of the site. Warmwater species in ponds.

Canoeing: Chipuxet River access is on SR 138, 2 mi. W of Kingston; 4-mi. paddle to Worden Pond. Usquepaug River access is 3 mi. W on SR 138, then 2 mi. S on SR 2; a 2-mi. paddle to the Charles River, then 2 mi. to Worden Pond.

PUBLICATION: Division of Fish and Wildlife map.

HEADQUARTERS: Rhode Island Division of Fish and Wildlife, Government Center, Tower Hill Rd., Wakefield, RI 02879; (401) 789-3094.

NINIGRET NATIONAL WILDLIFE REFUGE/NINIGRET
CONSERVATION AREA
U.S. Fish and Wildlife Service; Rhode Island Department of
  Environmental Management
407 acres; 174 acres.

> Between US 1 and Block Island Sound, near Charlestown. Refuge is off
> US 1; Conservation Area via East Beach Rd.

The Ninigret Refuge complex includes several satellite Refuges. We have separate entries for Trustom Pond and Sachuest Point, and for Block Island, on
which there is a small unit.

Ninigret Pond, 1,700 acres, is RI's largest salt pond, separated from Block
Island Sound by a long barrier beach with sand dunes. On the inland side,
the federal refuge occupies an abandoned airport, now an area of grassland,
shrubland, deciduous woodland, and freshwater ponds. The federal land also
includes a small tract on the barrier beach. There is foot travel only within
the Refuge.

The Conservation Area is a barrier beach more than 2 mi. long. Like most
public beaches, it attracts crowds in summer, but here there is a limitation:
The parking lot is closed when it reaches its capacity of about 100 cars. The
road beyond the parking lot is suitable for 4-wheel-drive vehicles only. At the
E end is a area of salt marsh.

Birds: The Refuge checklist of 289 species, plus 21 accidentals, includes reports from Trustom Pond, Sachuest Point, and Block Island as well as here.
It includes most of the species that occur in Rhode Island, and we have therefore used it in compiling the bird list in the state preface. Spring and fall are
the best seasons for wildlife viewing in all the units.

Woodcock courtship display flights are a feature here beginning in mid-
March. The warbler migration peaks in May.

Mammals: No checklist available. 40 species recorded. Often or occasionally
seen: red and gray foxes, chipmunk, deer. Coyotes have been seen.

Reptiles and Amphibians: No checklist available. Often or occasionally seen:
eastern painted turtle, garter snake.

INTERPRETATION: The Frosty Dew Nature Center, an independent, self-
supporting project, is in Ninigret Park, off US 1 on Old Post Road.

ACTIVITIES
Camping: In the Conservation Area, 50 sites for self-contained units.

Hiking: About 2 1/2 mi. of trails in the federal refuge. Kiosk at Foster Cove, off US 1, has a posted map. Hiking also on Grassy Point; access through Ninigret Park. Hiking on the barrier beach is best at low tide, with firm sand underfoot.

PUBLICATIONS
Federal Refuge site map.
Bird checklist.
When and Where to See Wildlife.

HEADQUARTERS: Ninigret National Wildlife Refuge, Box 307, Charlestown, RI 02813; (401) 364-9124. Rhode Island Department of Environmental Management, 22 Hayes St., Providence, RI 02908; (401) 277-2632.

POWDER MILL LEDGES WILDLIFE REFUGE
Audubon Society of Rhode Island
76 acres.

From Exit 7B on I-295, W of Providence, 1 mi. W on US 44, then 0.1 mi. S on SR 5.

This small but delightful site is also the Audubon Society's state headquarters. On the coastal plain, it is upland woodland, with almost pure stands of northern red oak, white pine, and pitch pine. It includes a small pond and red maple swamp.

Plants: Understory includes serviceberry, sweet pepperbush, sweetfern, huckleberry, witch hazel, elderberry, highbush blueberry, northern arrowwood. Seasonal wildflowers include jack-in-the-pulpit, wild sarsaparilla, pipsissewa, downy rattlesnake plantain, pink lady's-slipper, bunchberry, wild geranium, Indian cucumber-root, yellow pond-lily, false Solomon's-seal, larger blue flag. Peak season is early summer.

Birds: Checklist available. More than 150 species recorded, 50 known to nest on the Refuge.

Mammals: Checklist available. 14 species recorded include American opossum, gray fox, woodchuck, eastern chipmunk, eastern gray squirrel, red squirrel, cottontail, deer. Present but seldom seen: striped skunk, meadow and woodland jumping mice, shorttail shrew.

Reptiles and Amphibians: Checklist of 9 species available. Often or occasionally seen: eastern painted turtle, northern brown snake, eastern garter snake, American toad, green frog, bullfrog, wood frog.

Pets are prohibited.

INTERPRETATION
Audubon HQ has exhibits, films, talks, literature. Open Mon.–Sat., 9 A.M.–5 P.M.
2-mi. *nature trail* begins at HQ.

NEARBY: Snake Den State Park, 1 mi. away, is shown on the highway map but not included in 1987 State listings. It's open to hiking. (See entry.)

HEADQUARTERS: 12 Sanderson Rd., Smithfield, RI 02917; (401) 231-6444.

SACHUEST POINT NATIONAL WILDLIFE REFUGE/NORMAN BIRD SANCTUARY
U.S. Fish and Wildlife Service; Independent
242 acres; 250 acres.

E of Newport. Highway map shows several routes to Green End Ave. *For Refuge:* S on Paradise Ave., left at fork, then right. *For Sanctuary:* S on Third Beach Rd.

The Refuge is open daily, dawn to dusk. The Sanctuary is open Wed.–Sun., 1 to 4 P.M.

These adjoining sites are at the tip of land where the Sakonnet River enters Rhode Island Sound. The coast is rocky. The Refuge is mostly grassland and shrubland, with some marsh. It was established in 1970 to provide nesting, resting, and feeding habitat for migratory birds. The Sanctuary has rugged outcrops, ledges of pudding stone, open and reverting fields, swamp, pond, and woodland.

Three public beaches are along the access roads, so traffic in warm weather may be heavy.

Birds: Checklist available (for all units of the Ninigret Complex). This is one of RI's best birding areas. Fall and winter are the best seasons for birding. About 250 species have been recorded, 70 of them breeding here. More than 15 waterfowl species winter here. It's a good place to see the fall hawk migration. The Sanctuary has a woodcock singing ground. Refuge species of special interest include harlequin, eider, and oldsquaw ducks, snowy and short-eared owls.

Mammals: No checklist; 10 species recorded. Red fox and cottontail are often seen, striped skunk occasionally, harbor seal on rare occasions.

INTERPRETATION
Visitor center at the Refuge is staffed by volunteers, open intermittently, Sat. and Sun., 8 A.M.–4 P.M. Exhibits, films, talks, literature. *Three nature trails,* 0.8, 1.3, and 1.2 mi. *Guided walks,* no regular schedule.
Nature museum at the Sanctuary.

ACTIVITIES
Hiking: 3 mi. of trails at the Refuge; map posted at entrance kiosk. 5 mi. of trails at the Sanctuary.
Fishing: Surf. Excellent for bluefish, striped bass, tautog, in season.

REFERENCE: Weber, Ken. *Walks & Rambles in Rhode Island.* Woodstock, VT: Backcountry Publications, 1988.

HEADQUARTERS: Ninigret National Wildlife Refuge Complex, Box 307, Charlestown, RI 02813; (401) 364-9124. Norman Bird Sanctuary, Third Beach Rd., Middletown, RI 02840; (401) 846-2577.

SEAPOWET MARSH MANAGEMENT AREA/EMILIE RUECKER WILDLIFE REFUGE

Rhode Island Division of Fish and Wildlife; Audubon Society of Rhode Island
296 acres; 50 acres.

Eastern RI. From Tiverton, S on SR 77 to Seapowet Ave., then W toward Puncatest Rd. and entrances. Ruecker entrance is on Seapowet Ave.

The Marsh is on the Sakonnet River, the Eastern Passage of Narragansett Bay. The marsh is dissected by a number of narrow channels and includes several salt ponds.
The Refuge is on the N side of Seapowet Ave. It includes tidal flats, salt marsh, a freshwater pond, a small oak/hickory woodland, and a pine/spruce plantation.

Plants: Marsh vegetation is predominantly cordgrass, with saltmeadow grass, spike-grass, rushes, saltwort, seaside plantain, seaside goldenrod. On somewhat higher ground are shadbush, bayberry.

Birds: No checklist available. The several habitats and viewpoints make it a fine birding site. Species mentioned include waterfowl, pheasant, rails, ruffed grouse, screech owl, mourning dove, goldfinch, white-eyed vireo, great and little blue herons; cattle, snowy, and great egrets; glossy ibis, black-crowned night-heron, yellow-rumped and yellow warblers, redstart, yellowthroat.

ACTIVITIES

Hiking: Although it's smaller than the Management Area, the Refuge has 3 short, well-developed trails with a good trail guide. The Seapowet Marsh has a short trail across its midsection.

Hunting: In the Management Area only. Rails, pheasant, quail, waterfowl, dove.

Fishing: From the Management Area. Saltwater species.

Boating, canoeing: Unimproved ramp on Puncatest Neck Rd. Canoeing in marsh channels.

PUBLICATIONS

Management Area: map.
Refuge: trail guide with map.

REFERENCE: Weber, Ken. *Walks & Rambles in Rhode Island.* Woodstock, VT: Backcountry Publications, 1988.

HEADQUARTERS: Rhode Island Division of Fish and Wildlife, Government Center, Tower Hill Rd., Wakefield, RI 02879; (401) 789-3094. Audubon Society of Rhode Island, 12 Sanderson Rd., Smithfield, RI 02917; (401) 231-6444.

SNAKE DEN STATE PARK
Rhode Island Department of Environmental Management
744 acres.

From Providence, W on US 6 to Brown Ave., beyond I-295; then right.

As of 1988 this State land was undeveloped except for 170 acres leased to the Dame family for farming. Under the sponsorship of the Rhode Island Historical Farm Association, the farm is open to the public, with the request that visitors don't interfere with operations or trample crops.

The rest of the site, woodlands and reverting fields, is available for hiking. It's lightly used.

REFERENCE: Weber, Ken. *Walks & Rambles in Rhode Island.* Woodstock, VT: Backcountry Publications, 1988.

HEADQUARTERS: Department of Parks and Recreation, 22 Hayes St., Providence, RI 02908; (401) 277-2635.

TRESTLE TRAIL
Rhode Island Department of Environmental Management
6 1/2 miles.

E access at Coventry Center on Hill Farm Rd.

The Trail is shown on the official highway map, a green stripe extending W to the CT border. It was built on an abandoned railroad bed, so it's level, easy walking. Much of the route is on an embankment with woodlands on both sides, but there is considerable visual variety. Coventry Reservoir is at the E end. The Trail passes through cuts and rock ledges, crosses highway bridges and a trestle, and ends near Carbuncle Pond, where swimming is permitted.

Railroad rights-of-way and their adjacent banks and ditches are almost always rich in botanical variety, partly because of the effects of edges and variations in soil moisture, often because trains have transported seeds from place to place. The Trestle Trail is no exception. Species suppressed by railroad maintenance practices are now flourishing.

Unfortunately, the route is open to motor bikes, but apparently conflicts between hikers and cyclists haven't been serious.

In May 1988 we were informed that the State's lease agreement on part of this route had expired. The State owns several miles of the route near the CT border, and the entire route may still be available to hikers. The State has recently acquired 832 acres S of the Trail, E of the border, crossed by the Moosup River, where there is hiking on unmarked trails. Name: Nicholas Farm Management Area.

REFERENCE: Weber, Ken. *Walks & Rambles in Rhode Island.* Woodstock, VT: Backcountry Publications, 1988.

INFORMATION: Department of Environmental Management, 22 Hayes St., Providence, RI 02908; (401) 277-2632.

TRUSTOM POND NATIONAL WILDLIFE REFUGE
U.S. Fish and Wildlife Service
641 acres.

From US 1 near Perryville, S 1 mi. on Moonstone Beach Rd., right on Matanuck Schoolhouse Rd. 0.7 mi. to entrance on left.

Trustom Pond, 160 acres, is RI's only undeveloped salt pond. The Refuge was established in 1974 to provide nesting, resting and feeding habitat for migratory birds. Most of the site is upland habitat, once a farm, now reverting. It includes grassland, shrub, and coastal hardwood forest, fresh and brackish marsh, small freshwater ponds, and wooded swamp. Trustom Pond is separated from Block Island Sound by Moonstone Beach, a barrier beach of sand and dunes.

There is foot access only. Crowding is limited by the size of the parking lot. Moonstone Beach Rd. ends at a public beach, but there is no swimming within the Refuge.

Plants: About 10% of the site is forested. Prominent woodland, understory, and brush species include serviceberry, black cherry, oaks, red maple, viburnum, blueberry, bayberry, smilax, blackberry. Beach species include beachgrass, beach pea, roses, seaside goldenrod.

Birds: Best birding is in spring and fall. Checklist of the Ninigret NWR Complex (see entry) notes species occurring here. About 300 species have been recorded, including most of those listed in the RI Preface. Refuge management says there is "something good in each season," noting piping plover, least tern, and osprey in spring, wintering waterfowl.

Mammals: No checklist. 40-plus species recorded. Often or occasionally seen: red and gray fox, cottontail, eastern chipmunk, woodchuck, muskrat, deer. Coyote, mink, and otter are present but seldom seen.

Reptiles and Amphibians: No checklist. 20-plus species recorded, including painted and snapping turtles, bullfrog, garter snake, brown snake, smooth green snake, northern water snake.

INTERPRETATION
Information kiosk at trailhead.
Nature trails; 1.4 and 1.9 mi.

Fishing: Surf, chiefly for bluefish and stripers.

REFERENCE:
Weber, Ken. *Walks & Rambles in Rhode Island.* Woodstock, VT: Backcountry Publications, 1988.

HEADQUARTERS: Ninigret National Wildlife Refuge Complex, Box 307, Charlestown, RI 02813; (401) 364-9124.

WICKABOXET MANAGEMENT AREA
Rhode Island Division of Forest Environment
682 acres.

From I-95, Exit 5. NW on SR 102 to Plain Meeting House Rd., then N about 3 mi.

If you happen to pass this way, as we did, here is an opportunity for a short walk in woods seldom visited except in hunting season. The sign was missing, but a locked gate painted orange marks the entrance. From here a jeep road runs N across the site. What we first saw was rather flat land with mixed hardwood forest, but there are also steep slopes, rock ledges, and a scenic knob. Features include a stream and a swampy area. Birding is reasonably good. Wildflowers in season.

ACTIVITIES
Hiking: About 5 mi. of trails and woods roads.
Hunting: Raccoon, gray squirrel, grouse, snowshoe hare, deer.

PUBLICATION: Site map.

HEADQUARTERS: Division of Forest Environment, RR #1, Box 55, Hope Valley, RI 02832; (401) 539-2356.

CONNECTICUT

Only two states are smaller than Connecticut. Only three exceed its population density. For comparison: Montana's population density is 6 per square mile, Connecticut's 653. Fairfield County, closest to New York, has twice that.

Urbanization has burgeoned along the corridor between New York City and Boston. Of the 253-mi. shoreline, only a few fragments remain in public ownership. Connecticut has no National Park, no National Forest, two small National Wildlife Refuges. Even so, most of the state is green, with many quiet places to enjoy.

Connecticut measures 90 mi. W–E, 75 mi. N–S. It's hilly. The highest ground is in the NW, 1,000 to over 2,000 ft. Elevations in the SW and E are predominantly 300 to 1,000 ft. The Connecticut River bisects the state. The principal rivers flow S from Massachusetts, most often in steep-sided narrow valleys. Settlement and subsequent development followed the rivers upstream. Many dams have been built for flood control and power.

The National Climatic Center says CT's weather has more variety than monotony. "A 'normal' month, season, or year is the exception rather than the rule." On the average, the higher NW has 70 below-freezing days in a year, the central and coastal regions 25 to 30 days. Summer temperatures above 90°F occur about 10 days per year.

Average annual precipitation is 44 to 48 inches, with no regular dry or wet seasons. Most snow falls in Jan. and Feb. Away from the coast, most of the state has some snow cover from late Dec. through early Mar.

STATE LANDS

By the late nineteenth century, loggers had felled most of the primeval forest. Only one-fifth of the land remained forested. Today three-fifths of the land is tree-covered. In the new forests of mixed hardwoods with a scattering of conifers, stone walls mark the boundaries of fields once cultivated.

It was private land then and most of it is now. With no federal land to provide green space, wildlife habitat, and recreation, the State has done remarkably well on its own. Distributed over the state are more than a hundred State Forests and State Parks, the largest with over 23,000 acres. The Connecticut Audubon Society, The Nature Conservancy, and other private groups have acquired attractive preserves.

The State system has been planned to provide nearby green spaces and out-door recreation for Connecticut residents, and does so admirably. Outsiders who want to camp will find limited opportunities. Only 13 State Parks and 3 State Forests have campgrounds. Camping elsewhere on public land is pro-hibited. State and commercial campgrounds in resort areas are usually full on fine weekends. It's wise to have reservations. Distances are short, however, so any campground can be a base for exploring other sites.

State Parks without campgrounds may also be crowded, especially those offering water-based recreation. Parks in western Connecticut tend to be less crowded than those on or near the coast.

Most developed State Parks have entrance signs. So do the 3 Forest camp-grounds. Except at these developed sites, Forest roads often have no signs. Boundaries between State and private land are often unmarked. No matter—local hunters, fishermen, hikers, birders, and picnickers can tell you where to go.

If you are traveling to New England for outdoor adventures, Connecticut has few places we'd recommend over the larger and wilder natural areas far-ther north. If you are traveling through Connecticut, however, there are many places worth stopping for. We never ended a day without finding a delightful marsh, pond, waterfall, hemlock grove, or hilltop. Almost every day we hiked quiet trails, usually alone. For entries we've chosen places well worth visiting for an hour or a day.

TRAILS

We've seen nothing like it anywhere: a statewide system of blazed trails. It's astonishing to find it in a densely populated state, the more so that the system has been planned, built, and maintained by a private organization of volunteers, the Connecticut Forest and Park Association:

Connecticut Forest and Park Association, Inc.
16 Meriden Rd.
Middletown, CT 064557
(203) 346-2372

The Association began this work in 1929. It has persuaded many private landowners to allow trails to cross their properties. Today it can say to Con-necticut residents, "Go a few miles away from your home, and you can soon be on a forest trail."

The Association lists the Trail Chairmen who coordinate the volunteers caring for 68 trails and sections of trails. The 500-mile blue-blazed system has 15 principal trails and many feeders, loops, and spurs.

We considered including brief descriptions of the principal trails and decid-ed not to. Wherever you are in the state, trails are nearby, and there is no substitute for the 62 maps and 106 pages of trail descriptions in the *Connecticut Walk Book,* itself an impressive achievement. It describes not only main trails but numerous feeder trails and loops. It's loose-leaf, so maps and descriptions can be detached for field use.

Many trail segments are within State Parks and State Forests. Linking them is a never-ending task. The privilege of crossing private land is contingent on good behavior. It may be lost when a property changes hands. Where there's no open land, a trail may be routed along a public road, preferably a quiet way. Some trails have gaps. In general, the longest unbroken segments are in the northern half of the state.

Camping is forbidden except at designated sites. Some of these are the campgrounds of State Parks and Forests. There are a few shelters but not enough to support trips over several nights. Long-distance hikers use off-trail quarters.

The two other references listed overlap the *Connecticut Walk Book* in part, but their emphasis is on day hikes to places of special interest:

Hardy, Gerry and Sue. *Fifty Hikes in Connecticut.* Woodstock, VT: Back-country Publications, 1984.

Hicock, Shelton B., ed. *Connecticut Walk Book.* Middletown: Connecticut Forest and Park Association, 1984.

Keyarts, Eugene. *60 Selected Short Walks in Connecticut.* Chester, CT: Globe Pequot Press, 1979.

MAPS

The official State highway map serves most purposes. Although it shows only the general locations of State Forests and Wildlife Areas, we could usually find the ones we sought by cruising roads and, if necessary, inquiring. The map has a long list of public boat-launching areas, a chart showing the facilities in Parks and Forests, and other information. It's available from:

Connecticut Department of Transportation
P.O. Drawer A
Wethersfield, CT 06109

The Connecticut Office of State Parks and Recreation has site maps for a few of the State Parks and State Forests. The most complete series is available from the Wildlife Bureau. Their ninety-eight 8 1/2- by 11-inch maps include most of the State Forests. We found them helpful, despite inaccuracies. Path-finding is made more difficult by the lack of name signs on many local roads.

FLORA AND FAUNA

Only a few small groves of giant white pines remain. Groves of large hemlocks are somewhat more numerous. The predominant pattern of the new forest is mixed hardwoods with scattered white pines and hemlock groves. Most of the coastal salt marshes and freshwater wetlands have also vanished, but significant sites remain and are now protected by law.

Several preserves of the Connecticut Audubon Society and other private groups maintain and interpret the state's ecosystems. The society has annotated checklists of wildflowers and of birds. More than 200 bird species have been recorded in CT. Write to:

Connecticut Audubon Society
2325 Burr St.
Fairfield, CT 06430

The following two references are out of print, but we found copies:

Billard, Ruth Sawyer. *Places to Look for Birds.* Hartford: Department of Environmental Protection, 1972.

Proctor, Noble S. *25 Birding Areas in Connecticut.* Chester, CT: Globe Pequot Press, 1978.

After a drastic decline, the deer population recovered dramatically. Deer are hunted, subject to season and bag limits. Cougar and wolf are among the vanished species. The relatively abundant game mammals are gray squirrel, cottontail, snowshoe hare, raccoon, red and gray foxes, woodchuck, and opossum.

The following reference relates bird, mammal, amphibian, and reptile species to place, habitat, and season in New England:

DeGraaf, Richard M., and Deborah D. Rudis. *New England Wildlife: Habitat, Natural History, and Distribution.* General Technical Report NE-108. Broomwall, PA: U.S. Department of Agriculture, Forest Service, Northeastern Forest Experiment Station, 1986.

CAMPING

The season in State campgrounds is mid-Apr. to Sept. 30. Limited off-season camping is permitted at some locations, but not during the spring thaw: Mar. 1–Apr. 14. Emergency stopover space may be provided for out-of-state campers.

Reservations can be made at some State campgrounds, by mail only, during the period between Memorial Day and Labor Day. Request application from Connecticut Office of State Parks and Recreation.

Pets are prohibited in State Park campgrounds, permitted on leash in State Forests.

CANOEING, BOATING

Several rivers have flatwater and whitewater canoe runs. Few runs are longer than 10 miles. Some require portages around dams. Some are canoeable only during spring runoff. Three State canoe camps are on the lower Connecticut River (see entry). Our entries note canoeing and boating opportunities.

Connecticut's coast is on Long Island Sound, one of America's most popular waters for boating and fishing.

Lakes with no bordering State Park or State Forest aren't mentioned in entries. Public launch sites on lakes, rivers, and salt water are listed in the official highway map.

Borton, Mark C., ed. *The Complete Boating Guide to the Connecticut River.* Woodstock, VT: Backcountry Publications, 1985.

Schweiker, Roioli, ed. *AMC River Guide: Massachusetts, Connecticut, Rhode Island.* Boston: Appalachian Mountain Club, 1985.

Weber, Ken. *Canoeing Massachusetts, Rhode Island, and Connecticut.* Woodstock, VT: Backcountry Publications, 1980.

FISHING

River pollution curtailed some of CT's best fishing, but water conditions have improved substantially. Shad fishing in the Connecticut River was excellent until deterioration of the Enfield Dam, and there is still an annual shad derby.

Fishing is noted as an available activity in many public areas. Many streams and ponds are stocked. Most of the trout caught are from hatcheries. Other species include bass and pickerel.

Judging by the fleets of small boats we saw in harbors, saltwater fishing is extremely popular. Bluefish is a leading catch.

STATE AGENCIES

The Department of Environmental Protection has responsibility for all the state's natural resources. Among its numerous administrative units are the following, all at:

165 Capitol Ave.
Hartford, CT 06106

Office of State Parks and Recreation
(203) 566-2304

The Office of State Parks and Recreation is responsible for recreation areas in State Parks and State Forests. Its publications include
Connecticut State Park and Recreation Areas.

Camping in Connecticut.
Guide to State Boat Launch Areas.
Ski Touring.
Snowmobiling in Connecticut.

Wildlife Bureau
(203) 566-4683

The Wildlife Bureau manages the state's wildlife resources. Its publications include

Wildlife Area maps, including maps of most State Forests. Up to 5 free.
Hunting and Trapping Field Guide.

Fisheries Bureau
(203) 566-2287

Publications include the *Connecticut Angler's Guide.*

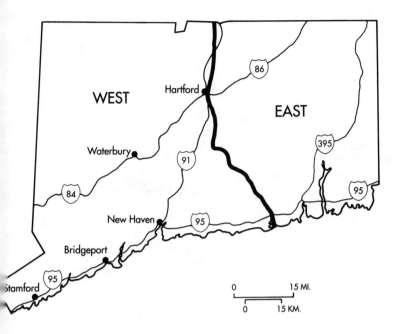

WEST

Hartford

86

EAST

Waterbury

91

395

84

New Haven

95

95

Bridgeport

Stamford

95

0   15 MI.

0   15 KM.

NATURAL AREAS IN CONNECTICUT

An Alphabetical Listing

Algonquin State Forest
West

Assekonk Swamp Wildlife
Management Area
East

Audubon Center in
Greenwich/Audubon Fairchild
Garden *West*

Barn Island Wildlife Management
Area *East*

Bigelow Hollow State Park
East

Bluff Point Coastal Reserve
East

Campbell Falls State Park
West

Chatfield Hollow State Park
West

Cockaponset State Forest
West

Connecticut River
West/East

Devil's Den Preserve
West

Devil's Hopyard State Park
East

Durham Meadows Wildlife
Management Area
West

Edward Steichen Memorial Wildlife
Preserve *West*

Ellithorpe Flood Control Area
East

Franklin Swamp Wildlife
Management Area
East

Gay City State Park
East

Hammonasset Beach State Park
West

Hopeville Pond State Park
East

Housatonic State
Forest/Housatonic Meadows
State Park *West*

Hurd State Park
East

James L. Goodwin State Forest
East

John A. Minnetto State Park
West

Kettletown State Park/Indian Well
State Park *West*

Macedonia Brook State Park
West

Mansfield Hunting Area/Mansfield
Hollow State Park
East

Mashamoquet Brook State Park
East

Mattatuck State Forest
West

Meshomasic State Forest
East

Mohawk State Forest
West

Morgan R. Chaney Sanctuary
East

Nassahegon State Forest
West

Natchaug State Forest
East

Nehantic State Forest
East

Nepaug State Forest
West

Nipmuck State Forest
East

Northeast Audubon Center
West

Pachaug State Forest
  East
Penwood State Park/Talcott
  Mountain State Park
  West
Peoples State Forest
  West
Quaddick State Forest and State
  Park   *East*
Quinebaug River Wildlife
  Management Area
  East
Rocky Neck State Park
  East
Roy and Margot Larsen Sanctuary
  West

Salmon River State Forest
  East
Salt Meadow National Wildlife
  Refuge   *West*
Satan's Kingdom State Recreation
  Area   *West*
Shade Swamp Sanctuary
  West
Shenipsit State Forest
  East
Sleeping Giant State Park
  West
Tunxis State Forest
  West
White Memorial Conservation
  Center   *West*

NATURAL AREAS IN CONNECTICUT

by Zones

West Zone

Algonquin State Forest
Audubon Center in
  Greenwhich/Audubon Fairchild
  Garden
Campbell Falls State Park
Chatfield Hollow State Park
Cockaponset State Forest
Connecticut River
Devil's Den Preserve
Durham Meadows Wildlife
  Management Area
Edward Steichen Memorial Wildlife
  Preserve
Hammonasset Beach State Park
Housatonic State
  Forest/Housatonic Meadows
  State Park
John A. Minnetto State Park

Kettletown State Park/Indian Well
  State Park
Macedonia Brook State Park
Mattatuck State Forest
Mohawk State Forest
Nassahegon State Forest
Nepaug State Forest
Northeast Audubon Center
Penwood State Park/Talcott
  Mountain State Park
Peoples State Forest
Roy and Margot Larsen Sanctuary
Salt Meadow National Wildlife
  Refuge
Satan's Kingdom State Recreation
  Area
Shade Swamp Sanctuary
Sleeping Giant State Park
Tunxis State Forest
White Memorial Conservation
  Center

East Zone

Assekonk Swamp Wildlife
  Management Area
Barn Island Wildlife Management
  Area
Bigelow Hollow State Park
Bluff Point Coastal Reserve
Connecticut River
Devil's Hopyard State Park
Ellithorpe Flood Control Area
Franklin Swamp Wildlife
  Management Area
Gay City State Park
Hopeville Pond State Park
Hurd State Park
James L. Goodwin State Forest

Mansfield Hunting Area/Mansfield
  Hollow State Park
Mashamoquet Brook State Park
Meshomasic State Forest
Morgan R. Chaney Sanctuary
Natchaug State Forest
Nehantic State Forest
Nipmuck State Forest
Pachaug State Forest
Quaddick State Forest and State
  Park
Quinebaug River Wildlife
  Management Area
Rocky Neck State Park
Salmon River State Forest
Shenipsit State Forest

ALGONQUIN STATE FOREST

West

Connecticut Department of Environmental Protection
2,947 acres.

> From Winsted, N on SR 8. About 1.6 mi. N of the Colebrook town line, turn left on Sandy Brook Rd. Look for access points on both sides.

The Forest is listed as "undeveloped." No woods roads or trails are shown on the Wildlife Bureau maps. The largest block, N of Sandy Brook Rd., is closed to hunting and lacks good fishing streams, so we found no informal trails. Bushwhacking is the way to go, or just stroll down the road.

Why go? One reason is birding. It's described in Billard's *Places to Look for Birds* as a good place to see warblers in spring and fall.

A separate 406-acre block is on both sides of US 44 along the Mad River, NW of Winsted, just beyond the dam. It has a parking area and river trail on the S side. Reverting fields, some mixed hardwoods, a small pond.

Fishing: Trout in Sandy Brook.

PUBLICATIONS: Wildlife Bureau maps; 3 sections.

REFERENCE: Billard, Ruth Sawyer. *Places to Look for Birds.* Hartford: Department of Environmental Protection, 1972.

HEADQUARTERS: DEP, Office of State Parks and Recreation, 165 Capitol Ave., Hartford, CT 06106; (203) 566-2304.

ASSEKONK SWAMP WILDLIFE MANAGEMENT AREA
Connecticut Department of Environmental Protection   East
700 acres.

SW of North Stonington. From intersection with SR 201, NE on SR 184 about 2.5 mi.; 0.25 mi. E of Jeremy Hill Road, left on dirt road. Open barway at 0.4 mi. and continue to parking area.

A wild, picturesque marsh; enough open water for canoeing; reverting fields; mixed hardwood forest. Parking area, trails, and open fields are on the W side of the site.

ACTIVITIES
Hunting: Pheasant, small game only. Closed to waterfowl hunting.
Canoeing: Access is across a field behind the North Stonington firehouse, at intersection of SR 2 and Rocky Hollow Rd. Not much open water in summer. Best birding is by canoe.

PUBLICATION: Wildlife Bureau map.

HEADQUARTERS: DEP, Eastern District, Wildlife Bureau, 209 Hebron Rd., Marlborough, CT 06447; (203) 295-9525.

AUDUBON CENTER IN GREENWICH/AUDUBON FAIRCHILD GARDEN
National Audubon Society   West
485 acres.

From I-684 in NY, Exit 3 or 3-N. N on SR 22 to light. Right on SR 433, 2 mi. to John St. For the Garden, continue S on Riversville Rd., left on N. Porchuck Rd.

Open 9 A.M.–5 P.M. Tues.–Sun. except holidays and holiday weekends.

The *Center* includes woods, old fields, deep ponds, wet meadows, clear streams, habitats with an abundance of birds and small mammals. Nature trails throughout the site include a wetland boardwalk. Guided walks are scheduled occasionally.

The *Garden* has deciduous woodland, a small pine forest, damp meadows, a pond, and open areas. Along its trails can be seen specimens of almost all the wildflowers, shrubs, ferns, and mosses indigenous to CT.

Birds: A checklist of 190 species is available. Bird blinds are available on request.

Pets, picnicking, and smoking are prohibited.

PUBLICATIONS
Maps: routing, Center, and Garden.
Bird checklist.
Trail guide.

HEADQUARTERS: Audubon Center of Greenwich, 613 Riversville Rd., Greenwich, CT 06831; (203) 869-5272.

BARN ISLAND WILDLIFE MANAGEMENT AREA
Connecticut Department of Environmental Protection   East
748 acres.

SE corner of CT. US 1 to traffic light at Greenhaven Rd. Right on Palmer Neck Rd. to parking.

On Little Narragansett Bay, between Wequetequock Cove and the Pawcatuck River. Tidal and brackish marsh grades into oak forest with reverting fields. Trails and unpaved roads across the marshes and in the upland areas.

Birds: Variety of waterfowl winter in the bay. Many shorebirds in spring and fall. Grouse, pheasant, woodcock, and quail in brushy areas. Many songbirds.

ACTIVITIES
Hunting: Waterfowl, other game birds, squirrel, cottontail.
Boating: Ramp at parking area. Saltwater canoeing in calm weather.

PUBLICATION: Wildlife Bureau map.

HEADQUARTERS: DEP, Eastern District, Wildlife Bureau, 209 Hebron Rd., Marlborough, CT 06447; (203) 295-9525.

BIGELOW HOLLOW STATE PARK
Connecticut Department of Environmental Protection   East
513 acres.

From Union, 2 mi. E on SR 197.

A State pamphlet describes this as "a large picnic area in a scenic, natural setting. . . ." It's on the Nipmuck Trail, thus a convenient trailhead, and it adjoins the Nipmuck State Forest (see entry).

Rolling forest land surrounds Lake Mashapaug, 1 1/2 mi. long, and Bigelow Pond, both good trout waters.

ACTIVITIES
Boating: Ramp on the lake. Hand-carried craft on the pond.
Swimming and scuba diving. No lifeguard.

HEADQUARTERS: DEP, Office of State Parks and Recreation, 165 Capitol Ave., Hartford, CT 06106; (203) 566-2304.

BLUFF POINT COASTAL RESERVE
Connecticut Department of Environmental Protection   East
806 acres.

From I-95, Exit 88. S on SR 117, right on US 1, left on Depot Rd., under railroad overpass to parking.

This is the last significant fragment of undeveloped shoreline in CT. We haven't seen it on a summer weekend, but we were told the half-mile walk from the parking area to the beach and lack of a developed swimming area deter crowds.

The Reserve is a bluff or headland overlooking Mumford Cove, Long Island Sound, and the Poquonock River. Highest point is 128 ft. above sea level. The wooded highland descends to tidal wetlands. A long, narrow sandspit curves westward, ending at Bushy Point, a small island. Beach vegetation includes beach plum, beach pea, red and white shore roses.

HEADQUARTERS: DEP, Office of State Parks and Recreation, 165 Capitol Ave., Hartford, CT 06106; (203) 566-2304.

CAMPBELL FALLS STATE PARK
Connecticut Department of Environmental Protection   West
102 acres.

On the MA border. From Torrington, N on SR 272. Beyond US 44, turn W on Spaulding Rd. to Park.

See entry in MA. A short trail through a fine hemlock forest leads to the MA parking area. At the concrete post, turn left to the short falls trail. The 50-ft. falls on Ginger Creek drops into a narrow ravine. Not much water was dropping when we visited, but it's obviously attractive in full flow.

REFERENCES

Billard, Ruth Sawyer. *Places to Look for Birds.* Hartford: Department of Environmental Protection, 1972.

Kulik, Stephen, Pete Salmansohn, Matthew Schmidt, and Heidi Welch. *The Audubon Society Field Guide to the Natural Places of the Northeast: Inland.* New York: Pantheon Books, 1984.

HEADQUARTERS: DEP, Office of State Parks and Recreation, 165 Capitol Ave., Hartford, CT 06106; (203) 566-2304.

CHATFIELD HOLLOW STATE PARK

Connecticut Department of Environmental Protection   West
102 acres.

This small park adjoins part of the Cockaponset State Forest (see entry) and provides access to over 18 mi. of hiking trails, including the blue-blazed Chatfield Trail. The site is a heavily wooded hollow with caves and ledges. A 7-acre pond provides fishing and swimming.

REFERENCE: Hicock, Shelton B., ed. *Connecticut Walk Book.* Middletown: Connecticut Forest and Park Association, 1984.

HEADQUARTERS: DEP, Office of State Parks and Recreation, 165 Capitol Ave., Hartford, CT 06106; (203) 566-2304.

COCKAPONSET STATE FOREST

Connecticut Department of Environmental Protection   West
15,652 acres.

From Chester, 3 mi. W on SR 148. Or from SR 9, Exit 8, then 1/2 mi. E on Beaver Meadow Rd.

CT's second largest State Forest extends for about 10 mi. N–S, in several blocks, on both sides of SR 9 in the western Connecticut River valley. As the State acquired the land, efforts to restore forest conditions began. The most intensive period was 1933–1941, when a large contingent of the Civilian Conservation Corps was quartered here.

Oak, hickory, and maple are now the predominant species on the higher ground, with beech, birch, oak, and tulip in stream valleys. Dogwood and laurel are conspicuous in the spring.

This is one of the 3 CT State Forests with campgrounds. It has a well-developed trail system.

Forest Headquarters is on Beaver Meadow Rd., just 1/2 mi. E of Exit 8 from SR 9. From here Filley Rd. runs S through the Turkey Hill block, passing Turkey Hill Reservoir and Pataconk Reservoir, the Forest's two largest water bodies, each about 3/4 mi. long. The area includes small streams, ponds, and marshes including a white-cedar swamp. Several mi. to the SW, S of I-95 on SR 146, are 2 small blocks of tidal waterfowl marsh on Great Harbor.

ACTIVITIES
Camping: 25 sites.
Hiking: The blue-blazed Cockaponset Trail runs N–S in the Turkey Hill block, about 7 1/2 mi., with alternate trails permitting circuit hikes. In the Killingworth block, which includes Chatfield Hollow State Park (see entry), are the 4 1/2-mi. Chatfield Trail and others.
Hunting: Grouse, cottontail, deer, squirrel, raccoon, waterfowl, other furbearers.
Fishing: Trout fishing is said to be fair to good.
Ski touring: Trails and unplowed roads.

ADJACENT: Chatfield Hollow State Park (see entry).

PUBLICATIONS
Maps, 8 1/2 × 11-inch, little detail:
Parks and Recreation: Turkey Hill block.
Wildlife Bureau: Turkey Hill block.
Madison block.
Spectacle Meadow block.
Great Harbor block.

REFERENCE: Hicock, Shelton, ed. *Connecticut Walk Book.* Middletown: Connecticut Forest and Park Association, 1984.

HEADQUARTERS: DEP, Office of State Parks and Recreation, 165 Capitol Ave., Hartford, CT 06106; (203) 566-2304.

CONNECTICUT RIVER
70 river miles.   West/East

MA border to Long Island Sound.

More than 400 mi. long, the Connecticut is New England's longest river. By the time it reaches the CT border, it has been polluted. Efforts have been made to reduce the pollution; anadromous fishes have reappeared in the lower river; and one hopes conditions will improve from year to year. As of this writing, the river water isn't fit to drink and is not recommended for swimming. Fishermen should seek current information on what's edible. Boating is popular, so much so that many launch sites are overcrowded.

The river bisects the state, with development on both sides. Few long sections of shoreline could be called natural. On warm weekends, power boat traffic is heavy near Hartford and other centers.

There are quiet times and places, however. The State provides opportunities for canoe camping along the lower river. Hurd State Park (see entry), 47 river miles below the MA line, 26 river miles S of Hartford, is the first State campsite, reserved for canoeists. Other State campsites are at Gillette Castle State Park (Mile 56) and Selden Neck State Park (Mile 58).

ACTIVITIES
Camping: Reservations must be made two weeks in advance, stating camping area, date, name and address of leader, number and ages of party members, type of boat, intended put-in and take-out points. Manager: Gillette Castle State Park, East Haddam, CT 06423; (203) 526-2336. One night only. No vehicle access.

Canoeing: Concession at Gillette provides outfitting and transportation. (203) 739-0791.

Boating: State launch sites at Enfield, Haddam Meadows, Old Saybrook, Salmon River, Suffield, and Windsor. Some riverside towns have ramps.

PUBLICATIONS
Canoe Camping.
Guide to State Boat Launch Areas.

REFERENCES

Schweiker, Roioli, ed. *AMC River Guide: Massachusetts, Connecticut, Rhode Island*. Boston: Appalachian Mountain Club, 1985.

Weber, Ken. *Canoeing Massachusetts, Rhode Island, and Connecticut*. Woodstock, VT: Backcountry Publications, 1980.

HEADQUARTERS: DEP, Office of State Parks and Recreation, 165 Capitol Ave., Hartford, CT 06106; (203) 566-2304.

DEVIL'S DEN PRESERVE

The Nature Conservancy   West

1,558 acres.

N of Norwalk. From Merritt Parkway or I-95, N on SR 57 or SR 53 to Weston Center. N on SR 53 to Godfrey Road West. Left 1/2 mi. to Pent Rd. and right to parking.

This is the largest wild area remaining in congested SW CT. The terrain is a series of rocky ridges rising from 260 to 610 ft., providing views of Long Island Sound. Intermittent streams flow through oak/maple woodland. Dense swamps are in the lowlands.

The Preserve has 15 mi. of trails, named and marked.

Plants: Vegetation studies have been published. The site is almost totally forested. Principal tree species are red maple, beech, red oak, white oak, hickory. Red maple dominates in wetlands, beech, birch, and maple on the lower slopes. The mid-slopes are dominated by red and white oak, chestnut oak above. 500 species of flowering plants have been recorded. Plant lists are available.

Birds: Preliminary list indicates seasonal abundance of warblers and other songbirds, woodcock, grouse. Relatively few birds of prey and waterfowl.

Mammals: Preliminary record includes most small mammals common to the region. Deer; occasional bobcat.

INTERPRETATION

Exhibits along trails. Old pond and mill site, charcoal site, Indian shelter, sawmill, farms.

Guided hikes are occasionally provided by volunteers, by appointment, mainly in spring and fall.

PUBLICATIONS
    Walk booklets ($3 each plus postage, handling):
    A Guide to Trails of Devil's Den Preserve.
    A Guide to Ferns and Fern Allies.
    A Guide to Winter Natural History.
    A Guide to the Trees and Shrubs.
    A Guide to the Spring Wildflowers.
    A Guide to the Summer and Fall Flowering Plants.
    Research studies:
    Geology and Geologic History.
    Soil Survey.
    Vegetation.
    Wildlife Survey.
    Archeological Investigations.

Pets are prohibited. Parking area may be full on fine spring or fall weekends.

HEADQUARTERS: Box 1162, Weston, CT 06833; (203) 226-4991.

DEVIL'S HOPYARD STATE PARK

Connecticut Department of Environmental Protection   East
860 acres.

S of Colchester. From the intersection of SR 156 and SR 82, 3 mi. N.

More than 100,000 visitors come here each year, but there are quiet days. The chief attraction is Chapman Falls, where Eight Mile River plunges down a 60-ft. escarpment. Around the splash pool at the base are several kettleholes. The river continues through handsome hemlock forest. Steep, wooded hillsides. Small marshes are in the E and SW portions of the Park.

ACTIVITIES
    Camping: 20 sites.
    Hiking: About 15 mi. of trails and woods roads.
    Fishing: Brook trout. American and lamprey eels travel to the base of the falls each spring.

PUBLICATION: Leaflet with map.

HEADQUARTERS: DEP, Office of State Parks and Recreation, 165 Capitol Ave., Hartford, CT 06106, (203) 566-2304.

DURHAM MEADOWS WILDLIFE MANAGEMENT AREA
Wildlife Bureau   West
571 acres.

S of Middletown. From Durham, S on SR 17. Entrance is 1/2 mi. beyond junction with SR 77. For N block, N on SR 17, W about 1 mi. on SR 147.

Most of the site is marsh along the Coginchaug River, partly overgrown in swamp maple. Also reverting fields, some old-growth hardwoods, open water. Three streams join the Coginchaug. Foot travel is difficult.

Birds: Include ducks, rail, marsh wren. Blue-winged teal nest.

ACTIVITIES
Hunting: Pheasant, woodcock, waterfowl, cottontail, squirrel.
Canoeing: Best in spring when water is high and before vegetation becomes thick. Put-in is on SR 147, W of N block entrance.

PUBLICATION: Wildlife Bureau map.

HEADQUARTERS: DEP, Western District, Wildlife Bureau, 230 Plymouth Rd., Harwinton, CT 06791; (203) 485-0226.

EDWARD STEICHEN MEMORIAL WILDLIFE PRESERVE
Connecticut Audubon Society   West
54 acres.

From US 7 at Topstone (between Georgetown and Danbury), turn right on Topstone Rd. Entrance is on the left just beyond Chestnut Woods Rd.

Edward Steichen, famous nature photographer, bought Huckleberry Swamp and other lands in 1928 and allowed natural succession to proceed. The Preserve includes a red maple swamp, shrubby swamp, and uplands. A boardwalk enters the swamp.

A 94-page ecological survey of the site traces its geological history and includes annotated lists of its flora and fauna.

PUBLICATIONS
Leaflet with site map.
Roth, Linda, Henry Woolsey, and Ellen Baum. *Huckleberry Swamp and Adjacent Uplands.* $3.

HEADQUARTERS: Connecticut Audubon Society, 2325 Burr St., Fairfield, CT 06430; (203) 259-6305.

ELLITHORPE FLOOD CONTROL AREA

Connecticut Department of Environmental Protection   East
400 acres.

Near the MA border. From Stafford Springs, N on SR 32 beyond SR 190.
Left on Crow Hill Rd. Park on near side of railroad tracks.

A quiet place for an easy walk through wetlands. Walk beside the tracks and
around a barrier to a dirt road on a dike. It's straight and level, with swamp,
swamp forest, and areas of open water on either side. Two local residents had
carried a small boat about half a mile to one snag-dotted pond. They said the
bass and pickerel fishing was fine. We had good birding.

NEARBY: Shenipsit State Forest (see entry).

PUBLICATION: Wildlife Bureau map.

HEADQUARTERS: DEP, Eastern District, Wildlife Bureau, 209 Hebron Rd.,
   Marlborough, CT 06447; (203) 295-9525.

FRANKLIN SWAMP WILDLIFE MANAGEMENT AREA

Connecticut Department of Environmental Protection   East
620 acres.

Between Franklin and North Franklin on SR 32.

Except in hunting season, if you're passing by, this is a pleasant spot for a
short walk. Headquarters and parking are well marked. A dirt road between
SR 32 and the parking leads toward HQ. Take the blacktop to the left through
a closed gate. On the left is a shooting range. Down the hill are trails, chiefly
jeep tracks. The site extends along Under Mountain Rd., through fields and
woodlands.

The moderately hilly terrain includes mixed forest, hardwood swamp, open
swale, and fields. (An unenthusiastic local resident said, "It's a lot of bram-
bles.") We saw two small ponds, a great horned owl, and no other visitors.

Hunting: Pheasant, cottontail, woodcock.

PUBLICATION: Wildlife Bureau site map.

HEADQUARTERS: DEP, Eastern District, Wildlife Bureau, 209 Hebron Rd., Marlborough, CT 06447; (203) 295-9525.

GAY CITY STATE PARK
Connecticut Department of Environmental Protection   East
1,569 acres.

From Bolton, 3 mi. S on SR 85.

Named for a vanished mill town, the park is crossed by the Blackledge River, which provided water power. A small pond at the park's center has a sand beach. The SW sector is a swamp.

Rolling and forested, the park has 10 numbered trails, offering a variety of loop hikes. Trails connect with the Shenipsit Trail, a short distance to the W, which runs from Cobalt through the Meshomasic and Shenipsit State Forests (see entries) to the MA border.

PUBLICATION: Map with text.

REFERENCES

Hardy, Gerry and Sue. *Fifty Hikes in Connecticut.* Woodstock, VT: Backcountry Publications, 1984.

Hicock, Shelton B., ed. *Connecticut Walk Book.* Middletown: Connecticut Forest and Park Association. Periodic new editions.

HEADQUARTERS: DEP, Office of State Parks and Recreation, 165 Capitol Ave., Hartford, CT 06106; (203) 566-2304.

HAMMONASSET BEACH STATE PARK
Connecticut Department of Environmental Protection   West
919 acres.

From I-95, Exit 62, then 1 mi. S.

With 2 mi. of fine beach on Long Island Sound and CT's largest State campground, easily reached from most CT cities, this is a crowded place in summer. Birders enjoy it in spring and fall. Meigs Point has shore and marsh birds. The extensive marsh on the Hammonasset River attracts waterfowl, herons, possibly clapper rail. The scrubby upland is habitat for thrashers, grackles, redwings, warblers. Part of the undeveloped acreage has been designated a Natural Area Preserve.

ACTIVITIES
Camping: 558 sites.
Fishing: Saltwater species.

HEADQUARTERS: DEP, Office of State Parks and Recreation, 165 Capitol Ave., Hartford, CT 06106; (203) 566-2304.

HOPEVILLE POND STATE PARK
Connecticut Department of Environmental Protection   East
554 acres.

From Connecticut Turnpike (SR 52), Exit 86. E on SR 201.

Driving in, we passed a great number of picnic tables scattered on the wooded shoreline of a small, attractive pond. The campground is on the opposite shore. The Park has heavy weekend use in season.

We include it because it adjoins the Pachaug State Forest (see entry), largest in CT, and serves as a bedroom and trailhead.

Camping: 81 sites.

HEADQUARTERS: DEP, Office of State Parks and Recreation, 165 Capitol Ave., Hartford, CT 06106; (203) 566-2304.

HOUSATONIC STATE FOREST/HOUSATONIC MEADOWS STATE PARK
Connecticut Department of Environmental Protection   West
9,543 acres/451 acres

Several tracts on both sides of the Housatonic River, between US 44 and Cornwall Bridge. The State Park is 1 mi. N of Cornwall Bridge on SR 7.

The Housatonic River Valley is one of CT's most scenic areas, although US 7 and a railroad run close to the river. Rising from the river are forested hills cut by ravines and streams, with nearby swamps and beaver flowages. Portions of the river are canoeable, when there's plenty of water. Friends told us about "rump-bumping," floating downstream in rubber tubes. (Swimming is not permitted at the State Park.)

The Forest includes almost a dozen blocks, the largest with more than 3,000 acres. The Appalachian Trail crosses portions of the Forest. About 2,300 acres are in small blocks, not shown on available maps.

The *State Park* is a narrow strip along the W shore of the river. Campsites are under pines near the river bank. One block of Forest land adjoins the W boundary of the Park. Another, across the river, rises more than 700 ft. to the N–S ridge of Mine Mountain. Both have trails. From the Park, Pine Knob Loop, 2 1/2 mi., climbs to a viewpoint at 1,160 ft.

The *Cream Hill block,* 2,290 acres, is E of the river. At West Cornwall, cross the covered bridge on SR 128 and take Cream Hill Rd. The block is hilly, forested, with laurel thickets, some swamp. Cream Hill's elevation is 1,503 ft. The Appalachian Trail crosses Cream Hill Rd. and Yelping Hill Rd. The Pine Knoll lean-to is on Wickwire Rd. *Dean Ravine* and *Barrack Mountain* are scenic destinations for day hikers.

The *Sharon Mountain block,* 3,030 acres, lies N of West Cornwall, E of the river. Access is from US 7 on Cornwall Rd. or Pine Swamp Rd. Mixed hardwoods, beaver flowages, some swamp. Local trails cross the site.

The *Canaan Mountain block,* 1,370 acres, is farthest N, between US 7 and East Canaan. Access is from US 44 via Lower Rd. Sometimes referred to as "wilderness," it is roadless and has no marked trails. Highest point is 1,962-ft. Bradford Mountain. Canaan Mountain, in the N sector, is 1,762 ft. The forest includes mixed hardwoods, white pine, and hemlock, with an unusual stand of red pine.

ACTIVITIES

Camping: 102 sites at State Park. Jan. 15–Apr. 15, (203) 927-3238; Apr. 15–Labor Day, (203) 672-6772.

Hiking, backpacking: Appalachian Trail, local trails, long-unused logging roads.

Hunting: Grouse, pheasant, woodcock, cottontail, gray squirrel, raccoon, deer, wild turkey; some waterfowl in Sharon Mountain block.

Fishing: Trout, chiefly in river. A 2-mi. section at the State Park is restricted to fly fishing.

PUBLICATIONS: Wildlife Bureau maps, 4 sections.

REFERENCES

Billard, Ruth Sawyer. *Places to Look for Birds.* Hartford: Department of Environmental Protection, 1972.

Hardy, Gerry and Sue. *Fifty Hikes in Connecticut.* Woodstock, VT: Backcountry Publications, 1984.

Hicock, Shelton B., ed. *Connecticut Walk Book.* Middletown: Connecticut Forest and Park Association, 1984.

Proctor, Noble S. *25 Birding Areas in Connecticut.* Chester, CT: Globe Pequot Press, 1978.

HEADQUARTERS: DEP, Office of State Parks and Recreation, 165 Capitol Ave., Hartford, CT 06106; (203) 566-2304.

HURD STATE PARK

Connecticut Department of Environmental Protection   East
884 acres.

On the E side of the Connecticut River, 3 mi. S of Cobalt on SR 151.

Hurd is the most northern of 3 State-operated canoe camps on the Connecticut River (see entry), 47 river miles S of the MA border. The bank is steep, with granite ledges, rising from about 10 ft. elevation to 266 ft. on Split Rock and 408 ft. on White Mountain. Hurd Brook drops to the river over cascades in a hemlock gorge.

For motorists, this is a day-use park, with picnic shelter and about 2 1/2 mi. of woodland trails in two loops, one riverside, the other to the Split Rock viewpoint. It has an interesting diversity of wildlife and fine display of colors in the fall.

ACTIVITIES

Camping: Boat access only. Primitive sites. Permit required, requested at least two weeks in advance from Manager, Gillette Castle State Park, East Haddam, CT 06423. State camping area, date, name and address of leader, number and ages of party members, intended put-in and take-out points. May 1–Sept. 30. One night limit. $2 per person.

Canoeing: This is not a put-in site; no vehicle access to the river.

HEADQUARTERS: DEP, Office of State Parks and Recreation, 165 Capitol Ave., Hartford, CT 06106; (203) 566-2304.

JAMES L. GOODWIN STATE FOREST & CONSERVATION CENTER

Connecticut Department of Environmental Protection   East
2,171 acres.

On US 6, 3 mi. E of South Chaplin.

The original forest was cut and the land farmed until about 1900. In 1913 the owner, James L. Goodwin, one of the first forestry graduates, began developing the site as a tree farm. He became a leader in promoting good forest management. In 1964 he gave the land to the State, dedicating it to conservation education. 80 acres were set aside for a conservation center.

It's a fine place to learn the history of CT woodlands and see how forest has been restored. At the Center, exhibits are open from 1 to 6 P.M., Wed. through Sun. An arboretum features woodland shrubs. Guided walks and field trips are available for groups, by appointment.

The site includes hardwood forest, softwood plantation, wildlife ponds, and flooded swamp.

ACTIVITIES

Hiking: Easy hiking trails and woods roads extend throughout the area. The Natchaug Trail crosses the Forest.

Fishing: Bass, bluegill, bullheads in ponds.

Boating: Canoeing on flooded swamps. Boats with electric motors on Pine Acres Pond.

ADJACENT: Natchaug State Forest (see entry).

PUBLICATION: Map.

HEADQUARTERS: DEP, Office of State Parks and Recreation, 165 Capitol Ave., Hartford, CT 06106; (203) 566-2304.

JOHN A. MINNETTO STATE PARK
Connecticut Office of State Parks and Recreation   West
678 acres.

Off SR 272 N of Torrington.

The site is a long, narrow strip of rolling, open land along Hall Brook, now a flood control area. A central portion serves the function of a municipal park, with such activities as picnicking, swimming, field sports, and winter sports. The other 500 acres are mostly wetland, with trails and good waterfowl viewing.

KETTLETOWN STATE PARK/INDIAN WELL STATE PARK

Connecticut Department of Environmental Protection   West
492 acres/153 acres.

5 mi. S of Southbury/2 mi. N of Shelton.

These two parks are linked by the Paugussett and Pomperaug Trails. Both are on the Housatonic River, Kettletown bordering for 2 mi. on an impoundment called Lake Zoar.

ACTIVITIES

Camping: At Kettletown, 80 sites.
Fishing, swimming: At both sites.
Boating: Ramp at Indian Well. State ramp a short distance upstream from Kettletown.

REFERENCE: Hicock, Shelton B., ed. *Connecticut Walk Book.* Middletown: Connecticut Forest and Park Association, 1984.

HEADQUARTERS: DEP, Office of State Parks and Recreation, 165 Capitol Ave., Hartford, CT 06106; (203) 566-2304.

MACEDONIA BROOK STATE PARK

Connecticut Department of Environmental Protection   West
2,300 acres.

From Kent, 4 mi. N on SR 341.

In mountainous terrain near the NY border, this is one of CT's largest and wildest State Parks, with little development other than campground and trails. It is crossed by 4 mi. of Macedonia Brook, with a deep gorge and upper and lower falls. Elevations range from 670 to 1,360 ft., with views of the Catskills and the Taconic Range from the heights.

The site is mostly forested with mixed hardwoods. Woodland bird species are abundant during migrations; birders often camp so they can be in the woods at dawn.

ACTIVITIES

Camping: 84 sites.

Hiking, backpacking: The Appalachian Trail traverses the Park, crossing Cobble Mountain and Pine Hill. Two lean-tos. Other trails are color-coded.
Fishing: Said to be good. Trout are stocked.

REFERENCES

Appalachian Trail Guide to Massachusetts/Connecticut. Harpers Ferry, WV: Appalachian Trail Conference, 1985.

Billard, Ruth Sawyer. *Places to Look for Birds.* Hartford: Department of Environmental Protection, 1972.

Hardy, Gerry and Sue. *Fifty Hikes in Connecticut.* Woodstock, VT: Backcountry Publications, 1984.

Hicock, Shelton B., *Connecticut Walk Book.* Middletown: Connecticut Forest and Park Association, 1984.

HEADQUARTERS: DEP, Office of State Parks and Recreation, 165 Capitol Ave., Hartford, CT 06106; (203) 566-2304.

MANSFIELD HUNTING AREA/MANSFIELD HOLLOW STATE PARK

Connecticut Department of Environmental Protection   East
2,500 acres.

1 mi. E of Mansfield Center off SR 89.

A flood-control dam on the Natchaug River created Mansfield Hollow Lake, covering 1,800 acres at full pool in summer. The Park surrounds the N portion of the impoundment, called Naubesatuck Lake. The more extensive Hunting Area is adjacent, extending upstream along the Natchaug and Fenton rivers.

The developed area of the Park is on a wooded bluff overlooking the lake. Swimming is not permitted because the lake is a public water supply, but picnicking, boating, and fishing are enough to attract crowds on fine weekends. The shallow lake is deep enough for boating. Water level is fairly constant in summer. We were there in a dry season, and the drawdown was less than 18 inches. The area is largely mixed hardwood forest, with reverting fields, brushy marsh, and beaver flowages. Wildlife is abundant.

ACTIVITIES

Hiking: Easy trails along the shoreline and through fields and forest. A spur extends to the Nipmuck Trail.

Hunting: Pheasant, grouse, quail, small game.

Fishing: Said to be one of CT's best areas for trout, smallmouth bass, bullhead, and chain pickerel.

Boating: Paved launching ramp. No hp limit.

PUBLICATIONS
Parks and Recreation: site map.
Wildlife Bureau: hunting area map.

HEADQUARTERS: DEP, 165 Capitol Ave., Hartford, CT 06106. Wildlife Bureau (203) 566-4683; Office of State Parks and Recreation (203) 566-2304.

MASHAMOQUET BROOK STATE PARK

Connecticut Department of Environmental Protection   East
942 acres.

From Putnam, 5 mi. SW on SR 44.

In the eastern highlands, this attractive Park is usually at capacity on summer weekends. We drove past many picnic tables to a swimming beach on a small pond. Not far away are Natchaug and James L. Goodwin State Forests, which have fine hiking trails but no campgrounds. Before and after the swimming season, the Park is a convenient base.

It includes the former Wolf Den and Saptree Run parks. Rolling woodlands in all stages of succession: reverting fields; stands of smooth alder, juniper, and young redcedar; birch replacing cedar; oak replacing birch. Beaver-flooded swamp has a short boardwalk. Table Rock and Indian Chair are large stone formations.

ACTIVITIES
Camping: Apr. 15–Oct. 14. Two campgrounds, 20 and 35 sites. Reservations.
Hiking: Short trails within the Park.

HEADQUARTERS: DEP, Office of State Parks and Recreation, 165 Capitol Ave., Hartford, CT 06106; (203) 566-2304.

MATTATUCK STATE FOREST

Connecticut Department of Environmental Protection   West
4,531 acres.

Several scattered tracts. The largest is N of Watertown, along the W side of SR 8, crossed by US 6. A second is across the river, crossed by SR 262. Others are E and N. Site maps are needed.

From the Naugatuck River, hills rise as much as 500 ft. The tracts of the Forest include several hills with bare granite crests, providing good vistas. Much of the area is forested, but the stands we saw were of poor quality. We wouldn't make this an entry were it not for the Mattatuck Trail, which begins near Wolcott and traverses portions of the Forest, including Mt. Tobe and Cedar Mountain, as well as Black Rock State Park.

PUBLICATIONS: Wildlife Bureau maps; 5 sections.

REFERENCE: Hicock, Shelton B., ed. *Connecticut Walk Book.* Middletown: Connecticut Forest and Park Association, 1984.

NEARBY: *Black Rock State Park,* on US 6 N of Watertown, 439 acres, adjoins part of the Forest. It has 90 campsites, pond fishing and swimming, and is usually crowded on warm weekends.

HEADQUARTERS: DEP, Office of State Parks and Recreation, 165 Capitol Ave., Hartford, CT 06106; (203) 566-2304.

MESHOMASIC STATE FOREST
Connecticut Department of Environmental Protection   East
7,886 acres.

N of SR 66 at Cobalt.

One of CT's largest land areas, undeveloped, in the rolling hills E of the Connecticut River. No highway crosses its main body but it has a modest network of local roads, several of which have unmarked trailheads. Best access is by Great Hill Rd., N of Cobalt, on its S boundary. Great Hill, ascended by trail, is a bare granite outcrop with a lookout. The Shenipsit Trail begins here; another trail ascends from Great Hill Pond. Mixed hardwood and conifer forest. Witch hazel is cut commercially. Several brooks drain W to the Connecticut River. Cobalt was once mined here. The area is of interest to rockhounds.

The State agencies have no site maps. The Shenipsit Trail maps in the *Connecticut Walk Book* are useful.

ACTIVITIES
Hiking: The Shenipsit Trail extends N through the Meshomasic and Shenipsit State Forests to the MA border, with some gaps.

Hunting: Deer, small game.

Fishing: We've seen no indication that pond or stream fishing is great, but trout are stocked.

Ski touring: Trails and unplowed roads.

REFERENCE: Hicock, Shelton B., ed. *Connecticut Walk Book.* Middletown: Connecticut Forest and Park Association, 1984.

HEADQUARTERS: DEP, Office of State Parks and Recreation, 165 Capitol Ave., Hartford, CT 06106; (203) 566-2304.

MOHAWK STATE FOREST
Connecticut Department of Environmental Protection   West
3,351 acres.

Closed at sundown.

From Goshen, 4 mi. W on SR 4.

Long ago, friends who had a summer place nearby brought us here for sight-seeing and a picnic. Both are popular. A good road ascends to the observation tower atop 1,683-ft. Mohawk Mountain, where the view is splendid. One can picnic there or at intermediate stops. Hillsides are moderately sloping to steep, some boulder-strewn, cut by deep ravines. Numerous streams. Several glacial eskers. The oak/beech/hickory forest includes white pine and is interspersed with handsome hemlock groves. The ski area on the NW slope isn't conspicuous. It has tows, lifts, snowmaking.

The 35-mi. Mattatuck Trail crosses the top. So did the Appalachian Trail until it had to be relocated because a landowner blocked the route. We hiked several short, pleasant trails.

Black Spruce Bog, near Forest HQ, has a trail and boardwalk. Pitcher-plant, sundew, mountain holly, other bog species.

Great Gulf Trail is a 1-mi. loop along a deep ravine. E of the Toumey Rd. entrance.

PUBLICATION: Map, 2 sections with text.

REFERENCES
Billard, Ruth Sawyer. *Places to Look for Birds.* Hartford: Department of Environmental Protection, 1972.

Hardy, Gerry and Sue. *Fifty Hikes in Connecticut.* Woodstock, VT: Back-country Publications, 1984.

Hicock, Shelton B., ed. *Connecticut Walk Book.* Middletown: Connecticut Forest and Park Association, 1984.

Keyarts, Eugene. *60 Selected Short Walks in Connecticut.* Chester, CT: Globe Pequot Press, 1979.

NEARBY: *Cathedral Pines,* a 42-acre property of The Nature Conservancy, is an impressive grove of huge white pines and hemlocks. From Cornwall, S on Pine St., turning or bearing left at intersections; about 1 mi.

HEADQUARTERS: DEP, Office of State Parks and Recreation, 165 Capitol Ave., Hartford, CT 06106; (203) 566-2304.

MORGAN R. CHANEY SANCTUARY

Connecticut Audubon Society   East
235 acres.

From I-395, Exit 77, drive NW on SR 85. Beyond Konomoc Lake, turn right on Turner Rd. to entrance on left.
Open dawn to dusk.

After three centuries of land clearing, cultivation, and pasturing in this region, few signs remain of the primeval ecosystem. The society has used the inherent characteristics of this site to develop a diversity of natural habitats. Stone walls, foundations, and the ruins of a dam are relics of earlier uses.

At 426 ft. elevation, the site overlooks the adjacent, town-owned Great Swamp, a public water supply. A hemlock ravine near the entrance has intermittent streams.

PUBLICATIONS
Leaflet with site map.
Information pages:
Regional Setting.
Geology.
Hydrology.

HEADQUARTERS: Connecticut Audubon Society, 2325 Burr St., Fairfield, CT 06439; (203) 259-6305.

NASSAHEGON STATE FOREST

Connecticut Department of Environmental Protection   West
1,226 acres.

From Burlington on SR 4, SE on Washington Turnpike, a local road.

This irregularly shaped Forest is of interest chiefly as a link in the Tunxis Trail, with several blazed local trails permitting loop hikes. Washington Turnpike bisects the site. Turn S on Stone Rd. to intercept the Trail, which crosses near the S boundary. The site is rolling, with low hills. Cover is mixed hardwoods with spruce and pine plantations.

REFERENCES

Hardy, Gerry and Sue. *Fifty Hikes in Connecticut.* Woodstock, VT: Backcountry Publications, 1984. (p. 132)

Hicock, Shelton B., ed. *Connecticut Walk Book.* Middletown: Connecticut Forest and Park Association, 1984.

HEADQUARTERS: DEP, Office of State Parks and Recreation, 165 Capitol Ave., Hartford, CT 06106; (203) 566-2304.

NATCHAUG STATE FOREST

Connecticut Department of Environmental Protection   East
12,935 acres.

4 mi. S of Phoenixville on SR 198.

Natchaug, which means "land between the rivers," is one of the largest State Forests. The land is rolling, largely covered by hardwood forest with occasional mixture of hemlock and pines. The understory includes much laurel, spectacular in the blooming season. Habitats include numerous marshes and riparian zones.

Most of the Forest is E of the Natchaug River. The well-signed entrance road crosses the river to Forest HQ. Just beyond is a beaver pond and wildlife marsh. Several gravel roads traverse the area. Driving in, we saw picnic tables widely spaced under trees beside the stream.

It's a hiker's forest and one of the few where backpacking is allowed, camping by permit at designated sites. The Nipmuck Trail extends about 26 mi. N from Mansfield Hollow State Park to SR 171 in Union, near the Bigelow Hollow State Park entrance; an extension to the Massachusetts state line is planned. The Natchaug Trail traverses the James L. Goodwin and Natchaug State Forests. With local trails and logging roads, they form a network available to horse riders, skiers, and snowmobilers as well as hikers. A horse camp is 2 mi. S of Phoenixville.

ACTIVITIES
Hiking, backpacking: About 55 mi. of trails.
Horse riding: Trails and roads. Horse camp has 28 sites; reservations.
Hunting: Deer, cottontail, squirrel, raccoon, grouse, woodcock, pheasant, waterfowl.
Fishing: Trout stocked. Natchaug River and streams.
Ski touring: Unplowed roads and trails.

PUBLICATIONS
Maps, simple, 8 1/2 × 11-inch:
    From Parks and Recreation:
        Site map.
        Backpack trails.
        Snowmobile trails.
    From Wildlife Bureau: site map.

REFERENCE: Hicock, Shelton B., ed. *Connecticut Walk Book.* Middletown: Connecticut Forest and Park Association, 1984.

ADJACENT: James L. Goodwin State Forest (see entry).

NEARBY: Mashamoquet Brook State Park (see entry) has a campground.

HEADQUARTERS: DEP, Office of State Parks and Recreation, 165 Capitol Ave., Hartford, CT 06106; (203) 566-2304.

NEHANTIC STATE FOREST
Connecticut Department of Environmental Protection   East
3,798 acres.

From the Connecticut Turnpike, N on SR 156. About 1 mi. S of Hamburg, turn right.

The directions are to the Tanney Hill block (also spelled "Tanny" and "Taney"). Other Forest acreage is to the NE. Falls Brook is on the S boundary of the Tanney Hill block, as are Uncas and Norwich ponds.

The forest has been recovering from heavy damage in a 1938 hurricane. Mixed hardwoods, small streams, marshes, reverting fields.

ACTIVITIES

Hiking: The Wildlife Bureau map shows trails throughout the area, used chiefly by hunters.

Hunting: Grouse, deer, squirrel, cottontail.

Fishing: Ponds, warmwater species.

PUBLICATION: Wildlife Bureau map.

HEADQUARTERS: DEP, Office of State Parks and Recreation, 165 Capitol Ave., Hartford, CT 06106; (203) 566-2304.

NEPAUG STATE FOREST

Connecticut Department of Environmental Protection   West

1,199 acres.

N of US 202, W of the Farmington River.

We spotted the Tunxis Trail sign on the N side of US 202, at a narrow dirt road that enters the Forest. The road didn't seem suitable for cars, but there's no barrier. We found no other road leading in. Pine Hill Rd., shown on the Wildlife Bureau map as traversing the Forest, is a dead-end stub.

Except for hunting, the Forest is of interest chiefly as a link on the Tunxis Trail. The Trail runs W along US 202 for a short distance before turning S.

PUBLICATION: Wildlife Bureau map.

REFERENCE: Hicock, Shelton B., ed. *Connecticut Walk Book.* Middletown: Connecticut Forest and Park Association, 1984.

HEADQUARTERS: DEP, Office of State Parks and Recreation, 165 Capitol Ave., Hartford, CT 06106; (203) 566-2304.

NIPMUCK STATE FOREST

Connecticut Department of Environmental Protection   East

8,058 acres.

On the MA border, both sides of I-84.

The Wildlife Bureau map shows the several Forest tracts but with little detail. It's not much help in pathfinding, out of date and with several inaccuracies.

We found one signed entrance about 1/2 mi. W of the intersection of SR 89 and SR 190. Just beyond is the signed entrance of Laurel Sanctuary. E of the intersection is the road in to Morey Pond. We had less success in finding Bear Den and Sessions Meadow marshes, but it was late in the day.

Terrain is rolling. The diverse habitats include mixed hardwood and conifer forest, evergreen plantations, wooded wetlands, wildlife marshes, ponds, brooks, beaver flowages.

Aside from trails, there is little development: a boat ramp at Morey Pond, a good road into the Laurel Sanctuary. It's a hiker's forest, featuring the Nipmuck Trail, with good birding plus hunting and fishing.

FEATURES

Laurel Sanctuary offers an extensive display of the state flower, blooming about the second week of June.

Morey Pond seemed isolated until we saw highway traffic on the opposite side. It's attractive, nonetheless, a forest setting, water-lilies massed at one end. Parking for about 6 cars, one picnic table. We saw two children swimming while their parents fished. No sign prohibits power boats, but the pond seemed too small for them.

Bear Den Marsh and Sessions Meadow Marsh are waterfowl areas W of I-84. Access is by Stickney Hill Rd. to Bear Den or Skopec roads. What we think was Bear Den Rd. unsigned, seemed too muddy for our motor home that day.

ACTIVITIES

Hiking: The Nipmuck Trail has two southern branches, both originating near Mansfield Center, soon joining, continuing N through Bigelow Hollow State Park into the Nipmuck State Forest, about 25 mi. Another trail links the Forest with the Natchaug Trail. Other trails and woods roads.

Hunting: Grouse, squirrel, snowshoe hare, deer, woodcock, raccoon.

Fishing: Trout stocked in ponds and streams.

Boating: Ramp on Morey Pond.

Ski touring: Trails and unplowed roads.

REFERENCE: Hicock, Shelton B., ed. *Connecticut Walk Book.* Middletown: Connecticut Forest and Park Association, 1984.

NEARBY: Bigelow Hollow State Park (see entry).

PUBLICATION: Wildlife Bureau map.

HEADQUARTERS DEP, Office of State Parks and Recreation, 165 Capitol Ave., Hartford, CT 06106; (203) 566-2304.

NORTHEAST AUDUBON CENTER

National Audubon Society   West
684 acres.

From Sharon, 2 mi. SE on SR 4.

Open Mon.–Sat., 9 A.M.–5 P.M.; Sun. 1 P.M.–5 P.M. Closed holidays.

Charcoal mounds and old stone walls in the woodlands tell of past landclearing and forest regeneration. Present-day habitats include pond and stream, field and forest, marsh and swamp. They can be visited along 11 mi. of trails. Almost two-thirds of the site is forested with hardwoods and white pine, with groves of large hemlocks.

More than 175 bird species have been recorded. Mammals include bobcat, mink, beaver, otter, red and gray foxes, squirrel, deer, cottontail.

Hal Borland Exhibit Room, other exhibits, library, and information about educational programs are available at headquarters.

PUBLICATIONS
   Center brochure.
   Otter Observer, quarterly.

HEADQUARTERS: Sharon, CT 06069; (203) 364-0520.

PACHAUG STATE FOREST

Connecticut Department of Environmental Protection   East
22,938 acres.

Eastern CT. Its several sections surround Voluntown. A principal entrance is on SR 49 N of Voluntown.

Largest of CT's public land areas, this was one of the most abused: logged, burned, allowed to erode, much of it flattened by a 1938 hurricane. Most of the area is again forested, partly by natural succession, elsewhere in more than 3,000 acres of plantations. The land is gently rolling, the highest point 441 ft., exposed rocks providing evidence of past erosion. Old cellar holes and miles of stone fence record a history of cultivation and grazing.

The Pachaug River crosses the area but is largely outside Forest boundaries. The Forest has numerous streams, 7 lakes, several impoundments, open and brushy marshes, white-cedar swamps.

The Forest is crisscrossed by graded and unimproved roads. Maps show no point as much as a mile from a road. They also show 35 miles of hiking trails, more than in any other CT Forest.

The Pachaug is one of the few CT Forests with campgrounds and one of the rare CT areas where backpacking is permitted. Overnight hikers must have permits and use designated shelters.

The typical lack of information signs cost us some sleep. At Green Falls we pulled into what seemed to be a campsite: parking slot, table, fire ring. After midnight we were awakened by one of the few unpleasant rangers we've ever met, who said camping was prohibited here. No sign said so, nor did any sign point to the camping area, toward which he gestured vaguely. Were there any vacant sites? He didn't know and obviously didn't care, just insisted that we get up and move on.

FEATURES

Green Falls, off SR 138, 3 mi. E of Voluntown, has only 18 campsites. It is chiefly a day-use area, often crowded in fine weather because it offers swimming and boating as well as fishing. We saw one trailhead on the access road marked "Green Falls Trail." The trail map shows the Pachaug and Narragansett Crossover trails at about this point but no Green Falls Trail. The Nehantic Trail is nearby.

H. H. Chapman Area is about 1 mi. N of Voluntown off SR 49. The area includes Forest headquarters, Beachdale Pond, and a boat launch site on the Pachaug River. Firetower Rd., W of Voluntown on SR 138, runs N to intersect Headquarters Rd., passing the parking area for Mt. Misery Overlook, highest point in the Forest. Nearby are the Mt. Misery campground, with 20 sites, a Rhododendron Sanctuary, blooms peaking about July 4, and access to the Pachaug and Nehantic trails.

Great Meadow complex is E of SR 49, N of the river. A 70-acre wildlife marsh, oak forest, hardwood swamps, hemlock stands, white pine plantations, open and reverting fields.

Hell Hollow-Sue Hopkins Area, further N, off SR 49 E of Ekonk, has a similar diversity of habitats.

ACTIVITIES

Camping: 2 campgrounds, 40 sites.

Hiking, backpacking: On the Nehantic, Quinebaug, and Pachaug trails. Four trailside camping zones are available. Backpackers are invited to arrange parking with the manager of Hopeville Pond State Park, rather than leaving vehicles at roadside. The Pachaug Trail extends for about 30 mi. from Green Falls Pond to Pachaug Pond. The Nehantic Trail, about 14 mi., runs from Green Falls Pond to Hopeville Pond. Quinebaugh is a 5 1/2-mi. trail linked with the Pachaug.

Horse riding: Trails are open to horse travel, and woods roads are also suitable. The Frog Hollow Horse Camp has 18 sites available by reservation. (203) 295-9523.

Hunting: deer, squirrel, cottontail, raccoon, grouse, pheasant, duck, fox, woodcock.

Fishing: In 7 lakes, 9 impoundments.

Canoeing: Lakes, Pachaug River.

Ski touring: On trails and unplowed roads.

PUBLICATIONS

Maps, simple 8 1/2- × 11-inch:
From Parks and Recreation:
Green Falls Area.
H. H. Chapman Area.
Backpack Trails.
Horse Trails.
From Wildlife Bureau: 3 sections.

REFERENCE: Hicock, Shelton B., ed. *Connecticut Walk Book.* Middletown: Connecticut Forest and Park Association, 1984.

NEARBY: Hopeville Pond State Park (see entry).

HEADQUARTERS: DEP, Office of State Parks and Recreation, 165 Capitol Ave., Hartford, CT 06106; (203) 566-2304.

PENWOOD STATE PARK/TALCOTT MOUNTAIN STATE PARK

Connecticut Department of Environmental Protection   West
787 acres/557 acres.

3 mi. W of Bloomfield on SR 185.

These contiguous parks, N and S of SR 185, attract hikers for their trails and sightseers for their fine vistas. They lie along the Talcott Mountain Range. The 45-mi. Metacomet Trail traverses both.

Penwood was given to the State in 1944; the donor required that it be left in natural condition. He and his wife had built many of the trails, as well as a road artfully designed to fit into the mountain contours, passing a high pond. The highest elevation is 741 ft.

The Talcott Mountain park, acquired 20 years later, has a famous landmark, the Heublein Tower, built by the former owner on a 1,000-ft. promontory, overlooking most of N central CT. The tower, open seasonally, is reached by a ridgeline foot trail.

Slopes are moderate to steep, forested, with rock outcrops. Seasonal wildflowers include dutchman's-breeches, trillium, bloodroot, hepatica, trailing arbutus, trout lily, wood anemone. Often-seen birds include turkey vulture, bald eagle, and pileated woodpecker.

PUBLICATIONS: Site maps.

REFERENCES

Billard, Ruth Sawyer. *Places to Look for Birds.* Hartford: Department of Environmental Protection, 1972.

Hardy, Gerry and Sue. *Fifty Hikes in Connecticut.* Woodstock, VT: Backcountry Publications, 1984.

Hicock, Shelton B., ed. *Connecticut Walk Book.* Middletown: Connecticut Forest and Park Association, 1984.

HEADQUARTERS: DEP, Office of State Parks and Recreation, 165 Capitol Ave., Hartford, CT 06106; (203) 566-2304.

PEOPLES STATE FOREST

Connecticut Department of Environmental Protection   West
2,942 acres.

From Winsted, E on US 44; turn E on SR 318 across the Farmington River, then N.

The Forest lies between East River Rd., beside the river, and Park Rd., about 1 1/2 mi. E. Greenwoods Rd. runs generally N–S, bisecting the site. Beaver Brook Rd. branches off Greenwoods at Beaver Swamp, following a trout stream.

The Park was acquired in 1923 thanks to the Connecticut Forest and Park Association. We judged that nine-tenths of the visitors are from nearby. Most of them gather at two recreation areas on East River Rd. The Matthies Grove area ("Peoples Recreation Area" on the site map), about a mile N of SR 318, has a large parking area, ball field, many picnic tables, and other facilities. Nearby is a grove of 200-year-old white pines. The Whittemore Area, farther N, is chiefly for picnicking. Both are on the river and convenient for trout fishermen and hikers.

Access to the two recreation areas is clearly signed. On East River Rd. and Park Rd., we saw unmarked roads that enter the Forest.

No point in the Forest is more than 1/4 mi. from a road, but the interior roads are lightly traveled. A network of trails offers opportunities for hikes of up to a half-day.

Elevations range from 500 ft. at the river to 1,200 ft. Most is rolling forest land, young mixed hardwoods with heavy stands of hemlock, white pine, and spruce. The trails are blazed, but those we saw are not well maintained.

It's a fine recreation resource for nearby residents. Visitors from other areas can find somewhat more attractive trails in the Tunxis State Forest (see entry) a few miles N.

NEARBY: The 782-acre American Legion State Forest is just across the river. Although much smaller and with only two short trails, it has a campground.

Pets are permitted in the campground only.

ACTIVITIES

Hiking, backpacking: Trailside camping in 4 Adirondack shelters.

Camping: 30 sites. Campground in American Legion SF, on West River Rd. N of Pleasant Valley.

Hunting: Grouse, cottontail, snowshoe hare, deer, squirrel, raccoon, some waterfowl.

Fishing: River. Trout stocked.

PUBLICATIONS

Map, Peoples and American Legion State Forests.
Wildlife Bureau maps.

REFERENCES

Billard, Ruth Sawyer. *Places to Look for Birds.* Hartford: Department of Environmental Protection, 1972.

Hardy, Gerry and Sue. *Fifty Hikes in Connecticut.* Woodstock, VT: Backcountry Publications, 1984.

Hicock, Shelton B., ed. *Connecticut Walk Book.* Middletown: Connecticut Forest and Park Association, 1984.

HEADQUARTERS: DEP, Office of State Parks and Recreation, 165 Capitol Ave., Hartford, CT 06106; (203) 566-2304.

QUADDICK STATE FOREST AND STATE PARK

Connecticut Department of Environmental Protection   East
972 acres/116 acres.

NE corner of CT. From US 44 at East Putnam, N on East Putnam Rd.

The chief attraction is Quaddick Reservoir, over 2 mi. long. The Park attracts visitors for water-based recreation, including swimming and sailing. It's sometimes crowded, but less so than parks closer to population centers. The Forest, N of the Park, is available for hiking.

NEARBY: Buck Hill and George Washington Management Areas, in RI. (See entries.)

HEADQUARTERS: DEP, Office of State Parks and Recreation, 165 Capitol Ave., Hartford, CT 06106; (203) 566-5524.

QUINEBAUG RIVER WILDLIFE MANAGEMENT AREA
Connecticut Department of Environmental Protection   East
1,219 acres.

From I-395 N of Plainfield, Exit 89. W on SR 14 about 2 mi. Follow signs on N to Quinebaug Hatchery. Just beyond hatchery, left to parking.

The directions given took us to the extreme S tip of the WMA. From here it extends N along the Quinebaug River almost to Wauregan, a narrow strip in the S, two broader areas further N. Where we saw the river it was shallow, 30 to 50 ft. wide.

The parking area where we stopped is among low hills. White pine, oak, and maple form a forest with sparse understory, open enough for easy walking. Nearby are a marsh, stream, and 2 small ponds. Next to the parking are several picnic tables, trash barrel, and latrines. They seemed to have had little recent use. It's a quiet, pleasant spot with good birding. Other portions of the site include open fields, mixed hardwoods, pine plantations, and swamps.

Parking areas for the larger N portion of the WMA are NW of Central Village on SR 14. We saw no signs; one needs a site map or local advice.

Hunting: Chiefly small game and pheasant.

PUBLICATION: Wildlife Bureau site map.

HEADQUARTERS: DEP, Eastern District, Wildlife Bureau, 209 Hebron Rd., Marlborough, CT 06447; (203) 295-9525.

ROCKY NECK STATE PARK

Connecticut Department of Environmental Protection   East
708 acres.

From Connecticut Turnpike, Exit 72, then S.

Don't come in summer if you dislike crowds. This is one of CT's few State beaches, a mile of gently sloping sand on Long Island Sound. Out of season it's delightful, and its several habitats provide interest for birders.

Back of the beach is mixed hardwood maritime forest. Bride Brook flows through the site, with salt and brackish marsh. A long stony ridge juts into the Sound.

ACTIVITIES
Camping: 169 sites.
Hiking: About 4 mi. of trails.
Fishing: Mackerel, striped bass, blackfish, flounder.

PUBLICATION: Leaflet with map.

HEADQUARTERS: DEP, Office of State Parks and Recreation, 165 Capitol Ave., Hartford, CT 06106; (203) 566-2304.

ROY AND MARGOT LARSEN SANCTUARY

Connecticut Audubon Society   West
152 acres.

From Merritt Parkway, Exit 44. Bear right, then immediate right turn onto Congress St. Follow Audubon signs to Fairfield Center on Burr St.

An extensive wilderness is best left undisturbed. In a small tract, skillful management can increase natural diversity. Thirty years ago, this site was covered with second-growth hardwoods. Now it also has ponds and open fields. Woodlands are managed. Species of plants, shrubs, and trees have been added to offer food and cover to birds and small mammals.

The purpose is environmental education. An illustrated guide to the 6 1/2 mi. of trails explains what visitors see. The Society sponsors nature education programs for adults and children. A recent addition is a trail for handicapped visitors.

No pets, horses, or picnicking.

PUBLICATIONS
 Walk Guide. $1.50.
 Trail map.
 Information pages:
  List of common trees and shrubs.
  Geology.
  Skiing guide.

REFERENCES
 Billard, Ruth Sawyer. *Places to Look for Birds.* Hartford: Department of Environmental Protection, 1972.
 Hardy, Gerry and Sue. *Fifty Hikes in Connecticut.* Woodstock, VT: Backcountry Publications, 1984.

HEADQUARTERS: Connecticut Audubon Society, 2325 Burr St., Fairfield, CT 06430; (203) 259-6305.

SALMON RIVER STATE FOREST
Connecticut Department of Environmental Protection   East
6,115 acres.

Several sections; W of Colchester, along the Salmon River.

The Wildlife Unit issues maps of 3 Forest tracts: Dickinson Creek and Bull Hill; Dickinson; and Larson Lot. Parks & Recreation issues a map centered on the Salmon River. Even with these we had difficulty finding and identifying Forest land. The total area shown on these maps is much less than 6,115 acres, but DEP could supply no other maps.

What we saw of the area is moderately hilly, predominantly in mixed hardwoods with occasional openings. On SR 149 E of Day Pond, we drove N on Shailor Hill Rd., continued on dirt beyond the blacktop, found a hunters' parking area that showed no sign of recent use, and continued on foot. It was pleasant, quiet, woodland hiking that would be enhanced by fall colors or spring flowers. This was part of the *Larson Lot,* which surrounds the State Park, N of SR 16. The Salmon River crosses the NW portion of this tract.

The *Salmon River* flows to the Connecticut. W of SR 16 it is close to Gulf Rd., E of SR 16 to River Rd., both on the N. Access to parking, picnic, and put-in sites are near SR 16.

Dickinson Creek and *Bull Run,* 1,000 acres. From SR 2 at Marlborough, W on SR 66 about 2 mi. to Flood Rd., left 0.5 mi. to fork, left 0.2 mi. This has mixed hardwood forest along Dickinson Creek with some hardwood swamp.

Dickinson area, 600 acres. From SR 2 at Marlborough, E on SR 66 about 1.5 mi., cross the Blackledge River, then left. More upland hardwood forest with small brooks and wetlands.

ACTIVITIES

Hiking: The Salmon River Trail has two loops, both originating at Day Pond. The *Connecticut Walk Book* trail map also shows the Shailor Hill Rd. and an old railroad grade beside the river. The Forest also has hiking opportunities on unmapped woods roads.

Fishing seems to attract the most visitors. The Salmon has excellent trout fishing, including a fly-fishing-only section.

Canoeing, kayaking: In early spring; about 5 mi. to the Connecticut River.

PUBLICATIONS: Maps, 8 1/2- × 11-inch; few details.

REFERENCE: Hicock, Shelton B., ed. *Connecticut Walk Book.* Middletown: Connecticut Forest and Park Association, 1984.

NEARBY

Day Pond State Park, 180 acres. Hike, fish, swim.

Wopowog Management Area, 473 acres. On the Salmon River SW of Day Pond, off SR 196 to Wopowog Rd. Hike, hunt.

HEADQUARTERS: DEP, Office of State Parks and Recreation, 165 Capitol Ave., Hartford, CT 06106; (203) 566-2304.

SALT MEADOW NATIONAL WILDLIFE REFUGE
U.S. Fish and Wildlife Service   West
183 acres.

From I-95 near Clinton, Exit 64. S about 1/4 mi., then left on Clinton Rd. 1 mi. to entrance on right.

Part of the Ninigret (RI) refuge complex (see entry), this site is near the coast but as much as 110 ft. above sea level. The Penn Central RR divides the area. The larger portion, N of the RR, is woodland, shrubland, and salt marsh. Prominent tree species are oaks, yellow poplar, and black cherry. The Menunketesuck River is on the SW boundary of this portion, and it forms the E boundary of the smaller, inaccessible, lower-lying tract, which is largely salt marsh.

This is a little-known and lightly used refuge, a gift to the federal government.

Birds: No checklist available. Over 200 species recorded. Osprey nest on a platform in the marsh.

Hiking: 3 mi. of trails, beginning at the entrance parking lot.

PUBLICATION: Trail map available from HQ.

HEADQUARTERS: Ninigret National Wildlife Refuge Complex, Box 307, Charlestown, RI 02813; (401) 364-9124.

SATAN'S KINGDOM STATE RECREATION AREA
North American Canoe Tours, Inc.   West
About 5 river miles.

On US 44 S of New Hartford.
Weekends May 23–June 20 and Sept. 7–20. Daily June 20–Sept. 7.

The sign calls it a State Recreation Area, but it's commercially operated. State leaflets don't list it. The only activity is tubing, floating in large tubes down the Farmington River for about 2 1/2 hrs. to the take-out N of US 202. The concessionaire provides tubes, other gear, and a shuttle bus. Some moderate whitewater. The setting is forest, with US 44 close by.

HEADQUARTERS: North American Canoe Tours, 65 Black Point Rd., Niantic, CT 06357; (203) 693-6465.

SHADE SWAMP SANCTUARY
Connecticut Department of Environmental Protection   West
(Trails managed by the Farmington Land Trust)
800 acres.

Near Farmington. W of the junction of US 6 and SR 10. Launch at the river, or continue on US 6 to parking on right.

On the Pequabuck River, this site has diverse habitats: open marsh, brushy marsh, hardwood swamp, mixed hardwood forest, evergreen plantations, open fields. Many birds and wildflowers. Two trails, but much of the area is best seen by canoe, from US 6 to Meadow Rd. in Farmington.

Canoeing: Pequabuck River.

Pets are prohibited. No smoking. Picnicking at roadside area only.

PUBLICATION: Field guide published by the Farmington River Watershed Association. Available in Farmington at the town hall, library, bookshops.

REFERENCE: Billard, Ruth Sawyer. *Places to Look for Birds.* Hartford: Department of Environmental Protection, 1972.

HEADQUARTERS: DEP, Office of State Parks and Recreation, 165 Capitol Ave., Hartford, CT 06106; (203) 566-2304.

SHENIPSIT STATE FOREST

Connecticut Department of Environmental Protection   East
6,126 acres.

From Stafford Springs, W about 6 mi. on SR 190. Left on Sodom Rd.

The Shenipsit has several blocks, generally W and N of Stafford Springs. Wildlife Bureau maps cover only 3 blocks encompassing 2,650 acres. These maps do not show private inholdings. Driving on several roads that cross Forest blocks, we saw houses on both sides and no markers identifying Forest land.

Sodom Rd. is marked as a Forest entrance. This is near the N end of the 30-mi. Shenipsit Trail, which extends S to Cobalt on SR 66. The road had been recently bladed when we visited. Several little-used woods roads branch off it. The forest in this area includes white pine and hemlock as well as hardwoods, trees apparently 30 to 50 years old, with a moderately dense understory.

The Trail crosses the Forest's highest point: 1,121-ft. Bald Mountain and 1,061-ft. Soapstone Mountain.

Terrain includes moderately steep slopes, rock outcrops, ledges, small streams and ponds.

FEATURES

Bald Mountain can be approached by Old Country Rd., N from SR 190 just E of Gulf Rd.

Soapstone Mountain can be reached by an unpaved road NW from SR 140 just W of Crystal Lake. The road continues to SR 190. Observation tower.

ACTIVITIES

Hiking: Shenipsit Trail, other trails, woods roads.
Hunting: Grouse, woodcock, cottontail, squirrel, deer.
Ski touring: Trails and unplowed roads.

PUBLICATIONS: Wildlife Bureau maps: Crow Hill Block; Tower and Bald Mountain blocks.

REFERENCE: Hicock, Shelton B., ed. *Connecticut Walk Book.* Middletown: Connecticut Forest and Park Association, 1984.

NEARBY: Ellithorpe Flood Control Area (see entry). The Wildlife Bureau map shows this as part of the Crow Hill Block.

HEADQUARTERS: DEP, Office of State Parks and Recreation, 165 Capitol Ave., Hartford, CT 06106; (203) 566-2304.

SLEEPING GIANT STATE PARK
Connecticut Department of Environmental Protection   West
1,439 acres.

From Hamden, 2 mi. N on SR 10.

Seldom have we read more entertaining trail guidance: "Its white paint blazes lead over the *right lower left leg . . . Pass along the upper right thigh,* cross the *waist* and go up onto the rocky slabs of the *left shoulder . . . " (Connecticut Walk Book).* Two miles of mountain top form the silhouette of the giant lying on his back. A 30-mi. trail network winds through mixed hardwood forest with mountain laurel, brooks, swamps. Highest point is 739 ft. on Mt. Carmel, providing a view of Long Island Sound. Observation tower.

ACTIVITIES
   Camping: Don't plan to camp here. One of the few campgrounds in a heavily populated region, it has only 8 sites, for tents and small vehicles.
   Hiking: The Quinnipiac Trail, oldest in the blue-blazed hiking trails system, 21 mi. long, passes over the Giant.
   Fishing: Stream.

REFERENCE: Hicock, Shelton B., ed. *Connecticut Walk Book.* Middletown: Connecticut Forest and Park Association, 1984.

HEADQUARTERS: DEP, Office of State Parks and Recreation, 165 Capitol Ave., Hartford, CT 06106; (203) 566-2304.

TUNXIS STATE FOREST
Connecticut Department of Environmental Protection   West
8,638 acres.

On the MA border. Blocks on both sides of Barkhamsted Reservoir. Crossed by SR 20.

The State lists it as "undeveloped" and provides no information other than Wildlife Bureau maps. The two maps given us cover only part of the Forest. Although useful, they are inaccurate and incomplete. The *Connecticut Walk Book* map is a good guide to the Tunxis Trail, but it doesn't show Forest boundaries and covers little of the area E of the reservoir. The Forest has no reservoir frontage. It adjoins the Granville State Forest in Massachusetts, but we found no trail connection.

It's delightful hiking country, and you won't meet many people there. To explore, take the well-marked Tunxis Trail N from its crossing on SR 219 E of the reservoir or cruise along lightly traveled SR 20 and look for side roads. We found two that were paved for a short distance, then became dirt or gravel. The Tunxis Trail leaves SR 20 on a woods road open to vehicles, but soon breaks away from it.

The area is gently rolling, most of it between 1,000 and 1,160 ft. elevation, a few hills rising above 1,200 ft. Pine Mountain, on the Tunxis Trail, reaches 1,391 ft., sufficient in this region to make it a good observation point for the hawk migration. Roaring Brook, dropping down to the reservoir on the E side, has an attractive waterfall. On the W side, a short walk S from SR 20, is a waterfall on Falls Brook.

Habitats include reverting fields, ponds, brooks and swamps, beaver flowages, and forest. We hiked through an open mixed hardwood forest and, on a slight rise, entered an extensive dark grove of hemlock. On the higher ground of Pine Mountain are moosewood, hobblebush, mountain ash, wood sorrel.

Howells Pond is popular with fishermen. From West Hartland, proceed NW on West St. The roads don't match those on the forest map, but we found the pond easily.

ACTIVITIES

Hiking: The Tunxis Trail is the best-known route, but we saw many inviting woods roads and informal trails. Although no postings prohibit trail bikes, we saw no tracks.

Hunting: Grouse, cottontail, snowshoe hare, gray squirrel, raccoon, wild turkey, some waterfowl.

PUBLICATIONS: Wildlife Bureau maps, Howells Pond area map.

REFERENCES

Billard, Ruth Sawyer. *Places to Look for Birds.* Hartford: Department of Environmental Protection, 1972.

Hicock, Shelton B., ed. *Connecticut Walk Book.* Middletown: Connecticut Forest and Park Association, 1984.

Keyarts, Eugene. *60 Selected Short Walks in Connecticut.* Chester, CT: Globe Pequot Press, 1979.

HEADQUARTERS: DEP, Office of State Parks and Recreation, 165 Capitol Ave., Hartford, CT 06106; (203) 566-2304.

WHITE MEMORIAL CONSERVATION CENTER
The White Memorial Foundation, Inc.   West
4,000 acres.

From Litchfield, 2.2 mi. W on US 202.

The Foundation owns and maintains this extensive preserve for conservation, education, recreation, and research. It has 60% of the shoreline of Bantam Lake, 2.4 mi. long, the largest natural lake in CT. In the Litchfield Hills, elevations are from 894 ft. to 1,120 ft. Habitats include forest, hardwood swamp, brushy to open marsh, open fields, beaver flowages, Bantam River, several streams and ponds.

Plants: About 60% of the area is forested with mixed hardwoods, white pine, and spruce. The understory includes mountain laurel, azalea, shadbush. Many wildflowers, ferns, and mosses, including wetland species.

Birds: Checklist available includes waterfowl, rails, herons, gulls, terns, hawks, owls, numerous songbirds.

Mammals: Common species include deer, beaver, cottontail, chipmunk, squirrel, raccoon. Less often seen: mink, weasel, bobcat, flying squirrel, fox.

FEATURES

Four areas totaling 200 acres are essentially undisturbed, including stands of old-growth white pine, hemlock, and hardwoods.

The *Museum,* once a private home, has natural history exhibits, live animals, learning centers, library. Nature education programs are offered for all age groups.

Weekend programs include nature walks and slide shows.

Nature trail, self-guiding. Also a nature trail for the handicapped.

Boardwalk around Little Pond.

ACTIVITIES

Camping: Two campgrounds, 48 and 20 sites. Mid-Apr. to mid-Oct. Reservations suggested. Write or call (203) 567-0089.

Hiking: About 25 mi. of woodland roads, 10 mi. of trails. Trails include a section of the Mattatuck Trail, a major N–S route that connects with the Appalachian Trail. Woodland roads may also be used for horse riding and ski touring.

Fishing: Bantam Lake. Northern pike, bass.

Swimming: Beach on Bantam Lake.

Boating: Marina opposite the Folly Point Campground has ramp and moorings.

Ski touring: Trails and woodland roads.

Off-road vehicles, including snowmobiles, are prohibited. No motor vehicles on woods roads. Pets must be leashed.

PUBLICATIONS

Trail map. $2.

Guide to Birding. Annotated list. $0.40.

Nature trail leaflet. $0.25.

A Guide to the Habitat Groups. $0.25.

Egler, F. E., and W. N. Neiring. *The Natural Areas of the White Memorial Foundation.* Litchfield: Friends of the White Memorial Conservation Center, 1976. $0.50.

REFERENCE: Hardy, Gerry and Sue. *Fifty Hikes in Connecticut.* Woodstock, VT: Backcountry Publications, 1984.

HEADQUARTERS: Route 202, Litchfield, CT 06759. Business office: (203) 567-0857. Conservation Center: (203) 567-0015.

INDEX

THE PERRYS, long residents of the Washington, DC., area, moved to Winter Haven, Florida, soon after work on these guides began. Their desks overlook a lake well populated with great blue herons, anhingas, egrets, ospreys, gallinules, and wood ducks, a nesting pair of bald eagles, and occasional pelicans, alligators, and otters.

Jane, an economist, came to Washington as a congressman's secretary and thereafter held senior posts in several executive agencies and presidential commissions. John, an industrial management consultant, left that work to spend ten years with the Smithsonian Institution, involved in overseas nature conservation.

They have hiked, backpacked, camped, canoed, and cruised together in all fifty states. They have written more than fourteen books and produced two dozen educational filmstrips, chiefly on natural history and ecology.

Their move to Florida marked a shift from international to local conservation action. They hold various offices in county Sierra Club and Audubon Society groups and the Coalition for the Environment. John is a trustee of the Florida Nature Conservancy.

The guide series keeps them on the road about three months each year, living and working in a motor home, accompanied by Tor II, a black Labrador.